Lonely Planet

D0728522 L

THE PACIFIC NORTHWEST'S
BEST TRIPS

32 AMAZING ROAD TRIPS

Becky Ohlsen, Robert Balkovich, Celeste Brash,
John Lee, Craig McLachlan, MaSovaida Morgan,
Brendan Sainsbury

SYMBOLS IN THIS BOOK

✔ Top Tips	📖 History & Culture	📷 Essential Photo
🔗 Link Your Trips	👫 Family	🏃 Walking Tour
💧 Tips from Locals	🍷 Food & Drink	✗ Eating
↪ Trip Detour	🌳 Outdoors	🛏 Sleeping

📞 Telephone Number	@ Internet Access	🅑 English-Language Menu
⊙ Opening Hours	🛜 Wi-Fi Access	👪 Family-Friendly
🅟 Parking	🌱 Vegetarian Selection	🐾 Pet-Friendly
✱ Nonsmoking		
✸ Air-Conditioning	🏊 Swimming Pool	

MAP LEGEND

Routes
- ▬▬ Trip Route
- ▬ ▬ Trip Detour
- ▨▨▨ Linked Trip
- ▬ Walk Route
- Tollway
- Freeway
- Primary
- Secondary
- Tertiary
- Lane
- Unsealed Road
- ▨▨ Plaza/Mall
- ····· Steps
-)= = Tunnel
- ═══ Pedestrian Overpass
- - - - Walk Track/Path

Boundaries
- --- International
- ---- State/Province
- ┬┬┬ Cliff

Hydrography
- ∿ River/Creek
- ∩‿ Intermittent River
- Swamp/Mangrove
- ∿ Canal
- Water
- Dry/Salt/ Intermittent Lake
- Glacier

Route Markers
- 🛡97 US National Hwy
- 🛡5 US Interstate Hwy
- 44 State Hwy

Trips
- 1 Trip Numbers
- 9 Trip Stop
- 🏃 Walking tour
- ↪ Trip Detour

Population
- ✪ Capital (National)
- ◉ Capital (State/Province)
- ● City/Large Town
- ● Town/Village

Areas
- Beach
- + + Cemetery (Christian)
- x x x Cemetery (Other)
- Park
- Forest
- Reservation
- Urban Area
- Sportsground

Transport
- ✈ Airport
- Ⓑ BART station
- Ⓣ Boston T station
- +Ⓔ+ Cable Car/ Funicular
- Ⓜ Metro/Muni station
- Ⓟ Parking
- Ⓢ Subway station
- +Ⓡ+ Train/Railway
- +Ⓣ+ Tram
- Ⓤ Underground station

2

Note: Not all symbols displayed above appear on the maps in this book

PLAN YOUR TRIP

ON THE ROAD

CONTENTS

British
Columbia
p267

Washington
p53

Oregon
p159

Contents cont.

ROAD TRIP ESSENTIALS

Classic Trips

Look out for the Classic Trips stamp on our favorite routes in this book.

WELCOME TO
THE PACIFIC NORTHWEST

What's the Pacific Northwest got that other regions don't? Plenty. Start with hundreds of miles of coastline and throw in a stunning natural landscape: thousands of years of geological events have dramatically shaped this region, leaving behind snowcapped mountain ranges, rocky islands, hundreds of waterfalls, natural hot springs and one particularly lovely gorge.

Because almost every drive in the Pacific Northwest is a scenic one, there's no better way to see it than by road trip. The great stops along the way range from historical sites to natural wonders to roadside attractions.

You can cruise along the coast, explore volcanic remnants, sample regional wines, or even travel in the footsteps of Lewis and Clark.

And if you've only got time for one trip, make it one of our eight Classic Trips, which take you to the very best of the Pacific Northwest. Turn the page for more.

Olympic National Park (p68), Washington
KEN CANNING/GETTY IMAGES ©

THE PACIFIC NORTHWEST HIGHLIGHTS

Classic Trip
26
Sea to Sky Highway Coastal towns to snowy peaks with classic BC sights and views en route. 1–2 DAYS

Classic Trip
30
Okanagan Valley Wine Tour Overflowing fruit stands, award-winning vineyards and amazing cuisine. 2 DAYS

Classic Trip
8
Cascade Drive Wild West towns, Bavarian villages and moody mountains. 4–5 DAYS

Classic Trip
3
Mountains to Sound Greenway Washington's only east–west interstate has a greenway. 1–2 DAYS

BRITISH COLUMBIA

CANADA
USA

WASHINGTON

Campbell River

Parksville

Nanaimo

Tofino

Vancouver Island

Duncan

Lake Cowichan

Victoria

Sooke

Strait of Georgia

Strait of Juan de Fuca

Cape Flattery

Réserve de Parc National du Canada Pacific Rim

Squamish

Whistler

Vancouver

Lillooet River

Fraser River

Merritt

Hope

Kelowna

Okanagan Lake

Okanagan River

Colville National Forest

Lake Roosevelt

Banks Lake

Moses Lake

Potholes Reservoir

Columbia River

Yakima

Ellensburg

Olympia

Tacoma

Bremerton

Seattle

Everett

Bellingham

Burlington

San Juan Islands

Puget Sound

Port Angeles

Aberdeen

Willapa Bay

Olympic National Park

Mt Olympus (7965ft)

Mt Rainier National Park

Mt Rainier (14,411ft)

Leavenworth

Wenatchee

Chelan

Lake Chelan

Glacier Peak (10,541ft)

Cascade Range

North Cascades National Park

Ross Lake

Methow River

Mt Baker (10,781ft)

Lake River

8

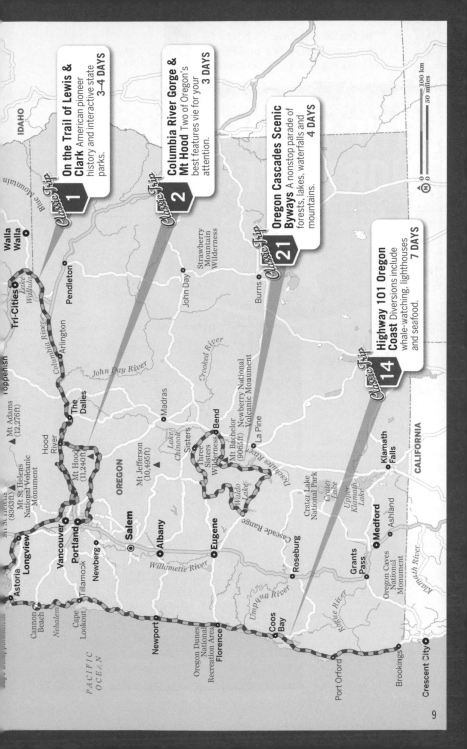

Classic Trip

1 On the Trail of Lewis & Clark American pioneer history and interactive state parks. **3–4 DAYS**

Classic Trip

2 Columbia River Gorge & Mt Hood Two of Oregon's best features vie for your attention. **3 DAYS**

Classic Trip

21 Oregon Cascades Scenic Byways A nonstop parade of forests, lakes, waterfalls and mountains. **4 DAYS**

Classic Trip

14 Highway 101 Oregon Coast Diversions include whale-watching, lighthouses and seafood. **7 DAYS**

IDAHO

Blue Mountain

Walla Walla

Toppenish

Tri-Cities

Lake Wallula

Pendleton

Arlington

Columbia River

The Dalles

Hood River

John Day River

John Day

Strawberry Mountain Wilderness

Burns

Crooked River

Madras

Sisters

Lake Chinook

Bend

Mt Bachelor (9065ft)

Newberry National Volcanic Monument

La Pine

Three Sisters Wilderness

Mt Jefferson (10,495ft)

Mt Hood (11,240ft)

Mt St Helens National Volcanic Monument

Mt Adams (12,276ft)

Mt St Helens (8363ft)

Longview

Vancouver

Portland

Astoria

Cannon Beach

Nehalem

Tillamook

Cape Lookout

Newberg

Salem

Albany

OREGON

Willamette River

Waldo Lake

Cascade Range

Deschutes River

Eugene

Roseburg

Umpqua River

PACIFIC OCEAN

Newport

Oregon Dunes National Recreation Area

Florence

Coos Bay

Port Orford

Brookings

Crescent City

Rogue River

Grants Pass

Oregon Caves National Monument

Medford

Ashland

Crater Lake National Park

Crater Lake

Upper Klamath Lake

Klamath Falls

Klamath River

CALIFORNIA

0   100 km
0   50 miles

9

The Pacific Northwest's best sights and experiences, and the road trips that will take you there.

THE PACIFIC NORTHWEST
HIGHLIGHTS

Coastal Highways

Cruising along the stunning Pacific Coast is an unforgettable experience. Lofty headlands reach out to the ocean, offering spectacular views, while steep mountains of rock jut offshore like giant sentinels. Stroll beaches, explore tide pools, watch for whales and eat your fill of fresh seafood on **Trip 14: Highway 101 Oregon Coast**, or get a taste of maritime history on **Trip 5: Graveyard of the Pacific Tour**.

Trips 5 14

Oregon Highway 101 (p163)

North Cascades National Park View from Diablo Lake overlook (p106)

Cascade Mountains

The Cascades stretch from British Columbia to California, and you don't have to leave the cities to enjoy them: snowcapped peaks make natural backdrops to the urban bustle in Seattle, Portland and Vancouver. Want to get closer? Explore the North Cascades on **Trip 8: Cascade Drive** and the Oregon Cascades on **Trip 21: Oregon Cascades Scenic Byways**.

Trips **8** **21**

John Day Fossil Beds

Within the soft rocks and crumbly soils of eastern Oregon's John Day region lies one of the world's greatest fossil collections. Over 2200 plant and animal species dating back millions of years have been identified at the John Day Fossil Beds, and the amazing rock formations make **Trip 17: Journey Through Time Scenic Byway** particularly memorable.

Trip **17**

Back Roads & Byways

Ditching the interstate is richly rewarded around these parts. Experience one of the West Coast's most spectacular coastal back roads on **Trip 7: Chuckanut Drive & Whidbey Island**. Get lost in a maze of forests, lakes and hot springs on **Trip 21: Oregon Cascades Scenic Byways**. Or go back in time with the amazing **Trip 17: Journey Through Time Scenic Byway**.

Trips **7** **17** **21**

John Day Fossil Beds Painted Hills (p197)

BEST ROADSIDE FUN

Oregon Vortex Defy physics at a classic roadside attraction. **Trips** 22 23

Prehistoric Gardens Where the dinosaurs are more fun than ferocious. **Trip** 14

Stonehenge Washington's answer to the UK monument. **Trips** 1 17

The Glass House A quirky house made of embalming-fluid bottles. **Trip** 13

Marsh's Free Museum Right across from the World's Largest Frying Pan. **Trip** 5

Willamette Wineries

Pinot Noir lovers unite! It's Oregon's most famous grape, finicky as a superstar and the foundation for some exceptional wine. Cruise around the towns of Newberg, Dundee and McMinnville and sample the local favorite, along with Chardonnay, Riesling and Pinot Gris. Bring a designated driver and hit all the high points on **Trip 16: Willamette Valley Wine Tour.**

Trip 16

Washington Mt St Helens (p119)

Volcanoes & Craters

Volcanoes have a way of wreaking havoc upon the landscape, but give them an eon or two to settle down and you get some gorgeous results. The eruption of Mt Mazama left behind the unique geological gift of Crater Lake, which you'll see on **Trip 23: Crater Lake Circuit**, or you can witness more recent volcanic aftermath on **Trip 10: Mt St Helens Volcano Trail**.

Trips 10 23

BEST HOT SPRINGS

Terwilliger Hot Springs
A popular place at Cougar Reservoir. **Trips** 20 21

Breitenbush Lovely, developed springs with on-site accommodations. **Trip** 20

McCredie One of the largest – and hottest – pools in Oregon. **Trip** 21

Umpqua An unbeatable location, perched on a cliff above the Umpqua River. **Trip** 23

Belknap A resort built around two giant pools. **Trip** 21

HIGHLIGHTS
★

Columbia River Gorge Multnomah Falls (p46)

Washington Camping in Olympic National Park (p68)

Columbia River Gorge

Carved out by the mighty Columbia as the Cascades uplifted, the Columbia River Gorge is a geological marvel. With Washington State to its north and Oregon to its south, the gorge provides both states with dramatic views, countless waterfalls and great hikes. Take your time following the gorge on **Trip 2: Columbia River Gorge & Mt Hood**.

Trip **2**

Olympic National Park

Within this park you can hike through old-growth forests, waltz through flower-filled meadows, swim in pure mountain lakes or try to summit Mt Olympus. You can even go trout fishing, beachcombing, hot-spring soaking and skiing. Learn about some of the park's best features, including the intensely green Hoh Rainforest, on **Trip 4: Olympic Peninsula Loop**.

Trip **4**

Waterfalls

Tiered falls, plunging falls, curtain falls, ribbon falls – hundreds of waterfalls in the Pacific Northwest give you ample opportunity to witness firsthand all the variations in the waterfall vernacular. You'll find abundant waterfall-peeping opportunities on **Trip 2: Columbia River Gorge & Mt Hood**, and you can even hit 10 falls within one state park on **Trip 20: To Bend & Back**.

Trips **2** **20**

17

Microbreweries

Love beer? Welcome to paradise. The Pacific Northwest has some of the best microbrews in the world and plenty of them. In fact, Portland (aka 'Beervana') holds the distinguished record of 'most microbreweries of any city in the world.' Almost any city worth its malt has multiple brews to sample; head out to Bend and check out its nine local microbreweries in **Trip 20: To Bend & Back**.

Trip **20**

Foodie Fun

The Pacific Northwest has some of the most inventive restaurants in the country, with chefs known for making the most of the region's bounteous produce and fresh seafood. Sample the latter on **Trip 14: Highway 101 Oregon Coast**, or go inland for decadent pairings of wine and fine dining on **Trip 16: Willamette Valley Wine Tour**. For a taste of several urban foodie hot spots, check out **Trip 22: Essential I-5**.

Trips **14** **16** **22**

(left) **Haida Gwaii** (p325)

(below) **McMinnville** Joel Palmer House (p191)

Island Exploration

Hundreds of islands litter the Pacific Northwest coastline, ranging from uninhabited to barely inhabited, and you'll feel like you've left the world behind the moment you drive onto the ferry. Go off the grid on **Trip 6: San Juan Islands Scenic Byway**, or make your escape with **Trip 31: Haida Gwaii Adventure**.

Trips

BEST SKIING

Whistler Follow in the ski tracks of the 2010 Winter Olympians. **Trip** 26

Methow Valley A cross-country skier's paradise with over 125 miles of groomed trails. **Trip** 8

Crystal Mountain Washington's largest ski resort, with more than 50 named runs. **Trip** 9

Mt Hood You can ski here every month of the year. **Trip** 2

19

Seattle Aquarium (p64)

History

History buffs can follow in the footsteps of Native Americans, explorers, pioneers and gold rush prospectors, and the area's maritime history is reflected all along the Pacific Coast. Too recent? Explore fossil beds that date back millions of years.

5 Graveyard of the Pacific Tour Lighthouses, nautical museums and shipwrecks illuminate maritime history.

1 On the Trail of Lewis & Clark Follow the trail of America's greatest explorers.

17 Journey Through Time Scenic Byway Dig deep into Oregon history with fossil beds, ghost towns and more.

25 Vancouver & the Fraser Valley East of Vancouver, learn more about British Columbia's pioneer past.

The Great Outdoors

It's no wonder the Pacific Northwest attracts outdoorsy types. The Great Outdoors is what the area is all about, whether you're trekking through forests, finding remote hot springs or biking down the coast.

4 Olympic Peninsula Loop From beaches to mountains, explore the treasures of the Olympic Peninsula.

6 San Juan Islands Scenic Byway Whale-watching, kayaking and biking are the main attractions in these islands off Washington's coast.

2 Columbia River Gorge & Mt Hood This area reveals some of Oregon's most dramatic work.

21 Oregon Cascades Scenic Byways Waterfalls, hot springs and lakes break up the almost nonstop greenery.

Food & Drink

The Pacific Northwest leads the continent in locally grown, sustainable and organic products. And since great wine demands great food, you can get your fill of both in the wine regions of Oregon, Washington and British Columbia, where tasting things is an art form.

7 Chuckanut Drive & Whidbey Island Nosh your way from cheese shops to oyster farms and farm-to-plate restaurants.

11 Washington Wine Tour Columbia Valley's laid-back wine country is emerging as a major wine-making destination.

16 Willamette Valley Wine Tour Oregon's wine country showcases some of the area's best food and wine.

30 Okanagan Valley Wine Tour Explore Canada's hill-lined, lakeside wine region.

Fort Stevens State Park Wreckage of the *Peter Iredale* (p80)

Family Fun

From aquariums full of sea life to cowboys riding bucking broncos, the Pacific Northwest will spark a child's imagination. Whether you head to the coast, the mountains or farmland, you'll be greeted with kindness by locals who know how to treat families right.

3 Mountains to Sound Greenway Waterfalls, aquariums and interesting museums make this trip fun for everyone.

14 Highway 101 Oregon Coast Enjoy tide pools, ocean surf and lots of small-town stops along the way.

22 Essential I-5 This trip packs in the fun, with stops that range from roadside attractions to light history.

26 Sea to Sky Highway The Britannia Mine Museum is a hit with road-weary kids.

Off-the-Beaten-Track Travel

No one does remote like the Pacific Northwest. It's easy to lose yourself out here, with undeveloped land masses that stretch on and on, from the unpopulated eastern regions of Washington and Oregon to the vast expanses of British Columbia.

13 International Selkirk Loop Find the forgotten corners of Washington, Idaho and British Columbia.

19 Hells Canyon Scenic Byway Few roads access the canyons in this remote corner of Oregon.

17 Journey Through Time Scenic Byway If ghost towns and a wide horizon are what you're after, this is the place.

29 Vancouver Island's Remote North Head north from Vancouver to see the less well-known side of the island.

Mountains

One of the benefits of being in a geological area known for earthquakes and volcanoes is the landscape they leave behind. Snow-capped ranges dominate the landscape, providing scenic backdrops and abundant recreational opportunities – from skiing to hiking to searching for Bigfoot.

8 Cascade Drive This altitudinous route through the northern Cascades is alive with rugged beauty.

9 Mt Rainier Scenic Byways At 14,411ft, volcanic Mt Rainier is the highest peak in the Cascades.

10 Mt St Helens Volcano Trail See the destruction left behind after its 1980 eruption.

21 Oregon Cascades Scenic Byways Gaze at the Three Sisters and other central Oregon peaks from various angles, with several hot springs as a bonus.

NEED TO KNOW

CELL PHONES
The US and Canada use GSM-850 and GSM-1900 bands. SIM cards are relatively easy to obtain in both countries.

INTERNET ACCESS
Wi-fi is available in most lodgings and cafes; some larger hotels add $10 to $20 for access, but this is increasingly rare.

FUEL
Gas stations are easy to find, except in national parks and some mountain areas. Expect to pay $2.50 to $4.50 per gallon.

RENTAL CARS
Budget (www.budget.com)

Enterprise (www.enterprise.com)

Hertz (www.hertz.com)

IMPORTANT NUMBERS
The following numbers apply to both the USA and Canada:

Country Code (☎1)

International Access Code (☎011)

Ambulance, Fire and Police (☎911)

Local Directory Assistance (☎411)

Climate

Desert, dry climate

Warm to hot summers, mild winters

Mild to hot summers, cold winters

Vancouver GO Jun–Sep

Victoria GO Jun–Sep

Seattle GO Jun–Sep

Eastern Washington GO May–Oct

Portland GO Jun–Sep

Eastern Oregon GO May–Oct

Oregon Coast GO Jun–Sep

When to Go

High Season (Jun–Sep)
» Sunny, warm days throughout the region.

» More crowds and higher prices for accommodations and sights.

» For ski resorts, busiest times are December to March.

Shoulder (Apr–May & Oct)
» Crowds and prices drop off.

» Temperatures remain mild.

» Services are more limited, but there's less competition for them.

Low Season (Nov–Mar)
» Colder days, less sunlight, more rain.

» Some services may close along the coast, and high passes can be blocked by snow.

» Indoor activities such as theater and music are at their best.

Your Daily Budget

Budget: Less than $100
» Inexpensive motel room/dorm bed: $85/30

» Food-cart meal: $5–10

Midrange: $100–$200
» Good hotel room: $125

» Meal in a midrange restaurant: $20–35

Top End: More than $200
» Upscale hotel room: $200 & up

» Fine-dining meal: $35–75

Eating

Food trucks Cheap, creative and often delicious.

Cafes Pick up a pastry with your morning coffee.

Roadside diners Cheap and simple.

Restaurants All price ranges and cuisine types are represented.

Vegetarians Most restaurants offer vegetarian (and often vegan) options.

Eating price indicators represent the cost of a main dish:

$	less than $15
$$	$15–$25
$$$	more than $25

Sleeping

Hostels Budget options let you share a room on the cheap.

Motels Cheaper than hotels and ubiquitous along highways.

B&Bs Personal service, often in former homes; breakfast included.

Hotels The higher the rate, the more amenities.

Sleeping price indicators represent the cost of a double room with private bathroom in high season. Lodging tax (6% to 16%) will be extra:

$	less than $100
$$	$100–$200
$$$	more than $200

Arriving in the Pacific Northwest

Sea-Tac Airport (Seattle)

Rental cars Reserve online and pick up at the airport.

Link light-rail Connects to downtown Seattle in 30 minutes for $2.25.

Shuttle Frequent services from $18 one way.

Taxi $45; about 25 minutes to downtown.

Portland International Airport

Rental cars Reserve online and pick up at the airport.

MAX light-rail Connects to downtown Portland in 40 minutes for $2.50.

Shuttle Frequent services from $14 one way.

Taxis $35 to $40; around 20 minutes to downtown.

Vancouver International Airport

Rental cars Reserve online and pick up at the airport.

SkyTrain Connects to downtown Vancouver in 25 minutes; C$2.50 to C$5.

Taxi C$35; around 30 minutes to downtown.

Money

ATMs are widely available. Credit cards are accepted at most hotels, restaurants and shops.

Tipping

20% to 25% of restaurant bill; 10% to 15% for taxis; $1 per drink or 20% for bartenders; $1 to $2 per bag for valets; $2 daily for housekeeping.

Useful Websites

Lonely Planet (www.lonely planet.com/the-pacific-northwest)

Seattle Tourism (www.seattle.gov)

Washington State Tourism (www.experiencewa.com)

Travel Portland (www.travelportland.com)

Oregon Tourism Commission (www.travel oregon.com)

Tourism British Columbia (www.hellobc.com)

Opening Hours

For Sights, Activities and Information, we mostly list high-season hours. Mid- or low-season hours will vary throughout the year. Standard business hours:

Post offices and banks 8am or 9am to 5pm Monday to Friday, some 8am or 9am to 2pm Saturday.

Restaurants 7am to 11:30am breakfast, 11:30am to 2:30pm lunch, 5pm to 9pm dinner.

Shops 9am or 10am to 5pm or 6pm (malls 9pm) Monday to Saturday, noon to 5pm Sunday.

Supermarkets 8am to 10pm, 24 hours in large cities.

For more, see Road Trip Essentials (p346).

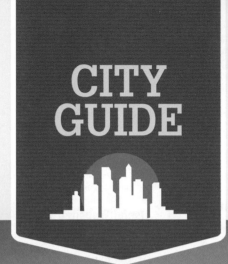

CITY GUIDE

SEATTLE

Lively, progressive and endlessly green, Seattle is Washington State's largest city. Rainy days are a great time to wander historic Pike Place Market or visit Seattle's most rocking museum, the Experience Music Project. When the sun comes out, head for the Olympic Sculpture Park or take our walking tour (p152).

Seattle Space Needle

Getting Around

Seattle traffic is heavy and chaotic, and downtown is hilly, with lots of one-way streets. All the city's taxicabs operate at the same rate, currently $2.60 at meter drop, then $2.50 per mile. Metro Transit buses (flat fare $2.50 for three hours) run from 5am to 1:30am.

Parking

Downtown parking is scarce and expensive, and some hotels charge a premium overnight, so check before booking. Metered parking goes from 8am to 6pm and extends until 8pm in popular areas; Sundays are free if you can find a spot, although some high-traffic areas limit you to two or four hours per spot.

Where to Eat

Some of Seattle's favorite restaurants are tucked into Pike Place Market, where you can also forage for picnic fixings. Historic Pioneer Square has a surprising number of budget-friendly dining options, and the International District has amazing Asian cuisine.

Where to Stay

Belltown and the Pike Place Market area offer lots of choices ranging from hostels to boutiques to large chains. The University District offers more budget-conscious options, and Capitol Hill is a good choice for inns and B&Bs.

Useful Websites

Lonely Planet (www.lonelyplanet.com/usa/seattle)

Visit Seattle (www.visitseattle.org)

Trips Through Seattle 3 9

TOP EXPERIENCES

➡ Browse in Pike Place Market

Seattle's landmark is more than just a market – it's a living community, complete with flying fish, mysterious shops, buskers, and a wall of chewing gum.

➡ Speed Up the Space Needle

On a clear day, views from this iconic 1962 World's Fair tower are well worth the price of admission.

➡ Rock Out at the EMP

Paul Allen's music museum introduces the musical legends who've shaped the Seattle sound for generations, from Bing Crosby to Jimi Hendrix to Kurt Cobain.

➡ Sample the Coffee Culture

This is, after all, the birthplace of Starbucks. Hundreds of micro-roasters, cafes, baristas and connoisseurs make sure the city's coffee culture keeps buzzing.

➡ Explore Capitol Hill

In Seattle's most colorful neighborhood, there's beer-flavored ice cream and coffee-flavored beer, dogs with dyed pink streaks in their fur, and enough vinyl and books to make you think Amazon.com never happened.

➡ Chow Down in Belltown

This funky little neighborhood, where grunge was born, is now known for its huge number and variety of restaurants. Most have a strong emphasis on 'locavore' cuisine, with ingredients sourced from Seattle's nearby waters and farms. It's a compact enough area to do a mini-tour through several menus.

Portland Kennedy School (p243)

PORTLAND

Laid-back Portland has a compact downtown and several charming residential neighborhoods. People-watching is a favorite pastime, best enjoyed while noshing at food carts, sipping microbrews at a sidewalk table, or wandering the aisles of Powell's Books. Check out all the city has to offer on our walking tour (p260).

Getting Around

Transit buses, the streetcar and the MAX light-rail system all link up and can get you nearly everywhere (www.trimet.org). Bicycling is a great way to see Portland; there's a good network of bike lanes and a bike-share program (look for the bright-orange fleets). The city has also added several fleets of electric scooters available to rent via mobile app.

Parking

You can get lucky with metered street parking, but there are six convenient SmartPark buildings downtown that charge $1.80 per hour. Check www.portlandonline.com/smartpark for locations and hours.

Where to Eat

Downtown offers everything from fine dining to food carts where you can find the perfect combination of good, cheap and fast. For decent midrange options, including great brunches and a mélange of ethnic cuisines, head across the river to Northeast and Southeast Portland.

Where to Stay

You'll find Portland's swankiest digs downtown, along with some nice midrange options. On the east side of town are some of the city's coolest independent hotels, as well as lots of midrange and budget chain offerings near the convention center.

Useful Websites

Travel Portland (www.travelportland.com) What to do, where to go, how to save.

Portland Mercury (www.portlandmercury.com) Alt-weekly paper with news and culture.

Willamette Week (www.wweek.com) Long-established news weekly with event listings.

Trips Through Portland

2 15 22

VANCOUVER

Vancouver is a sparkling, cosmopolitan city set against a backdrop of rugged natural beauty. Its welcoming downtown (see our walking tour p340) is flanked by the forested seawall of Stanley Park, and the neighborhoods contain easily walkable shopping streets. Wander historic Gastown, artsy Granville Island and the colorful West End 'gayborhood.'

Getting Around

You don't really need a car in Vancouver: it's easy enough to get around on foot, by bus or by cab. TransLink network – which includes buses, SkyTrain and SeaBus – starts at CAN$3 for travel within one zone. An all-day, all-zone pass costs CAN$10.50.

Parking

Parking is at a premium downtown. Some streets have metered parking (up to CAN$6 per hour), but your best bet is to head for pay-parking lots (from CAN$5 per hour). For an interactive map of parking-lot locations, check EasyPark (www.easypark.ca).

Where to Eat

Top streets include downtown's Robson St for Japanese *izakaya,* Yaletown's Hamilton and Mainland Sts for splurge-worthy dinners, Gastown for resto-bars, Commercial Dr for ethnic-flavored joints, and the West End's Denman and Davie Sts for midrange options.

Where to Stay

Swanky sleepovers abound downtown, as do midrange options. To split the geographical difference between downtown and the great outdoors, head to the North Shore. Hostels are scattered across the city; there are good digs near the University of British Columbia (UBC).

Useful Websites

Tourism Vancouver (www.tourismvancouver.com) Official tourism site.

City of Vancouver (www.vancouver.ca) Resource-packed official city site.

Inside Vancouver (www.insidevancouver.ca) What to do in and around the city.

Trip Through Vancouver 25

THE PACIFIC NORTHWEST
BY REGION

If one thing defines the Pacific Northwest, it's variety: roads here will take you to charming coastal villages, lush rainforests, alpine lakes, craggy mountain peaks, wide-open wheat fields and arid deserts, plus some of the most appealing cities in the US. Here's your guide to each region.

British Columbia (p267)

Canada's westernmost province wows visitors with its mighty mountains, deep forests and dramatic coastlines. But there's much more to British Columbia than nature-hugging dioramas – take for example cosmopolitan Vancouver, a city that fuses cuisines and cultures from Asia and beyond. Wherever you head, the great outdoors will always call.

Explore Vancouver on Trip 25

Go island-hopping on Trip 28

Washington (p53)

Washington State is the heart of the Pacific Northwest, from the lush, green Olympic Peninsula to the white peaks of the Cascade Mountains and the whale-surrounded San Juan Islands. Further east, the state leans more cowboy than boutique. The biggest urban jolt is Seattle, but Spokane, Bellingham and Olympia are equally worthy.

Explore a rainforest on Trip 4

Peek at peaks on Trip 8

Oregon (p159)

Oregon's landscape ranges from rugged coastline and thick evergreen forests to barren, fossil-strewn deserts, volcanoes and glaciers. And then there are the towns: funky Portland, dramatic Ashland, beer-loving Bend and beyond.

Eat like royalty on Trip 16

Gaze upon Crater Lake on Trip 23

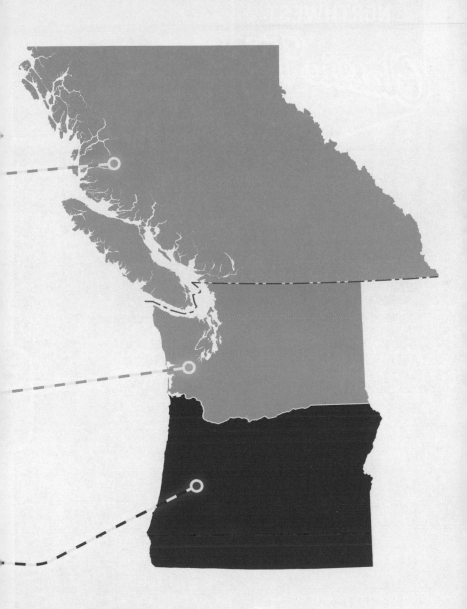

THE PACIFIC NORTHWEST

Classic Trips

CHECUBUS/SHUTTERSTOCK ©

8

What is a Classic Trip?

All of our trips show you the best of the region, but we've chosen some as our all-time favorites. These are our Classic Trips – the ones that lead you to the most iconic sights, the top activities and the uniquely Pacific Northwest experiences. Turn the page to see our cross-regional Classic Trips, and look out for more Classic Trips throughout the book.

Left: Historic Route 30 near Rowena Crest (p47)
Above: Downtown Leavenworth (p101)

Classic Trip

On the Trail of Lewis & Clark

Follow the Columbia River on this historic drive that marks the climax of American explorers Lewis and Clark's cross-continental 1805 journey as they stumbled toward the Pacific and instant immortality.

1

TRIP HIGHLIGHTS

340 miles

Cape Disappointment
Rocky end-of-the-continent cliff-top where Lewis and Clark first sighted the Pacific

107 miles

Stonehenge
Four thousand years newer than the English original but still impressive

3–4 DAYS
385 MILES / 620KM

GREAT FOR...

BEST TIME TO GO
Year-round – if you don't mind frequent rain, the Columbia River valley is always open.

ESSENTIAL PHOTO
Indian Beach, Ecola State Park – the Oregon coast epitomized.

BEST FOR HISTORY
The Lewis & Clark Interpretive Center in Cape Disappointment State Park.

10

Astoria

12 **FINISH**

7

The Dalles

2

Tri-Cities

Ecola State Park
Quintessential Oregon coastal scenery beloved by surfers and hikers

385 miles

Beacon Rock
This steep-sided rock rises like a mini-Gibraltar above the Columbia

182 miles

1

On the Trail of Lewis & Clark

It would take most people their combined annual leave to follow the Lewis and Clark trek in its entirety from St Louis, MO, to Cape Disappointment. Focusing on the final segment, this trip documents the mix of crippling exhaustion and building excitement that the two explorers felt as they struggled, worn out and weather-beaten, along the Columbia River on their way to completing the greatest overland trek in American history.

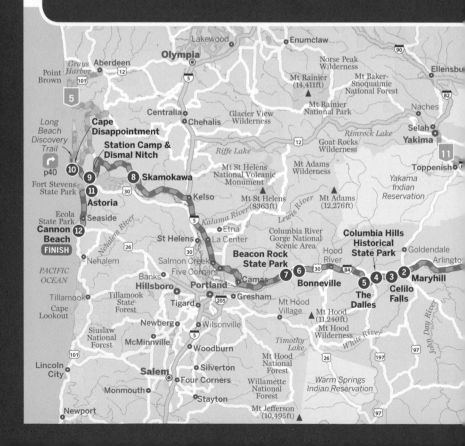

❶ Tri-Cities

This trip's start point has a weighty historical significance. The arrival of Lewis and Clark and the Corps of Discovery at the confluence of the Snake and Columbia Rivers on October 16, 1805, marked a milestone achievement on their quest to map a river route to the Pacific. After a greeting by 200 Native Americans singing and drumming, the band camped at this spot for two days, trading clothing for dried salmon. The **Sacajawea State**

Park Interpretive Center (☎506-545-2361; www. parks.state.wa.us/250; 2503 Sacajawea Park Rd; suggested donation $1; ☺10am-5pm late Mar-Nov 1; ♿), situated at the river confluence 5 miles southeast of present-day Pasco, relates the story of the expedition through the eyes of Sacajawea, the Shoshone Native American guide and interpreter the Corps had recruited in North Dakota.

The Drive ❱❱ Head south on I-82 before switching west at the Columbia River on SR 14, aka the Lewis & Clark Hwy. Here, in dusty sagebrush country, you'll pass a couple of minor sites – Wallula Gap, where the Corps first spotted Mt Hood, and the volcanic bluff of Hat Rock, first named by William Clark. Maryhill is 107 miles from Tri-Cities.

✕ 🛏 p41, p134

- - - - - - - - - - - - - - - -

TRIP HIGHLIGHT

❷ Maryhill

Conceived by great Northwest entrepreneur and road builder Sam Hill, the **Maryhill Museum of Art** (☎509-773-3733; www.maryhillmuseum.org; 35 Maryhill Museum Dr; adult/ child $12/5; ☺10am-5pm mid-Mar–mid-Nov) occupies a mansion atop a bluff overlooking the Columbia River. Its eclectic art collection is enhanced by a small Lewis and Clark display, while its peaceful gardens are perfect for a classy picnic punctuated by exotic peacock cries. Interpretive signs point you to fine views down the Columbia Gorge to the riverside spot (now a state park) where Meriwether Lewis and William Clark camped on October 21, 1805. The park is just one of several along this trip where you can pitch a tent within a few hundred yards of the Corps' original camp.

Another of Hill's creations – a life-size, unruined replica of **Stonehenge** (Hwy 97) – lies 2 miles to the east.

The Drive ❱❱ Continue west from Maryhill on SR 14 for 5 miles to the site of the now submerged Celilo Falls.

§ **LINK YOUR TRIP**

5 **Graveyard of the Pacific Tour**

Lewis and Clark survived, but others didn't. Find out about the tumultuous maritime history of southwest Washington's coast.

11 **Washington Wine Tour**

After all that Lewis and Clark history, you'll need a glass of wine. Break off in the Tri-Cities for some relaxed quaffing opportunities.

Classic Trip

③ Celilo Falls

A vivid imagination can be as important as sunscreen when following the 'Trail.' One example of this is the turnout 5 miles west of Maryhill that overlooks what was once the Native American salmon fishing center of Celilo Falls. The explorers spent two days here in late October 1805, lowering their canoes down the crashing falls on elk-skin ropes. A century and a half later, the rising waters of the dammed Columbia drowned the falls – which were the sixth-most voluminous in the world – destroying a centuries-old fishing site and rendering much of Clark's description of the region unrecognizable.

The Drive » Head west on SR 14, paralleling the mighty Columbia, for another 15 miles to Columbia Hills Historical State Park.

④ Columbia Hills Historical State Park

Native American tribes like the Nez Percé, Clatsop and Walla Walla were essential to the success of the Lewis and Clark expedition, supplying them with food,

horses and guides. One of the best places to view tangible traces of the region's Native American heritage is the Temani Pesh-wa (Written on Rocks) Trail at **Columbia Hills Historical State Park** (☑509-439-9032; Hwy 14, Mile 85; day-use $10; ⊙Apr-Oct), which highlights the region's best petroglyphs. Reserve a spot in advance on the free guided tours on Friday and Saturday at 10am to view the famous but fragile pictograph of the god Tsagaglalal (She Who Watches). The park is also a popular site for rock climbers and windsurfers.

The Drive » Two miles west of Horsethief Lake, turn south onto US 197, which takes you across the Columbia River into The Dalles in Oregon. Two miles upriver sits The Dalles Dam, which completely submerged the once magnificent Celilo Falls and rapids on its completion in 1957.

⑤ The Dalles

Once the urban neighbor of the formidable Celilo Falls, The Dalles has a more mundane image these days. The local economy focuses on cherry-growing, computer technology and outdoor recreation. Notwithstanding, the city hosts one of the best Lewis and Clark–related museums along this stretch of the Columbia, sited in the Columbia

Gorge Discovery Center (p47) on the western edge of town. Displays detail the 30 tons of equipment the Corps dragged across the continent and the animals they had to kill to survive (including 190 dogs and a ferret). Kids will get a kick from dressing up in Lewis and Clark period costume.

The Drive » You can continue west from The Dalles on either side of the Columbia (the expedition traveled straight down the middle by canoe) via SR 14 (Washington), or the slower, more scenic SR 30 (Oregon). En route to Bonneville, 46 miles away, look for views down to macabre Memaloose Island, where Native Americans would leave their dead in canoes of cedar.

🍴 🛏 p41

⑥ Bonneville

There are two Bonnevilles: Bonneville, Oregon, and North Bonneville, Washington. At this stage in their trip, Lewis and Clark were flea-infested and half-starved from a diet of dog meat and starchy, potatolike wapato roots. Fortunately, 21st-century Bonneville – which is famous for its Depression-era dam, completed in 1938 – has some tastier culinary offerings to contemplate.

The Drive » Just west of North Bonneville on SR 14 lies Beacon Rock State Park.

7 Beacon Rock State Park

On November 2, 1805, a day after passing modern Bonneville, Clark wrote about a remarkable 848ft-tall monolith he called Beaten Rock, changing the name to Beacon Rock on his return. Just over a century later, Henry Biddle bought the rock for the bargain price of $1 (!) and you can still hike his snaking 1-mile trail to the top of the former lava plug in **Beacon Rock State Park** (☎509-427-8265; www.parks.state.wa.us/474; Hwy 14, Mile 35; day-use $10). As you enjoy the wonderful views, ponder the fact that you have effectively climbed up the *inside* of an ancient volcano. For the Corps, the rock brought a momentous discovery, for it was here that the excited duo first noticed the tide, proving at last that they were finally nearing their goal of crossing the American continent.

The Drive » Your next stop along SR 14 should be the Cape Horn overview, with its fantastic views of the flood-carved gorge and its impressive cascades. From here, it's a straight shot on I-5 to Kelso and then over the Lewis and Clark Bridge to parallel the Columbia River westward on SR 4. Skamokawa is 103 miles from the state park.

LEWIS & CLARK HISTORICAL PARK

The so-called **Lewis & Clark National Historical Park** (☎503-861-2471; www.nps.gov/lewi; 92343 Fort Clatsop Rd; adult/child $5/free; ⊙9am-6pm mid-Jun–Aug, to 5pm Sep–mid-Jun) combines 10 different historical sites clustered around the mouth of the Columbia River, each of which relates to important facts about the Corps of Discovery and its historic mission to map the American West. It was formed through the amalgamation of various state parks and historic sites in 2004, and is run jointly by the National Park Service (NPS) and the states of Washington and Oregon. Highlights include Cape Disappointment, Fort Clatsop and the 6.5-mile **Fort to Sea trail** linking Clatsop and the ocean at Sunset Beach.

8 Skamokawa

For most of their trip down the Columbia River, Lewis and Clark traveled not on foot but by canoe. There's nowhere better to paddle in the Corps' canoe wake than at **Pillar Rock**, where Clark wrote of his joy at finally being able to camp in view of the ocean. **Columbia River Kayaking** (☎360-747-1044; www.columbiariverkayaking.com; 957 Steamboat Slough Rd; half-day tours from $59; ⊙noon-4pm Fri-Sun) in the town of Skamokawa offers one- and two-day kayak tours to this site, as well as Grays Bay.

The Drive » Continue on SR 4 northwest out of Skamokawa. In Naselle, go southwest on SR 401. From Skamokawa to Dismal Nitch is 35 miles, along the north bank of the Columbia River.

9 Station Camp & Dismal Nitch

Just east of the Astoria–Megler Bridge on the north bank of the Columbia River, a turnout marks Dismal Nitch, where the drenched duo were stuck in a pounding weeklong storm that Clark described as the most disagreeable time he had ever experienced. The Corps finally managed to make camp at Station Camp, 3 miles further west, now an innocuous highway pullout, where they stayed for 10 days while the two leaders, no doubt sick of each other by now, separately explored the headlands around Cape Disappointment.

The Drive » You're nearly there! Contain your excitement as you breeze the last few miles west along US 101 to Ilwaco and the inappropriately named Cape Disappointment.

WHY THIS IS A CLASSIC TRIP
BECKY OHLSEN, WRITER

This is about as classic as an American road trip gets: retracing the steps of Lewis and Clark, the great explorers who, with their Corps of Discovery, plunged into the wilderness of the 'New World' in a spirit of curiosity more than conquest. To get the most out of the trip, bring a copy to read along the way of the journals they kept during the expedition.

Above: Cannon Beach (p40), Ecola State Park
Left: Stonehenge (p35), Maryhill
Right: North Head Lighthouse, Cape Disappointment State Park

TRIP HIGHLIGHT

⑩ Cape Disappointment

Disappointment is probably the last thing you're likely to be feeling as you pull into blustery cliff-top **Cape Disappointment State Park** (☎360-642-3078; www. parks.state.wa.us/486; Hwy 100; Discover Pass required; ☺dawn-dusk). Find time to make the short ascent of Mackenzie Hill in Clark's footsteps and catch your first true sight of the Pacific. You can almost hear his protracted sigh of relief more than two centuries later.

Located on a high bluff inside the park not far from the Washington town of Ilwaco, the sequentially laid-out **Lewis & Clark Interpretive Center** (www.capedisappointment.org; Hwy 100; adult/child $5/2.50; ☺10am-5pm Wed-Sun Oct-Mar, daily Apr-Sep) faithfully recounts the Corps of Discovery's cross-continental journey using a level of detail the journal-writing explorers would have been proud of. Information includes everything from how to use an octant to what kind of underpants Lewis wore! A succinct 20-minute film backs up the permanent exhibits. Phone ahead and you can also tour the impressive end-of-continent **North Head Lighthouse** (☎360-

642-3029; www.northhead lighthouse.com; tours $2.50; ☺10am-5pm May-Sep) nearby.

The Drive » From Ilwaco, take US 101 back east to the 4.1-mile-long Astoria–Megler Bridge, the longest continuous truss bridge in the US. On the other side, 18 miles from Cape Disappointment, lies Astoria in Oregon, the oldest US-founded settlement west of the Mississippi.

 p81

⑪ Astoria

After voting on what to do next – a decision often described as the first truly democratic ballot in US history, since everyone in the party had a say – the Corps elected to make their winter bivouac across the Columbia River in present-day Oregon. A replica of the original **Fort Clatsop** (adult/child $7/free; ☺9am-6pm Jun-Aug, to 5pm Sep-May), where the Corps spent a miserable winter in 1805–06, lies 5 miles south of Astoria. Also on site are trails, a visitor center and buckskin-clad rangers who wander the camp between mid-June and Labor Day sewing moccasins (the Corps stockpiled an impressive 340 pairs for their return trip), tanning leather and firing their muskets.

> ### DETOUR:
> ### LONG BEACH
> ### DISCOVERY TRAIL
>
> **Start: ⑩ Cape Disappointment**
> Soon after arriving in 'Station Camp', the indefatigable Clark, determined to find a better winter bivouac, set out with several companions to continue the hike west along a broad sandy peninsula. They came to a halt near present-day 26th St in Long Beach, where Clark dipped his toe in the Pacific and carved his name on a cedar tree for posterity. The route of this historic three-day trudge has been re-created in the Long Beach Discovery Trail, a footpath that runs from the small town of Ilwaco, adjacent to Cape Disappointment, to Clark's 26th St turnaround. Officially inaugurated in September 2009, the trail has incorporated some dramatic life-size sculptures along its 8.2-mile length. One depicts a giant gray whale skeleton, another recalls Clark's recorded sighting of a washed-up sea sturgeon, while a third re-creates in bronze the original cedar tree (long since uprooted by a Pacific storm).

The Drive » From Fort Clatsop, take US 101, aka the Oregon Coast Hwy, south through the town of Seaside to Cannon Beach, 25 miles from Astoria.

✕ ⊨ p41, p81, p174

TRIP HIGHLIGHT

⑫ Cannon Beach

Mission accomplished – or was it? Curiosity (and hunger) got the better of the Corps in early 1806 when news of a huge beached whale lured Clark and Sacajawea from a salt factory they had set up near the present-day town of Seaside down through what is now Ecola State Park to Cannon Beach.

Ecola State Park (☎503-436-2844; www. oregonstateparks.org; day-use $5) is the Oregon you may have already visited in your dreams: sea stacks, crashing surf, hidden beaches and gorgeous pristine forest. Crisscrossed by paths, it lies 1.5 miles north of Cannon Beach, the high-end 'antiresort' resort so beloved by Portlanders.

Clark found the whale near **Haystack Rock**, a 295ft sea stack that's the most spectacular landmark on the Oregon coast and accessible from the beach. After bartering with the Tillamook tribe, he staggered away with 300lb of whale blubber – a feast for the half-starved Corps of Discovery.

✕ ⊨ p41, p174

Eating & Sleeping

Tri-Cities ❶

✗ Atomic Ale Brewpub & Eatery   Pub $

(📞509-946-5465; www.atomicalebrewpub.
com; 1015 Lee Blvd, Richland; mains $10-17;
🕐11am-9pm Mon-Thu, to 10pm Fri & Sat, to
9pm Sun) The first brewpub in the Tri-Cities
has hearty fare like quesadillas, pretzels (with
'nuclear sauce'!) and pizza, but locals rave
about the potato soup. Start with a B-17 Brown
or Atomic Amber – the beers might not blow
your mind, but this is a fun, friendly hangout.

The Dalles ❺

✗ Baldwin Saloon   American $$

(📞541-296-5666; www.baldwinsaloon.com; 205
Court St; mains $11-29; 🕐11am-9pm Mon-Thu,
to 10pm Fri & Sat) This 1876 building has been a
bar, a brothel and a coffin-storage warehouse.
Today it's a casual, popular establishment
with a beautiful brick interior full of large oil
paintings, and a historic dark-wood bar. Food
choices include a dozen cut-above-average-in-
The Dalles salads, sandwiches, burgers, pasta
and seafood dishes.

⌂ Celilo Inn   Motel $$

(📞541-769-0001; www.celiloinn.com; 3550 E 2nd
St; d $95-159; 😊❄🎦❄🐾) The beautifully
remodeled Celilo Inn is now a slick and trendy
stay with gorgeous contemporary rooms, many
offering views of The Dalles' bridge and dam
(worth it at only $10 to $20 more). Luxurious
touches include flat-screen TVs and a pool for
those hot summer days. Discount on weekdays.

Astoria ⓫

✗ Astoria Coffeehouse & Bistro   American $$

(📞503-325-1787; www.astoriacoffeehouse.
com; 243 11th St; breakfast & lunch mains $6-18,
dinner mains $15-32; 🕐7am-9pm Sun, to 10pm
Mon-Thu, to 11pm Fri & Sat) Small, popular
cafe with attached bistro offering an eclectic
menu. Everything is made in-house, even the
ketchup. There's sidewalk seating and excellent
cocktails. Expect a wait at dinner and Sunday
brunch. Excellent and changing $5 breakfast
and lunch specials available daily.

✗ Fort George Brewery   Pub Food $

(📞503-325-7468; www.fortgeorgebrewery.
com; 1483 Duane St; mains $7-17, pizzas $14-26;
🕐11am-11pm, from noon Sun) One of the
state's best and most reliable craft brewers. Its
atmospheric brewery-restaurant is in a historic
building that was the original settlement site of
Astoria. Apart from the excellent beer, you can get
gourmet burgers, housemade sausages, salads
and, upstairs, wood-fired pizza. Head to the Lovell
Taproom for views over the production line.

⌂ Commodore Hotel   Boutique Hotel $$

(📞503-325-4747; www.commodoreastoria.com;
258 14th St; d with/without bath from $164/89;
🅿😊🎦) This stylish hotel offers attractive
but small, minimalist rooms. Choose a room
with bathroom or go Euro style (sink in room,
bathroom down the hall; 'deluxe' rooms have
better views). There's a lounge-style lobby with
cafe, free samples of local microbrews from
5pm to 7pm, a movie library and record players
to borrow.

Cannon Beach ⓬

✗ Irish Table   Irish $$$

(📞503-436-0708; www.theirishtable.com;
1235 S Hemlock St; mains $26-30; 🕐5:30-9pm
Fri-Tue) Excellent restaurant hidden at the back
of Sleepy Monk Coffee (📞503-436-2796;
www.sleepymonkcoffee.com; drinks & snacks
$2-7; 🕐8am-3pm Mon, Tue & Thu, to 4pm
Fri-Sun), serving a fusion of Irish and Pacific
Northwest cuisine made with local and seasonal
ingredients. The menu is small and simple, but
the choices are tasty.

⌂ Ocean Lodge   Hotel $$$

(📞503-436-2241; www.theoceanlodge.com;
2864 S Pacific St, d $219-369; 😊❄🎦🐾)
This gorgeous place has some of Cannon
Beach's most luxurious rooms, most with ocean
view and all with fireplace and kitchenette.
A complimentary continental breakfast, an
800-DVD library and pleasant sitting areas are
available to guests. Located on the beach at the
southern end of town.

Classic Trip

Columbia River Gorge & Mt Hood

2

Towering waterfalls, excellent hiking, hot springs, fruit farms – what else could you want from a long weekend? Add shimmering lakes and snowcapped Mt Hood, and the diversity becomes almost surreal.

TRIP HIGHLIGHTS

65 miles

Hood River
Hip, active town with great beer on tap

25 miles

Bonneville Dam & Fish Hatchery
Tour Portland's fish-filled power center

7

5 Cascade Locks

START Troutdale

11

FINISH Portland

Sandy **Mt Hood Village**

13

150 miles

Timberline Lodge
Hike, dine or stay overnight in alpine bliss

Hwy 35
Pick fruit and lavender, pet an alpaca and taste wine

125 miles

3 DAYS
215 MILES / 346KM

GREAT FOR...

BEST TIME TO GO
May to October: fruit is in season and all roads are open.

ESSENTIAL PHOTO
Multnomah Falls: one of the country's highest cascades.

BEST FOR VIEWS
Enjoy a panorama of the gorge's lushest part from Vista House.

Classic Trip

2

Columbia River Gorge & Mt Hood

Few places symbolize the grandeur of the Pacific Northwest like the Columbia River Gorge and Mt Hood. Start along this massive cleft in the Cascade Range that measures up to 4000ft deep and is graced by 77 waterfalls. Meanwhile, Mt Hood peeks out from behind it all in its 11,240ft glory. As you drive up the mountain from the gorge, you'll be treated to a heaven of fruit farms and vineyards.

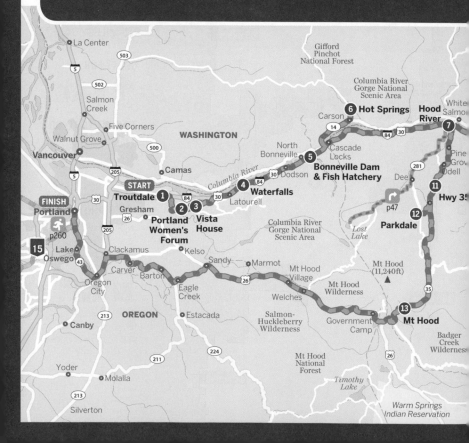

❶ Troutdale

Although the metal arch over Troutdale isn't the official entrée to the Historic Route 30 (which starts a few miles west from here), this is the logical place to turn off I-84 from Portland and begin a journey into the Columbia Gorge's moss-covered wonderland. Troutdale's center is adorably early 20th century and a pleasant place to stretch your legs before the drive.

The Drive ›› Continue through town then turn right

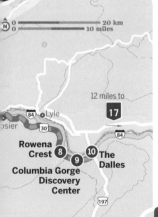

(inland) after the bridge, following the signs for Historic Route 30 toward Corbett. The road follows the forested Sandy River before veering left. Follow this road through a few sleepy hamlets.

🛏 p51

❷ Portland Women's Forum

Pull into this parking lot for your first view of the Columbia Gorge. This spot was once the site of the Chanticleer Hotel, built in 1912. It was here, in 1913, that the plans were made for building Hwy 30, which would become Oregon's first modern paved road. Unfortunately the hotel burned down in 1931, but the panoramas are as splendid as ever. This is arguably the best drive-to viewpoint in the Columbia Gorge.

The Drive ›› Turn left from the parking lot, drive along the ridge and watch as Hwy 30 turns into classic Columbia Gorge country, with increasing mossy lushness.

❸ Vista House

Built between 1916 and 1918, this stone road-side rotunda sits atop Crown Point, 733ft above the Columbia River, and offers magnificent 180-degree views. From the outside, the building looks like it only houses a small information center, but there's a worthwhile historical **museum** (📞503-344-1368; www.vistahouse.com; ⏰9am-4pm Oct-Apr, to 6pm May-Sep) and gift shop hidden down a staircase underground. Weather permitting, you can also go upstairs to the fabulous outdoor viewing deck. Be warned: the winds here can be outrageously strong.

The Drive ›› Take a right directly out of the parking lot and head downhill as the road winds along the old highway and its stone barriers into increasing greenery.

❹ Waterfalls

Welcome to a land so lush and vibrantly green that it looks more like

LINK YOUR TRIP

15 **Three Capes Loop** Head back through Portland and go west on Hwy 26 toward the coast.

17 **Journey Through Time Scenic Byway** From The Dalles, it's about 30 miles east along Hwy 84 and the Columbia River Gorge to Maryhill.

something described in a fantasy novel than reality. This 9-mile section of Hwy 30 could easily be nicknamed 'Waterfall Alley' for the excessive number of spectacular cascades tumbling over mossy basalt cliffs. The falls are at their gushiest in spring. If you're into hiking, you could easily spend a day or two exploring this area, or you can take short walks to the easier-access places. **Multnomah Falls** is the highest in Oregon and the busiest stop – you'll find more peace and quiet around the lesser-known spots.

The Drive ≫ Keep heading east on Hwy 30 until it merges with I-84 shortly after Ainsworth State Park. After a few miles, take exit 40 toward Bonneville Dam.

TOP WATERFALLS

The following are all off Hwy 30, listed from west to east.

Latourell Falls (249ft) The first major waterfall as you come east on Hwy 30. Hike 10 minutes to reach it, or go a mile to the top.

Bridal Veil Falls (140ft) Two-tiered falls reached via an easy half-mile walk. A separate wheelchair-accessible trail passes through a meadow.

Wahkeena Falls (242ft) Hike up the Wahkeena Trail, join Trail No 441 and head down to Multnomah Falls. Return via the road for the 5-mile loop.

Multnomah Falls (642ft) The gorge's top attraction. Trail No 411 leads to the top (1 mile). Continue up foresty Multnomah Creek and the top of Larch Mountain (another 7 miles).

Oneonta Falls (75ft) Located within the lovely half-mile Oneonta Gorge. Carefully scamper over logjams and wade in water up to waist-high. Fun and worth it!

Horsetail Falls (176ft) Just east of Oneonta Gorge. A 4.5-mile loop begins here, passing through Ponytail Falls and Triple Falls. Walk a half-mile east on Hwy 30 (passing the Oneonta Gorge) to return.

Elowah Falls (289ft) More isolated but pretty falls, located about a mile off the highway. Hike to the top, then take a 0.7-mile side trail to McCord Creek Falls (2.5 miles round-trip).

TRIP HIGHLIGHT

❺ Bonneville Dam & Fish Hatchery

Upon its completion in 1938, Bonneville became the first dam on the Columbia River, permanently altering one of the continent's mightiest rivers, as well as one of the world's most important salmon runs. It's worth stopping here to check out the **visitor center** (☏541-374-8820; I-84 exit 40; ☺9am-5pm), which has good exhibits, free tours to the powerhouse throughout the day and a theater showing videos of the dam's history. The underwater viewing room into the fish ladder is a highlight. Afterwards, stroll the nearby fish hatchery, making sure to visit the 11ft-long sturgeon named Herman, who has survived a kidnapping, a knife attack and even the 2017 wildfires.

The Drive ≫ Get back on I-84 and drive about 3.5 miles upstream to exit 44, which leads you to the Bridge of the Gods (toll $2 each way) into Washington State. Turn east on Hwy 14, then left on Wind River Rd from the highway, and finally right on Hot Springs Ave.

❻ Carson Hot Springs

Feel like a nice warm soak to ease your car-stiff bum? Carson Hot Springs

Resort (p51) is hardly fancy, but its modesty is its finest feature; the first-come, first-served mineral baths are a true escape from any kind of hype.

The Drive » Backtrack over the Bridge of the Gods, then head east on I-84.

🛏 p51

TRIP HIGHLIGHT

7 Hood River

Your next stop is the windy riverside town of Hood River, one of the world's top windsurfing and kiteboarding destinations. It's also one very attractive town, thanks to its old homes and stunning setting on the Columbia River. Plus Mt Hood, with its hiking trails and ski runs, is only a stone's throw away. It should come as no surprise that Hood River has a youthful, adrenaline-hungry population and a main drag packed with good restaurants, boutique shops and adventure sports stores.

The Drive » Get back on I-84 E for around 10 miles, then take exit 69 to Mosier. This links you back up with Historic Route 30 for another incredibly scenic 9 miles.

🍴 🛏 p51

8 Rowena Crest

The summit of this portion of Historic Route 30

DETOUR: LOST LAKE

Start: 7 **Hood River**

For a classic Mt Hood photo op, detour 25 miles south of Hood River to the spectacular Lost Lake. Flanked by forest, this stunning blue body of mountain water frames the white cone of Mt Hood like a perfect postcard. Along with fabulous views, the detour offers respite from the heat when the gorge gets too hot. To get there from Hood River, take Hwy 281 to Dee and follow the signs. Allow at least half a day for the excursion.

has a parking lot with views over the Columbia Gorge, which at this point is losing its lushness to windy, barren hillsides and steep, stratified cliff faces. There are two hiking trails: the **Tom McCall Point Trail** (3 miles round-trip) will get you glimpses over the rolling hills of the plateau and Mt Adams; and the easier **Rowena Plateau Trail** (2.5 miles round-trip) is a particularly good spot for May wildflowers and leads to the waterfowl-filled **Rowena Pond**.

The Drive » Historic Route 30 winds down the hill back to river level. Follow the signs to the Columbia Gorge Discovery Center.

9 Columbia Gorge Discovery Center

The informative **Columbia Gorge Discovery Center** (☎541-296-8600; www.gorgediscovery.org;

5000 Discovery Dr; adult/child $9/5; ⊙9am-5pm) covers the history of the gorge from its creation by cataclysmic floods, through its Native American inhabitants, to the early pioneers, settlers and eventual damming of the river. Whether you're a gorge fanatic or a first-time visitor, the center will undoubtedly increase your appreciation for one of the Pacific Northwest's most amazing natural landscapes.

The Drive » Go back out to Historic Route 30 or I-84 (they run parallel to each other from here, but Historic Route 30 is more scenic), then east a couple of miles to The Dalles.

10 The Dalles

Though steadfastly unglamorous, The Dalles offers decent camping and hiking, and the fierce winds are excellent for windsurfing and kiteboarding. Sights here

Classic Trip

WHY THIS IS A CLASSIC TRIP
CELESTE BRASH, WRITER

Few routes take in this much beauty in such a small space – and it all starts only a half-hour from Portland! The waterfall strip of the Columbia Gorge is one of the most beautiful places I know, and Mt Hood's sharp snowy peak is symbolic of the region. The hiking is phenomenal, the people are down to earth, and you can pick fruit and drink fabulous beer and wine.

Above: Mt Hood (p50)
Left: Rainbow Trout, Bonneville Dam & Fish Hatchery (p46)
Right: Multnomah Falls (p46), Columbia River Gorge

DANITA DELIMONT/GETTY IMAGES ©

include the fascinating **Fort Dalles Museum** (☏541-296-4547; www.fort dallesmuseum.org; 500 W 15th St; adult/child $5/1; ⊘10am-5pm Mar-Oct, closed Mon-Thu Nov-Feb), Oregon's oldest museum, which is full of historical items. Built in 1957, **The Dalles Dam & Lock** produces enough electricity to power a city of a million inhabitants. **The Dalles Dam Visitor Center** (☏541-296-9778; Clodfelter Way; ⊘9am-5pm May-Sep) contains the expected homage to hydroelectricity, along with a fish cam to view migratory salmon – it's east on the frontage road from exit 87 off I-84.

The Drive » From here you'll backtrack on Historic Route 30 or I-84 (the faster option) to Hood River. Take exit 64 and follow the signs for Hwy 35, which leads inland toward Mt Hood.

✕ ⏢ p41

- - - - - - - - - - - - - - - - - -

TRIP HIGHLIGHT

⓫ Highway 35

The first 16.5 miles of Hwy 35 to Parkdale is the first leg of the 'Fruit Loop,' named for all its agriculture. Wind past scenic fertile lands, easy-to-spot family fruit stands, U-pick orchards, lavender fields, alpaca farms and winery tasting rooms. There are blossoms in spring, berries in summer, and apples and pears in fall – with plenty of festivals and

celebrations throughout the seasons (except for winter). It's a good way to sample the area's agricultural bounties while appreciating the local scenery too – try not to get in an accident from ogling the larger-than-life Mt Hood when it's in view.

The Drive 》 Enjoy the scenery of endless orchards and vineyards, and stop whenever you feel the whim – there are over 30 businesses to choose from.

⑫ Parkdale

Your ascent ends at the little town of Parkdale, a great stop for lunch. You can also visit the

tiny **Hutson Museum** (📞541-352-7434; 4967 Baseline Dr; $1; 🕐noon-3pm Thu-Sun Apr-Oct, hours vary other months) in a country-perfect red farmhouse. It has displays of rocks and minerals, Native American artifacts and local memorabilia – plus a garden of native plants.

The Drive 》 Return to Hwy 35 and follow it south for 27 miles around grand, white-capped Mt Hood to Hwy 26.

✕ ⊨ p51

TRIP HIGHLIGHT

⑬ Mt Hood

At 11,240ft, Mt Hood is the highest peak in Oregon. Its pyramid shape makes it peek out from behind many hills, enhancing the view. The best place to enjoy this alpine world is Timber-

line Lodge, a handsome wooden gem from the 1930s, offering glorious shelter and refreshments to both guests and nonguests (and yes, some exterior shots of *The Shining* were filmed here). In summer, wildflowers bloom on the mountainsides and hidden ponds shimmer in blue, making for some unforgettable hikes; in winter, downhill and cross-country skiing dominates people's minds and bodies.

From here there's also convenient access to the **Pacific Crest Trail** (PCT). Whether you hike 2 miles or 12 miles along the PCT, the views of Mt Hood are incredible. The trail is easy to find – follow the signs to the right of the lodge.

⊨ p51

MT HOOD RAILROAD

If you're tired of the road, the **Mt Hood Railroad** (📞800-872-4661; www.mthoodrr.com; 110 Railroad Ave; adult/child from $35/30) also starts here and runs scenically from Hood River up a similar route to Hwy 35, past the towns of Odell and Dee before its terminus in Parkdale. The views are spectacular, the cars are beautifully restored and the food is memorable. You can also choose to go on special train excursions that include wine tasting and visits to museums.

Eating & Sleeping

Troutdale ❶

🛏 McMenamins Edgefield   Hotel $$

(📞503-669-8610; www.mcmenamins.com;
2126 SW Halsey St; dm $35, s/d without bath
from $60/155; 🐾🛜) This former county poor
farm is now a one-of-a-kind, 38-acre complex
with a dizzying variety of services. There's a
wine-tasting room, a cinema, a glassblowing
studio, a golf course, live music, gardens and
restaurants. Rooms are European style (no TVs
or phones; wi-fi in common areas), some with
bathrooms down the hall.

Carson Hot Springs ❻

🛏 Carson Hot Springs Resort   Hotel $$$

(📞509-427-8292; www.carsonhotspringresort.
com; 372 St Martin Rd; r $169-350; 🛜🐾) This
rustic, locally loved resort has standard hotel
rooms and a charming historic bathhouse
where you can soak in a mineral bath and then
be wrapped up like a burrito to sweat out your
worries (mineral bath and wrap $30 to $35).

Hood River ❼

🍴 Celilo
Restaurant & Bar   Northwestern US $$$

(📞541-386-5710; www.celilorestaurant.com; 16
Oak St; mains lunch $12-15, dinner $24-28; ⏱5-
9pm daily, 11:30am-3pm Fri-Sun) For upscale
dining with an emphasis on locally sourced
ingredients, this modern restaurant has walls
that open to the sidewalk on warm afternoons.
Main dishes include housemade pastas, salads,
and lots of fish and seafood dishes. Lunch is
more affordable but the half-price happy hour
(5pm to 6pm) small plates are a scrumptious
steal.

🍴 Double Mountain Brewery   Pub $$

(📞541-387-0042; www.doublemountainbrewery.
com; 8 4th St; sandwiches $8-12, pizzas $10-26;
⏱11am-10pm Sun-Thu, to 11pm Fri & Sat; 🎵🐾)
For a casual bite, step into this popular brewpub-
restaurant for a tasty sandwich or excellent
brick-oven pizza. The menu is limited, but the

food is great and the beer even better. Outside
tables are pet-friendly.

🛏 Columbia Gorge Hotel   Hotel $$$

(📞800-345-1921; www.columbiagorgehotel.
com; 4000 Westcliff Dr; r $99-439;
🐾❄@🛜🐾) Hood River's most famous
place to stay is this historic Spanish-style hotel,
set high on a cliff above the Columbia. The
atmosphere is classy and the grounds lovely,
and there's a fine restaurant on the premises.
Rooms have antique beds and furnishings.
River-view rooms cost more but are worth it.

🛏 Society Hotel – Bingen   Hotel $

(📞503-445-0444; www.thesocietyhotel.com;
cnr Franklin & Cedar St, Bingen; dm $40-52, r
without bath $110-146, cabins $239-309; 🛜🐾)
It's a historic hotel, it's a hostel, it's a retreat
center and it's a spa. Whoever you are, there's
a space for you on beautiful grounds amongst
modern, cozy architecture. The dorm and
shared-bath rooms are in a restored schoolhouse
that includes a massive activities area, while the
newly built cabins surround a spa complete with
hot and cold pools.

Parkdale ⑫

🍴 Apple Valley BBQ   Barbecue $$

(4956 Baseline Dr; mains $10-15; ⏱11am-8pm
Wed-Sun) Fill up on barbecue ribs, pulled pork,
burgers, salads and homemade pie in a lively
1950s flashback setting. Tables out front make
for excellent street viewing on a warm day.

Mt Hood ⑬

🛏 Timberline Lodge   Lodge $$$

(📞800-547-1406; www.timberlinelodge.com;
27500 Timberline Rd; bunk r $165-221, d from
$180; 🐾🛜🐾) As much a community treasure
as a hotel, this gorgeous historic lodge offers a
variety of rooms, from dorms that sleep up to 10
to deluxe fireplace rooms. There's a year-round
heated outdoor pool, and the ski lifts are close
by. Enjoy awesome views of Mt Hood, nearby
hiking trails, two bars and a good dining room.
Rates vary widely.

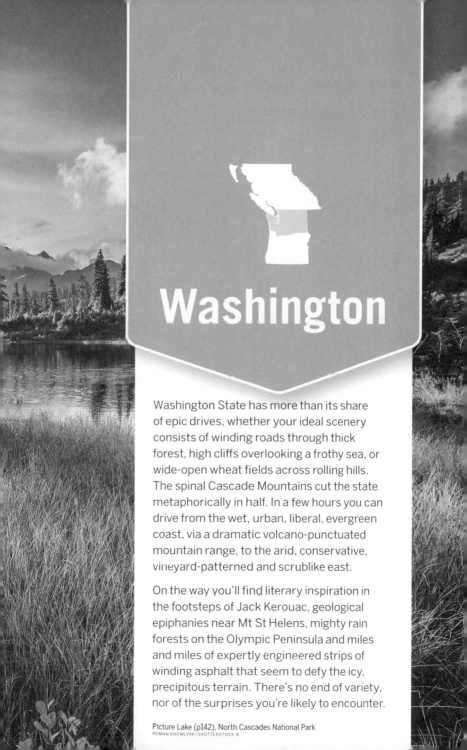

Washington

Washington State has more than its share of epic drives, whether your ideal scenery consists of winding roads through thick forest, high cliffs overlooking a frothy sea, or wide-open wheat fields across rolling hills. The spinal Cascade Mountains cut the state metaphorically in half. In a few hours you can drive from the wet, urban, liberal, evergreen coast, via a dramatic volcano-punctuated mountain range, to the arid, conservative, vineyard-patterned and scrublike east.

On the way you'll find literary inspiration in the footsteps of Jack Kerouac, geological epiphanies near Mt St Helens, mighty rain forests on the Olympic Peninsula and miles and miles of expertly engineered strips of winding asphalt that seem to defy the icy, precipitous terrain. There's no end of variety, nor of the surprises you're likely to encounter.

Picture Lake (p142), North Cascades National Park
ROMAN KHOMLYAK/SHUTTERSTOCK ©

Washington

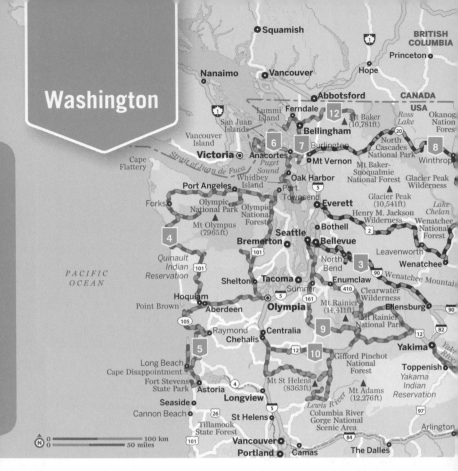

 DON'T MISS

Ross Lake Resort

A floating hotel on a wilderness lake; no wonder Kerouac loved the cold, almost terrifying, beauty on Trip 8

Cape Disappointment

Few leave Cape Disappointment disappointed, thanks to its spectacular end-of-the-continent setting. Drop by on Trips 1 5

Leavenworth

German theme towns rarely work in the US except when the alpine backdrop looks positively German. See it on Trip 8

Northwest Railway Museum

Snoqualmie community saves a slice of American heritage: a moving museum on a train. Visit on Trip 3

North Woven Broom

Long before Harry Potter, North Woven Broom was making artisan broomsticks. Sweep by on Trip 13

9 **Mt Rainier Scenic Byways 2–3 Days**
The Northwest's hulking emblem circumnavigated.

10 **Mt St Helens Volcano Trail 3 Days**
The fieriest of US volcanoes is a giant outdoor science lab.

11 **Washington Wine Tour 3 Days**
Is Washington the next Sonoma? Ply the Yakima Valley wineries for clues.

12 **Mt Baker & Lummi Island 1–2 Days**
An icy sentinel overlooking an island of culinary wizardry.

13 **International Selkirk Loop 3 Days**
Some of Washington's weirdest roadside attractions and a bit of Canada.

Classic Trip

Mountains to Sound Greenway

3

Busy I-90 zaps you from the Yakima Valley to the metro sophistication of Seattle in less than two hours. But meander off the main road and more serendipitous adventures await you.

TRIP HIGHLIGHTS

95 miles

Northwest Railway Museum
Five-mile retrospective train rides between Snoqualmie and North Bend

90 miles

Mt Si
North Bend's 'twin peaks' is Washington's most popular hike

FINISH
11

8 **6**

5

Snoqualmie Pass

Ellensburg
START

Pike Place Market
Every facet of Seattle contained in one raucous market

120 miles

John Wayne Pioneer Trail
A cycling thoroughfare along an old railroad

80 miles

1–2 DAYS
120 MILES / 193KM

GREAT FOR...

BEST TIME TO GO
May to September: open museums and predictable weather.

ESSENTIAL PHOTO
Snoqualmie Falls' raw power and *Twin Peaks* flashbacks.

BEST FOR FAMILIES
Northwest Railway Museum and its train rides.

Classic Trip

3 Mountains to Sound Greenway

Dramatic changes in scenery and radically contrasting ecosystems are par for the course in Washington, a land bisected by the climate-altering Cascade Mountains. With I-90 as its main artery, this drive ferries you from the dry east to the wet west via the 3046ft Snoqualmie Pass on an ostensibly busy road. But a mile or two off the interstate a parallel 'greenway' of bucolic trails and small-town preservation societies prevails.

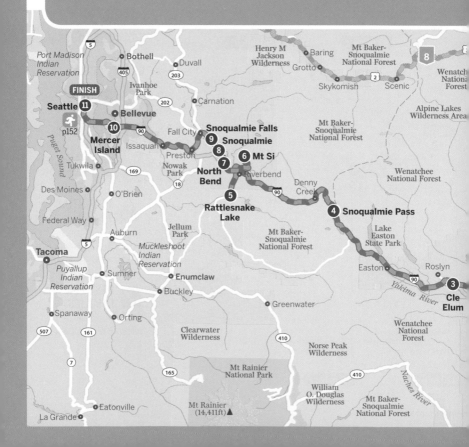

❶ Ellensburg

Take an archetypal American rodeo town with a smattering of historic buildings and add a stately college. Welcome to Ellensburg, a place of juxtapositions. Here, erudite college undergraduates rub shoulders with weekend cowboys in a small yet salubrious collegiate town where two-thirds of the 18,000 population are registered students. Ellensburg is at its busiest during the annual **rodeo** (☎800-637-2444; www.ellensburgrodeo.com; 1010 E 8th Ave; tickets $16-36; ⏱Labor Day weekend Aug-Sep), the biggest of its kind in the Pacific Northwest. Like most Washington towns, Ellensburg has its fair share of peripheral motel/mall infestations, but body-swerve the familiar big boxes and you'll uncover a compact but select cluster of venerable red-brick buildings in a downtown **historic district**. Also worth checking out is the **Kittitas County Historical Museum** (☎509-925-3778; www.kchm.org; 114 E 3rd Ave; by donation; ⏱10am-4pm Mon-Sat), housed in the 1889 Cadwell Building, known mostly for its petrified-wood and gemstone collections, but also hosting a cleverly laid out history section documenting the backgrounds of Croatian, Arabic and Welsh immigrants.

The Drive » To avoid the clamor of the busy interstate, take US 97 northwest out of town before branching onto SR 10 to the small rural settlement of Thorp, 9 miles from Ellensburg.

✕ ⛿ p65

❷ Thorp Grist Mill

In the small town of Thorp (population 297), the **Thorp Grist Mill** (☎509-964-9640; www.thorp.org; 11640 N Thorp Hwy; ⏱tours noon-4pm Wed-Fri, 11am-4pm Sat & Sun May-Aug) was once a de facto meeting place for local farmers. Today, its well-preserved shell gives an interesting insight into the pioneer farmers who plowed the fields of the Kittitas Valley in the late 19th century. Converted to a rural museum, the mill originally dates from 1879 when its primary purpose was to grind flour using water power from the nearby Yakima River. It ceased operation in 1946, but, thanks to the foresight of local community activists, was placed on the National Register of Historic Places in 1977.

The Drive » Continue northwest on SR 10 through

Winton

Wenatchee National Forest

ns Club Park

Leavenworth

Cashmere

Sunnyslope

Wenatchee Confluence State Park

enatchee ational Forest

Squilchuck State Park

Liberty

istol

❷ Thorp Grist Mill

Ellensburg ❶ START

16 miles to 11

0 | 20 km
0 | 10 miles

§ LINK YOUR TRIP

8 Cascade Drive
Both ends of this trip will deposit you close to entry points for the Cascade Drive, another mountain-punctuated driving extravaganza.

11 Washington Wine Tour
Do this drive backward, starting in Seattle, and the essence of local wine in Ellensburg might inspire you to travel on to Yakima and beyond.

quiet bucolic farmland to Cle Elum, 18 miles from Thorp.

---

❸ Cle Elum

Cle Elum's location on the cusp of the Eastern Cascades and the bald treeless grasslands of the Kittitas Valley pulls in two radically different types of visitor. Seattle-ites regularly cross Snoqualmie Pass to sup the local wine and enjoy seemingly endless summer sunshine. Eastern-ers stop by to gaze west at the snowier, more topographically interesting mountains. A posh resort, the **Suncadia** (☎509-649-6400; www. suncadiaresort.com; 3600 Suncadia Trail; d from $210; 🛜🐾), just west of Cle Elum and complete with golf, spa and winery, caters for both groups.

Though small, the town has a couple of esoteric museums conceived and maintained by vivacious community groups.

Up the road 3.5 miles, **Roslyn** stood in for Alaska in the 1990s TV show *Northern Exposure* (plot spoiler: there's more TV nostalgia four stops further on).

The Drive 》 Time to brave I-90! Access the road at exit 84 and motor 30 miles progressively uphill

to Snoqualmie Pass. Just before the summit you'll pass Keechelus Lake, the source of the Yakima River, on your left.

---

❹ Snoqualmie Pass

One of the easier routes across the Cascades and the only one to carry an interstate (I-90), Snoqualmie was first prospected by white settlers in the 1850s. By the 1930s a fledgling road was being plowed year-round and the pass had spawned a nascent ski area, which has since morphed into four separate areas known (and managed) communally as the **Summit at Snoqualmie** (☎425-434-7669; www.summitatsnoqualmie. com; 1001 SR 906; day pass adult/youth $95/62; ☺9am-10pm late Nov-Apr). This is the nearest day-use ski area to Seattle (read: long lines). Should you summit the pass in summer, consider a hike. The **Pacific Crest Trail** briefly descends to the hustle of the interstate here but blissful tranquility stretches for many miles in either direction.

The Drive 》 Descend on I-90 until exit 32, 22 miles from the pass. Go south on 436th Ave SE, which becomes Cedar Falls Rd. Within 3 miles you will be deposited at Rattlesnake Lake.

TRIP HIGHLIGHT

❺ Rattlesnake Lake

An important nexus on the Mountains to Sound Greenway, tranquil Rattlesnake Lake was once a more tumultuous place. A town called Moncton existed here until 1915 before it was flooded, evacuated and condemned after an abortive damming project. From 1906 to 1980 an erstwhile railway, the 'Milwaukee Road,' passed through. The railroad bed has been reworked into a non-motorized thoroughfare known as the **John Wayne Pioneer Trail**, which is popular with cyclists. From here, with a bike or walking, you can descend to the lake, a journey that includes careering through the 2.3-mile Snoqualmie tunnel (bring headlamps). The lake is also the starting point for the **Snoqualmie Valley Trail** and a 4-mile round-trip hike up to Rattlesnake Ridge. There are toilets and a kayak launch lakeside, and a small interpretive center.

The Drive 》 Return to I-90 but this time, rather than join it, head underneath on 436th Ave SE to the junction with E North Bend Way. Turn left and then go right on SE Mt Si Rd. This leg of the trip is 10 miles.

TRIP HIGHLIGHT

❻ Mt Si

Brooding moodily behind the town of North Bend, 4167ft Mt Si is allegedly the most climbed mountain in the state (approximately 40,000 hike it every year) and an annual fitness test for many Seattleites. The trail starts 2.5 miles down SE Mt Si Rd from a parking lot and is an 8-mile round-trip, including 3150ft of ascent. Though popular and predictably crowded in summer, the switchbacking path is no piece of cake. Dress appropriately for the mountains and bring water. The lofty meadow that acts as the summit for most walkers (the actual summit is a precipitous haystack-shaped rock) is revered for its hard-earned Puget Sound views.

The Drive » Retrace your route along SE Mt Si Rd to the intersection with E North Bend Way, where you turn right into North Bend, about 4 miles away.

----

❼ North Bend

If you're one of the many fans of a certain cult-classic TV show, your first sight of North Bend might make you do a double-take. This is where David Lynch's weird and wonderful *Twin Peaks* was filmed, both the original run in the early 1990s and the final season in 2017. The town – a sleepy, if salubrious, place these days – is still milking its fame. **Twede's** (☏425-831-5511; www.twedescafe.com; 137 W North Bend Way; mains $8-11; ⏰8am-8pm Mon-Fri, from 6:30am Sat & Sun), the 'Double R Diner' in the TV show, proudly advertises its *Twin Peaks* credentials with cherry pie and 'a damn fine cup o' coffee,' along with 50 – yes 50 – different types of burger. Down the road, the **Snoqualmie Valley Historical Museum** (www.snoqualmievalleymuseum.org; Bendigo Blvd; ⏰1-5pm Sat-Tue Apr-Oct, noon-4pm Mon & Tue Nov-Mar) charts the pre-Lynchian history of the valley with pioneer and Native American exhibits.

The Drive » From North Bend take Bendigo Blvd, cross the South Fork of the Snoqualmie River and continue 3 miles into Snoqualmie.

TWIN PEAKS

Recognize *that* Snoqualmie Valley mountain, *that* waterfall, *that* cafe and *that* hotel? If so, you're not alone. By now, *Twin Peaks* probably needs very little introduction. The TV drama series conceived, written and directed by Mark Frost and legendary US film director David Lynch has long since moved beyond cult status to become an almost mainstream cultural phenomenon. Laura Palmer, Agent Cooper and the log lady are widely beloved characters. David Lynch (*Blue Velvet, Wild at Heart*) has become so influential that he has his own adjective: 'Lynchian' denotes anything that's surreal, dreamy, unsettling and – occasionally – freakishly funny.

Twin Peaks originally ran for 30 episodes over two seasons between 1990 and 1991, then returned for a final season in 2017. The show was set in a fictional Washington town of the same name (and filmed in North Bend and Snoqualmie). It starred Kyle MacLachlan as FBI agent Dale Cooper, investigating the mysterious death of a pretty blonde homecoming queen. The series, with its complex plot and surreal, but suspenseful, story line, quickly gained a large audience and won numerous Golden Globe and Emmy nominations and several awards. Time has done little to diminish its appeal. The third season was wildly anticipated, and praised by fans and critics alike.

As for those recognizable landmarks? The mountain (the fictional 'Twin Peaks') is Mt Si, the waterfall (seen in the show's opening credits) is Snoqualmie Falls, the cafe (where Kyle MacLachlan extolled the virtues of hot black coffee) is Twede's and the hotel (the Great Northern in the show) is the Salish Lodge & Spa (p65).

WHY THIS IS A CLASSIC TRIP
BECKY OHLSEN,
WRITER

This trip takes in a good sampling of Washington's unusually varied pleasures, from the cowboy town of Ellensburg to the skiing and hiking haven of Snoqualmie Pass; from a waterfall made famous by a trippy TV show to a rewardingly tough mountain hike. (The route has several great hiking opportunities, in fact.) And it all wraps up in the world-class city of Seattle.

Above: View from Mt Si (p60) near North Bend
Left: Steam train, Northwest Railway Museum
Right: Pike Place Market (p64)

TRIP HIGHLIGHT

⑧ Snoqualmie

Located a mile east of the famous falls, Snoqualmie is a diminutive town of eclectic shopfronts that ply hardware, organic coffee and Native American art. Across the tracks, the lovingly restored **Northwest Railway Museum** (www.trainmuseum.org; 38625 SE King St; ⊙10am-5pm) is the largest of its type in Washington. Its hook is its retro steam-train trips (adult/child $20/10), which chug (Saturdays and Sundays from April to October) 5 miles down the line to North Bend and another equally cute Thomas-the-Tank-Engine station.

Snoqualmie is also an ideal place to jump onto the **Snoqualmie Valley Trail**, the region's longest greenway (31 miles), which parallels the Snoqualmie River along the course of an old railway line. Access is best gained from the north end of Meadowbrook Way SE.

The Drive » From Snoqualmie follow Railroad Ave northwest out of town and within a mile you'll be at Snoqualmie Falls.

⑨ Snoqualmie Falls

Come between April and June during the spring snow melt and you'll see why this 268ft mini Niagara has been producing hydroelectric power since 1899. Observation decks and an overlook park stand face-on against the supersonic spray, while perched awfully close to the giant falls' rim is the luxurious Salish Lodge & Spa, the second incarnation of a hotel that was first built here in 1918.

A half-mile trail drops down through spray-fed rain forest to the **Snoqualmie Falls Hydroelectric Museum** (☑425-831-4445; SE 69th Pl; ☺10am-5pm Wed-Sun Jun-Sep), housed in the old train depot and chronicling the history of the power plant.

The Drive ≫ Take the Fall City–Snoqualmie Rd to Fall City, where you turn left onto the Preston–Fall City Rd opposite the Fall City Roadhouse and Inn. Merge west onto I-90 again at Preston (exit 22) to reach Mercer Island, 23 miles from Snoqualmie Falls.

🛏 p65

❿ Mercer Island

You don't have to get out of your car to experience Mercer Island's greatest engineering marvel. The community's two colossal parallel bridges that carry traffic over to metro Seattle are the second- and fifth-longest floating bridges in the world. An initial bridge, built here in 1939, was destroyed by a storm in 1990. The current structures, the **Homer M Hadley Memorial Bridge** (westbound traffic) and the **Lacey V Murrow Memorial Bridge** (eastbound) were built in 1989 and 1993 respectively.

The Drive ≫ Coming off the floating bridges, traffic is directed through the Baker Tunnel before coming out with surprising suddenness in Seattle's downtown core close to King Street Station.

TRIP HIGHLIGHT

⓫ Seattle

Put aside some time to enjoy Seattle at the end of this drive, which deposits you on the cusp of downtown and its cluster of craning skyscrapers, great to explore on foot (p152). For dazzling city views ascend the **Columbia Center** (☑206-386-5564; www.skyviewobservatory.com; 701 5th Ave; adult/child $20/14; ☺10am-10pm late May-early Sep, to 8pm rest of year; ☒Pioneer Sq), which, at 932ft high, is the loftiest building in the Pacific Northwest and a lot cheaper than the Space Needle. Pioneer Square is Seattle's oldest quarter and home to the **Klondike Gold Rush National Historical Park** (☑206-553-3000; www.nps.gov/klse; 319 2nd Ave S; ☺9am-5pm daily Jun-Aug, 10am-5pm Tue-Sun Sep-Feb, 10am-5pm daily Mar-May; ☒First Hill Streetcar), a shockingly good free museum about the 1897 Alaska gold rush. Another good family-orientated attraction is the **aquarium** (☑206-386-4300; www.seattleaquarium.org; 1483 Alaskan Way, Waterfront; adult/child $34.95/24.95; ☺9:30am-5pm; 👶; ☒University St), the centerpiece of which is a glass-domed room. For a post-drive picnic, decamp to **Pike Place Market** (☑206-682-7453; www.pikeplacemarket.org; 85 Pike St; ☺9am-6pm Mon-Sat, to 5pm Sun; ☒Westlake) for artisan cheeses, Russian pastries and Italian deli meats.

✕ 🛏 p65

HAY IS FOR HORSES

As you drive the rural roads around Ellensburg and then again as you descend into the Snoqualmie Valley, you're sure to see fields of Timothy grass, a tall, rolled-form grass farmed for hay that's considered top-notch cattle and horse feed as well as tasty grub for rabbits and guinea pigs. Surprisingly, hay is one of the highest-valued crops in Washington and around 35% of the harvest is shipped internationally, mostly to Asia. The grass is cut two times per year, usually in June and September.

Eating & Sleeping

Ellensburg ❶

✖ Red Pickle
Guatemalan, Fusion $

(📞509-367-0003; 301 N Pine St; mains from $10, cocktails $8; ⏰11am-9pm Wed-Sun, 4-9pm Tue) Ellensburg's favorite food truck now has a bricks-and-mortar location, inside an old filling station (formerly D&M Coffee). There's no sign, so it's extra-delightful to stumble upon the place, with its delicious, creative food (Guatemalan hot dogs piled high with spicy toppings, street tacos stuffed with flavorful pork and homemade salsa, wasabi fries, burgers, fried chicken), cheerful staff and perfect cocktails.

⌂ Rainbow Motel
Motel $

(📞509-933-7100; 1025 W University Way; s/d from $65/75; 🛜) This place is so authentically and unintentionally retro, it's as if it's been in a plastic bubble since the '60s – you'll either love it or hate it. Rooms have a perfumed or smoky odor (even though they're all nonsmoking), original wood paneling, terrible landscape paintings on the walls and worn mid-century furniture straight out of Mad Men.

Snoqualmie Falls ❾

⌂ Salish Lodge & Spa
Hotel $$$

(📞info 425-888-2556, reservations 800-272-5474; www.salishlodge.com; 6501 Railroad Ave; d from $459; P🛜🐾) Here is a beautiful resort that sits atop 268ft Snoqualmie Falls. This hotel doesn't rest on its well-located laurels: the modern amenities combined with rustic Pacific Northwest charm (imagine enjoying the warmth of a fireplace while lounging on a memory foam mattress) make this a quintessential luxury lodge getaway.

Seattle ⓫

✖ Top Pot Hand-Forged Doughnuts
Cafe $

(www.toppotdoughnuts.com; 2124 5th Ave, Belltown; doughnuts from $1.29; ⏰6am-

7pm Mon-Fri, 7am-7pm Sat & Sun; 🚇13) Sitting pretty in a glass-fronted former car showroom with art deco signage and immense bookshelves, Top Pot's flagship cafe produces the Ferraris of the doughnut world. It might have morphed into a 20-outlet chain in recent years, but its hand-molded collection of sweet rings are still – arguably – some of the best in the city. The coffee's pretty potent too.

✖ Wild Ginger
Asian $$$

(📞206-623-4450; www.wildginger.net; 1401 3rd Ave, Downtown; mains $19-34; ⏰11:30am-10pm Mon-Thu, to 11pm Fri & Sat, 4-9pm Sun; 🚇University St) A tour of the Pacific Rim – via China, Indonesia, Malaysia, Vietnam and Seattle, of course – is the wide-ranging theme at this highly popular downtown fusion restaurant. The signature fragrant duck goes down nicely with a glass of Riesling. The restaurant also provides food for the swanky Triple Door (📞206-838-4333; www.thetripledoor.net; 216 Union St) dinner club downstairs.

✖ Zeitgeist Coffee
Cafe $

(📞206-583-0497; www.zeitgeistcoffee.com; 171 S Jackson St, Pioneer Sq; ⏰6am-7pm Mon-Fri, from 7am Sat, 8am-6pm Sun; 🛜; 🚇First Hill Streetcar) Possibly Seattle's best (if also busiest) indie coffee bar, Zeitgeist brews smooth doppio macchiatos to go with its sweet almond croissants and other luscious baked goods. The atmosphere is trendy industrial, with brick walls and large windows for people-watching. Soups, salads and sandwiches are also on offer.

⌂ Belltown Inn
Hotel $$

(📞206-529-3700; www.belltown-inn.com; 2301 3rd Ave, Belltown; r from $234; 🐾❄@🛜; 🚇RapidRide D Line) The reliable Belltown Inn is a popular midrange place to stow your suitcase – good on the basics, if a little light on embellishments. That said, there's a roof terrace, free bike rentals and some rooms have kitchenettes. Both downtown and the Seattle Center are within easy walking distance.

Olympic Peninsula Loop

Freakishly wet, fantastically green and chillingly remote, the Olympic Peninsula looks like it has been resurrected from a wilder, pre-civilized era.

4

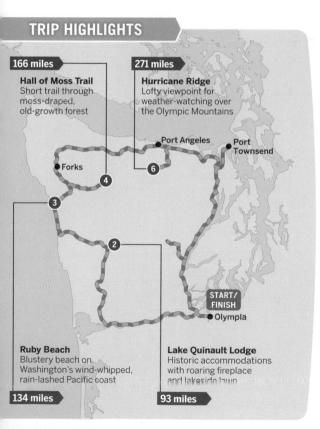

166 miles

Hall of Moss Trail
Short trail through moss-draped, old-growth forest

271 miles

Hurricane Ridge
Lofty viewpoint for weather-watching over the Olympic Mountains

● Port Angeles

Port Townsend

● Forks

4

6

3

2

START/ FINISH

● Olympia

Ruby Beach
Blustery beach on Washington's wind-whipped, rain-lashed Pacific coast

134 miles

Lake Quinault Lodge
Historic accommodations with roaring fireplace and lakeside lawn

93 miles

---

4 DAYS
435 MILES / 700KM

GREAT FOR...

BEST TIME TO GO
June to September, when deluges are slightly less likely.

 ESSENTIAL PHOTO

Hoh Rainforest to see greens you've never imagined.

 BEST FOR WILDLIFE

Roosevelt elk at the Hoh Rainforest.

4 Olympic Peninsula Loop

Imagine pine-clad beaches fused with an American Mt Olympus, with a slice of Stephenie Meyer's *Twilight* saga thrown in for good measure and you've got an approximation of what a drive around the Olympic Peninsula looks like. This is wilderness of the highest order, where thick forest collides with an end-of-the-continent coastline that hasn't changed much since Juan de Fuca sailed by in 1592. Bring hiking boots — and rain gear!

❶ Olympia

Welcome to Olympia, city of weird contrasts, where street-side buskers belt out acoustic grunge, and stiff bureaucrats answer their ringtones on the lawns of the expansive state legislature. A quick circuit of the **Washington State Capitol** (☏360-902-8880; www.olympiawa.gov/ community/visiting-the-capitol. aspx; 416 Sid Snyder Ave SW; ⊙7am-5:30pm Mon-Fri, 11am-4pm Sat & Sun), a huge Grecian temple of a building, will give you a last taste of civilization before you depart. Then load up the car and head swiftly for the exits.

The Drive » Your basic route is due west, initially on US 101,

then (briefly) on SR 8 before joining US 12 in Elma. In Grays Harbor, enter the twin cities of Aberdeen and Hoquiam, famous for producing William Boeing and the grunge group Nirvana. Here, you swing north on US 101 (again!) to leafier climes at Lake Quinault, 88 miles from Olympia.

✗ p73

❷ Lake Quinault

Situated in the extreme southwest of the **Olympic National Park** (www.nps. gov/olym; 7-day access per vehicle $30, pedestrian/cyclist $15, 1yr unlimited entry $55), the thickly forested Quinault River Valley is one of the park's least-crowded corners. Clustered on the south shore of deep-blue glacial Lake Quinault is the tiny village of **Quinault**, complete with the luscious Lake Quinault Lodge (p73), a US Forest Service (USFS) office and a couple of stores.

A number of short **hiking trails** begin just below Lake Quinault Lodge; pick up a free map from the USFS

office. The shortest of these is the **Quinault Rain Forest Nature Trail**, a half-mile walk through 500-year-old Douglas firs. This brief trail adjoins the 3-mile Quinault Loop Trail, which meanders through the rainforests before circling back to the lake. The Quinault region is renowned for

LINK YOUR TRIP

5 Graveyard of the Pacific Tour

Continue down the coast from Aberdeen, where you'll begin a coastal drive along a watery ship cemetery.

7 Chuckanut Drive & Whidbey Island

Across from Port Townsend, Whidbey is a gentler and – traditionally – drier contrast to the Olympics.

its huge trees. Close to the village is a 191ft Sitka spruce tree (supposedly over 1000 years old), and nearby are the world's largest red cedar, Douglas fir and mountain hemlock trees.

The Drive >> West from Lake Quinault, US 101 continues through the Quinault Indian Reservation before entering a thin strip of national park territory that protects the beaches around Kalaloch (klay-lock). This is some of the wildest coastal scenery in the US accessible by road; various pullovers allow beach forays. After a total of 40 miles you'll reach Ruby Beach.

🛏 p73

TRIP HIGHLIGHT

❸ Ruby Beach
Inhabiting a thin coastal strip that was added to the national park in 1953, Ruby Beach is accessed via a short 0.2-mile path that leads down to a large expanse of windswept coast embellished by polished black stones and wantonly strewn tree trunks. To the south toward Kalaloch, other accessible beaches include unimaginatively named Beach One through to Beach Six, all of which are popular with beachcombers. At low tide, rangers give talks on tidal-pool life at **Beach Four** and on the ecosystems of the Olympic coastal strip.

The Drive >> North of Ruby Beach, US 101 swings sharply

northeast and inland, tracking the Hoh River. Turn right off US 101 onto the Hoh River Rd to explore one of the national park's most popular inner sanctums, the Hoh Rainforest. It's 14 miles from Ruby Beach to the turnoff, then 19 miles further to the Hoh visitor center.

🛏 p73

TRIP HIGHLIGHT

❹ Hoh Rainforest
Count yourself lucky if you arrive on a day when it isn't raining! The most popular detour off US 101 is the 19-mile paved road to the Hoh Valley, the densest, wettest, greenest and most intensely surreal temperate rainforest on earth. The essential hike here is the short but fascinating **Hall of Moss Trail**, an easy 0.75-mile loop through the kind of weird, ethereal scenery that even JRR Tolkien couldn't have invented. Old-man's beard drips from branches above you like corduroy fringe, while trailside licorice ferns and lettuce lichens overwhelm the massive fallen trunks of maple and Sitka spruce. Rangers lead interesting free guided walks here twice a day during summer and can help you spot some of the park's 5000-strong herd of **Roosevelt elk**.

The Drive >> Rejoining US 101, motor north to the small and relatively nondescript but handy settlement of Forks. Press

on through as US 101 bends north then east through a large logging area before plunging back into the national park on the shores of wondrous Lake Crescent, which is 66 miles from the Hoh Rainforest visitor center.

❺ Lake Crescent
Before you've even had time to erase the horror of teenage vampires from your mind, the scenery shifts again as the road winds along the glittering pine-scented shores of glacier-carved Lake Crescent. The lake looks best from water level, on a rental kayak, or from high above at

Olympic Peninsula Ruby Beach

its eastern edge on the **Storm King Mountain Trail** (named after the peak's wrathful spirit), accessible via a steep, 1.7-mile ascent that splits off the Barnes Creek Trail. For the less athletic, the **Marymere Falls Trail** is a 2-mile round-trip to a 90ft cascade that drops down over a basalt cliff. Both hikes leave from a parking lot north of US 101 at the **Storm King Ranger Station** (📞360-928-3380; 343 Barnes Point Rd; ⏰May-Sep). The area is also the site of the Lake Crescent Lodge (p73), the oldest of the park's trio of celebrated lodges, which opened in 1916.

The Drive » From Lake Crescent take US 101 22 miles east to the town of Port Angeles, a gateway to Victoria, Canada, which is reachable by ferry. Starting in Race St, the 18-mile Hurricane Ridge Rd climbs up 5300ft toward extensive wildflower meadows and expansive mountain vistas often visible above the clouds.

🔖 p73

- - - - - - - - - - - - - - - - - -

TRIP HIGHLIGHT

6 Hurricane Ridge

Up above the clouds, stormy Hurricane Ridge lives up to its name with fickle weather and biting winds made slightly more bearable by the park's best high-altitude views. Its proximity to Port Angeles is another bonus; if you're heading up here be sure to call into the museum-like **Olympic National Park Visitor Center** (📞360-565-3130; www.nps.gov/olym; 3002 Mt Angeles Rd; ⏰9am-6pm Jul & Aug, to 4pm Sep-Jun) first. The smaller **Hurricane Ridge Visitor Center** (📞360-565-3131; www.nps.gov/olym; ⏰9:30am-5pm daily summer, Fri-Sun winter) has a snack bar, gift shop and toilets, and is the starting point for various

THE TWILIGHT ZONE

It would have been impossible to envisage 15 years ago: diminutive Forks, a depressed lumber town full of hard-nosed loggers, reborn as a pilgrimage site for 'tweenage' girls following in the ghostly footsteps of two fictional sweethearts named Bella and Edward. The reason for this weird metamorphosis was, of course, the *Twilight* saga, a four-part book series by US author Stephenie Meyer about love and vampires on the foggy Olympic Peninsula that in just a few years shifted more than 100 million books and spawned five Hollywood movies. With Forks acting as the book's main setting, the town was catapulted to international stardom, and the cachet has yet to wear off.

hikes. **Hurricane Hill Trail** (which begins at the end of the road) and the **Meadow Loop Trails** network are popular and moderately easy. The first half-mile of these trails is wheelchair accessible.

The Drive » Wind back down the Hurricane Ridge Rd, kiss the suburbs of Port Angeles and press east through the retirement community of Sequim (pronounced 'skwim'). Turn north on SR 20 to reach another, more attractive port, that of Port Townsend. From the ridge visitor center to Port Townsend is 65 miles.

- - - - - - - - - - - - - - - - - -

❼ Port Townsend

Leaving the park momentarily behind, ease back into civilization with the cultured Victorian comforts of Port Townsend, whose period charm dates from the railroad boom of the 1890s, when the town was earmarked to become the 'New York of the West.' That never happened, but you can pick up a historic walking tour map from the **visitor center** (📞360-385-2722; www.ptchamber.org; 2409 Jefferson St; ⏰9am-5pm Mon-Fri, 10am-4pm Sat & Sun) and wander the waterfront's collection of shops, galleries and antique malls. Don't miss the gorgeously renovated **Rose Theatre** (www.rosetheatre.com; 235 Taylor St; tickets $10-12), which has been showing movies since 1908, and the fine Victorian mansions on the bluff above town, where several charming residences have been turned into B&Bs.

The Drive » From Port Townsend, head back to the junction of US 101, but this time head south passing Quilcene, Brinnon, with its great diner, and the Dosewallips Park entrance. You get more unbroken water views here on the park's eastern side courtesy of the Hood Canal. Track the watery beauty to Hoodsport where signs point west off US 101 to Staircase, 67 miles from Port Townsend.

✕ 🛏 p73

- - - - - - - - - - - - - - - - - -

❽ Staircase

It's drier on the park's eastern side and the mountains are closer. The Staircase park nexus, accessible via Hoodsport, has a ranger station, a campground and a decent trail system that follows the drainage of the North Fork Skokomish River and is flanked by some of the most rugged peaks in the Olympics. Nearby **Lake Cushman** has a campground and water-sports opportunities.

Eating & Sleeping

Olympia ❶

✗ Spar Cafe Bar
Pub, Diner $$

(☎360-357-6444; www.mcmenamins.com; 114 4th Ave E; breakfast $9-18, lunch & dinner mains $10-18; ⊘7am-midnight Sun-Thu, to 1am Fri & Sat) This legendary local cafe-pub has an authentic wood-panel interior. There's a snug, a long bar counter, curtained booths and window-facing tables: take your pick. You could spend all morning here eating brunch, shooting pool and admiring the cigar collections. Beer is brewed on-site with water from the artesian well in the basement.

Lake Quinault ❷

🛏 Lake Quinault Lodge
Historic Hotel $$$

(☎360-288-2900; www.olympicnationalparks. com; 345 S Shore Rd; r $250-450; ❄ 🛜 🍽) Everything you could want in a historic national-park lodge and more, the suspended-in-time Quinault, built in 1926, has a massive fireplace, a manicured cricket-pitch-quality lawn, huge, comfy leather sofas, a regal reception area, and a dignified lake-view restaurant serving upscale American cuisine. Trails into primeval forest leave from just outside the door.

Ruby Beach ❸

🛏 Kalaloch Lodge
Historic Hotel $$$

(☎360-962-2271; www.thekalalochlodge.com; 157151 US 101, Kalaloch; r from $299; ❄ 🛜 🍽) The Kalaloch (built in 1953) makes up for a relatively unassuming facade with a spectacular setting perched on a bluff overlooking the crashing Pacific. In addition to rooms in the old lodge, there are log cabins and motel-style units. The family-friendly Creekside Restaurant has great breakfasts and great ocean views.

Lake Crescent ❺

🛏 Lake Crescent Lodge
Lodge $$

(☎888-896-3818; www.olympicnationalparks. com; 416 Lake Crescent Rd; lodge r from

$139, cottage from $245; ⊘May-Nov, limited availability winter; 🅿 ❄ 🛜 🍽) This turn-of-the-century lodge is handsomely furnished with antiques and surrounded by giant fir trees. There's a wide variety of lodging available, but the most popular (and the only ones open in winter – weekends only) are the cozy cottages. Sumptuous Northwestern-style food is served in the lodge's ecofriendly restaurant.

Port Townsend ❼

✗ Doc's Marina Grill
American $$

(☎360-344-3627; www.docsgrill.com; 141 Hudson St; mains $13-28; ⊘11am-11pm) With a great location by Port Townsend's marina, Doc's offers something for everyone. There are burgers, fish-and-chips, various salads, pastas, steaks, seafood and a few vegetarian options. It's housed in a historic building that was a nurses' barracks back in the 1940s.

🛏 Palace Hotel
Historic Hotel $$

(☎360-385-0773; www.palacehotelpt.com; 1004 Water St; r from $150, 🛜 🍽) Built in 1889, this beautiful Victorian building was once a brothel run by the locally notorious Madame Marie, who did business out of the 2nd-floor corner suite. It's been reincarnated as an attractive, character-filled period hotel with antique furnishings (plus all the modern amenities). Pleasant common spaces; kitchenettes available. The cheapest rooms share a bathroom. Rates are higher on festival weekends.

Brinnon ❼

✗ Halfway House
Diner $

(☎360-796-4715; 41 Brinnon Lane; mains $8-16; ⊘7am-7pm Tue-Sun, to 8pm Fri) Popping up out of nowhere just when you're desperate for coffee and a slice of pie, this place looks rough from outside but is bright and cheery indoors. Service is fast, the burgers are good and the crusty fruit pies ($4.75 per slice) taste like they were made by someone's grandma. It sits aside Hwy 101 in Brinnon, halfway between Port Townsend and Staircase.

Graveyard of the Pacific Tour

5

The wild Pacific Ocean turns positively fiendish where tide meets current at the mouth of the Columbia River. Explore shipwrecks and lighthouses in this landlubber's tour of the nautical Northwest.

TRIP HIGHLIGHTS

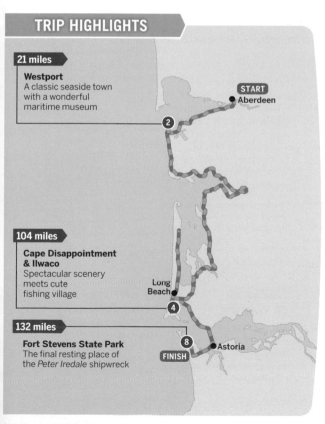

21 miles

Westport
A classic seaside town with a wonderful maritime museum

START
Aberdeen

104 miles

Cape Disappointment & Ilwaco
Spectacular scenery meets cute fishing village

Long Beach

132 miles

Fort Stevens State Park
The final resting place of the *Peter Iredale* shipwreck

FINISH

Astoria

2 DAYS
132 MILES / 212KM

GREAT FOR...

BEST TIME TO GO
April to September for the best weather.

 ESSENTIAL PHOTO

The wreckage of the *Peter Iredale*.

 BEST SHIP SIGHTING

The tall ship *Lady Washington* docks along the coast.

Fort Stevens State Park Wreckage of the *Peter Iredale* (p80)

5 Graveyard of the Pacific Tour

They call it the Graveyard of the Pacific. The area from northern Oregon to Vancouver Island is known for its unpredictable weather, unforgiving coastline and bad habit of gobbling up ships. Thousands of vessels have been lost, from war ships to barges to countless smaller craft. Dive in to this area with its unique seafaring character and fascinating maritime history.

❶ Aberdeen

Start your trip in Aberdeen's Grays Harbor, home port of the tall ship **Lady Washington** (☏360-532-8611; www.historicalseaport.org; 500 N Custer St; suggested donation for tours $5), the Official Ship of the State of Washington. This impressive reproduction of a 1788 tall ship – featured in *Pirates of the Caribbean* if that helps give you a visual – is available for dockside tours and adventure sails all along the state's coast. Check the website to find out where along the way you might catch her.

Fans of Nirvana front man **Kurt Cobain** might be interested in the self-guided walking tour at www.aberdeen-museum.org/kurt.htm. It includes the store where Kurt's uncle bought him his first guitar and several seen-better-days former residences.

The Drive ❯❯ From Aberdeen, take US 101 across the Chehalis River bridge, then follow Grays Harbor southwest on SR 105 for 20 miles to reach the coastal town of Westport.

TRIP HIGHLIGHT
❷ Westport

The seaside town of Westport has two worthwhile stops. First, head to **Grays Harbor Lighthouse** (☏360-268-0078; 1020 West Ocean Ave; $5; ⊙10am-4pm Thu-Mon Jun-Aug, noon-4pm Sat & Sun Sep-Nov, noon-4pm Fri-Sun Feb-May, closed Dec & Jan), the tallest lighthouse in Washington. It's always there for photo ops, and tours up the 135-step circular staircase (pant, wheeze) are available seasonally.

Next, head over to the **Westport Maritime Museum** (☏360-268-0078; www.westportmaritimemuseum.com; 2201 Westhaven Dr; adult/child $5/3; ⊙10am-4pm Thu-Mon Jun-Aug, noon-4pm Thu-Mon Sep-May), a noteworthy Cape Cod–style building at the northern tip of town. It offers your typical array of nautical knickknacks, but most impressive is the authentic Fresnel lighthouse lens. It's a first-order lens, which as anyone who knows about lens rankings will attest, is really impressive; loosely translated, that means it's big enough to need its own separate building.

The Drive ❯❯ Continue on SR 105, following the coast 30 miles southeast to Raymond.

✕ 🛏 p81

---

❸ Raymond

Raymond is home of the **Willapa Seaport Museum** (☏360-942-4149; www.willapaseaportmuseum.com; 310 Alder St; suggested donation $5; ⊙10am-4pm Tue-Sat, closed Tue in winter). It looks more like a cross

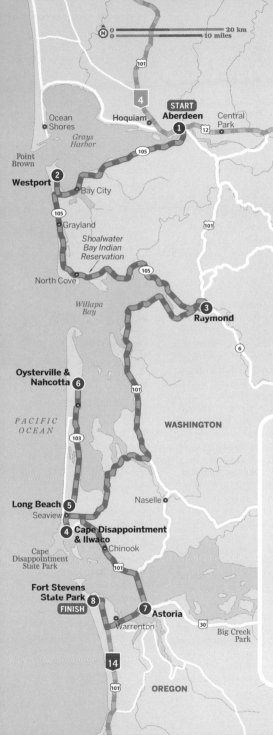

between a fisherman's garage sale and Disney's Pirates of the Caribbean ride than a formal museum, but that's part of its charm, and it's a good leg-stretch on your way to your next stop. Let the salty ol' museum owner lead you around if you've got an hour or more.

Before you leave, though, you might want to stop to pay your respect to Willie Keils at **Willie Keils Grave State Park** (443 Hwy 6; ☉ dawn-dusk), just south of town. Nineteen-year-old Willie died in 1855 right before his family left Missouri, but they couldn't bear leaving him; instead, they filled his coffin with whiskey and brought him along, turning their wagon train into a very slow funeral procession.

§ LINK YOUR TRIP

4 Olympic Peninsula Loop

From Aberdeen, pick up this loop that features the best of northwest Washington, including more coastline and Olympic National Park.

14 Highway 101 Oregon Coast

Hook up with this trip at Fort Stevens State Park, continuing down the coast for seafood, razor clams, tide pools and lighthouses.

The Drive ≫ Pick up US 101 west and head 45 miles south. When you get to Seaview, follow the signs for Cape Disappointment, 2 miles further south.

- - - - - - - - - - - - - - - - - -

TRIP HIGHLIGHT

❹ Cape Disappointment & Ilwaco

Although little remains of the original Fort Canby that once stood in **Cape Disappointment State Park** (☏360-642-3078; www.parks.state. wa.us/486; Hwy 100; Discover Pass required; ☉dawn-dusk), 2 miles southwest of Ilwaco, the area does hold the excellent **Lewis & Clark Interpretive Center** (www.capedisap pointment.org; Hwy 100; adult/child $5/2.50; ☉10am-5pm Wed-Sun Oct-Mar, daily Apr-Sep), some wild beach, around 8 miles of coastal, forested hiking trails and two dramatic lighthouses. It's a short walk from the interpretive center to the small **Cape Disappointment Lighthouse**, perched on a particularly vertiginous cliff over crashing seas. You could also take a short trail on the other side of the park to **North Head Lighthouse**, which offers tours in summer and is the oldest lighthouse in use on the west coast.

Just north, you'll pass through the cute seaside village of Ilwaco, deco-rated with driftwood, glass floats and fishing nets. It's an excellent place to stop for fresh seafood.

The Drive ≫ Head back north on US 101, which continues on to become SR 103; Long Beach is just 6 miles north of Cape Disappointment.

🛏 p81

- - - - - - - - - - - - - - - - - -

❺ Long Beach

Need a break from all the nautical history? Wee Long Beach packs in the roadside fun and is a big hit with road-weary kids. **Marsh's Free Museum** (☏360-642-2188; www. marshsfreemuseum.com; 409 Pacific Ave S; ☉9am-8pm Mon-Thu, to 9pm Fri & Sat, to 7pm Sun) dates back to the 1930s and isn't a museum so much as a place where souvenirs and seashells intermingle with sideshow-worthy attractions and oddities. The real star of the show is **Jake the Alligator Man**, media darling of the *Weekly World News*. Half-alligator, half-man, his suspiciously plaster-like remains hold packs of tweens in his thrall. Across the street from Marsh's is the **World's Largest Frying Pan**, measuring over 18ft tall.

Want to find out just how long Long Beach is? Primary **beach access** points in Long Beach are off 10th St SW and at the end of Bolstad Ave;

GARY WEATHERS/GETTY IMAGES ©

a 0.25-mile boardwalk links the two entryways.

The Drive ≫ Head north up the peninsula for 15 miles to find the quiet, undeveloped part of Willapa Bay.

✗ p81

- - - - - - - - - - - - - - - - - -

❻ Oysterville & Nahcotta

Purists might prefer the Willapa Bay side of the peninsula, with its old towns, oyster beds and wildlife viewing. The charm of these old communities – the only ones on the bay side of the Long Beach Peninsula – derives not only from

Cape Disappointment North Head Lighthouse

their history but also from the absence of the beachfront towns' carnival atmosphere.

Tiny Oysterville stands largely unchanged since its heyday in the 1870s, when the oyster boom was at its peak. The town is filled with well-preserved Victorian homes including the 1863 **Red Cottage** (Territory Rd, Oysterville), near Clay St, which served as the first Pacific County courthouse, and the **Big Red House** (cnr Division St & Territory Rd), built in 1871. Other historic buildings include a one-room schoolhouse and the 1892 **Oysterville Church** (www.oysterville. org; cnr Clay St & Territory Rd); pick up a walking-tour brochure here.

The Drive » Head back south down the Long Beach Peninsula, then take US 101 south. After 9 miles you'll cross the Columbia River and arrive in Astoria.

 p81

- - - - - - - - - - - - - - - -

❼ Astoria

Astoria sits at the mouth of the Columbia River, where you'll find some of the most treacherous waters of the Pacific, thanks to river currents rushing out where ocean tide is trying to get in. The town has a long seafaring history and has seen its old harbor attract fancy hotels and restaurants in recent years, thanks in part to Astoria's popularity as a film location. *Kindergarten Cop, Free Willy* and *Into the Wild* were all filmed here, and fans of the cult hit *The Goonies* can seek out the house where Brandon and Mikey Walsh lived.

You can explore both flotsam and jetsam at **Columbia River Maritime Museum** (📞503-325-2323; www.crmm.org; 1792

TOP TIP:
WHICH WAY TO
THE PETER IREDALE?

Shipwrecks don't have addresses: here's how to find the *Peter Iredale*. Cross the bridge from Astoria to Hammond and turn right on East Harbor Dr, which becomes Pacific Dr. Take a left at Lake Dr then a right at the KOA campground and go straight until you see the signs.

Marine Dr; adult/child $14/5; ☺9:30am-5pm; 🚻). It sits right on the edge of the Columbia River, offering a look at everything from old boats to maritime mementos that have washed up in the area. A Coast Guard exhibit – featuring a rescue boat plying dramatic, fake waves – makes you really appreciate the danger of their job.

The Drive ≫ Head west for the 10-mile drive to Hammond and Fort Stevens State Park.

✕ 🏠 p81, p174

TRIP HIGHLIGHT

8 Fort Stevens
State Park

Thousands of vessels have been lost in the Graveyard of the Pacific, from warships to barges to freighters, and those are just the ones on record. There are likely countless smaller craft littering the ocean floor. A few are still visible occasionally at low tide, but the easiest one to spot is the **Peter Iredale**, resting peacefully at Fort Stevens State Park. The ship was driven onto the shore by rough seas on October 25, 1906, and the wreckage has sat embedded in the sand for over a century. Today, kids have made a jungle gym out of the rusted skeleton and families picnic and build sandcastles on the nearby sand at low tide. (As a reassuring side note, no lives were lost in the shipwreck, so don't let the thought of ghostly sailors dampen your fun.)

Eating & Sleeping

Westport ❷

✖ Blackbeard's Brewery   Pub Food $$

(📞360-268-7662; www.blackbeardsbrewing.
com; 700 W Ocean Ave; pizzas $15-23;
🕐11:30am-8:30pm Thu-Mon, to 9pm Fri & Sat)
Blackbeard's offers a Seattle-worthy selection
of craft beers, wine by the glass and hard cider,
plus a housemade root beer for kids. The wood-
fired pizzas are the best thing to eat in town and
the ambience is small-town friendly.

🛏 Loge at the Sands   Hotel, Hostel $$

(📞360-268-0091; www.logecamps.com; 1416 S
Montesano St; s/d from $115/120, dm from $45,
tent sites from $40; 🛜🍽) This Insta-worthy
surfers' hangout is a combination hotel, hostel
and super-chic campground, decked out in
tiny lights and reclaimed wood. Choose from
queen and king kitchenette rooms, dorms,
covered campsites or primitive tent sites. Add
to that an outdoor kitchen, firepits, seasonal
cafe, cruiser bicycles to borrow, surfboard and
wetsuit rentals, hot showers, laundry and some
seriously chill vibes.

Cape Disappointment & Ilwaco ❹

🛏 Cape Disappointment State Park Campground   Campground $

(📞360-642-3078; www.parks.state.wa.us;
Hwy 100; tent sites $27-37, RV sites $35-50,
yurts & cabins from $69) The campground has
nearly 250 sites in two zones: by the beach
and around a lake near the park entrance.
Coin-operated hot showers and flush toilets are
within easy reach. Yurts and cabins (each can
accommodate up to six) are also available.

🛏 Inn at Harbor Village   Hotel $$

(📞360-642-0087; www.innatharborvillage.
com; 120 Williams Ave NE; r $109-199; 🛜) This
is a gorgeously refurbished 1928 Presbyterian
church, with sloped ceilings and nine exquisite
rooms. The parlor has an old grandfather
clock, plus you can enjoy the delights of a
complimentary breakfast and wine. The inn is
set in woodland, an easy walk from Ilwaco port.

Long Beach ❺

✖ Depot   Northwestern US $$$

(📞360-642-7880; www.depotrestaurantdining.
com; 1208 38th Pl, Seaview; small plates $12-19,
mains $25-42; 🕐from 5pm) This cute, narrow
restaurant inhabits the historic Seaview train
depot, originally built in 1888 (though the
current building dates from 1905), and the menu
is part 'land food' (think: wild-boar-stuffed quail),
part seafood (Dungeness crab mac, inventive
takes on prawns, clams and oysters).

Oysterville & Nahcotta ❻

✖ Bailey's Bakery & Café   Bakery, Cafe $

(📞360-665-4449; www.baileysbakerycafe.
com; 26910 Sandridge Rd, Nahcotta; snacks from
$3; 🕐9am-3pm Wed-Sun) Sharing digs with
Nahcotta post office, this small nook serves
espresso from Astoria, sandwiches on freshly
baked bread, and, on Sundays, the lauded
'thunder buns': currants, pecans, honey-butter
glaze and a whole lot of bun.

Astoria ❼

✖ Baked Alaska   Seafood $$$

(📞503-325-7414; www.bakedak.com; 1 12th St;
mains $14-29; 🕐11am-10pm) One of Astoria's
finest restaurants, Baked Alaska sits right atop
a pier on the water – views are excellent. Lunch
means 0.5lb gourmet burgers and blackened
sirloin salad, while dinner mains range from
grilled wild salmon to the 10oz rib-eye steak.
Great happy hour 3pm to 6pm daily.

🛏 Cannery Pier Hotel   Hotel $$$

(📞503-325-4996; www.cannerypierhotel.com;
10 Basin St; d from $329; 🐾🛜) Located on
a pier at the west end of town, this luxurious
hotel offers fine rooms right over the water,
with balconies, bridge views, contemporary
furnishings and bathtubs that open to the
room. Perks include afternoon wine socials,
continental breakfast and a free ride in a vintage
car. Spa and Finnish sauna on the premises.

San Juan Islands Scenic Byway

6

More a float trip than a drive, this voyage will leave you swearing that you've dropped off the edge of the American continent and landed somewhere less clamorous.

TRIP HIGHLIGHTS

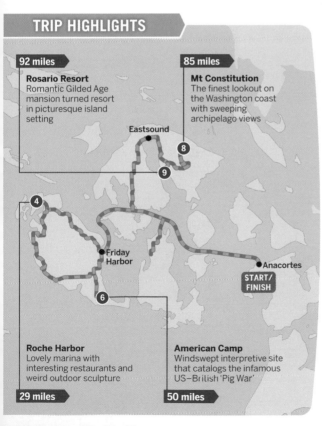

92 miles

Rosario Resort
Romantic Gilded Age mansion turned resort in picturesque island setting

85 miles

Mt Constitution
The finest lookout on the Washington coast with sweeping archipelago views

Eastsound

8

9

4

Friday Harbor

Anacortes

START/ FINISH

6

Roche Harbor
Lovely marina with interesting restaurants and weird outdoor sculpture

29 miles

American Camp
Windswept interpretive site that catalogs the infamous US–British 'Pig War'

50 miles

3 DAYS
136 MILES / 220KM

GREAT FOR...

BEST TIME TO GO
April to September for calmer seas and common whale sightings.

ESSENTIAL PHOTO
View from atop Mt Constitution, Orcas Island.

 BEST FOR WILDLIFE
Whale-watching trips from Friday Harbor.

San Juan Islands Orca (killer whale; p85)

6

San Juan Islands Scenic Byway

A thousand metaphorical miles from the urban chaos surrounding Puget Sound, the San Juan archipelago conjures up flashbacks from another era (the 1950s, perhaps?). Crime barely registers here, fast-food franchises are a nasty mainland apparition, and cars are an optional luxury on the three ferry-reachable islands of Orcas, Lopez and San Juan.

❶ Anacortes

This voyage starts at **Anacortes Ferry Terminal** (www.wsdot.wa.gov/ferries; 2100 Ferry Terminal Rd; ⏱7am-9pm), where you'll board the ferry for Friday Harbor. Drivers might end up waiting for hours in the busy summer months (hint: reserve ferry tickets online). Two alternatives are to spend the night in Anacortes and get to the ferry early, or park at the terminal and make the trip on foot or by bike.

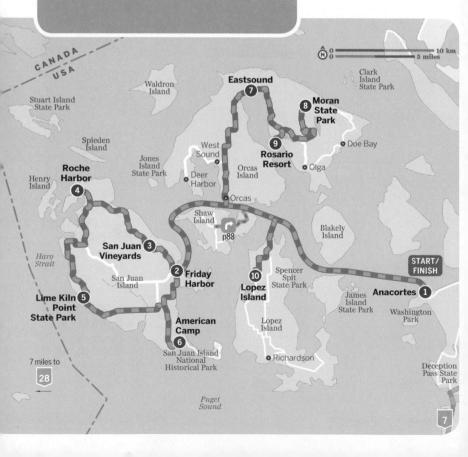

The Drive » If you're taking your car, today's drive is limited to sliding in slow motion onto the ferry where you'll be packed tightly in with several hundred others. Don't stay put; rather climb upstairs and enjoy the 80-minute journey (and it is a great journey) from the passenger lounge.

❷ Friday Harbor

You'll land at Friday Harbor, the San Juans' only real town and a blueprint for the archipelago as a whole, where the worst kind of hassle you're likely to face is a badly pitched baseball. Restaurants, shops and a couple of interesting museums embellish the

LINK YOUR TRIP

7 Chuckanut Drive & Whidbey Island

A short hop from Anacortes, this pastoral trip acts like a decompression chamber before re-entering metro Puget Sound.

28 Southern Vancouver Island Tour

Located a handful of watery miles from Vancouver Island, the San Juans provide an ideal opportunity to visit Canada by sea.

settlement's diminutive grid.

San Juan Island has the good fortune to be right in the migration path of three pods of orcas (aka killer whales), unimaginatively named the J, K and L pods. (Pod members' names aren't much better: 'K-17, meet L-9.') To learn more about the island's unofficial mascots, stop by the **Whale Museum** (☎360-378-4710; www.whale-museum.org; 62 1st St; adult/child $9/4; ☺9am-6pm Sun-Thu, to 8pm Fri & Sat). To see the real thing – a regional highlight – hook up with **San Juan Excursions** (☎360-378-6636; www.watchwhales.com; whale-watching tours $99), which stands by its boast: 'see whales or come again free.'

The Drive » Navigation on San Juan Island is a no-brainer. Take Roche Harbor Rd northwest out of Friday Harbor as far as Sportsmans Lake. It's 3 miles from the harbor to the vineyards.

 p89

❸ San Juan Vineyards

The premier **vineyard** (☎844-243-6359; www.sanjuanvineyards.com; 3136 Roche Harbor Rd; ☺11am-5pm Thu-Mon) in the islands has a tasting room adjacent to its on-site, 1896-vintage schoolhouse. The vineyard also has an outlet in town.

For the real home-grown stuff, you're looking at Siegerrebe and Madeleine Angevine varietals with the occasional Pinot Noir thrown in. The vineyard also makes wines using grapes imported from East Washington.

The Drive » Continue northwest on Roche Harbor Rd. At the T-junction with West Valley Rd, 4.5 miles from the vineyard, turn right.

TRIP HIGHLIGHT

❹ Roche Harbor

A sublime rurally inclined 'resort,' Roche Harbor is a scenic mix of swanky yachts, historic houses and picnicking vacationers. At the entrance gate sits the eccentric **Westcott Bay Sculpture Park** (www.sjisculpturepark.com; cnr Westcott Dr & Roche Harbor Rd; ☺dawn-dusk) where you can wander among more than 100 sculptures scattered over 20 acres. Half the fun is the sheer variety: each was made by a different artist, and materials range from aluminum to granite to recovered redwood.

Around the corner, Roche Harbor proper has a lovely marina packed with millionaire boats and backed by the historic buildings of the lime-mining McMillan clan, the oldest of which dates from 1886. Explore the manicured gardens, browse the plush shops or even play boules.

The Drive » From Roche Harbor to Lime Kiln Point State Park is about 10 miles. Heading back down the Roche Harbor Rd, take the West Valley Rd south at the first junction. Just past the alpaca farm, turn right on Mitchell Bay Rd and then left on West Side Rd, which skirts the lapping waters of Haro Strait.

❺ Lime Kiln Point State Park

Clinging to the island's rocky west coast, this beautiful park overlooks the deep Haro Strait and is one of the best places in the world to view whales from the shoreline. There is a small **interpretive center** in the park, open from Memorial Day to Labor Day, along with trails, a restored lime kiln and the landmark **Lime Kiln lighthouse** built in 1919. Orca and minke whale sightings are more common in summer after the June salmon run. Offering exceptional views of Vancouver Island and the Olympic Mountains, the park is best enjoyed at sunset, camera poised.

The Drive » West Side Rd swings east and becomes Bailer Hill Rd and Little Rd before joining with Cattle Point Rd. Turn right here toward the island's wild treeless southern tip. It's 9 miles from Lime Kiln Point State Park to the American Camp visitor center.

TRIP HIGHLIGHT

❻ American Camp

On the southern flank of the island, the American Camp hosts a small **visitor center** (⊙8:30am-5pm Jun-Aug, to 4:30pm Sep-May) and is a good place to learn about the islands' history and the infamous 'Pig War' with Britain in 1859, a military standoff ignited after an American settler shot a pig belonging to a homesteading Irishman on San Juan Island. The ensuing squabble led to a border dispute and near conflict between Britain and the US. Among the remnants of an old fort are the officers' quarters and a laundress' house, while a series of interpretive trails lead to earthwork fortifications, a British farm from the dispute era and desolate **South Beach**. The 1.8-mile trail along the ridge of **Mt Finlayson** makes for a pleasant hike, with splendid views and unlimited birdwatching potential.

The Drive » Head north on Cattle Point Rd back to Friday Harbor and catch an interisland ferry to Orcas Island, where you'll find a wilder, less manicured landscape than on San Juan Island. There's not a lot to see or do around the ferry landing so head straight down Orcas Rd for just over 8 miles to Eastsound.

SEASTOCK/SHUTTERSTOCK ©

❼ Eastsound

Orcas Island is shaped like a pair of saddlebags, with the main town, Eastsound, diplomatically in the middle. This is where you'll find most of the dining options. The town shuts down early though, so don't wait till you're hungry to plan dinner.

Paddling around the island gives you an entirely different view of things. **Shearwater Adventures** (☏360-376-4699; www.shearwaterkayaks.com/tours; 138 N Beach Rd; 3hr tours per adult/child $85/55) offers guided excursions

Moran State Park View from Mt Constitution

from the north side of the island. Take anything from a quick, one-hour splash-about to an all-day outing in its hand-crafted, Aleut-style kayaks.

The Drive >> East of Eastsound, Olga Rd gives access to the island's eastern saddlebag, dominated by Moran State Park, 4.5 miles from Eastsound.

✗ ⊨ p89

TRIP HIGHLIGHT

❽ Moran State Park

Ex-Seattle mayor Robert Moran's generous gift to the island was **Moran State Park** (☏360-376-6173; 3572 Olga Rd; Discover Pass required at some parking lots per day/year $10/35; ⏱6:30am-dusk Apr-Sep, 8am-dusk Oct-Mar), **where** more than 5000 acres of forest lie draped over two mountains. On a clear day, the view from **Mt Constitution** is incomparable; you can see mountains, islands, even Vancouver. Sadly, on a foggy day, you can only see the person standing next to you. Thirty miles of trails give you ample opportunity to explore on foot, but there's also a road straight to the top if you have a ferry to catch.

The Drive >> Just after exiting the park's northern gate a road turns left to the Rosario Resort, 1.5 miles south.

TRIP HIGHLIGHT

❾ Rosario Resort

Orcas' resort (p89) is a refined place, unsullied by modern clamor, where seaplanes dock, kayaks launch and discerning vacationers bask in a heady kind of F Scott Fitzgerald–style romance. Its centerpiece is the seafront Rosario mansion, built by former shipbuilding magnate Robert Moran in 1904. A **museum** (Rosario Way, Rosario;

DETOUR: SHAW ISLAND

Start: ❼ Eastsound

The quietest and smallest of the four main San Juan Islands, tranquil Shaw is famous for its restrictive property laws and handsome Benedictine monastery. Ferries arrive here daily from Orcas Island (car and driver $28), but with only one campsite offering just 12 overnight berths, opportunities to linger are limited. For the curious, Shaw is worth a slow spin on a mountain bike or an afternoon of quiet contemplation on a pebbly beach. History buffs can break the reverie at the **Shaw Island Historical Museum** (Blind Bay Rd; by donation; ☺2-4pm Tue, 11am-1pm Thu, 10am-noon & 2-4pm Sat), while perennial peace-seekers can find lazy solace on quiet South Beach in **Shaw Island County Park** (☎360-378-1842; www.sanjuanco.com/523; Squaw Bay Rd; tent sites $22), a stop and potential camping spot on the aquatic Cascadia Marine Trail – doable on nonmotorized boats and kayaks – which starts in southern Puget Sound.

☺9am-9pm) encased in the mansion tells the life and times of Moran, a former Seattle mayor who lived here from 1906 until 1938. Look out for the ship memorabilia and the huge custom-made organ.

The Drive » There's only one way back to the ferry terminal – the way you came! Interisland ferries leave five times daily for Shaw and Lopez Islands.

🛏 p89

❿ Lopez Island

Lopez – or *Slow-pez* as it's sometimes known – is the ultimate friendly isle where local motorists give strangers the 'Lopezian wave' (two fingers raised from the steering wheel) and you can leave your bike outside the village store and it'll still have both wheels when you return several hours later. A leisurely pastoral spin can be tackled in a day with good overnight digs available in the clustered settlement that passes for the main village. If you arrive bike-less, call up **Lopez Bicycle Works** (☎360-468-2847; www.lopezkayaks.com; 2847 Fisherman Bay Rd; per day from $35; ☺10am-6pm May-Sep), which can deliver a bicycle to the ferry terminal for you.

🍴 🛏 p89

Eating & Sleeping

Friday Harbor ➋

✖ Market Chef   Deli $

(☏360-378-4546; 225 A St; sandwiches from $9; ⊙10am-4pm Mon-Fri) Super popular and famous for its delicious sandwiches, including its signature curried-egg salad with roasted peanuts and chutney, or roast beef and rocket. Salads are also available; local ingredients are used. If you're in town on a Saturday in summer, visit Market Chef at the San Juan Island Farmers Market (10am to 1pm).

🛏 Earthbox Inn & Spa   Motel $$

(☏360-378-4000; www.earthboxmotel.com; 410 Spring St; r from $169; 🛜🖾🐾) Earthbox is a hybrid of simplicity and sophistication as a former motor inn made over to resemble a deluxe hotel. The result: a variety of funky, cleverly designed rooms with comfy beds and colorful yet minimalist undercurrents. Other bonuses include a pool, spa, fitness room, bike rental and fine gardens.

Eastsound ➐

✖ Inn at Ship Bay   Seafood $$$

(☏877-276-7296; www.innatshipbay.com; 326 Olga Rd; mains $27-36; ⊙5-10pm Tue-Sat) Locals unanimously rate this place as the best fine-dining experience on the island. The chefs work overtime preparing everything from scratch using the freshest local ingredients. Seafood is the specialty and it's served in an attractive 1860s orchard house a couple of miles south of Eastsound. There's also an on-site 11-room hotel (doubles from $195). Reservations recommended.

🛏 Outlook Inn   Hotel $$

(☏360-376-2200; www.outlookinn.com; 171 Main St; r/ste from $109/250; @🛜🐾)

Eastsound's oldest and most eye-catching building, the Outlook Inn (1888) is an island institution. Budget rooms are cozy and neat (try for room 30), while the luxurious suites have fireplaces, Jacuzzi tubs and stunning water views from their balconies. Excellent attached cafe.

Rosario Resort ➒

🛏 Rosario Resort & Spa   Resort $$

(☏360-376-2222; www.rosarioresort.com; 1400 Rosario Rd, Eastsound; r from $199; 🌼🛜🐾) This magnificent seafront mansion built by former shipbuilding magnate Robert Moran in 1904 is now the centerpiece of an upscale resort. The 180 modern rooms sprawl across the grounds surrounding the old mansion, and the complex includes tennis courts, a swimming pool, a marina and a spa.

Lopez Island ➓

✖ Holly B's Bakery   Bakery $

(www.hollybsbakery.com; Lopez Rd, Lopez Village; pastries around $3; ⊙7am-4pm Fri-Mon, longer hours summer) Holly's handles the early-morning latte and pastry rush while harnessing the slow island vibe and thus remaining effortlessly low-key. The seasonal fruit pastries are worthy of any swanky Seattle patisserie.

🛏 Lopez Islander Resort   Resort $$

(☏360-468-2233; www.lopezfun.com; 2864 Fisherman Bay Rd; r from $159; 🛜🐾) Equipped with restaurant, swimming pool, Jacuzzi, gym and 'tiki lounge bar,' this so-outdated-it's-kind-of-cool 'resort' sits alongside a marina in Fisherman Bay, where eagles glide. What it lacks in intimacy it makes up for in amiability and good service.

Chuckanut Drive & Whidbey Island

Veer off the congested interstate at Bellingham and you quickly enter a parallel universe of sinuous back roads, tulip fields and spectacular ribbons of coastal asphalt.

TRIP HIGHLIGHTS

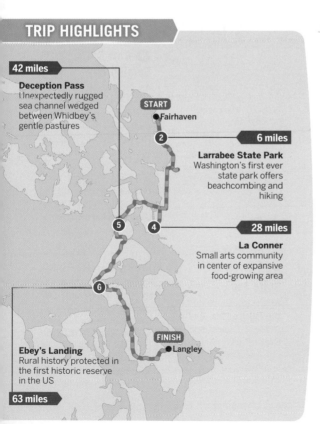

42 miles

Deception Pass
Unexpectedly rugged sea channel wedged between Whidbey's gentle pastures

START
● Fairhaven

② **6 miles**

Larrabee State Park
Washington's first ever state park offers beachcombing and hiking

④ ⑤

④ **28 miles**

La Conner
Small arts community in center of expansive food-growing area

⑤ ⑥

FINISH
● Langley

Ebey's Landing
Rural history protected in the first historic reserve in the US

63 miles

1–2 DAYS
89 MILES / 143KM

GREAT FOR...

BEST TIME TO GO

March to June when spring flowers bloom.

ESSENTIAL PHOTO

The daffodil and tulip fields around La Conner are the best this side of Holland.

BEST FOR FOOD

La Conner – food from farm to plate in yards, not miles.

La Conner Daffodil field

7 Chuckanut Drive & Whidbey Island

Short but sweet, this winding sojourn along Chuckanut Dr and through Whidbey Island is the kind of dreamy drive you see in car commercials: sunlight through trees, sparkling ocean and a dozen broccoli-colored islands shimmering in the mid-distance. If you've got a convertible, it's roof-down time, weather permitting, as you glide between oyster restaurants, beaches and scenic state parks.

1 Fairhaven

Of Bellingham's four original towns, Fairhaven is the best preserved; a four-square-block historic district of handsome redbrick Victorians testifies to a rich, if sometimes rambunctious, past. Today, the same buildings harbor bookstores, cafes and arty nooks – they're lovely to explore on foot (p154). Fairhaven is also an important transport nexus, and home of Bellingham's Amtrak station and ferry terminal, with regular ferries up the Inside Passage to Alaska.

The Drive » You don't have to wait long for the beauty of

Chuckanut Dr to unfold. Vistas open out immediately south of Fairhaven, where homes hug million-dollar lots high above Puget Sound. Cut into the cliff, the road winds spectacularly through trees that frame island-speckled water views; to the right is the railway. After 6 miles you come to Larrabee State Park.

✗ ⊨ p97

TRIP HIGHLIGHT

2 Larrabee State Park

At the southern end of the Interurban Trail (p96) sits **Larrabee State Park** (www.parks. state.wa.us/536; Chuckanut Dr; ☺dawn-dusk), a square chunk of emerald-green forest that spills into the bay at popular Clayton

Beach and Wildcat Cove. Poking around in the tide pools or hiking up to **Fragrance Lake Trail** (5.1 miles return) are the most popular activities, though the trails can be crowded at weekends.

The Drive » Chuckanut's precipitous topography continues for a few miles after Larrabee. Then, with dramatic suddenness, the landscape opens out into the flat agricultural pastures of the Skagit River Valley. Pass the Oyster Bar and Chuckanut Manor (both on the right) and, almost 9 miles from Larrabee State Park, you'll arrive at Bow Hill Rd, the first main intersection since Fairhaven.

3 Bow & Samish Bay

As you continue the drive south several pullouts lure you with fine views over Samish Bay as they explain the history of the road and its oyster industry. Oysters adore the brackish waters of the bay, and nearby **Taylor Shellfish Farms** (www. taylorshellfish.com; 2182 Chuckanut Dr; oysters around $1.50; ☺9am-6pm) has been hand harvesting and shucking 1800 acres of seabed here since the 1880s. Staff can lead you through oyster etiquette as you learn to differentiate between a buttery Shigoku or a creamy Kumamoto.

Both Taylor and nearby Blau, across the

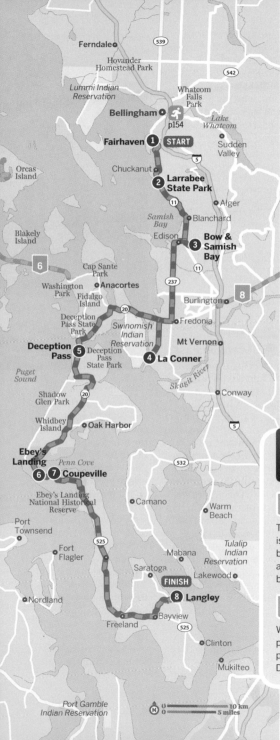

bay on Samish Island, deliver their freshest catch to a pair of Chuckanut Dr restaurants that between them boast the region's most hypnotic views: the **Oyster Bar** (📞360-766-6185; www.the oysterbar.net; 2578 Chuckanut Dr; mains $32-36, oysters from $2.95; 🕐11:30am-10pm) and **Chuckanut Manor** (www.chuckanutmanor.com; 3056 Chuckanut Dr; mains $14-35, oysters from $2.75; 🕐11:30am-9pm Tue-Sun).

South of Blanchard Mountain, Bow junction holds a few surprises, including the gourmet Goudas (and other treats) of **Samish Bay Cheese** (www.samishbay cheese.com; 15115 Bow Hill Rd; cheese boards from $9; 🕐10am-5pm Mon-Sat, 11am-5pm Sun), available for tasting at its tiny store.

 LINK YOUR TRIP

6 **San Juan Islands Scenic Byway**

The San Juan archipelago is never out of view as you breeze down Chuckanut Dr and across Whidbey Island, begging you to visit.

8 **Cascade Drive**

Bisected by SR 20, Whidbey Island, though physically flat, is actually part of the official Cascade Drive. Join it in Burlington.

The Drive » Back at the Bow Hill Rd–Chuckanut Dr intersection, take the W Bow Hill Rd through the pinprick community of Edison, whose artisan bread store and Tweets Café merit a quick stopover. Continue south on the ruler-straight Farm to Market Rd to busy SR 20, which you join briefly heading west before turning left onto the La Conner–Whitney Rd. This section of the drive is 16 miles.

TRIP HIGHLIGHT

❹ La Conner

Celebrated for its tulips, wild turkeys, erudite writer's colony and (among other culinary treats) soccer-ball-sized cinnamon buns, La Conner's myriad attractions are hard to categorize. Jammed with gift shops and classy B&Bs, it also has three decent museums; the best is the **Museum of Northwest Art** (www.monamuseum.org; 121 1st St; ☺10am-5pm Tue-Sat, noon-5pm Sun & Mon). The zenith of La Conner's cultural calendar is during the annual **Tulip Festival** and surrounding months, when the nearby fields are embellished with a colorful carpet of daffodils (March), tulips (April) and irises (May). To see the flowers in all their artistic glory, detour a few miles to the **Roozengaarde Display Garden** (www.tulips.com; 15867 Beaver Marsh Rd; $10; ☺9am-7pm Apr, 9am-6pm Mon-Sat, 11am-4pm Sun rest of year),

halfway between La Conner and Mt Vernon. This renowned 3-acre garden plants 250,000 tulip bulbs annually and, with Mt Baker in the background, photo opportunities abound.

The Drive » Retrace your tracks north to SR 20 and turn left with the Anacortes traffic toward the San Juan Islands ferry terminal. After crossing the Swinomish Channel turn left to stay on SR 20, following signage to Whidbey Island. Deception Pass is 13 miles from La Conner. You're now on Fidalgo Island, separated from the mainland by a narrow sea channel.

✗ ⊨ p97

TRIP HIGHLIGHT

❺ Deception Pass

Emerging from the flat pastures of Fidalgo Island, Deception Pass leaps out like a mini Grand Canyon, its precipitous cliffs overlooked by a famous bridge made all the more dramatic by the sight of the churning, angry water below. The bridge consists of two steel arches that span Canoe Pass and Deception Pass, with a central support on Pass Island between the two. Visitors to the 5.5-sq-mile **Deception Pass State Park** (☎360-675-2417; www.parks.state. wa.us/497; 41229 N State Hwy 20; day pass $10; ☺dawn-dusk) usually introduce themselves to the spectacular land- and

CHECUBUS/SHUTTERSTOCK ©

seascape by parking at the shoulders on either end and walking across the bridge. Built during the 1930s by the Civilian Conservation Corps, the bridge was considered an engineering feat in its day.

Besides the dramatic bridge overviews, the park's attractions include over 15 miles of saltwater shoreline and 27 miles of forest trails. **Deception Pass Tours** (☎888-909-8687; www. deceptionpasstours.com; 1hr Deception Pass tour adult/child $40/35) organizes jet-boat tours through

the turbulent waters daily.

The Drive » Deception Pass disappears almost as quickly as it materialized and you're soon in the pastoral fields that characterize Whidbey Island. After passing the entrance to the Naval Air station on your right, you'll skirt the rather ugly mall infestations of Oak Harbor. Traffic lights will slow your progress. Keep on SR 20 to Ebey's Landing, 16 miles from Deception Pass.

- - - - - - - - - - - - - - - - - -

6 Ebey's Landing

The nation's first National Historic Reserve, listed in 1978, was created in order to preserve Whidbey Island's historical heritage from the encroaching urbanization that had already partly engulfed Oak Harbor. Still 90% privately owned, **Ebey's Landing** (360-678-6084; www.nps.gov/ebla; 162 Cemetery Rd, Coupeville) comprises 17,400 acres encompassing working farms, four historic blockhouses, two state parks and the small historic town of Coupeville. A series of interpretive boards shows visitors how the patterns of croplands, woods and even roads reflect the activities of those who have peopled this scenic landscape, from its earliest indigenous inhabitants to 19th-century settlers.

The museum in Coupeville distributes a brochure on suggested driving and cycling tours through the reserve. Highly recommended is the 3.6-mile **Bluff Trail**, which starts from a small parking area at the end of Ebey Rd. The energetic can walk or cycle here from Coupeville, thus crossing

INTERURBAN TRAIL

For a break from the car, you can join Bellingham's fleece-wearing weekend warriors and savor a bit of Chuckanut Dr by bike along the 6-mile Interurban Trail, a deliciously flat former electric trolley bed that parallels the tarmac passing deep forest and lovely views of Chuckanut Bay to Larrabee State Park. **Fairhaven Bicycles** (✆360-733-4433; www.fairhavenbicycles.com; 1108 11th St, Bellingham; ◷10am-6pm Mon & Wed-Sat, 11am-5pm Sun; bike rental per day from $50) will set you up with a bike ($25 for four hours) for the easy two-hour ride.

the island at one of its narrowest points.

The Drive ›› Veer off SR 20 just past Penn Cove to visit Coupeville, just 2.5 miles north.

---

❼ Coupeville

Tiny Coupeville is Whidbey Island personified: fresh mussels and clams, old-world B&Bs, historic clapboard shop fronts, and instant access to a National Historical Reserve. Call in at the **Island County Historical Society Museum** (908 NW Alexander St; ◷10am-4pm Mon-Sat, from 11am

Sun) for the lowdown on Washington State's second-oldest settlement (founded in 1852) and walking-tour maps of the town's handsome vintage homes.

The Drive ›› SR 20 veers east at the southern end of Ebey's Landing toward the Keystone Ferry and Fort Casey State Park. The latter was part of an early 1900s military defense system and features old cement batteries, tunnels and a lighthouse. Continue south on SR 525 through Freeland to Bayview, where you take a left for Langley, 26 miles from Coupeville.

✕ ⛐ p97

---

❽ Langley

Langley, like Coupeville, is a small seafront community that is little changed since the late 19th century. Encased in its attractive historical center are small cafes, antique furniture shops, funky boutiques and a couple of decent B&Bs. While there's little to do here activity-wise, Langley provides a perfect antidote to the hustle and bustle of nearby Seattle and is a great place to relax and unwind.

Langley is 8 miles north of **Clinton** and the 20-minute ferry service from **Mukilteo** (✆206-464-6400; www.wsdot.com/ferries; 64 S Ferrydock R; person/bike/car $5/6/9), making this the closest of the Whidbey Island communities to the urban areas of northern Seattle.

✕ p97

Eating & Sleeping

Fairhaven ❶

✕ Colophon Cafe — Cafe $

(1208 11th St; sandwiches $8-16, soups $8-10; ⊙9am-8pm Mon-Thu, 9am-9pm Fri & Sat, 10am-7pm Sun) Linked with Fairhaven's famous literary haven, Village Books (p155), the Colophon is a multiethnic eatery for people who like to follow their panini with Proust. Renowned for its African peanut soup and chocolate brandy cream pies, the cafe has indoor seating along with an outside wine garden and is ever popular with the local literati.

🛏 Fairhaven Village Inn — Hotel $$

(☎360-733-1311; www.fairhavenvillageinn.com; 1200 10th St; r from $179; ❄ 🤖) Downtown Bellingham lacks a decent number of well-appointed independent hotels, but one good option is this prime place in genteel Fairhaven. In keeping with the tone of the historic district, the inn is a class above the standard city hotels; its spacious, tastefully decorated rooms have views of either the harbor or the village.

La Conner ❹

✕ Seeds Bistro & Bar — Modern American $$

(☎360-466-3280; www.seedsbistro.com; 623 Morris St; brunch dishes $8-18, dinner mains $13-28; ⊙11am-8pm Sun-Thu, to 9pm Fri & Sat; 🖊) With a freshened-up stylish interior and new owners, this long-standing farm-to-table favorite serves inventive, decadent yet semihealthy dishes made from locally sourced ingredients. (Suppliers are listed on a chalkboard on the wall.) Try the lemon-ricotta French toast or any of the veggie bowls for brunch, or roasted beets, wedge salad or pan-seared duck breast for dinner.

🛏 Heron Inn & Day Spa — B&B $$

(☎360-399-1074; www.theheroninn.com; 117 Maple Ave; r from $150; ❄ 🤖🛁) Some of the 10 rooms here have fireplaces, others have Jacuzzi tubs or a view (choose from the garden, the surrounding farmlands or snowcapped Mt Baker). Above-and-beyond service is propped up by the on-site spa (massages, scrubs and more) and lovingly home-cooked breakfasts.

Coupeville ❼

✕ Christopher's — Seafood $$

(☎360-678-5480; www.christophersonwhidbey.com; 103 NW Coveland St; lunch mains $12-16, dinner mains $16-26; ⊙11:30am-2pm & 5-8pm Sun, Mon, Wed & Thu, to 8:30pm Fri & Sat) The mussels and clams are the best in town (no mean feat in Coupeville), and the seafood Alfredo pasta is wonderfully rich. Try the Penn Cove seafood stew – prawns, scallops, mussels and clams in a tomato broth – or just go for the huge plate of mussels in a white-wine cream sauce.

🛏 Captain Whidbey Inn — Inn $$

(☎360-678-4097; www.captainwhidbey.com; 2072 W Captain Whidbey Inn Rd; r/cabins from $205/420; 🤖) The beautifully forest-clad Captain Whidbey Inn was built in 1907 and has all the creaky floors and enchantingly rustic log construction to match. Lodging is in 12 sea-galleon-style guest rooms (with shared bathrooms) in the main lodge, as well as wood-heated cottages and a more modern building with verandas facing a lagoon. It's worth paying a little more for a view.

Langley ❽

✕ Useless Bay Coffee Roasters — Cafe $

(☎360-221-4515; https://uselessbaycoffee.com; 121 2nd St; ⊙7:30am-4:30pm) You'll smell the rustic scent of roasting beans long before you see this place. The vast, industrial-meets-1950s diner interior spills out to outdoor picnic tables, and the coffee is great, as are the burgers and sandwiches (mains $8 to $13). Any food preferences from gluten- to dairy-free are very well catered to.

Cascade Drive

Rugged and inaccessible for half the year, this brawny mountain drive is etched with the kind of monumental, Alaskan-style beauty that once inspired Jack Kerouac.

8

TRIP HIGHLIGHTS

276 miles

Diablo Lake Overlook
Staggering natural view of a man-made reservoir

250 miles

Rainy Pass
Towering, seasonally accessible road amid sawtoothed Cascade peaks

FINISH
Burlington

9

8

6

START
Everett

Stevens Pass

Chelan

3

Leavenworth
Bavarian 'theme' town blessed with an authentic alpine backdrop

100 miles

Sun Mountain Lodge
One of the best places to stay in Washington State

215 miles

4–5 DAYS
350 MILES / 563KM

GREAT FOR...

BEST TIME TO GO
June to September when roads are snow-free and passable.

 ESSENTIAL PHOTO
View from the Sun Mountain Lodge.

 BEST FOR HIKING
The Maple Pass Loop Trail from Rainy Pass.

---

rth Cascades National Park Washington Pass (p103)

8 Cascade Drive

Nature defies modern engineering in the North Cascades, where high-altitude roads succumb to winter snow storms, and the names of the mountains – Mt Terror, Mt Fury, Forbidden Peak – whisper forebodingly. Less scary are the scattered settlements, small towns with eclectic distractions such as Bavarian Leavenworth and 'Wild West' Winthrop. Fill up the tank, put on your favorite Springsteen track and prepare for one of the rides of your life.

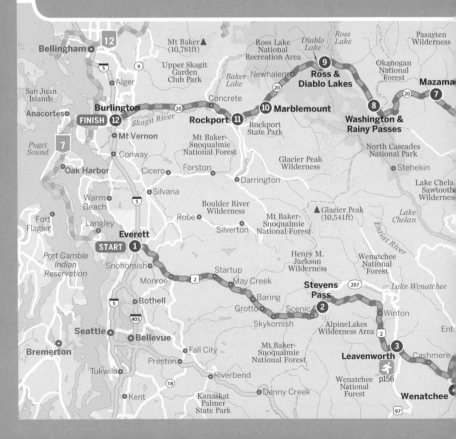

1 Everett

This drive incorporates four-fifths of the popular 'Cascade Loop.' You can complete the other fifth by taking in the second half of the trip through Whidbey Island (p91). There's not much to detain you in Everett, the route's starting point, 30 miles north of Seattle. It's known mainly for its Boeing connections and as the genesis of countless Seattle-region traffic jams. Head directly east and don't stop until Stevens Pass.

The Drive » Everett marks the starting point of US 2, a 2579-mile cross-continental road that terminates in Maine. Crossing I-5, the route, which parallels the Great Northern Railway and Skykomish River for much of its journey, passes the towns of Startup, Sultan and Index, climbing toward Stevens Pass, 66 miles away. There are a number of drive-through espresso huts en route.

2 Stevens Pass

Accessible year-round thanks to its day-use **ski area** (📞206-812-4510; www.stevenspass.com; US 2, Skykomish; day pass adult/child from $84/56), Stevens Pass was only 'discovered' by white settlers as recently as 1890. Despite its lofty vantage – at 4061ft it is over 1000ft higher than Snoqualmie Pass – it was chosen for the Great Northern railroad's cross-Cascade route, but you won't see any train tracks here. Instead, the railway burrows underneath the pass via North America's longest rail tunnel (7.8 miles). The long-distance

Pacific Crest Trail also crosses the highway here. Tempted?

The Drive » From Stevens Pass the descent begins immediately with subtle changes in the vegetation; the cedars and hemlocks of the western slopes are gradually replaced by pine, larch and spruce. For 35 miles, the road threads through the steep-sided Tumwater canyon alongside the turbulent Wenatchee River. Suddenly, German-style houses start to appear against an eerily familiar alpine backdrop.

TRIP HIGHLIGHT

3 Leavenworth

Blink hard and rub your eyes. This isn't some strange Germanic hallucination. This is Leavenworth, a former lumber town that underwent a Bavarian makeover in the 1960s after the re-routing of the cross-continental railway threatened to put it permanently out of business. Swapping loggers for tourists, Leavenworth today has successfully reinvented itself as a traditional *Romantische*

🔗 LINK YOUR TRIP

7 Chuckanut Drive & Whidbey Island

For a break from the mountain madness, veer north in Burlington to Bellingham and sample the coastal and pastoral joys of Puget Sound.

12 Mt Baker & Lummi Island

For more mountain madness, head north to Bellingham and then inland into another North Cascadian wilderness.

Strasse village, right down to the beer and bratwurst. The *Sound of Music*-style setting helps, as does the fact that Leavenworth serves as the main activity center for sorties into the nearby **Alpine Lakes Wilderness** (☑425-888-1421; www.recreation.gov/permits/233273; overnight permits per day $5) and Wenatchee National Forest.

A surreal stroll (p156) through the gabled alpine houses of Leavenworth's Front St with its dirndl-wearing waitstaff, wandering accordionists and European cheesemongers is one of Washington State's oddest, but most endearing, experiences. For white-water rafting trips, call by **Osprey Rafting Co** (☑509-548-6800; www.ospreyrafting.com; 4342

Icicle Rd; rapids trip from $105, 3hr float from $60).

The Drive » The 22 miles between Leavenworth and Wenatchee highlight one of the most abrupt scenery changes in the state. One minute you're in quasi-Bavaria surrounded by crenellated alpine peaks, the next you're in a sprawled couldn't-be-anywhere-but-America town amid bald hills and a wide river valley. East of Leavenworth, US 2 shares the road briefly with US 97.

✕ 🛏 p107

---

❹ Wenatchee

Fruit stands start peppering the highway soon after you leave Leavenworth, paving your entry into Wenatchee, the self-proclaimed – and who's arguing? – Apple Capital of the World. Something of an ugly sister after cute Leavenworth, Wenatchee's a place to go local and taste the apples from the nearby orchards before swinging north. The best fruit stands enliven US 2/97 on the way to Chelan.

As an overture to your tasting experience, check out the **Washington Apple Commission Visitors Center** (www.bestapples.com; 2900 Euclid Ave; ⊘9am-5pm Mon-Fri) on the way into town, where you can bone up on the relative merits of a Gala versus a Braeburn over a surprisingly interesting video.

The Drive » US 2/97 plies the east side of the Columbia River for 39 miles between Wenatchee and Chelan. This is one of the best places to 'shop' at impromptu seasonal fruit outlets run by enterprising local farmers who haul their freshly plucked produce from the nearby fields and orchards to sell roadside from semi-permanent stores, carts or just plain old boxes.

---

❺ Chelan

Lake Chelan shelters some of the nation's cleanest water and has consequently become one of Washington's premier water recreation areas. Not surprisingly, the place is packed cheek by jowl in summer, with all number of speedboats, Jet Skis and power-craft battling it out for their own private slice of water. To avoid any high-speed collisions, try renting a kayak from **Lake Rider Sports** (☑509-885-4767; www.lakeridersports.com; Lakeshore Waterfront Park; single/double kayak rental per day $70/90; ⊘10am-4pm weekends, by appointment weekdays) and paddling up the lake to see some

---

KEROUAC & THE VOID

A turnout at milepost 135 on US 20 offers the drive's only roadside views of **Desolation Peak**. The peak's lookout tower was famously home to Zen-influenced Beat writer Jack Kerouac who, in 1956, spent 63 days here in splendid isolation, honing his evolving Buddhist philosophy, raging at 'the Void' of nearby Hozomeen Mountain (also visible from the turnout) and penning drafts of *Desolation Angels*. It was the last time Kerouac would enjoy such anonymity; the following year saw the publication of *On the Road*, and his propulsion to the status of literary icon.

undiluted Cascadian nature firsthand.

There are public beaches at **Lakeside Park**, near the west side of Chelan town, and at **Lake Chelan State Park**, 9 miles west on S Lakeshore Rd.

If you have kids, don't even think they'll let you sneak past **Slidewaters Water Park** (www.slide waters.com; 102 Waterslide Dr; day pass adult/child $25/20; 10am-7pm May-Sep;), located on a hill above the boat dock.

The Drive » Rejoin US 97 and follow it north through the grand coulees of the Columbia River valley to the small town of Pateros. From here SR 153, aka the Methow Hwy, tracks the younger, faster-flowing Methow River north to Twisp. At a junction with US 20 turn left, and continue on the highway into Winthrop, 61 miles from Chelan.

TRIP HIGHLIGHT

❻ Winthrop

Winthrop is – along with Leavenworth – one of two themed towns on this Cascade Drive. Once a struggling mining community, it avoided ghost town status in the 1960s when it was made over to look like a cowboy settlement out of the Wild West. Although on paper it sounds like a corny Hollywood gambit, the Gary Cooper touches feel surprisingly authentic. Winthrop's *High Noon* shopfronts hide a genuine frontier spirit (the road ends in winter not far

LOCAL KNOWLEDGE: METHOW VALLEY TRAILS

The Methow's combination of powdery winter snow and abundant summer sunshine has transformed the valley into one of Washington's primary recreation areas. You can bike, hike and fish in the summer, and cross-country ski on the second-biggest snow-trail network in the US in the winter. The 125 miles of trails are maintained by a nonprofit organization, the **Methow Valley Sport Trails Association** (MVSTA; 509-996-3287; www.methowtrails.org; 309 Riverside Ave, Winthrop; 8:30am-3:30pm Mon-Fri), and in the winter it provides the most comprehensive network of hut-to-hut (and hotel-to-hotel) skiing in North America.

beyond here), along with some fantastic accommodations and places to eat.

The facades of downtown Winthrop are so realistic it's easy to miss the collection of homesteader cabins that make up the **Shafer Museum** (285 Castle Ave; admission by donation; 10am-5pm Memorial Day-Labor Day). But best of all is the unmissable Sun Mountain Lodge (p107), a sporting and relaxation dreamscape 10 miles out of town overlooking the valley.

The Drive » Out of Winthrop, SR 20 enters the most bucolic and endearing stretch of the Methow Valley. Here the broad valley floor, scattered with farms, gives little hint of the jagged wilderness that lies beyond. If you thought Winthrop was small, don't blink when, in 14 miles, you reach Mazama, a small cluster of wooden buildings reminiscent of a gunslinger movie.

✕ ⊨ p107

❼ Mazama

The last outpost before the desolate North Cascades, Mazama's half-dozen wooden abodes sit at the western end of the Methow Valley. Fuel up on brownies at the **Mazama Store** (www.themazamastore. com; 50 Lost River Rd; 7am-6pm), a deli/espresso bar for locals that's a great place to pick up trail tips.

The Drive » You'll be working through your gears soon after Mazama as the North Cascade Mountains start to close in. This part of US 20 is unlike any other trans-Cascade road. Not only is the scenery more spectacular, but the road itself (closed November to May) is a major engineering feat. You have 22 miles to enjoy it before reaching Rainy Pass.

TRIP HIGHLIGHT

❽ Washington & Rainy Passes

Venture less than 100yd from your car at the

Classic Trip

CONNIE COLEMAN/GETTY IMAGES ©

WHY THIS IS A CLASSIC TRIP
BECKY OHLSEN, WRITER

Washington's wild coastline has its defenders, but for my money, the state's crown jewel is the mighty Cascade Range. This trip takes you into and over some of the region's most spectacular mountain scenery, from narrow, vertiginous passes to charming little alpine towns that specialize in gearing you up for adventure. Speaking of which, you should definitely stop somewhere along this route to explore on foot, too.

Above: Gas station, Winthrop (p103)
Left: Bavarian-style buildings, Leavenworth (p101, p156)
Right: Diablo Lake (p106), North Cascades National Park

Washington Pass overlook (5477ft) and you'll be rewarded with fine views of the towering Liberty Bell and its Early Winter Spires, while the highway drops below you in ribbonlike loops. By the time the highway reaches **Rainy Pass** (4875ft) a couple of miles further west, the air has chilled and you're well into the high country, a hop and a skip from the drive's highest hiking trails. The 6.2-mile **Maple Pass Loop Trail** is a favorite, climbing 2150ft to aerial views over jewel-like Lake Ann. The epic **Pacific Crest Trail** also crosses US 20 nearby, so keep an eye open for wide-eyed and bushy-bearded throughhikers popping out of the undergrowth. Perhaps the best choice if you want to shake the crowds is the excellent climb up to **Easy Pass** (7.4 miles return), hardly 'easy,' but offering spectacular views of Mt Logan and the Fisher Basin below.

The Drive » Surrounded by Gothic peaks, the North Cascades Scenic Hwy makes a big swing north shadowing Granite Creek and then Ruby Creek, where it swings back west and, 20 miles from Rainy Pass, enters the Ross Lake National Recreation Area near Ruby Arm.

TRIP HIGHLIGHT

⑨ Ross & Diablo Lakes

The odd thing about much of the landscape

on this trip is that it's unnatural, born from the construction of three huge dams that still supply Seattle with a large proportion of its electricity. The wilderness that surrounds it, however, is the rawest you'll get outside Alaska. **Ross Lake** (Hwy 20, Mile 134) was formed in the 1930s after the building of the eponymous dam. It stretches north 23 miles into Canada. Soon after the **Ross Lake overlook**, a path leads from the road to the dam. You'll see the unique Ross Lake Resort (p107) floating on the other side.

A classic photo opportunity comes a couple of miles later at the **Diablo Lake overlook** (ferry round-trip $20). The turquoise lake is the most popular part of the park, offering beaches, gorgeous views and a boat launch at **Colonial Creek Campground** (206-386-4495; www.nps.gov; Hwy 20, Mile 130; campsites from $16), with nearby hikes to Thunder Knob (3.6 miles return) and Thunder Creek (12 miles return).

The Drive » From Diablo, head west alongside the sinuous Gorge Reservoir on US 20. Pass through Newhalem (where you can stop at the North Cascades Visitor Center). As the valley opens out and the damp west coast air drifts in from the Pacific, you'll enter Marblemount, 23 miles from Diablo Lake.

🛏 p107

---

⑩ Marblemount

There's not much to the town of Marblemount, but the thought of buffalo burgers may entice you to pull over at the **Buffalo Run Restaurant** (www.buffaloruninn.com; 60084 Hwy 20; mains $10-34; ⊘11am-9pm May-Oct; ⊞), the first decent restaurant for miles, as long as you don't mind being greeted by the sight of several decoratively draped animal skins and a huge buffalo head mounted on the wall.

The Drive » The Skagit River remains your constant companion as you motor the 8 miles from Marblemount to equally diminutive Rockport. Look out for rafters, floaters and bald eagles.

🛏 p107

---

⑪ Rockport

As the valley widens further you'll touch down in Rockport, where the mirage-like appearance of an Indonesian-style Batak hut, aka **Cascadian Farms** (www.cascadianfarm.com; Hwy 20, Mile 100; milkshakes $6; ⊘10am-6pm May & Oct, 9am-7pm Jun-Sep), begs you to stop for organic strawberries, delicious fruit shakes and lifesav-ing espresso, which you can slurp down on a short self-guided tour of the farm.

Nearby, a 10-mile stretch of the Skagit River is a wintering ground for over 600 bald eagles who come here from November to early March to feast on spawning salmon. January is the best time to view them, ideally on a winter float trip with **Skagit River Guide Service** (888-675-2448; www.skagitriverfishingguide.com), whose boats use propane heat and are equipped with comfy cushioned seats. Three-hour trips run early November to mid-February.

The Drive » From Rockport, head west for 37 miles on US 20 through the Cascade Mountain foothills and the ever-broadening Skagit River valley to the small city of Burlington, which sits just east of busy I-5.

---

⑫ Burlington

The drive's end, popularly known as the 'Hub City,' is not a 'sight' in itself (unless you like shopping malls), although the settlement's location in the heart of the Skagit River valley means it acts as a hub for numerous nearby attractions, including the tulip fields of La Conner (p94), Chuckanut Dr (p91; which officially ends here) and the San Juan Islands (p83).

Eating & Sleeping

Leavenworth ❸

✕ Watershed Cafe   Northwestern US $$

(📞509-888-0214; www.watershedpnw.com;
221 8th St; mains $17-32; ⏲5-9pm Thu-Mon)
Farm to table, locally sourced – all the right
buzzwords can be found at this friendly and
elegant little cafe. There's a focus on local
seafood, but buffalo, organic chicken and pork
tenderloin are also likely to show up on the
menu, which changes with the seasons.

🛏 Hotel Pension Anna   Hotel $$

(📞509-548-6273; www.pensionanna.com;
926 Commercial St; r from $240; 🛜) The
most authentic Bavarian hotel in town is also
spotless and incredibly friendly. Each room is
kitted out in imported Austrian decor, and the
European-inspired breakfasts (included) may
induce joyful yodels. A recommended room
is the double with hand-painted furniture, but
the spacious suite in the adjacent St Joseph's
chapel is perfect for families.

Winthrop ❻

✕ Old Schoolhouse
Brewing   Pub Food $

(www.oldschoolhousebrewery.com; 155 Riverside
Ave; mains $14-17; ⏲3-9pm Mon-Thu, noon-
10pm Fri & Sat, noon-9pm Sun) Carb-load on
beer in this unusual pub that occupies a little
red former schoolhouse on the main street. You
can choose from an impressive range of home-
brewed ales; aficionados opt for the light bodied
Black Canyon Porter or the heavier, darker
Grampa Clem's Brown Ale. Classic pub-grub
highlights include outlaw chili, and fish-and-
chips with a Japanese twist.

🛏 Sun Mountain Lodge   Lodge $$$

(📞509-996-2211; www.sunmountainlodge.com;
604 Patterson Lake Rd; r from $285, cabins from
$415; ❄🛜✈) Without a doubt one of the best
places to stay in Washington, Sun Mountain
Lodge has an incomparable natural setting,
perched like an eagle's nest high above the
Methow Valley, and its assorted cabins provide
luxury without pretension. The 360-degree
views from its highly lauded restaurant are awe-
inspiring, and people travel from miles around
just to enjoy breakfast here.

Ross & Diablo Lakes ❾

🛏 Ross Lake Resort   Historic Hotel $$$

(📞206-486-3751; www.rosslakeresort.com;
503 Diablo St, Rockport; cabins $205-385;
⏲mid-Jun–late Oct; 🚗) The floating cabins at
this secluded resort were built in the 1930s for
loggers working in the valley soon to be flooded
by Ross Dam. There's no road in – either hike
the 2-mile trail from Hwy 20 (then call for a
quick $2 boat ride across the lake) or take the
ferry from the parking area near Diablo Dam.
Cabins vary in size and facilities, but all feature
electricity, plumbing and kitchenettes.

Marblemount ❿

🛏 Buffalo Run Inn   Motel $

(📞360-873-2103; www.buffaloruninn.com;
58179 Hwy 20; r with/without bath from $129/69;
🚗🛜) Across the street from the restaurant
of the same name, on a sharp bend on Hwy 20,
the Buffalo doesn't look much from outside. But
within its wooden walls is a clean and friendly
motel (kitchenettes, TVs and comfy beds). Five
of the 15 rooms share bathrooms and a sitting
area.

Mt Rainier Scenic Byways

Emblazoned on every Washington license plate and visible throughout the western part of the state, Rainier is the contiguous USA's fifth-highest peak and, arguably, its most awe-inspiring.

TRIP HIGHLIGHTS

260 miles

Sunrise
Flower meadows extraordinaire with four Cascadian volcanoes as backdrop

237 miles

Tipsoo Lake
Glorious triumvirate of alpine lake, Rainier view and high mountain pass

START/FINISH
Seattle

Nisqually Entrance

15 · 14

5 · 8

White Pass

Packwood

93 miles

Longmire
Pitch into the woods in Rainier's forested lowland nexus

104 miles

Paradise
A national park inn and visitor center amid high-altitude trails

2–3 DAYS
354 MILES / 570KM

GREAT FOR...

BEST TIME TO GO
June to October, when alpine flowers bloom.

  ESSENTIAL PHOTO
Rainier's snow-topped summit reflected in Reflection Lakes.

 BEST FOR ALPINE MEADOWS
A toss-up between Paradise and Sunrise.

Mt Rainier Scenic Byways

Wrapped in a 368-sq-mile national park, and standing 2000ft higher than anything else in the Pacific Northwest, Rainier is a mountain of biblical proportions. Circumnavigate it by car and you'll quickly swap the urban melee of Seattle for forest-covered mountain foothills strafed with huge trees and imbued with Native American myth. Closer to Paradise, flower meadows shimmer beneath Rainier's summit during an intense summer season.

❶ Seattle

Seattle is an appropriate place to start this epic circuit around what locals refer to reverentially as 'the Mountain.' Before heading off, take some time to walk around (p152), seeking out the soul of the city at Pike Place Market (p64). On the days when Rainier reveals itself from the cloudy heavens (a minority annually), you can also wander down to the waterfront for a glimpse of the

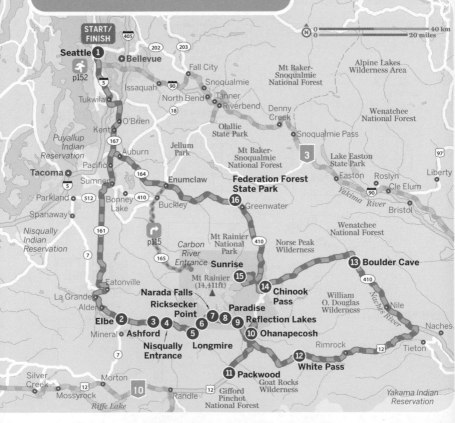

high-altitude glories to come.

The Drive ››› There is little to delay you beyond Seattle until the tiny town of Elbe, 72 miles away. Drive south on I-5 to exit 154A, then east on I-405, and south again on SR 167 and SR 161. Just southwest of Eatonville, SR 161 merges with SR 7; follow this road into Elbe on the cusp of the national park.

 p65

➋ Elbe

The pinprick settlement of Elbe has two claims to fame: its tiny white Lutheran **church** built by German immigrants in 1906 (and positively ancient by Pacific Northwest standards), and the heritage **Mt Rainier Scenic Railroad** (📞360-492-5588; www.mtrainier railroad.com; 54124 Mountain

LINK YOUR TRIP

10 **Mt St Helens Volcano Trail**

A logical link and an easy one given the proximity of the two mountains – Packwood, near Rainier's Ohanapecosh entrance, serves both drives.

3 **Mountains to Sound Greenway**

Seattle is the finish point of this roller-coaster drive, which is equally spectacular if done in reverse.

Hwy E; adult/child $41/21; ☺May-Sep) that runs summer steam trains between Elbe and Mineral (7 miles south). Trips depart three times daily from May to September. Aping the railway theme is the **Hobo Inn & Diner** (📞360-569-2500; www.rrdiner.com/the-hobo-inn; 54106 Mountain Hwy E, Elbe; d from $115), whose restaurant, bar and rooms all inhabit vintage, but lovingly tended, cabooses (train carriages).

The Drive ››› From Elbe take SR 706 (the National Park Hwy) 8 miles due east to Ashford.

➌ Ashford

Situated a couple of miles outside the busy Nisqually entrance, Ashford is the national park's main service center with some standard accommodations, an info center and Whittaker's Motel & Bunkhouse (p117), a hostel-cafe conceived by legendary local mountaineer Lou Whittaker in the early 1990s. It would be heresy to leave town without popping inside for an espresso before grabbing brunch (or lunch) down the road at the Copper Creek Inn (p117), where the wild blackberry pies have fuelled many a successful summit attempt.

The Drive ››› Two miles east of Ashford on SR 706 you'll

encounter the park entrance gate.

 p117

➍ Nisqually Entrance

The southwestern Nisqually entrance (named for the nearby river, which in turn is named after a local Native American tribe) is the busiest in **Mt Rainier National Park** (www.nps.gov/mora; car $30, pedestrian & cyclist $15, 1yr pass $55) and the only year-round entry gate. The simple entrance arch was built in 1922. Pay your park fee at the ticket window. As you drive through the entrance, you'll notice how, almost immediately, the trees appear denser and older. Many of these moss-covered behemoths date back over 700 years and measure up to 200ft in height.

The Drive ››› Follow the road alongside the Nisqually River for a couple of miles to Kautz Creek, where the summit of Rainier appears like a ghostly apparition. Six miles east of the park entrance, you'll reach Longmire.

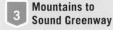

➎ Longmire

Worth a stop to stretch your legs or gain an early glimpse of Rainier's mossy old-growth forest, Longmire was the brainchild of a certain James Longmire who first came here in 1883 during a climbing trip when he noticed the hot mineral springs that bubbled up in a lovely meadow opposite the present-day National Park Inn (p117). He and his family returned the following year and established Longmire's Medicinal Springs, and in 1890 he built the Longmire Springs Hotel. Since 1917 the National Park Inn has stood on this site – built in classic 'parkitecture' style – and is complemented by a small store, the tiny **Longmire Information Center & Museum** (☎360-569-6575; Hwy 706; ⏰museum 9am-4:30pm year-round, info center May-Oct) and a number of important trailheads. For a laid-back look at some old-growth forest and pastoral meadows, try the **Trail of the Shadows** loop, a 0.8-mile circuit that begins across the road from the museum.

The Drive ❯❯ After Longmire the road slowly starts to climb, passing the Cougar Rock campground and Christine Falls, both on the left. A couple of miles after the falls, bear right onto a short stretch of summer-only one-way road (signposted 'Viewpoint') for a view stop at Ricksecker Point, 6.5 miles from Longmire.

🛏️ p117

⑥ Ricksecker Point

One of the park's premier viewpoints, beloved by photographers, professional or otherwise, Ricksecker Point is a fine place to study five of Rainier's 26 glaciers – Nisqually, Pyramid, Success, Kautz and Wilson. The summit you see here is actually a false one (Point Success); the obscured *true* summit is 257ft higher. Equally majestic to the southeast is the sawtoothed Tatoosh range.

The Drive ❯❯ Rejoin the main road and continue uphill for 2.5 miles.

⑦ Narada Falls

Eight miles east of Longmire, a parking area marks the starting point for a steep 0.2-mile trail that leads down through flowers and ferns to the misty 168ft Narada Falls. The falls, often embellished by brilliant rainbows, carry the Paradise River over a basalt cliff. In high season, expect to get a face-full of water spray and an earful of oohing and ahhing as this is the park's most popular waterfall. In winter the falls freeze over and attract daring ice-climbers.

The Drive ❯❯ Soon after the falls, the road forks; stay left for Paradise. Follow the winding asphalt for another 2 miles to the Upper Parking Lot, where

NADIA YONG/SHUTTERSTOCK ©

you'll find the Paradise Inn and Henry M Jackson Visitor Center.

TRIP HIGHLIGHT

⑧ Paradise

The daughter of park pioneer James Longmire unintentionally named this high mountain nirvana when she exclaimed what a paradise it was on visiting the spot for the first time in the 1880s. Suddenly, the area had a name, and a very apt one at that. One of the snowiest places on earth, 5400ft-high **Paradise** (Paradise Valley Rd) remains

the park's most popular draw with its famous flower meadows backed by dramatic Rainier views on the days when the mountain decides to take its cloudy hat off. Aside from hiding numerous trailheads and being the starting point for most summit hikes, Paradise guards the iconic Paradise Inn (p117; built in 1916) and the informative **Henry M Jackson Visitor Center** (☎360-569-6571; ⏱10am-5pm daily May-Oct, Sat & Sun Nov-Apr). Park naturalists lead free interpretive hikes from the visitor center daily in summer,

and snowshoe walks on winter weekends.

The Drive ≫ Drive out of the east end of the Paradise Upper Parking Lot, cross the Paradise River (looking out for marmots) and descend the one-way road for 2 miles to a junction. Turn left and rejoin the main two-way road for 1.5 miles toward Reflection Lakes and Steven's Canyon.

🛏 p117

- - - - - - - - - - - - - - -

❾ Reflection Lakes

Rainier eyes itself in the mirror on calm cloudless days at Reflection Lakes, formed during a violent volcanic eruption nearly 6000 years ago.

You can pull over for double-vision photos of the mountain framed by tufts of precious wildflowers. The main lake used to have a boat concession, but now it's deliciously tranquil bar the odd passing tour bus.

The Drive ≫ Avalanche chutes plague the U-shaped Steven's Canyon Rd in winter, ensuring it remains closed outside peak season (unlike Paradise on the western side). Seen from above, the canyon is rather spectacular. Stop for a bird's-eye view a mile or so after Reflection Lakes before the trees close in. From here it's downhill to Ohanapecosh, 20 miles from the lakes.

113

SUMMER WONDERLAND

You've circumnavigated it in a car; now how about walking it? Rainier is not only encircled by a road; you can also hike around it via the long-distance **Wonderland Trail**. Laid out in 1915, the 93-mile-long precipitous path initially served as a patrol beat for park rangers and in the 1930s it was briefly earmarked as a paved ring road for cars. Fortunately, the plan never reached fruition and today the unbroken trail (which gains 21,000ft in cumulative elevation) is one of the most challenging and iconic hikes in the Pacific Northwest. You'll need food, camping gear, eight to 12 free days and a permit from the Longmire Information Center (p112) to do Wonderland. Longmire is a popular start point. There are 18 backcountry campgrounds en route; reservations ($20) are advisable in peak season (July and August). The official park page (www.nps.gov/mora) has more information.

🔟 Ohanapecosh

Ohanapecosh (o-*ha*-nuh-peh-*kosh*) – the name means 'at the edge' – in the park's southeastern corner is usually accessed by the small settlement of Packwood, 11 miles to the southwest on US 12, which harbors a small number of eating and sleeping options. Shoehorned between Mt Rainier and its two southern neighbors, Mt St Helens and Mt Adams, this is a good base for travelers wanting to visit two or more of the mountains.

Just inside the Steven's Canyon gate, you'll find the 1.5-mile **Grove of the Patriarchs Trail**, one of the park's most popular short hikes. The trail explores a small island in the Ohanapecosh River replete with craning Douglas fir, cedar and hemlock trees, some of which are over 1000 years old. To reach the **Ohanapecosh Visitors Center** (☎360-569-6581; Hwy 123; ⊙9am-5pm Jun–mid-Oct), turn right at the Steven's Canyon entrance onto SR 123 and drive 1.5 miles south. Alternatively, you can hike down from the Grove of the Patriarchs.

The Drive ≫ Go right at the Steven's Canyon entrance and follow SR 123 south past the visitor center to the intersection with US 12. For Packwood, bear right for 11 miles.

🔟 Packwood

A service center for Mt St Helens, Mt Rainier and the nearby ski area of White Pass, Packwood is what in the Old West they called a 'one-horse town.' A few low- to mid-ranking eating joints and accommodations glued to US 12 provide a good excuse to pull over and mingle with other road-trippers. Chinwaggers congregate at **Mountain Goat Coffee** (☎360-494-5600; 105 E Main St; pastries from $2; ⊙7am-5pm), where you may run into a park ranger or two.

The Drive ≫ Retrace your route to the intersection of US 12 and SR 123. The 20-mile climb to White Pass begins here. Stop at a pullover soon after the intersection to appreciate the indelible sight of Mt Rainier as it appears briefly above the trees.

🛏 p117

🔟 White Pass

Higher than Snoqualmie and Stevens Passes to the north, White Pass carries a quieter, open-year-round road that, at various points, offers glimpses of three Cascadian volcanoes: Mt Rainier, Mt Adams and Mt St Helens. The pass itself, perched at 4500ft, is home to an understated **ski area** (☎509-672-3100; www.skiwhitepass.com; 48935 US 12; day pass adult/child $69/49), which has one condo complex for overnighters. Otherwise, people stay in nearby

Packwood or drive up for the day from Yakima.

The Drive ›› A classic east–west Washington scenery shift kicks in soon after White Pass as you follow US 12 amid increasingly scattered trees and bald, steep-sided river coulees. At the intersection with SR 410, swing north on the Chinook Scenic Byway just west of the town of Naches to reach Boulder Cave, 65 miles from White Pass.

🛏 p117

⓭ Boulder Cave

Among the many excuses to pull over on this stretch of the Chinook Scenic Byway is **Boulder Cave** (Hwy 410; ⊙May-Oct), a rarity in the relatively cave-free terrain of the Pacific Northwest and doubly unique due to its formation through a combination of volcanic and erosive processes. A 2-mile round-trip trail built by the Civilian Conservation Corps in 1935 leads into the cave's murky interior, formed when Devil's Creek cut a tunnel through soft sedimentary rock, leaving hard volcanic basalt on top. Up to 50 rare big-eared bats hibernate in the cave each winter, when it is closed to the public. Bring a flashlight.

The Drive ›› Continue west and uphill toward Chinook Pass, 25 miles from Boulder Cave, as the air cools and the snowdrifts pile up roadside.

TRIP HIGHLIGHT

⓮ Chinook Pass

Closed until May and infested with lingering snowdrifts well into July, Chinook Pass towers 5430ft on Rainier's eastern flank. The long-distance **Pacific Crest Trail** crosses the highway here on a pretty stone bridge, while nearby **Crystal Mountain** (www.skicrystal.com; 33914 Crystal Mountain Blvd; lift tickets adult/child $79/59; 🚡) comprises Washington's largest ski area and only bona fide overnight 'resort.' Rather than stop at the pass, cruise

a few hundred yards further west to **Tipsoo Lake**, another reflective photographer's dream where a paved trail will return the blood to your legs.

The Drive ›› From Tipsoo Lake the road winds down to relatively 'low' Cayuse Pass (4694ft). Turn north here and descend a further 1000ft in 3 miles to the turning for Mt Rainier's White River entrance. This is the gateway to Sunrise, 16 miles uphill via a series of switchbacks.

TRIP HIGHLIGHT

⓯ Sunrise

Sunrise, at 6400ft, marks the park's highest

DETOUR: CARBON RIVER ENTRANCE

Start: ⓰ Federation Forest State Park

The park's northwest entrance is its most isolated and undeveloped corner, with two unpaved (and unconnected) roads and little in the way of facilities, save a lone ranger station and the very basic **Ipsut Creek Campground** (☎360-829-5127; Carbon River Rd; camping free; ⊙year-round, weather permitting). But while the tourist traffic might be thin on the ground, the landscape lacks nothing in magnificence.

Named for its coal deposits, Carbon River is the park's wettest region and protects one of the few remaining examples of inland temperate rainforest in the contiguous USA. Dense, green and cloaked in moss, this verdant wilderness can be penetrated by a handful of interpretive trails that fan off the Carbon River Rd.

Getting here takes you part of the way back to Seattle. Take US 410W to 116S (Carbon River Rd) then turn left. After about 15.5 miles you'll come to the Carbon River ranger station just before the entrance.

road. Thanks to the superior elevation, the summer season is particularly short and snow can linger into July. It is also noticeably drier than Paradise, resulting in an interesting variety of subalpine vegetation, including masses of wildflowers.

The views from Sunrise are famously spectacular and – aside from stunning close-ups of Rainier itself – you can also, quite literally, watch the weather roll in over the distant peaks of Mt Baker and Mt Adams. Similarly impressive is the glistening Emmons Glacier, which, at 4 sq miles, is the largest glacier in the contiguous USA.

A trailhead directly across the parking lot from the **Sunrise Day Lodge** (Sunrise Park Rd; mains $6-12; ⏰10am-7pm Jul & Aug, 11am-3pm Sat & Sun Sep) cafeteria provides access to **Emmons Vista**, with good views of Mt Rainier, Little Tahoma and the glacier. Nearby, the 1-mile **Sourdough Ridge Trail** leads to pristine subalpine meadows for stunning views over other volcanic giants.

The Drive ≫ Coast downhill to the White River entrance and turn north onto the Mather Memorial Pkwy in order to exit the park. In the small community of Greenwater on SR 410 you can load up with gas and food. Federation Forest State Park is 36 miles from Sunrise.

- - - - - - - - - - - - - - - - - - -

16 Federation Forest State Park

Just when you thought you'd left ancient nature behind, up springs Federation Forest State Park, created by a foresighted women's group in the 1940s in order to preserve a rapidly diminishing stock of local old-growth forest from logging interests. Today its fir, spruce, hemlock and cedar trees cluster around the lackadaisical White River, while the **Catherine Montgomery Interpretive Center** (www.parks.state.wa.us/502; ⏰8am-dusk Fri-Sun Jun-Aug) offers a rundown of the contrasting ecosystems of east and west Washington State. There's also a bookstore and 12 miles of trails, most of them family-friendly.

Eating & Sleeping

Ashford ❸

✕ Copper Creek Inn   American $$
(📞360-569-2326; www.coppercreekinn.com; 35707 SR 706 E; breakfast $9-14, burgers $11-15, dinner mains $12-28; ⏰11am-8pm Mon-Fri, 8am-9pm Sat, 8am-8pm Sun, opens earlier summer) Forget the historic inns. This is one of the state's great rural restaurants, and breakfast is an absolute must if you're heading off for a lengthy hike inside the park. Situated just outside the Nisqually entrance, the Copper Creek has been knocking out pancakes, wild-blackberry pie and its own home-roasted coffee since 1946.

🛏 Whittaker's Motel & Bunkhouse   Hostel $
(📞360-569-2439; www.whittakersbunkhouse. com; 30205 SR 706 E; dm $40, d $90-145; 🛜) Part of Rainier's 'furniture,' Whittaker's is the home base of legendary Northwestern climber Lou Whittaker, who first summited the mountain at the age of 19 and has guided countless adventurers to the top in the years since. Down-to-earth and comfortable, this place has a good old-fashioned youth-hostel feel, with cheap sleeps available in six-bed dorms. The alluring on-site **Whittaker's Café & Espresso** (breakfast from $3; ⏰6:45am-8pm, weekends only winter) is a fine place to hunker down for breakfast.

🛏 Nisqually Lodge   Motel $$
(📞888-674-3554, 360-569-8804; www. whitepasstravel.com; 31609 SR 706 E; r from $200; 🆇🛜🏊) With an expansive lobby complete with crackling fireplace and huge, well-stocked rooms, this lodge is far plusher than an average motel. The outdoor Jacuzzi, simple help-yourself breakfast and easy access to the park pretty much seal the deal. Rates drop in winter.

Longmire ❺

🛏 National Park Inn   Inn $$
(📞360-569-2275; Hwy 706; r with/without bath from $203/138; 🆇) The National Park Inn, parts of which date from 1911, goes out of its way to be rustic, with no TVs or telephones and small yet cozy facilities. But who needs cable when you've got fine service, fantastic surroundings, and complimentary afternoon tea and scones served in the comfortable dining room? Reserve in summer.

Paradise ❽

🛏 Paradise Inn   Historic Hotel $$
(📞360-569-2275; r with/without bath from $182/123; ⏰mid-May–Oct; 🦽) Designed to blend in with the environment and constructed almost entirely of local materials, including the exposed cedar logs in the Great Room, the historic Paradise Inn (1916) was an early blueprint for National Park–rustic architecture. Following a two-year, $30 million, earthquake-withstanding revamp, the smallish rooms retain their close-to-the-wilderness essence, while the communal areas are nothing short of regal.

Packwood ⓫

🛏 Cowlitz River Lodge   Motel $
(📞360-494-4444; www.whitepasstravel.com/ cowlitzriverlodge; US 12, cnr Skate Creek Rd; r from $130; 🆇🛜) Probably the most convenient accommodations for both Mt Rainier and Mt St Helens, the Cowlitz is the sister motel to Ashford's Nisqually Lodge and offers 32 above-average motel rooms along with the obligatory outdoor Jacuzzi.

White Pass ⓬

🛏 White Pass Village Inn   Condo $$
(📞509-672-3131; www.staywhitepass.com; 48933 US 12; studios from $100; 🛜🆇) Adjacent to the White Pass Ski Area (p114), this condo complex is open year-round, meaning it's also good for sorties into Mt Rainier National Park (12 miles away). Condo sizes range from studio to deluxe, and all have kitchenettes and private bathrooms. The outdoor pool is heated to spa temperatures in the winter, and there's a store and laundry next door.

Mt St Helens Volcano Trail

Fiery infamy was made in 1980 when Mt St Helens blew megatons of molten ash into the atmosphere. Its devastated but recovering landscape looks like nothing else on earth.

TRIP HIGHLIGHTS

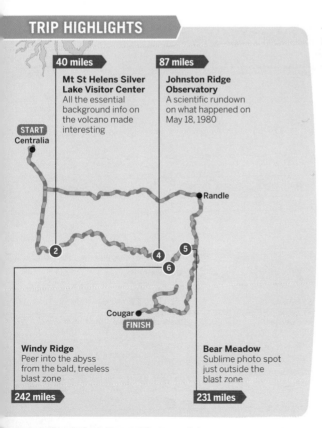

40 miles

Mt St Helens Silver Lake Visitor Center
All the essential background info on the volcano made interesting

87 miles

Johnston Ridge Observatory
A scientific rundown on what happened on May 18, 1980

START
Centralia

Randle

② ④ ⑤ ⑥

Cougar ●
FINISH

Windy Ridge
Peer into the abyss from the bald, treeless blast zone

242 miles

Bear Meadow
Sublime photo spot just outside the blast zone

231 miles

3 DAYS
366 MILES / 589KM

GREAT FOR...

BEST TIME TO GO
July to October – the mountain's best sights and roads are open.

 ESSENTIAL PHOTO
Mountain view from Bear Meadow.

 BEST FOR FAMILIES
Silver Lake Visitor Center's interactive exhibits.

10 Mt St Helens Volcano Trail

The name Mt St Helens has a fearful resonance for anyone who was alive on May 18, 1980, when a massive volcanic eruption set off the largest landslide in human history. Nearly 40 years later, you can drive through the embattled but slowly recovering landscape that makes up the Mt St Helens National Monument, stopping at interpretive centers that document the erstwhile environmental carnage. It's a unique if sometimes disconcerting ride.

❶ Centralia

The main reason to make this rather mundane mining and lumber town the starting point for your volcanic excursion is to stay at a converted brothel. The Olympic Club Hotel (p125) – a 'venue hotel' run by Portland's McMenamin brothers – dates from 1908 when it opened as a 'gentlemen's resort' designed to satisfy the various drinking, gambling and sexual vices of transient miners and loggers. In

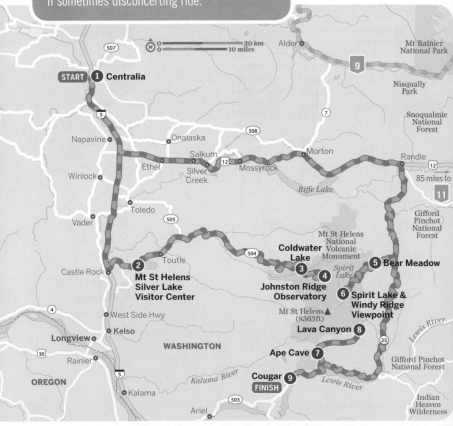

1996 the turn-of-the-century building was taken over by the McMenamins, who restored the brothel to its former glory complete with creaking floorboards, Tiffany lamps and art deco murals (but without the erstwhile night-time shenanigans).

The Drive » Steer south out of Centralia on I-5 for 32 miles to exit 49, where you proceed east 6 miles on SR 504, aka the Spirit Lake Memorial Hwy.

 p125

TRIP HIGHLIGHT

❷ Mt St Helens Silver Lake Visitor Center

Situated 5 miles east of Castle Rock on SR 504, the **Silver Lake Visitor**

LINK YOUR TRIP

9 Mt Rainier Scenic Byways

St Helens' taller, potentially more lethal mountain twin is easily accessible via its southeastern Ohanapecosh entrance.

11 Washington Wine Tour

Head east in Randle and continue on to Yakima on the cusp of a sunny valley full of grapes and wineries. Say no more.

Center (✆360-274-0962; www.parks.state.wa.us/245; 3029 Spirit Lake Hwy; adult/child $5/free; ☺9am-4pm Mar–mid-May & mid-Sep–Oct, to 5pm mid-May–mid-Sep, 9am-4pm Thu-Mon Nov-Feb; ♿) is the best introduction to the monument. There's a classic film and various exhibits, including a mock-up of the volcano; duck beneath the cone for displays on the subterranean workings of the mountain. Outside is the mile-long **Silver Lake Wetlands Trail**. If you're in need of a break, try the Fire Mountain Grill located on the 504.

The Drive » Continue east on the Spirit Lake Memorial Hwy (SR 504) until you get to the Forest Learning Center at milepost 33. The center runs an interesting film about the eruption. Soon after, you enter the blast zone near Elk Rock viewpoint. About 16 miles from Hoffstadt Bluffs you'll reach Coldwater Lake.

 p125

❸ Coldwater Lake

You're now categorically in the blast zone. Coldwater Lake, 43 miles east of Castle Rock, was created in 1980 when water backed up behind a dam caused by debris brought down by the eruption. The recreation area here (rest rooms, phone, boat launch) is the starting point of the 0.6-mile **Birth of a Lake Trail** (No 246), a paved

interpretive hike that seeks to demonstrate the regrowth of vegetation in the area. Look out for beavers and their handiwork.

The Drive » Follow the increasingly winding Spirit Lake Memorial Hwy (SR 504) 5.8 miles through the denuded landscape to the end of the road.

TRIP HIGHLIGHT

❹ Johnston Ridge Observatory

Situated at the end of SR 504 and looking directly into the mouth of the crater, this famous **observatory** (✆360-274-2140; www.fs.usda. gov; 24000 Spirit Lake Hwy; day-use $8; ☺10am-6pm mid-May–Oct) has exhibits that take a more scientific angle than the Silver Lake Visitor Center, depicting the geological events surrounding the 1980 blast and how they advanced the science of volcano forecasting and monitoring. The paved 1-mile round-trip **Eruption Trail** (No 201) offers once-in-a-lifetime views over toward the crater.

The Drive » Retrace your steps 52 miles to Castle Rock. Go north on I-5 and, at exit 68, east on US 12. Refuel in the tiny settlement of Randle. Turn right off US 12 onto SR 131, which soon becomes USFS Rd 25. Just past Iron Creek Falls, turn right onto USFS Rd 99. This section is 124 miles total.

5 Bear Meadow

Bear Meadow, just outside the blast zone, is where Gary Rosenquist took his infamous photographs of Mt St Helens erupting on May 18, 1980. The four quick-succession shots which Rosenquist started snapping at 8:32am are reproduced on an interpretive board and show the mountain, 11 miles away, with its northern slopes literally sliding away. Rosenquist, who was camping in the area at the time, was lucky and got out alive, driving north through thick ash. The blast zone stopped less than a mile away from the meadow, as the stands of still healthy trees in the foreground testify.

The Drive » Two miles further on, you'll enter the blast zone marked by eerie dead trees. Press on 12 miles from Bear Meadow, past various trailheads to the end of the road.

6 Spirit Lake & Windy Ridge Viewpoint

More remote but less crowded than Johnston Ridge is the harder-to-reach **Windy Ridge viewpoint** on the mountain's eastern side, accessed via USFS Rd 99. Here visitors get a palpable, if eerie, sense of the destruction that the blast wrought, with felled forests, desolate mountain slopes and the rather surreal sight of lifeless **Spirit Lake**, once one of the premier resorts in the South Cascades. There are toilets and a snack bar at the viewpoint parking lot, which is often closed until June. More than 350 steps ascend the hillside for close-up views of the crater 5 miles away. A stubbly green carpet covers the ridge slopes in summer as dwarf plants struggle back to life more than 30 years later. A few miles down the road you can descend 600ft on the 1.5-mile **Harmony Trail** (No 224) that leads to Spirit Lake.

The Drive » Retrace your steps to USFS Rd 25; turn right (south) and drive over Elk Pass and past the Clearwater viewpoint to Pine Creek information center. Turn west on USFS Rd 90 and drive along the north shore of Swift Reservoir before going right onto USFS Rd 83 and left onto USFS Rd 8303, a total distance of 56 miles.

7 Ape Cave

Ape Cave, on the south flank of Mt St Helens, is a 2-mile-long lava

MT ST HELENS INSTITUTE

The not-for-profit **Mt St Helens Institute** (📞360-449-7883; www.mshinstitute.org; 42218 NE Yale Bridge Rd, Amboy) is one of the most admired educational and conservation groups in the nation. Look out for the institute's expert volunteers at various interpretive sites around the mountain, where they organize hikes, talks, films and fundraisers, all related to the volcano and its geology.

Mt St Helens National Volcanic Monument Hoffstadt Creek Bridge on Spirit Lake Memorial Hwy

tube formed 2000 years ago by a lava flow that followed a deep watercourse. It's the longest lava tube in the Western Hemisphere. Hikers can walk and scramble the length of the cave on either the 0.8-mile **Lower Ape Cave Trail** or the 1.5-mile **Upper Ape Cave Trail**, which requires a certain amount of scrambling over rock piles and narrower passages. Bring your own light source. Free ranger-led explorations depart from **Apes' Headquarters** (☏360-449-7800; Forest Rd 8303; ⊗10am-5pm mid-Jun–early Sep), located at the entrance to the caves, several times daily in summer.

The Drive » Retrace your route to USFS Rd 83. Turn left and drive to the road's terminus at Lava Canyon, 14 miles from Ape Cave.

- - - - - - - - - - - - - - - - -

❽ Lava Canyon

The geology class continues on Mt St Helens' southeast side. Although the mountain's 1980 lateral blast blew north, the heat of the massive explosion melted its eastern glaciers and created a huge mud flow. Water, boulders and trees came flooding down **Muddy Creek**, scouring it out and revealing much older lava basalt underneath. This fascinating geological demolition can be seen at Lava Canyon, where a short 0.5-mile **interpretive trail** leads through new-growth trees to an overlook. To get closer, take a steeper path that zigzags down into the canyon, which you can cross on a bouncy suspension bridge built in 1993. **Lava Canyon Falls** crashes below. The trail continues further along the Canyon (though it's extremely exposed) to Smith Creek.

MT ST HELENS NATIONAL VOLCANIC MONUMENT

Mt St Helens is one of only two National Volcanic Monuments in the nation. The unique park, which measures 110,000 acres, was set aside in 1982 and is mostly comprised of land in the so-called 'blast zone' – the plan being that anything inside the park boundary is to be left to recover as nature intends. The monument, which is closely monitored, acts like a massive outdoor scientific laboratory.

The Drive » Track back along USFS Rd 83 to the junction with USFS Rd 90. Turn right (west) and head into the small settlement of Cougar, 21 miles from Lava Canyon, on Yale Lake.

⑨ Cougar

A 'town' with virtually no residents, lowly Cougar (population 120-ish), the nearest settlement to Mt St Helens, was mercifully spared the carnage of the 1980 eruption – though it was temporarily evacuated. Since 1953 it has sat on the shores of **Yale Lake**, a reservoir created after the construction of the Yale Dam on the Lewis River. It is a good pit stop courtesy of its Lone Fir Resort & Café, convenience store (with gas), grill restaurant and peaceful lakeside tranquility. Climbers making a St Helens summit bid often psyche up here.

✕ ⊨ p125

Eating & Sleeping

Centralia ❶

✗ Berry Fields — American $

(📞360-736-1183; www.berryfieldscafe.com; 201 S Pearl St; mains $7-14; ⏱7am-5pm) Centralia isn't known for its great restaurants, but here's an exception. This brunch spot, situated in Centralia's biggest antiques mall, offers formidable egg concoctions and enormous cinnamon buns.

🛏 Olympic Club Hotel — Hotel $

(📞360-736-5164; www.mcmenamins.com; 112 N Tower Ave; bunk/queen/king $65/75/85; 📶) This historic brothel with a McMenamins makeover (read: old-world class with quirky touches) offers bunks and double rooms with shared bathrooms. Bonus: you can eat, drink, shoot pool (or even snooker), play shuffleboard, see a live band and go to the cinema, all in the same evening – and all without having to leave the hotel.

Mt St Helens Silver Lake Visitor Center ❷

✗ Fire Mountain Grill — American $

(www.fmgrill.com; 9440 Spirit Lake Hwy, Toutle; mains $10-16; ⏱10am-8pm) A typical American grill menu of burgers, fish-and-chips, salads and steaks is enhanced here by its unexpectedness (there's nothing else for miles around), plus great views and a locally famous fruit cobbler for dessert.

🛏 Blue Heron Chateau — Inn $$$

(📞360-274-9595; www.blueheronchateau.com; 2846 Hwy 504; d from $250; 📶) A welcome B&B in an accommodation-light area, the Blue Heron offers seven rooms, including a Jacuzzi suite, in a large house almost opposite the Silver Lake Visitor Center on Hwy 504. Rooms are clean if unspectacular, but the views of Silver Lake and Mt St Helens – weather permitting – are spellbinding.

🛏 Eco Park Resort — Campground $

(📞360-274-7007; www.ecoparkresort.com; 14000 Spirit Lake Hwy, Toutle; campsites $25, 6-person yurts $95, cabins $150; 🐾) The closest full-service accommodations to the blast zone offers campsites and RV hookups, basic two- or four-person cabins and a yurt that sleeps six. Reservations are required. There's also a cafe-restaurant. The resort is owned by the family whose Spirit Lake Lodge was swept away by the 1980 eruption.

Cougar ❾

✗ Cougar Grill — American $

(📞360-238-5252; 16849 Lewis River Rd; mains $10-17; ⏱10am-9pm Mon-Thu, to 10pm Fri, 8am-10pm Sat & Sun) Before or after your hike, load up with a green-chili Cougar Burger or a slab of chicken-fried steak smothered in gravy at this divey little roadside cafe, the only game in town. What better way to reward yourself for slogging your way to the summit than a burger and a cold beer?

🛏 Lone Fir Resort & Café — Motel $$

(📞360-238-5210; www.lonefirresort.com; 16806 Lewis River Rd; tent/RV sites $30/41, r from $130, cabins from $203; ❄ 🏊) There's not a lot to choose from on Mt St Helens' south side in the noncamping genre, so thank your lucky stars that this place, in the rather lonesome settlement of Cougar, backs up its RV park with a pleasantly sited motel, cafe (pizzas and burgers, mainly) and swimming pool. Rustic's the word.

Washington Wine Tour

11

From the mellow Bordeaux reds of the sunny Yakima Valley to the big, bold flavors of pastoral Walla Walla, Washington wines are as luscious as the landscapes surrounding them.

TRIP HIGHLIGHTS

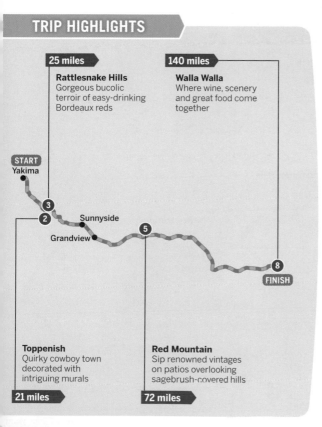

25 miles

Rattlesnake Hills
Gorgeous bucolic terroir of easy-drinking Bordeaux reds

140 miles

Walla Walla
Where wine, scenery and great food come together

START
Yakima

3
2

Sunnyside

Grandview

5

8
FINISH

Toppenish
Quirky cowboy town decorated with intriguing murals

21 miles

Red Mountain
Sip renowned vintages on patios overlooking sagebrush-covered hills

72 miles

3 DAYS
140 MILES / 225KM

GREAT FOR...

BEST TIME TO GO
April to October for weather and flowers.

ESSENTIAL PHOTO
Terra Blanca – views over grapevines from a grand villa.

✓ BEST FOR FOODIES
Walla Walla has top-notch restaurants.

Red Mountain Vineyards (p131)

11 Washington Wine Tour

Napa? Too crowded. France? Too far. Fortunately, the Yakima and Walla Walla valleys have emerged as major wine-making destinations. Learn about terroir and viticulture, or dedicate yourself to sampling lush reds and crisp whites in your search for your favorite appellation (you can always spit to manage consumption). For now this is still an unpretentious, small-town scene with bucolic scenery all around, but the wines are nothing less than extraordinary.

❶ Yakima

Yakima is a sprawling, flat mid-century-feeling city that doesn't have much allure, but it's a pleasant enough place to start your trip. It's also home to some of the only bubbles available in this region. Start the day at **Treveri Cellars** (www.trevericellars.com; 71 Gangl Rd, Wapato; ☾noon-5pm Mon-Thu, to 6pm Fri & Sat, to 4pm Sun), whose sparkling wines are so good they've been served at the White House.

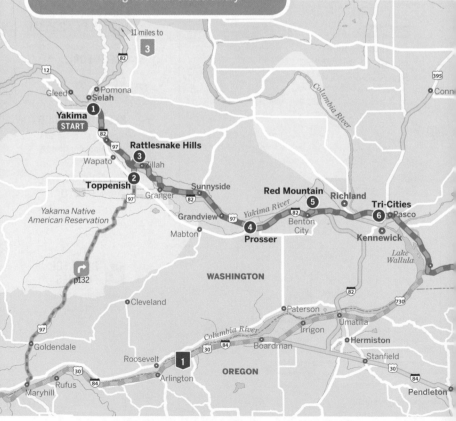

The Drive » From I-82E, take exit 50 toward Toppenish. Turn right on Buena Way off the exit and continue about 3 miles to 1st St, the main drag of downtown Toppenish.

✕ 🍴 p134

TRIP HIGHLIGHT

❷ Toppenish

Toppenish makes up for its lack of wineries with its kooky personality. The antique, distinctly Wild West brick and timber buildings are further beautified by some 70 **murals** within the downtown area.

Scenes include Native Americans, cowboys and early settlers as well as artistic hat-tipping to the majority Latinx population. Country-and-western music is pumped via loud-speaker into the streets. While here, stop at the **American Hop Museum** (📞509-865-4677; www.americanhopmuseum.org; 22 S B St; adult/child $5/3; ⏱10am-4pm Wed-Sat, 11am-4pm Sun May-Sep) to think about beer for a while, and the **Yakama Nation Museum & Cultural Center** (📞509-865-2800; www.yakamamuseum.com; 280 Buster Rd; adult/child $6/4; ⏱8am-5pm Mon-Fri, 9am-5pm Sat & Sun) to see crafts from the area's original artists.

The Drive » Go back toward I-82E but instead of getting on the freeway, cross over it. Cross the Yakima Valley Hwy, then at the crossroads turn left (this is still Buena Way). Take the third right on Highland Rd, up a hill through orchards to Bonair Winery in Rattlesnake Hills, 18 miles from Toppenish.

TRIP HIGHLIGHT

❸ Rattlesnake Hills

Lazing next to the tiny town of Zillah, the warm, rolling Rattlesnake Hills grow thick with grapevines and apple orchards. Nary a rattlesnake has been found in recent memory but you will find plenty of smooth and delicious Bordeaux reds at any of the dozen or so wineries. Start at wonderfully welcoming **Bonair Winery** (📞509-829-6027; www.bonairwine.com; 500 S Bonair Rd, Zillah; winery/vineyard tours $10/20, tasting $5; ⏱10am-5pm May-Nov, 11am-4pm Dec-Apr), one of the oldest in the area, where you're heartily encouraged to picnic on the lawn overlooking the pond – or grab a table in front of the buttery-yellow chateau for tapas.

Just north of Bonair, **Silver Lake Winery** (www.silverlakewinery.com; 1500 Vintage Rd, Zillah; tasting $7; ⏱noon-5pm Mon-Fri, 10am-5pm Sat & Sun Apr-Oct, noon-4pm Thu-Sun Nov-Mar)

LINK YOUR TRIP

1 On the Trail of Lewis & Clark

From Pasco, you can head west through the Yakima Valley or east to Walla Walla.

3 Mountains to Sound Greenway

Drive 36 miles from Yakima to Ellensburg via the Yakima River valley.

sits at the top of a hill overlooking the whole valley, making it a prime location for weddings and fancy-schmancy events.

The Drive » You can choose to take I-82E to exit 80 (about 30 miles) to get to Prosser, or take the Yakima Valley Hwy, which leads more slowly through scenic farmlands. With this second option, the Yakima Valley Hwy turns into Wine Country Rd at Grandview, which parallels I-82 and continues on to Prosser.

- - - - - - - - - - - - - - - - - -

④ Prosser

The historic center of Prosser is a small grid of brick buildings worthy of a 1950s-era movie set – it's a choice stop for lunch or the night. Stop in at picture-book pretty **Chinook Wines** (www.chinookwines.com; 220 W Wittkopf Loop; tasting $5; ☉ tastings noon-5pm Sat & Sun May-Oct), with a flower-filled yard and picnic area. The winery has been in operation since 1983 and is known for its classy Chardonnay and Sauvignon Blanc. It's just off Wine Country Rd to the east out of town.

Walla Walla Wine-tasting (p133)

Prosser sprawls less scenically across I-82, where you'll find **Vintner's Village**, a collection of excellent wineries in flat, housing-community-like surroundings. If you make one stop here, make it **Airfield Estates** (☎509-786-7401; www.airfieldwines.com; 560 Merlot Dr; tasting $7-10; ⏰11am-5pm Nov–mid-Apr, 11am-5pm Mon-Thu, 10am-6pm Fri-Sun

mid-Apr–Oct), known for its esteemed whites including a zesty, easy-to-love unoaked Chardonnay.

The Drive ❯❯ Back on I-82E, another 17 miles of highway brings you to Benton City and the Red Mountain AVA. Take exit 96 then turn left on SR 224, veering left again when the road forks.

✖ p134

TRIP HIGHLIGHT

❺ Red Mountain

Red Mountain, just next to Benton City, is the tiniest American Viticultural Area (AVA) in the state, coveted for its vintages brought to perfection on sun-drenched slopes. It's a California-esque landscape of hills covered in vineyards, golden grass and sagebrush. Meander up N Sunset Rd, making your first stop at humble **Cooper Wine Company** (www.cooperwinecompany. com; 35306 N Sunset Rd, Benton City; tasting $5; ◷noon-5pm), whose L'Inizio Bordeaux blend is anything but boring. Next, sample the highly regarded Bordeaux blends at **Hedges Family Estate** (☏509-588-3105; www.hedgesfamilyestate.com; 53511 N Sunset Rd, Benton City; tasting $5; ◷11am-5pm Wed-Sun Apr-Nov, 11am-5pm Tue-Sat Dec-Mar) in a French-inspired mansion; then drive up further to **Tapteil Estate** (www.tapteil.com; 20206 E 583 PR NE, Benton City; tasting $5-10; ◷11am-5pm Fri-Sun Apr-Dec), where you'll find delicious Syrah and Cabernet Sauvignons to sip over views of the valley.

Last, take a detour to the grandest estate on this trip, **Terra Blanca** (☏509-588-6082; www. terrablanca.com; 34715 N DeMoss Rd, Benton City; tasting $15; ◷10am-6pm), on N DeMoss Rd, which runs parallel to N Sunset Rd toward Benton. Try the reds and dessert wines in the castle-like tasting room or out on the terrace overlooking manicured gardens, a pond, the valley and mountains.

The Drive » It's a journey of about 12 miles from Red Mountain to Richland. Go back out to your friend I-82, take the I-182 exit toward Richland and then take exit 3. Turn right on Queensgate Dr and an immediate left onto Columbia Park Trail, then another left onto Tulip Lane.

- - - - - - - - - - - - - - - - -

⑥ Tri-Cities

Next stop? The Tri-Cities: Richland, Kennewick and Pasco.

DETOUR: YAKAMA SCENIC BYWAY

Start: ② **Toppenish**

This byway leads 63 miles down US 97 from Toppenish to Maryhill. You'll pass through native Yakama country and up through the desolate Simcoe Mountains. Highlights between them include the **St John's Monastery & Bakery** (www.stjohnmonastery. org; 5 Timmer Lane, Goldendale; ◷9am-6pm Mon-Sat) and **Goldendale Observatory State Park** (☏509-773-3141; www.goldendaleobservatory.com; Maryhill Stonehenge Visitor Center, 87 Stonehenge Dr, Goldendale; ◷shows 4pm & 8:30pm Fri-Sun Apr-Sep).

Nicknamed the Tri-Windies for the pushy gusts of wind that scoot you into the tasting rooms, the trio of towns is home to another batch of wineries just off the freeway, among them **Barnard Griffin** (☏509-627-0266; www.barnardgriffin. com; 878 Tulip Lane, Richland; tasting $10; ◷10am-5pm). You don't have to ask if they've won any awards; the medals are practically used as decor.

The Drive » Get ready for a change of scenery and wine style. Take US 12 south then east for about an hour to the Walla Walla Valley.

✕ ⌂ p41, p134

- - - - - - - - - - - - - - - - -

⑦ West Walla Walla

About 11 miles before you get to Walla Walla you'll find **L'Ecole No 41** (☏509-525-0940; www. lecole.com; 41 Lowden School Rd; tasting $10; ◷10am-5pm). The building alone, an early-1900s schoolhouse, is worth a visit, but the Syrah and Bordeaux earn an easy 'A' among wine lovers.

Back on the road about another mile toward Walla Walla is **Waterbrook Wine** (☏509-522-1262; www. waterbrook.com; 10518 W US 12; tasting $5-15; ◷11am-5pm Sun-Thu, to 6pm Fri & Sat) with an afternoon-devouring outdoor patio by a pond and authentic, mouthwatering tacos available on Friday and

Saturday. Imbibe a long selection of wines in the fresh air.

The Drive » Continue east on US 12 for about 10 miles into central Walla Walla. The center of town is at Main St and 2nd Ave.

TRIP HIGHLIGHT

8 Walla Walla

Walla Walla, more than any Washington town, has fermented the ingredients to support a burgeoning wine culture, including a historic Main St, a handsome college, a warm summer climate and a growing clutch of wine-loving restaurants. If it's time to let the pedal off the metal for a day or two, this is where to do it. The downtown area has lots of tasting rooms. A good one if you're on a stroll is **Otis Kenyon** (☎509-525-3505; www.otiskenyonwine.com; 23 E Main St; tasting $10; ☺11am-5pm Thu-Mon) – ask about its quirky story.

The Drive » Take SR 125 south out of town and turn right on Old Milton Hwy. In just

DETOUR: DAYTON & WAITSBURG

Start: 8 Walla Walla

Dayton (32 miles north of Walla Walla on US 12) and Waitsburg (21 miles from Walla Walla on the same highway) are a pair of quiet small towns with well-preserved buildings and a handful of places to eat and drink – though the expected boom in chic eateries from a few years back doesn't seem to have panned out, and several pioneering establishments have closed. They're more ghost towns than lively hubs at this point, but the countryside is pretty enough to make it well worth driving out.

a couple of miles you'll find yourself passing numerous orchards and wineries.

 p135

----

9 South Walla Walla

The southern part of the Walla Walla wine-growing region is the most scenic, with wineries off the highway and tucked within apple orchards or within their own vineyards. Fabulous wines are served in a low-key garden patio and tasting room (actu-ally a part of the owner's home) at **Dusted Valley Wines** (1248 Old Milton Hwy; ☺noon-5pm Thu-Mon Apr-Nov). Just down the road is the not-to-miss **Amavi Cellars** (☎509-525-3541; www.amavicellars.com; 3796 Peppers Bridge Rd; tasting $10; ☺10am-4pm), whose wines make headlines in the viticulture world. Indulge in its addictive Syrah and Cabernet Sauvignon on the classy yet comfortable outdoor patio, admire the view out to the Blue Mountains and toast to the end of your tour.

Eating & Sleeping

Yakima ❶

✕ Birchfield Manor Restaurant
Fusion $$$

(☎509-452-1960; www.birchfieldmanor.com; 2018 Birchfield Rd; prix fixe per person $49-65; ⏲7pm seatings Thu-Sat) The revered Birchfield is a dining experience offered in an intimate 1910 B&B. While the accommodations are considered top end, the food is even better. Reservations must be made in advance and seating is at a set time, but everything from the bread to the after-dinner chocolates to the knowledgeable service is impeccable. The highlights are the mains – salmon in puff pastry with Chardonnay sauce, steak Diane in a brandy-cream sauce – all expertly paired with local wines (the place has its own cellar).

🛏 Ledgestone Hotel
Hotel $

(☎509-453-3151; www.ledgestonehotel.com; 107 N Fair Ave; ste from $139; ❄ @ 🛜) The Ledgestone looks like another roadside chain hotel, but it's not. All its rooms are one-bedroom suites with mini kitchens, lounge areas, bathrooms and separate bedrooms. There's even a little office nook. Happily, the suites are sold at standard room prices, and there's also a fitness room and laundry service.

Prosser ❹

✕ Bern's Tavern
Pub Food $

(618 6th St; burgers from $8; ⏲noon-1:30am) In Prosser, a setting worthy of a mid-century movie, your best stop for lunch, beer and burgers is charmingly divey Bern's.

✕ Wine O'Clock
American $$

(☎509-786-2197; 548 Cabernet Ct; wine flights from $15, pizzas $16-18, mains $16-30; ⏲noon-8pm Thu-Mon Nov-Apr, expanded hours summer) Chic wine bar with a patio serving flatbread pizzas, cheese plates and light meals to nibble alongside wine flights from the Bunnell Family Cellar winery. Reservations are a good idea, especially in low season, when hours are more limited.

Tri-Cities ❻

✕ Taverna
Fusion $$$

(☎509-628-0020; www.tagariswines.com; Tagaris Winery, 844 Tulip Lane, Richland; pizzas $14-16, dinner mains $19-52; ⏲11am-close) The sophisticated dining room at Tagaris Winery is impressive, but on a pretty day the patio rules. The seasonal menu includes beautifully plated seafood, steak, and wood-fired flatbread pizzas.

🛏 Clover Island Inn
Hotel $$

(☎509-586-0541; www.cloverislandinn.com; 435 Clover Island Dr, Kennewick; r/ste from $93/249; ❄🛜♿🐾) You won't have trouble finding a basic chain motel in the Tri-Cities, but if you want something a little plusher, hit the locally owned Clover Island Inn, which occupies its own island on the Columbia River. This unique establishment boasts 152 rooms and suites, its own boat dock, and panoramic views from the top-floor Crow's Nest Restaurant. You can borrow bikes to use on the abundant paths for free.

Walla Walla ❽

✗ Andrae's Kitchen American $

(☎509-572-0728; www.andraeskitchen.com;
706 W Rose St; mains $10-15; ⏱6am-8pm
Mon-Sat, to 4pm Sun) Yep, it's inside a gas
station. You got a problem with that? Well,
you won't after you eat here. Super-creative
burgers, tacos, po'boys, gyros, all made from
scratch...this is not gas-station food. Even the
coleslaw has a complex flavor profile. Anything
with smoked pork is a good bet; Andrae
himself might be here running the smoker or
chatting with locals.

✗ Saffron Mediterranean Kitchen Mediterranean $$$

(☎509-525-2112; www.
saffronmediterraneankitchen.com; 125 W
Alder St; flatbreads $14-16, mains $25-45;

⏱2-9pm Mon-Fri, noon-9pm Sat & Sun) This
place isn't about cooking, it's about alchemy:
Saffron takes seasonal, local ingredients and
turns them into pure gold. The Med-inspired
menu lists dishes such as asparagus-fontina
flatbread, wood-grilled quail with dates and
olives, and eggplant, lamb and pork-belly
lasagna. Then there are the intelligently paired
wines – and gorgeous atmosphere. Reserve.

🛏 Inn at Abeja Inn $$$

(☎509-522-1234; www.abeja.net; 2014 Mill
Creek Rd; r from $319; ☎🐾) If you have your
own transportation and feel like spoiling
yourself, spend a night at this historic
farmhouse and winery set in the foothills of
the Blue Mountains, 4 miles east of Walla
Walla. Luxury accommodations are in
impeccably restored self-contained houses
that each played a historical role at the farm
(hayloft, mechanic's shed etc). Wine tastings
by appointment.

Mt Baker & Lummi Island

12

From seascape to snow in 84 miles, this journey takes you from a lesser-known Puget Sound island to Mt Baker, the white sentinel that frames every northwest Washington vista.

TRIP HIGHLIGHTS

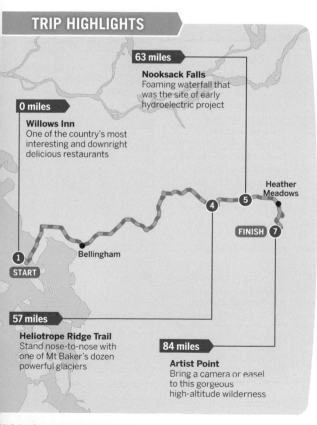

63 miles

Nooksack Falls
Foaming waterfall that was the site of early hydroelectric project

0 miles

Willows Inn
One of the country's most interesting and downright delicious restaurants

Heather Meadows

4 **5**

FINISH **7**

Bellingham

1
START

57 miles

Heliotrope Ridge Trail
Stand nose-to-nose with one of Mt Baker's dozen powerful glaciers

84 miles

Artist Point
Bring a camera or easel to this gorgeous high-altitude wilderness

---

1–2 DAYS
84 MILES / 135KM

GREAT FOR...

BEST TIME TO GO
Mid-July to September, when the whole road is open.

ESSENTIAL PHOTO

Mt Shuksan with Picture Lake in the foreground.

BEST FOR HIKING

Heliotrope Ridge Trail.

12 Mt Baker & Lummi Island

The 57-mile Mt Baker Scenic Byway that winds east from metropolitan Bellingham to the otherworldly flower meadows of Artist Point is one of the Northwest's most magic-invoking drives, replete with moss-draped forests and gurgling creeks. Affix Lummi Island onto the start of the trip with its slow-motion traffic and feisty insularity, and you have pretty much every facet the Pacific Northwest has to offer.

Langley

Blaine

Birch Bay

Ferndale

Lummi Indian Reservation

Lummi Island

① START

Bellingham Bay

Fairhaven

Orcas Island

Lummi Island

Sam Ba

Cypress Island

Guemes Island

TRIP HIGHLIGHT

① Lummi Island

Not technically one of the San Juan Islands but with them in spirit, Lummi acts as a bucolic buffer to the fast-spreading tentacles of American outlet-mall culture that plagues I-5. A slender green finger of land measuring approximately 9 miles long by 2 miles wide, and supporting a population of just under 1000, this tranquil dose of rural realism is home to the world's only reef-net salmon fishing operation, a pioneering agritourism project and an unhurried tempo of life best epitomized by the island's maximum speed limit – a tortoise-like 25mph.

One of the main reasons to come to Lummi is to sample the food at the reservations-only Willows Inn (p143) restaurant. The chefs forage for many of the locally grown ingredients, and the place has garnered international accolades in recent years.

The Drive >> Take the island's loop road to Lummi's small ferry terminal on the east shore. The five-minute crossing runs every 20 minutes (hourly at weekends) to Gooseberry Point on the mainland. From here, head north on Haxton Rd and right on Slater Rd to join I-5. Head south and exit to Bellingham, which is 17 miles from Gooseberry Point.

✗ p143

② Bellingham

Imagine a slightly less eccentric slice of Portland, Oregon, broken off and towed 250 miles to the north. Welcome to laid-back Bellingham,

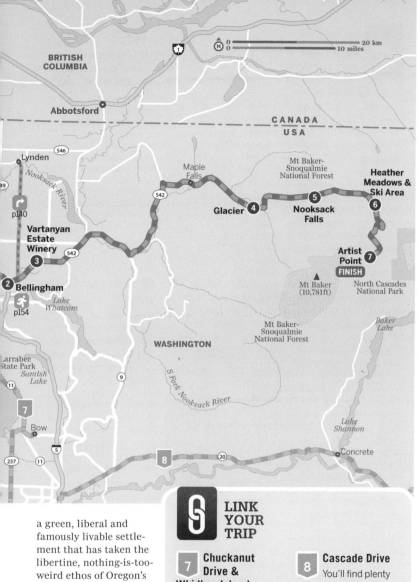

BRITISH COLUMBIA

Abbotsford

CANADA
USA

Lynden

Nooksack River

p140

Maple Falls

Mt Baker-Snoqualmie National Forest

Heather Meadows & Ski Area

Vartanyan Estate Winery

Glacier

Nooksack Falls

Artist Point
FINISH

Bellingham

p154

Lake Whatcom

Mt Baker (10,781ft)

North Cascades National Park

Baker Lake

WASHINGTON

Larrabee State Park

Samish Lake

S Fork Nooksack River

Mt Baker-Snoqualmie National Forest

Bow

Lake Shannon

Concrete

a green, liberal and famously livable settlement that has taken the libertine, nothing-is-too-weird ethos of Oregon's largest city and given it a peculiarly Washingtonian twist.

Mild in both manners and weather, the 'city of subdued excitement,' as a local mayor once

LINK YOUR TRIP

7 Chuckanut Drive & Whidbey Island

If you enjoyed Lummi Island, veer off along Chuckanut Drive for more pastoral scenery.

8 Cascade Drive

You'll find plenty more Cascade giants starting in Everett, 60 miles south down I-5.

DETOUR: GO DUTCH

Start: ❷ Bellingham

Washington State has an interesting stash of small towns that harbor a palpable European influence. Leavenworth, in the Eastern Cascades, draws in thousands of tourists annually with an authentic Bavarian look (not to mention its beer and sausages); Poulsbo, near Seattle, has a detectable Norwegian flavor. Lynden, meanwhile, located a few miles north of the Mt Baker Scenic Byway in the agricultural lowlands of the Nooksack Valley, is unmistakably Dutch.

First settled in the 1850s, the area received its first wave of Dutch settlers in the early 1900s – a steady trickle of Calvinist farmers who arrived from the Netherlands via brief stopovers in the Midwest. United by raspberries (the town produces 60% of the US crop), they formed a Christian Reform Church and set up mixed farms on the kind of flat pastoral fields that would have had Van Gogh reaching for his paint palette.

As well as competing for the prize of 'cleanest town in the US,' Lynden also excels in historical preservation. Handsome Front St includes a 72ft windmill, a mall with a canal, various Dutch eateries and the inspired **Lynden Pioneer Museum** (www.lyndenpioneermuseum.com; 217 Front St; adult/child $10/5; ◷10am-4pm Mon-Sat), which eloquently catalogs the pioneer experience.

Rumor has it that people from as far away as California plan pie sorties to **Lynden Dutch Bakery** (www.lyndendutchbakery.com; 421 Front St; pastries $1-6, breakfast dishes $5-9; ◷8:30am-5pm Mon-Sat) a few doors down. Try the split-pea soup or humongous rhubarb and raspberry pie.

spots and – in genteel Fairhaven – a rejuvenated historic district. It's an ideal place to stretch your legs (p154).

The Drive » The Mt Baker Scenic Byway officially begins at exit 255 of I-5 on Sunset Dr, which, within a mile, becomes the Mt Baker Hwy. Here the road dips into the pastoral Baker foothills. At the Hannegan Rd intersection you can detour north to the town of Lynden. Otherwise, continue 6 miles to Noon Rd and turn north for half a mile.

✕ ⊨ p143

❸ Vartanyan Estate Winery

Wrong side of the Cascade Mountains for grape-growing, you're thinking. Think again! The **Vartanyan Estate Winery** (☎360-756-6770; www.vewinery.com; 1628 Huntley Rd; tasting fee $7; ◷1-5pm Fri-Sun) is one of dozens of wineries that form the Puget Sound AVA (American Viticultural Area), the state's only wine-growing region west of the Cascade Mountains. The cool, wet, year-round climate here favors the sowing of mainly white grape varietals such as Siegerrebe and Madeleine Angevine. Wine-tasting here is a mellow, understated affair. Let curiosity get the better of you and check out Vartanyan's tasting room for a general sense of the region's offerings.

dubbed it, is historically four different towns – Fairhaven, Sehome, Whatcom and Bellingham – that amalgamated into a single metro area in the late 19th century. Despite vestiges of an ugly industrial past along the waterfront, and a flirtation with an out-of-town 1980s mall development directed mainly toward bargain-hunting Canadians, Bellingham's downtown has been revitalized in recent years with intra-urban trails, independent food co-ops, fine brunch

Picture Lake View of Mt Shuksan (p142)

The Drive » Retrace your
steps south to the well-
signposted Scenic Byway (SR
542), which tracks the North
Fork of the Nooksack River from
where it splits near Denning.
Ignore various turnoffs in the
small settlements of Kendall
and Maple Falls, and continue
due east to Glacier, 30 miles
from Vartanyan Winery. Maple
Falls is your last potential gas
stop until you return.

④ Glacier

A tiny service center and
the last proper settle-
ment before Mt Baker,
Glacier is basically a
ranger station, two
restaurants, a ski shop
and a small store.
This is where SR 542
enters the **Mt Baker-
Snoqualmie National
Forest**. Consequently,
many of Mt Baker's best
trails start near here. A
highlight is the 7.4-mile
out-and-back **Helio-
trope Ridge Trail**, which
begins 8 miles down
unpaved USFS Rd 39, 1
mile east of Glacier. The
trail takes hikers from
thick old-growth forest
to flower-filled mead-
ows and, ultimately, a
breathtaking Coleman
Glacier overlook. At the
2 mile point, the path
for the Coleman Glacier
ascent of Mt Baker
branches to the left. Call
into the excellent ranger
station for maps, trail
information and forest
passes ($5).

The Drive » You're now
in the Mt Baker-Snoqualmie
National Forest, where the
trees tell a different story: tall
moss-covered behemoths
that look like ghostly old men
sporting green beards. Keep
straight on the highway for 6
miles to the Wells Creek Rd.
Turn right here and follow the
forest road for half a mile to a
parking area and the Nooksack
Falls viewpoint.

✗ ⊨ p143

❺ Nooksack Falls

Powerful Nooksack Falls drop 175ft into a deep gorge. This was the site of one of the oldest hydropower facilities in the US, built in 1906 and abandoned in 1997. Sharp-eyed movie nerds will recognize it from one of the hunting scenes in the 1978 film, *The Deer Hunter*.

The Drive >> Rejoin the Scenic Byway and continue east paralleling the Nooksack River. Beyond milepost 48, the road leaves the river valley and starts to climb via a series of switchbacks. Mt Shuksan soon comes into view and at the road's 52 milepost you'll spy the Mt Baker Ski Area's White Salmon Day Lodge on the left, 12 miles from the falls.

❻ Heather Meadows & Ski Area

Receiving record-breaking annual snowfall and enjoying one of the longest seasons in the US, the **Mt Baker Ski Area** (☎360-734-6771; www.mtbaker.us; lift tickets adult/child $61/38) prides itself on being the classic 'nonresort' ski area and a rustic antidote to Whis-

tler in Canada. While luxury facilities are thin on the ground, the fast, adrenaline-fueled terrain has garnered many dedicated admirers. It was also one of the first North American ski locations to accommodate and encourage snowboarders.

There are two day lodges, both equipped with restaurants/cafeterias: the Cascadian-flavored **White Salmon Day Lodge** at milepost 52 and the **Heather Meadows Day Lodge**, 4 miles higher up.

In high summer, **Picture Lake** is the object of most people's affections. The view of **Mt Shuksan** reflected in its iridescent waters is an Instagram staple. You can wander for a half-mile around its shore taking follow-up snaps, or drive 1 mile further up to the **Heather Meadows Visitor Center** and plenty more trailheads.

The Drive >> Stay right when the road forks at Picture Lake. The last 3 miles (mileposts 55 to 58) of the byway are only open from around mid-July to September and subject to a $5 fee. The road terminates at a parking lot at Artist Point, 3.5 miles from the ski area.

❼ Artist Point

A picnic-spot extraordinaire, surrounded by perhaps the best high-altitude wilderness area in the US that is accessible by road, Artist Point at 5140ft is *high* – so high that in 2011 it remained snowed-in all year. Various hikes fan out from here, overlooked by the dual seductresses of Mt Baker and Mt Shuksan. Some are appropriate for families and most are snow-free by mid-July.

The interpretive **Artist Ridge Trail** is an easy 1-mile loop through heather and berry fields with the craggy peaks of Baker and Shuksan scowling in the background. Other options are the 0.5-mile **Fire and Ice Trail** adjacent to the Heather Meadows Visitor Center, which explores a valley punctuated by undersized mountain hemlock, and the 7.5-mile **Chain Lakes Loop** that starts at the Artist Point parking lot before dropping down to pass a half-dozen icy lakes surrounded by huckleberry meadows.

Eating & Sleeping

Lummi Island ❶

✖ Willows Inn
American $$$

(☎360-758-2620; www.willows-inn.com; 2579 West Shore Dr; tasting menu $225, breakfast per person $45; ⏱ dinner Wed & Thu mid-Mar-Dec) The ultimate in locavore dining with most ingredients sourced from within several miles. Think: mussels, clams and salmon, locally grown herbs and vegetables, farm eggs and homemade bread. It's a special-occasion place, with an 18-item tasting menu of food as art: pink scallops with black radish, root veggies in razor-clam sauce, flower-bedecked halibut and the like.

Bellingham ❷

✖ Mount Bakery
Breakfast $

(www.mountbakery.com; 308 W Champion St; mains $7-18; ⏱8am-3:30pm; 📶) This is where you go on Sunday mornings with a copy of the *New York Times* for Belgian waffles, crepes and organic eggs done any way you like. Plenty of gluten-free options. There's a second location in Fairhaven.

✖ Pepper Sisters
Modern American $$

(☎360-671-3414; www.peppersisters.com; 1055 N State St; mains $11-17; ⏱4:30-9pm Tue-Thu & Sun, to 9:30pm Fri & Sat; 👶) This cheerful, colorful restaurant serves innovative food that is hard to categorize – let's call it New Mexican cuisine with a Northwestern twist. Try the grilled eggplant tostada, chipotle-and-pink-peppercorn enchilada or Southwest pizza (with green chilies, jack cheese and tomatillo sauce); there's even a chicken-strip-free kids menu.

🛏 Hotel Bellwether
Boutique Hotel $$$

(☎360-392-3100; www.hotelbellwether.com; 1 Bellwether Way; r from $250; 😊❄@📶🐾) Bellingham's finest and most charismatic hotel lies on the waterfront and offers views of Lummi Island. Standard rooms (some with water views) come with Italian furnishings and Hungarian-down duvets, but the finest pick is the 900-sq-ft lighthouse suite (from $599), a converted three-story lighthouse with a wonderful private lookout. There's a spa and a restaurant on the premises.

Glacier ❹

✖ Milano's Restaurant & Deli
Italian $$

(9990 Mt Baker Hwy; dinner mains $15-26; ⏱4-8pm, to 9pm Fri & Sat) In common with much of the Mt Baker area, Milano's doesn't win any 'wows' for its decor. But when the pasta's al dente, the bread's oven fresh and you've got an appetite that's been turned ravenous by successive bouts of white-knuckle snowboarding, who's complaining?

✖ Rifugio's Country Italian Cuisine
Italian $$

(☎360-592-2888; www.ilcafferifugio.com; 5415 Mt Baker Hwy, Deming; mains $15-28; ⏱4-9pm Thu-Sat, to 8pm Sun, brunch 10am-3pm Sat & Sun) Just when you thought you were entering the wilderness, a bit of urban foodie culture pops up. In rural Deming, this Euro-centric cafe-restaurant offers big-city quality with a personable vibe and field-to-plate freshness. Choose from handmade pumpkin-stuffed ravioli, steak and polenta, rack of lamb, and breakfast carbonara – there's more than enough to fuel whatever adventures await you.

🛏 Winter Creek B&B
B&B $

(☎360-599-2526; www.wintercreekbandb.com; 9253 Cornell Creek Rd; r $145) Blessed with an outstanding view of Mt Baker, this simply furnished cabin-in-the-woods, two-bedrooms-only place is as friendly and cozy as B&Bs come. The 5-acre property holds horses and mules, and you'll surely meet the resident dog and cat. Warm up in the dry sauna in the shared bathroom. Discounts if you stay two nights or more. Cash or check only.

International Selkirk Loop

13

Covering two American states and one Canadian province, and juxtaposing fabulous scenery with idiosyncratic towns, the Selkirk is the great unsung byway of the Pacific Northwest.

TRIP HIGHLIGHTS

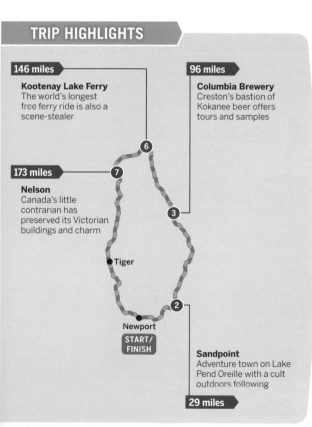

146 miles

Kootenay Lake Ferry
The world's longest free ferry ride is also a scene-stealer

96 miles

Columbia Brewery
Creston's bastion of Kokanee beer offers tours and samples

173 miles

Nelson
Canada's little contrarian has preserved its Victorian buildings and charm

6

7

3

● Tiger

● Newport
START/ FINISH

2

Sandpoint
Adventure town on Lake Pend Oreille with a cult outdoors following

29 miles

3 DAYS
287 MILES / 462KM

GREAT FOR...

BEST TIME TO GO
May to October for sun-dappled lake views.

  ESSENTIAL PHOTO
Anything with the sapphire waters of Kootenay Lake in it.

✓ **BEST FOR ROADSIDE ATTRACTIONS**
The Glass House, an icon made completely out of glass bottles.

Borders are arbitrary in the Selkirks, a more remote and geologically older antidote to the Rockies, where curious roadside attractions verge on the esoteric and the word 'clamorous' means the occasional moose blocking your views of so-clear-you-can-drink-it Kootenay Lake. Pack your passport, shake off the crowds and plunge into this wildly scenic two-nation loop through the forgotten corners of Washington, Idaho and British Columbia.

❶ Newport

Newport, a Washington State lavender-growing and logging town, faces off against Oldtown (the town's original incarnation), which sits across the state line in Idaho. The visitor center is situated next to the **Pend Oreille County Historical Museum** (☏509-447-5388; www.pochsmuseum.org; 402 S Washington Ave; adult/child $5/free; ◷10am-4pm late May-Sep), housed in a 1908 train depot and filled with local farming

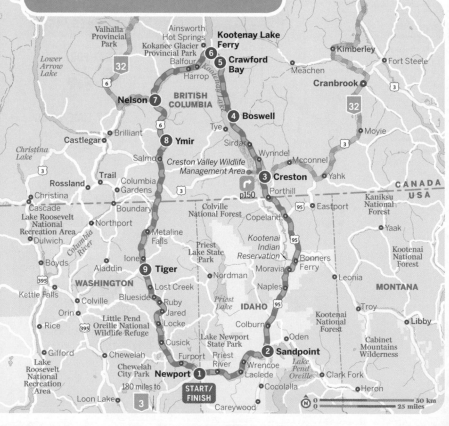

and railway paraphernalia. Both look out onto carefully manicured Centennial Plaza, which sits majestically at the head of Washington Ave (US 2), your ticket out of town.

The Drive >> Follow US 2 east for 29 miles (47km) on the north bank of the Pend Oreille River through the town of Priest River to Sandpoint.

TRIP HIGHLIGHT

2 Sandpoint

Within 45 minutes of leaving Washington at Newport you hit one of the Northwest's rarest jewels, Sandpoint, whose 7500 Idahoans make up the largest US town on

LINK YOUR TRIP

3 Mountains to Sound Greenway

Drive west via Spokane and I-90 to the next spectacular mountain range, the volcano-punctuated, snow-enveloped Cascades. From Spokane it's 172 miles to Ellensburg, where this trip begins.

32 Around the Kootenays

Since you brought your passport all this way, you might as well use it further north and keep the rugged mountain theme going.

this loop. Squeezed between the downhill runs of Schweitzer Mountain and the deep waters of Lake Pend Oreille, Sandpoint is the most discovered 'undiscovered' town in the nation (countless magazines list it on their 'hidden jewel' lists). Budget a couple of hours to stroll the bars, restaurants and shops of 1st Ave and sup vino and enjoy fresh fare at the **Pend D'Oreille Winery** (☎208-265-8545; www.powine.com; 301 Cedar St; ⊙11am-8pm), which also offers tours of its *très français* production process.

Sandpoint is right on Lake Pend Oreille ('hanging from the ears,' pronounced 'ponderay'), and the white sand and Jet Skis of City Beach are the closest the Idaho Panhandle ever gets to Miami. Bring a swimsuit and preferably some kind of boat.

The Drive >> US 95 heads to Bonners Ferry, originally built on stilts during the gold rush, and continues north past ranches, Christmas-tree farms and the world's largest hop farm at Elk Mountain. Branch onto SR 1 and cross into Canada at the Porthill–Rykerts border crossing, where you join Canadian Hwy 21 to Creston. The total journey is 67 miles (108km).

TRIP HIGHLIGHT

3 Creston

Creston advertises its premier business with a

statue of a 7ft Sasquatch (Bigfoot) making off with a six-pack. Fear not: this is the home of the **Columbia Brewery** (☎250-428-9344; www.columbiabrewery.ca; 1220 Erikson St; tours C$5; ⊙9:30am-3pm Jul & Aug, to 2:30pm Mon–Fri mid-May–Jun & Sep–mid-Oct), creator of the mass-market Kokanee and Kootenay brands. The brewery offers tours (four to six daily) and visits to the sample room. These mild lagers are consumed by the barrel during hockey season.

Creston's other pulls are fruit (apples and cherries dominate) and murals (local artists have instituted an art walk and mural tour). The downtown's art deco-heavy architecture is interrupted by two grain elevators – the only two city-center silos left in Canada.

The Drive >> The long, shimmering fjord of Kootenay Lake bursts into view a few miles (145km) outside Creston. This 90-mile slice of sapphire framed by the peaks of the Selkirk and Purcell ranges has water pure enough to drink. The 30-mile (48km) Creston–Boswell section is the most stunning of the drive and is enjoyed by drivers and riders for its many curves.

✕ 🛏 p151

---

4 Boswell

The wackiest sight on Kootenay Lake's eastern

shore is without doubt Boswell's **Glass House** ([📞]250-223-8372; 11341 Hwy 3A; adult/child C\$12/6; [🕐]8am-8pm Jul & Aug, 9am-5pm May, Jun & Sep–mid-Oct). With a mortician's sense of humor, funeral director David H Brown decided to build his dream retirement home out of used embalming-fluid bottles – half a million of them in total (and, more incredibly, then persuaded his wife this was a good idea). The result is a whimsy of turrets, towers, bridges and even a garden shed, all made from recycled bottles. Brown then topped this off with an interior decorated with fearless 1970s panache and a small army of garden gnomes.

The Drive » Keep on lake-hugging Hwy 3A for 17.4 miles (28km) to Crawford Bay.

- - - - - - - - - - - - - - - - - -

❺ Crawford Bay

Wizards and muggles (non-wizards) with a penchant for Harry Potter will find empathy in Crawford Bay at **North Woven Broom** ([📞]250-227-9245; www.northwovenbroom.com; Hwy 3A; [🕐]10am-5pm Mar–mid-Oct; [♿]), maker

of traditional brooms since 1975. One can only assume that orders have gone through the roof since the late 1990s when the word 'Quidditch' (a fictional sport in the *Potter* books that is played on broomsticks) entered the language. Numerous US colleges, including Harvard, now compete in real-life Quidditch cups and the workshop's owners once made 50 Nimbus 2000s (Harry Potter's prized broomstick) for a Vancouver book launch. The workshop's feathery golden hues and musky broomcorn fragrance are surprisingly beguiling, almost sensual, and there's something comforting about its almost total lack of modernity. While you're here, check out the glassblowers, blacksmith's forge and weavers' studio across the road.

The Drive » The highway runs out 3 miles (5km) west of Crawford Bay, and it's time for the ferry.

- - - - - - - - - - - - - - - - - -

TRIP HIGHLIGHT

❻ Kootenay Lake Ferry

Bridges are over-rated. Go slow on the

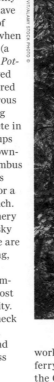

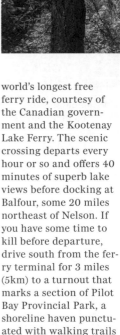

world's longest free ferry ride, courtesy of the Canadian government and the Kootenay Lake Ferry. The scenic crossing departs every hour or so and offers 40 minutes of superb lake views before docking at Balfour, some 20 miles northeast of Nelson. If you have some time to kill before departure, drive south from the ferry terminal for 3 miles (5km) to a turnout that marks a section of Pilot Bay Provincial Park, a shoreline haven punctuated with walking trails and the charming white

BORDER CROSSING

US citizens traveling between the US and Canada need a passport, enhanced driving license or NEXUS card. Returning to the US you can claim up to C\$800 of goods without duty after 48 hours.

clapboard 1907 **Pilot Bay lighthouse**.

The Drive » At the ferry landing, take SR 31 alongside Kootenay Lake's West Arm for around 20 miles (32km) to Nelson.

- - - - - - - - - - - - - - -

 TRIP HIGHLIGHT

❼ Nelson

Nelson has always flirted with contrarianism. It kept its early 20th-century boomtown buildings when everyone else was tearing theirs down, and it's happy to pursue anything outside of the mainstream.

Outdoorsy, alternative and organic, the historic former mining town has a tangible Victorian air, and is considered by many to be the most interesting and creative hangout east of Vancouver. Pick up a free **architectural walking tour** pamphlet to track down the most interesting of the town's 360 heritage buildings and stroll the waterfront pathway 1.2 miles to the lovely beaches of Lakeside Park, returning on the restored century-old 'Streetcar No 23.'

Revel in the mélange of cultures on Baker St, enjoying sitar music and intriguing boutiques. Pause to absorb the lake and mountain views. Choose from cafes with superb coffee, browse a farmers market, try some creative seasonal cuisine and hear local talent at one of Nelson's bars (where you'll also find some fine microbrews).

The Drive » Leaving Nelson in your rear-view mirror, the final day's drive takes you 18 miles (29km) south along Hwy 6 to Ymir, past remote,

DETOUR: CRESTON VALLEY WILDLIFE AREA

Start: ③ Creston

Nature lovers and birders should detour 6 miles (9.7km) west of Creston to the **Creston Valley Wildlife Management Area** (www.crestonwildlife.ca; 1760 West Creston Rd; ⏰dawn-dusk), part of the region's most important wildlife corridor. Walk the boardwalks and spot osprey, tundra swans, pelicans or great blue herons from the two birding towers, or sign up for an hour-long guided canoe paddle through the wetlands. Dawn and dusk are the best times to spot wildlife, including the occasional moose chomping in the shadows. Don't miss the very sweet 'turtle crossing' road sign.

formalities at the low-key Nelway–Metaline border crossing, 23.5 miles (38km) from Ymir, continue straight down the Washington SR 31 for 26.5 miles (42.6km) through the town of Metaline Falls to the Tiger junction.

🛏 p151

----

❾ Tiger

The fiercely named ex-town of Tiger, 4 miles (5.4km) south of Ione, has been reduced to one last remnant, the 1912 clapboard **Tiger Historical Center & Museum** (Tiger Store; ☎509-442-4656; www.facebook.com/tigerhistorical; 390372 Hwy 20; ⏰10am-4pm Thu-Mon Jun-Sep), which functions as a gift shop, cafe, information center and museum of the milling/railway town that once was. Glued to the junction of SR 31 and SR 20, it serves as a welcome apparition on this final part of the loop, aka the Pend Oreille Scenic Byway.

forested (and slightly odd) communities.

 p151

----

❽ Ymir

The oddest of the odd is historic Ymir (pronounced 'why-mur,' though grinning locals may well try to persuade you the name stands for 'Why Am I Here?'). It's weirdly named after a hermaphroditic giant from Norse mythology, though its history has more to do with gold mining than an Icelandic creature. Boomtown Ymir – founded as Quartz Creek in 1897 – once listed 10,000 inhabitants. Now there's little more than two hotels and a store. Check out the unusual Hotel Ymir (p151; built in 1916).

The Drive » After completing your US border

Eating & Sleeping

Creston ❸

✕ Retro Cafe   French $

(📞250-428-2726; www.retrocafe.ca; 1431 NW Blvd; mains from C$8; ⏰7am-4pm Mon-Fri, to 3pm Sat) A French mirage in Creston, 'retro' will probably be the last thing on your mind as you scour the hand-scrawled blackboard and tuck into *très délicieux* crepes.

🛏 Valley View Motel   Motel $

(📞250-428-2336; www.valleyviewmotel.info; 216 Valley View Dr; r from C$75; P ♿ ❄ 🛜) In motel-ville Creston, this is your best bet. On a view-splayed hillside, it's clean, comfortable and quiet.

Nelson ❼

✕ All Seasons Cafe   Fusion $$$

(📞250-352-0101; www.allseasonscafe.com; 620 Herridge Lane; mains from C$22; ⏰5-10pm) Sitting on the patio here beneath little lights twinkling in the huge maple above you is a Nelson highlight; in winter, candles inside provide the same romantic flair. The eclectic menu changes with the seasons but always celebrates BC foods. Presentations are artful; service is gracious.

🛏 Dancing Bear Inn   Hostel $

(📞250-352-7573; www.dancingbearinn.com; 171 Baker St; dm/r from C$29/59; P ♿ 🛜) The brilliant management here offers advice and smooths the stay of guests in the 14 shared and private rooms, all of which share bathrooms. There's a gourmet kitchen, library, patio and laundry.

🛏 Hume Hotel & Spa   Hotel $$

(📞250-352-5331; www.humehotel.com; 422 Vernon St; r incl breakfast from C$120; P ♿ ❄ 🛜) This 1898 classic hotel maintains its period grandeur. The 43 rooms vary greatly in shape and size; ask for the huge corner rooms with views of the hills and lake. Rates include a delicious breakfast. It has several appealing nightlife venues.

Ymir ❽

🛏 Hotel Ymir   Historic Hotel $

(📞250-357-9611; www.hotelymir.com; 7104 1st Ave; r from C$49; ♿ 🛜) Connoisseurs of the unusual should pop into Hotel Ymir, a 1916 flophouse that stands frozen in time. Try to imagine a Western saloon-style boarding house run by Bela Lugosi and you'll get an idea of the vibe here.

STRETCH YOUR LEGS
SEATTLE

Start/Finish King Street Station/EMP Museum

Distance 2 miles

Duration 3½ hours

Successive mayors have tried hard to alleviate Seattle's car chaos, and – hills and drizzly rain aside – this is now a good city for walking. Strategically placed coffee bars provide liquid fuel for urban hikers.

Take this walk on Trips

King Street Station

Seattle's **King Street Station** (303 S Jackson St; International District/Chinatown) was designed to imitate St Mark's bell tower in Venice. Now dwarfed by loftier towers, it was the tallest structure in Seattle upon its completion in 1906. It lay neglected until the late 2000s when restoration work revealed a once grandiose interior.

The Walk » From the station entrance, head around the corner onto S Jackson St.

Zeitgeist Coffee

Start this walk the way Seattleites start each day: with a latte. You'll find chain coffee shops on every corner, but Zeitgeist Coffee (p65), in a converted warehouse, is one of the better options in the city.

The Walk » Go west on S Jackson St and right on 1st Ave S, admiring the historic redbrick buildings.

Pioneer Square

Seattle was born in the muddy shores of Elliott Bay and reborn here post the catastrophic 1889 fire. The handsome redbrick buildings remain, built in a style known as Richardson Romanesque in the 1890s. Yesler Way was America's original 'Skid Row,' so named as they used to skid logs down the thoroughfare toward the harbor.

The Walk » Walk north on 1st Ave into the modern downtown core.

Seattle Art Museum

While it may be dwarfed by scenes in places like New York and LA, Seattle has its own unique arts culture. The **Seattle Art Museum** (SAM; 206-654-3210; www.seattleartmuseum.org; 1300 1st Ave; adult/student $25/15; 10am-5pm Wed & Fri-Mon, to 9pm Thu; University St) is the best place to dive into. The collection contains contemporary exhibitions, and a bounty of Native American art, among other things.

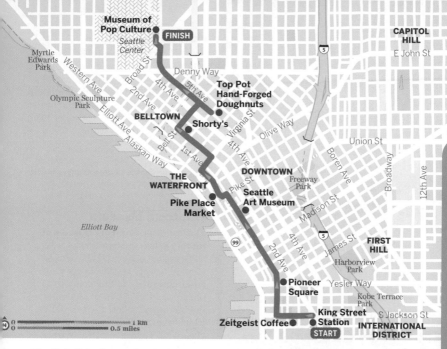

The Walk >> Continue north on 1st Ave two blocks to Pike Place Market.

Pike Place Market

The soul of the city is encased in Pike Place Market (p64), first launched in 1907. You'll need an early start if you want to spend more time dodging flying fish and less time dodging hordes of people. The big neon sign is a quintessential Seattle photo op.

The Walk >> Exit the north end of Pike Pl and you're in Belltown.

Shorty's

An early pulpit for grunge music, Belltown, north of downtown, has gone upscale since the 1990s with new condo developments and huddles of restaurants. A relic of old Belltown is **Shorty's** (☎206-441-5449; www.shortydog.com; 2222 2nd Ave; ☺noon-2am; ▣13), a cross between a pinball arcade and a dive bar.

The Walk >> Turn right on Bell St and right again on 5th Ave.

Top Pot Hand-Forged Doughnuts

Inhabiting an old car showroom, Top Pot Hand-Forged Doughnuts (p65) has done for doughnuts what Champagne did for wine. The coffee isn't bad either.

The Walk >> Walk along 5th Ave to the intersection with Denny Way. Hang a left and you'll see the Seattle Center and Space Needle in front of you.

Museum of Pop Culture

It's hard to miss the huge, crazily colorful building at the foot of the Space Needle. That would be the **Museum of Pop Culture** (www.mopop.org; 325 5th Ave N; adult/child $28/19; ☺10am-5pm Jan-late May & Sep-Dec, 10am-7pm late May-Aug; ▣Seattle Center), a fun place to immerse yourself in artifacts from the world of rock and roll, sci-fi, horror movies and cultural phenomena for one admission price.

The Walk >> To get back to the start, simply catch bus 131 ($2.75) from Wall St and 3rd Ave, which drops you in S Jackson St near King Street Station.

STRETCH YOUR LEGS
BELLINGHAM

Start/Finish Hotel Bellwether/Village Books

Distance 4 miles

Duration 3½ hours

Bellingham's all-American downtown is made for walking, with intra-urban trails, uncrowded streets and, in genteel Fairhaven, a rejuvenated historic district. Views of the gray or glittering sound and the San Juan Islands are highlighted by refreshing to icy sea breezes.

Take this walk on Trips

Hotel Bellwether

Kick off outside the Hotel Bellwether (p143), on a redeveloped part of the waterfront with water-hugging paths and views toward the whale-like hump of Lummi Island. The adjacent marina is a good place to ogle at other people's multimillion-dollar yachts.

The Walk » From the marina, walk down Bellwether Way onto Roeder Ave; turn right and then left, crossing the railway tracks onto W Holly St. Cut up through the Maritime Heritage Park toward the redbrick of Whatcom City Hall.

Whatcom Museum

The well-kept **Whatcom Museum of History & Art** (www.whatcommuseum.org; 121 Prospect St; adult/child $10/5; ☺ noon-5pm Wed-Sun; ⟨⟩) is spread over three buildings: historic Whatcom City Hall, the adjacent Syre Education Center and the innovative Lightcatcher building, which incorporates a spectacular 37ft glass wall. There are a rich array of exhibits.

The Walk » From the Lightcatcher building, head one block along Commercial St to the junction of W Champion St.

Mt Baker Theatre

With its minaret-like tower and elaborate interior, the grand **Mt Baker Theatre** (www.mountbakertheatre.com; 106 N Commercial St), built in 1925, harks back to an era when form was as important as function. Showcasing everything from live music to plays, the theater regularly draws in quirky national talent.

The Walk » Cross W Champion St and walk the half block to W Magnolia St. Turn left and continue two blocks to the corner of Railroad Ave, Bellingham's bike-friendly main thoroughfare. Numerous one-of-a-kind shops and cheap eating joints will detain you here.

Mallard

The start (or end) point of many a Bellingham date night, lurid **Mallard** (www.mallardicecream.com; 1323 Railroad Ave; scoops from $2; ☺ 11am-10:30pm Mon-Thu, to 11pm

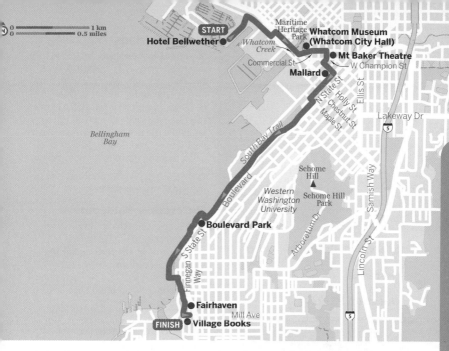

Fri-Sun) is a 1950s-style ice-cream parlor with a zillion flavors.

The Walk » Continue southwest on Railroad Ave, stopping for a microbrew in the Boundary Bay Brewery & Bistro, if you wish. At the T-junction with E Maple St, hang right and proceed half a block to the South Bay Trail.

Boulevard Park

The epitome of Bellingham's waterside rejuvenation, this park – accessed via a footbridge over the railway line – is cherished by locals for its San Juan Island views and sunsets. There's an outdoor theater and chic outlet of **Woods Coffee**, the sustainable local roasters. The **South Bay Trail**, which bisects the park, travels out on a boardwalk over the water before swinging back to land on the cusp of Fairhaven.

The Walk » Cross the railway, go right on 10th St and you're quickly in Fairhaven.

Fairhaven

Bellingham's history is enshrined in the Fairhaven district, once a separate city founded in the 1880s but later amalgamated with its big brother to the north. These days Fairhaven's handsome cluster of redbrick buildings have been reincarnated as specialty shops, European-style cafes and offbeat art galleries. A map/brochure gives the rundown of every building.

The Walk » Make your way over to the corner of Mill Ave and 11th St.

Village Books

Bellingham has long nurtured bookish inclinations and sports almost a dozen bookstores. Ruling the roost is **Village Books** (www.villagebooks.com; 1210 11th St; ⊙9am-9pm Mon-Sat, 10am-7pm Sun), a sprawling community resource with the popular **Colophon Cafe** (p97) next door.

The Walk » To return to the start, take bus 401 from Fairhaven to Bellingham station (on Railroad Ave). Change here onto bus 4 and get off at the Holly St/Broadway St junction for Bellwether Way.

STRETCH YOUR LEGS
LEAVENWORTH

Start/Finish München Haus

Distance 2 miles

Duration 1½ hours

Beer, sausages, nutcrackers, gabled Bavarian hotels and even some leafy forest – there aren't many places in the US where you can enjoy such a condensed exposure to German culture. Get out of your car and say *guten tag* to Leavenworth.

Take this walk on Trips

München Haus

Sizzling **München Haus** (☎509-548-1158; www.munchenhaus.com; 709 Front St; brats $4-7; ⊗11am-8pm, to 10pm Fri & Sat) is 100% alfresco, meaning the hot German sausages and pretzels served up here are essential stomach-warmers in the winter, while the Bavarian brews and casual beer-garden atmosphere do a good job of cooling you down in the summer.

The Walk ≫ Exit München Haus, turn right and wander half a block down Front St.

Nutcracker Museum

If you have a penchant for obscure, highly specialized museums, you'll want to stop by the **Nutcracker Museum** (www.nutcrackermuseum.com; 735 Front St; adult/child $5/2; ⊗1-5pm), which exhibits more than 6000 nutcrackers.

The Walk ≫ Cross the road to Front Street Park.

Front Street Park

A feature sadly absent in many American small towns is the good old main square. Leavenworth likes to be different, furnishing the strip facing Front St with lawns, an elegant bandstand, elaborate flower displays and a maypole. Numerous festivals enliven the space year-round.

The Walk ≫ Keep straight on Front St to the intersection with 10th St.

Icicle Brewery

Ditch Bavaria for a moment at **Icicle Brewery** (www.iciclebrewing.com; 935 Front St; snacks $2.50-12, beer flights $7-8; ⊗11am-10pm, to 11pm Fri & Sat), which has a funky outdoor patio and a distinctly Pacific Northwest–feeling modern-rustic interior (the tasting room) that's hard to resist. Pop in to sample the Khaos (the home-brewed beer, not the atmosphere, which is relaxed). Brewery tours are offered on Saturdays at noon.

The Walk ≫ Cut down 10th St (Festhallen Strasse) for one block and turn right on Commercial St (Markt Strasse).

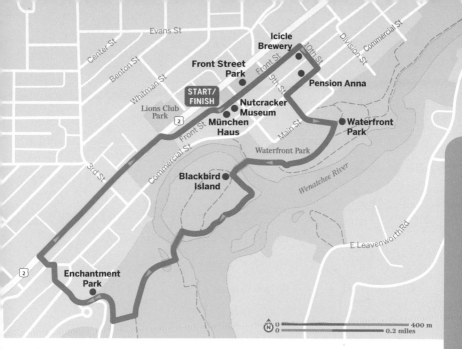

Pension Anna

For Leavenworth's most quintessentially Bavarian architectural creation, stop by to admire Hotel Pension Anna (p107). Examine the gabled roof, timbered balconies and geranium-filled flower boxes, and – should you decide to stay – slip inside to see the hand-painted Austrian furniture. The onion-domed St Joseph's chapel is let out as a luxury hotel suite.

The Walk » Turn left on 9th St (Alpen Strasse) and follow the slope down into the trees, lured by the melodious tinkle of the Wenatchee River. Suddenly this urban stroll has gone rural.

Waterfront Park

Tucked out of view but surprisingly close, this green area provides access to the Wenatchee River. Follow the leafy domain from 9th St to catch a glimpse of **Sleeping Lady Mountain**, ringed by a border of green foliage. Interpretive signs furnish the route and help explain the local plant and animal life. In sum-

mer, people launch inner tubes from the riverbanks, while in winter it's an informal cross-country skiing park.

The Walk » Follow the path through the trees and cross the footbridge onto Blackbird Island.

Blackbird Island

You're just as likely to spot an osprey as a blackbird on this small bird-filled nodule of land formed by a silt vacuum from a mill pond in the 1930s.

The Walk » Take the left fork and follow the main trail alongside the river to a second footbridge. Cross it and proceed to the lawns and sports grounds of Enchantment Park.

Enchantment Park

Connected by Enchantment Bridge to Blackbird Island, this park has various trailheads, a playground and rest rooms. Take the steep path up the grassy knoll and through the residential quarter to return to the main drag (US 2).

The Walk » Turn right and stroll past the gabled hotels to the walk's start point, München Haus.

Oregon

Laid-back Oregon concedes only two interstate highways to those with a misplaced sense of urgency. The real joy in Oregon is lazily crisscrossing the state along back roads and scenic byways. And boy, are they scenic. The Cascades are dense with natural wonders, including mountains, waterfalls, mighty rivers, forests and hot springs. The Oregon coast offers a completely different experience, with miles and miles of coastal highway stringing together charming seaside towns.

If sparsely populated Oregon still feels too busy for you, head to the remote eastern part of the state. In the land of fossils and pioneer relics, you can't help but think, 'Where am I, and what have they done with all the towns?' High desert and empty roads await.

Highway 101 (p163) near Cape Sebastian
MATT MUNRO/LONELY PLANET ©

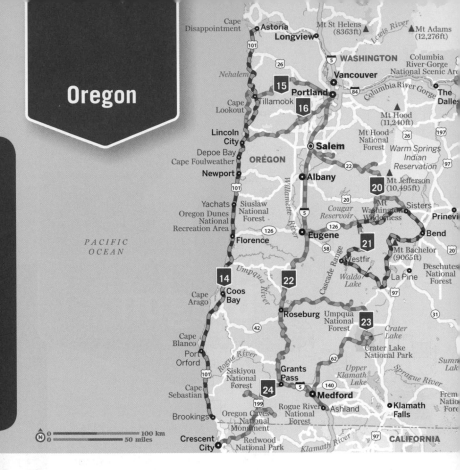

Oregon

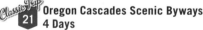
 DON'T MISS

Cape Perpetua

The best coast view isn't on the highway; drive to the top of Cape Perpetua for dizzying vistas on Trip 14

Kennedy School

Roam the halls of this former Portland school where you can spend the night, drink in the cafeteria and watch movies in the gym on Trip 22

Thomas Condon Paleontology Center

Get a fascinating lesson in history and paleontology on Trip 17

Golden State Heritage Site

Not all ghost towns are in remote locations. This abandoned mining town is amazingly located right off I-5 on Trip 23

Oregon Caves National Monument

After showing off with waterfalls and mountains, nature goes underground at the 'Marble Halls of Oregon.' Check them out on Trip 24

Classic Trip

Highway 101 Oregon Coast

14

Routes like Hwy 101 are the reason road trips were invented. It meanders the length of the Oregon coast past sandy beaches, colorful tide pools and nearly a dozen lighthouses.

TRIP HIGHLIGHTS

START

1

0 miles

Astoria
Cute Victorian town at the mouth of the Columbia

Tillamook

161 miles

Cape Perpetua
Hands-down the best views on the Oregon coast

9

134 miles

Newport
Tide pools and two lighthouses make this a coastal favorite

11

Florence

283 miles

Port Orford
Hike Humbug Mountain and meet some prehistoric creatures

Coos Bay

17

Brookings

FINISH

7 DAYS
340 MILES / 547KM

GREAT FOR...

BEST TIME TO GO

July to October, when the weather is more cooperative.

 ESSENTIAL PHOTO

Silhouette of Haystack Rock in Cannon Beach.

 BEST HIKING
Cape Perpetua offers several breathtaking hikes.

Cape Perpetua (p169)

163

Classic Trip

14 Highway 101 Oregon Coast

Scenic, two-lane Hwy 101 follows hundreds of miles of shoreline punctuated with charming seaside towns, exhilarating hikes, and ocean views that remind you you're on the edge of the continent. On this trip, it's not about getting from point A to point B. Instead, the route itself is the destination. And everyone from nature lovers to gourmands to families can find their dream vacation along this exceptional coastal route.

TRIP HIGHLIGHT

① Astoria

We begin our coastal trek in the northwestern corner of the state, where the Columbia River meets the Pacific Ocean. Ever so slightly inland, Astoria doesn't rely on beach proximity for its character. It has a rich history, including being a stop on the Lewis and Clark trail. Because of its location, it also has a unique maritime history, which you can explore at the **Columbia River Maritime Museum** (☎503-325-2323; www.crmm.org; 1792 Marine Dr; adult/child $14/5; ☉9:30am-5pm; ⊕).

Astoria has been the location of several Holly-wood movies, making it a virtual Hollywood by the sea: it's best known as the setting for cult hit *The Goonies*. Fans can peek at the **Historic Clatsop County Jail** (Oregon Film Museum; www.oregonfilmmuseum.com; 732 Duane St; adult/child $6/2; ☉11am-4pm Oct-Apr, 10am-5pm May-Sep; ⊕).

The Drive 》 Head south on Hwy 101 for 14.5 miles to Gearhart.

✕ ⊨ p41, p81, p174

② Gearhart

Check your tide table and head to the beach; Gearhart is famous for its razor clamming at low tide. All you need are boots, a shovel or a clam gun, a cut-resistant glove, a license (available in Gearhart) and a bucket for your catch. Watch your fingers – the name razor clam is well earned. Boiling up a batch will likely result in the most memorable meal of your trip. For information on where, when and how to clam, visit the Oregon Department of Fish & Wildlife's online guide (www.myodfw.com/crabbing-clamming).

The Drive 》 Don't get too comfortable yet: Seaside is just 2.4 miles further down the coast.

③ Seaside

Oregon's biggest and busiest resort town delivers exactly what you'd expect from a town called

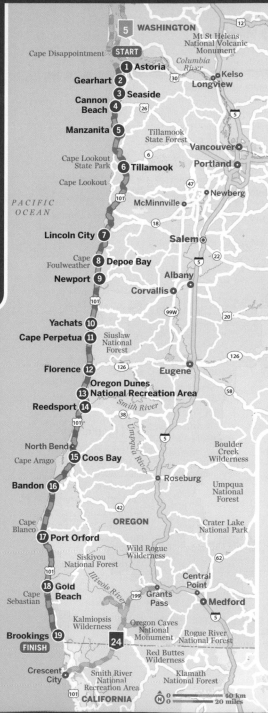

Seaside, which is wholesome, Coney Island–esque fun. The 2-mile boardwalk – known as 'the Prom' – is a kaleidoscope of seaside kitsch, with surrey rentals, video arcades, fudge, elephant ears, caramel apples, saltwater taffy and more. It's also where you'll find the **Seaside Aquarium** (☎503-738-6211; www.seasideaquarium. com; 200 N Promenade; adult/child $8.50/4.25; ☻9am-7pm, closes earlier winter; ♿). Open since 1937, the privately owned aquarium isn't much more than a few fish tanks, a touch pool and a small indoor seal tank where you can feed the splashy critters, but it's a fun stop for inquisitive kids.

The Drive » Leave the beach behind for a bit as you veer inland for the 8.8-mile drive to Cannon Beach.

✗ p174

LINK YOUR TRIP

5 **Graveyard of the Pacific Tour**

Continue your coastal adventure with this trip that starts in Astoria and heads north into Washington.

24 **Caves of Highway 199**

Pop down to Crescent City, CA, for a short but lovely trip cast that delivers you back to I-5.

4 Cannon Beach

Charming Cannon Beach is one of the most popular beach resorts on the Oregon coast. The wide sandy beach stretches for miles, and you'll find great photo opportunities and tide-pooling possibilities at glorious **Haystack Rock**, the third-tallest sea stack in the world. (What's a sea stack, you might ask? It's a vertical rock formation – in this case, one that's shaped like a haystack.) For the area's best coastal hiking, head immediately north of town to **Ecola State Park** (☑503-436-2844; www.regonstateparks.org; day-use $5), where you can hike to secluded beaches.

The Drive › Follow the coast 14.4 miles through Oswald West State Park to reach your next stop.

✗ ⌂ p41, p174

5 Manzanita

One of the more laid-back beach resorts on Oregon's coast is the hamlet of Manzanita – much smaller and far less hyped than Cannon Beach. You can relax on the white-sand beaches, or, if you're feeling more ambitious, hike on nearby **Neahkahnie Mountain**, where high cliffs rise dramatically above the Pacific's pounding waves. It's a 3.8-mile climb to the top, but the views are worth it: on a clear day, you can see 50 miles out to sea.

The Drive › Drive 27 miles from Manzanita along Nehalem and Tillamook Bays to reach inland Tillamook.

6 Tillamook

Not all coastal towns are built on seafood and sand. Tillamook has an entirely different claim to fame: cheese. Thousands stop annually at the **Tillamook Cheese Factory** (☑800-542-7290; www.tillamookcheese.com; 4175 N US 101; ☺8am-6pm Mon-Fri, to 8pm Sat & Sun) for free samples. You might choose to skip the dairy altogether and head to the two interesting museums: the **Pioneer Museum** (☑503-842-4553; www.tcpm.org; 2106 2nd St; adult/child $4/1; ☺10am-4pm Tue-Sun) has antique toys, a great taxidermy room (check out the polar bear) and a basement full of pioneer artifacts; and just south of town, the **Tillamook Naval Air Museum** (☑503-842-1130; www.tillamookair.com; 6030 Hangar Rd; adult/child $10.50/7.25; ☺10am-4pm Wed-Sun) has a large collection of fighter planes and a 7-acre blimp hangar.

The Drive › South of Tillamook, Hwy 101 follows the Nestucca River through pastureland and logged-off mountains 44 miles to Lincoln City.

7 Lincoln City

The sprawling modern beach resort of Lincoln City serves as the region's principal commercial center. In addition to gas and groceries, the town does offer a unique enticement to stop: from mid-October to late May, volunteers from the Visitor and Convention Bureau hide brightly colored glass floats – which have been hand-blown by local artisans – along the beaches, making a memorable souvenir

YAQUINA HEAD LIGHTHOUSE

If Yaquina Head Lighthouse in Newport seems a little creepier than a lighthouse ought, that's because it featured in the 2002 horror film starring Naomi Watts, *The Ring*. Built in 1873, it was originally called Cape Foulweather Lighthouse, but in the movie it was known as the Moesko Island Lighthouse. The lighthouse was also in the 1977 masterpiece *Nancy Drew: Pirate's Cove*.

for the resourceful and diligent vacationer.

The Drive » It's back to the coast for the 12-mile drive south to Depoe Bay.

 p174

❽ Depoe Bay

Though edged by modern timeshare condominiums, Depoe Bay still retains some original coastal charm. It lays claim to having the 'world's smallest navigable harbor' and being the 'world's whale-watching capital' – pretty big talk for such a pint-sized town. Whale-watching and charter fishing are the main attractions in the area, though 5 miles south of town there is the **Devil's Punchbowl**, an impressive collapsed sea cave that churns with waves and offers good tide pools nearby.

The Drive » Another 12.8 miles brings you to the lively tourist city of Newport.

TRIP HIGHLIGHT

❾ Newport

Don your marine-biologist cap and head to **Yaquina Head Outstanding Natural Area** (☎541-574-3100; www.blm.gov/yaquina; 750 NW Lighthouse Dr; vehicle fee $7; ⏱8am-sunset, interpretive center 10am-6pm), a giant spit of land that protrudes

nearly a mile into the ocean. This headland is home to some of the best touch pools on the Oregon coast. You'll also get a good look at the tallest lighthouse in Oregon, **Yaquina Head Lighthouse** (not to be confused with **Yaquina Bay Lighthouse**, 3 miles south).

Also worth a stop: the cutting-edge **Oregon Coast Aquarium** (☎541-867-3474; www.aquarium.org; 2820 SE Ferry Slip Rd; adult/3-12yr/13-17yr $25/15/20; ⏱10am-6pm Jun-Aug, to 5pm Sep-May; 🚻). The seals and sea otters are cute as can be, and the jellyfish room is a near-psychedelic experience. But what really knocks this place off the charts is the deep-sea exhibit that lets you walk along a Plexiglas tunnel through sharks, rays and other fish.

DETOUR: HACETA HEAD LIGHTHOUSE

Start: ⓫ **Cape Perpetua**

Picturesque **Heceta Head Lighthouse** (☎541-547-3416; www.hecetalighthouse.com; day-use $5; ⏱11am-3pm, to 2pm winter), 14 miles south of Yachats and 12 miles north of Florence, is one of the most photographed lighthouses on the Oregon coast. You can't see it from the highway, but you can park at Heceta Head State Park for great views from afar, as well as a trail leading past the former lightkeeper's quarters – now a bed-and-breakfast (p175) – and up to the lighthouse.

The Drive » It's 24 miles to Yachats along the edge of the Siuslaw National Forest.

 p174

❿ Yachats

One of the Oregon coast's best-kept secrets is the friendly little town of Yachats (ya-*hots*), which kicks off about 20 miles of spectacular shoreline. This entire area was once a series of volcanic intrusions, which resisted the pummeling of the Pacific long enough to rise as ocean-side peaks and promontories. Acres of tide pools are home to starfish, sea anemones and sea lions. Definitely stop in at the delicious Yachats Brewing & Farmstore (p175) for a bite to eat and some local flavor.

The Drive » Just 3 miles down the coast the dramatic Cape Perpetua begins.

 p175

Classic Trip

WHY THIS IS A CLASSIC TRIP
CELESTE BRASH, WRITER

There's nowhere else on the West Coast that matches the road-tripping perfection of this curving route alongside empty beach coves and waves of evergreen forest. Pull over and find a silent patch of sandy bliss, a mountain trail to climb or trundle along admiring the views with the windows open. I love looking for whales offshore and experiencing the changes in weather, from wild and stormy to perfect sunshine.

Above: Haystack Rock (p166), Cannon Beach
Left: Sandboarding, Oregon Dunes National Recreation Area (p170)
Right: Walking trail, Cape Perpetua

DAVID MADISON CREATIVE/GETTY IMAGES ©

⑪ Cape Perpetua

Whatever you do, don't miss the spectacular scenery of the **Cape Perpetua Scenic Area** (www.fs.usda.gov; Hwy 101; day-use $5), just 3 miles south of Yachats. You could easily spend a day or two exploring trails that take you through moss-laden, old-growth forests to rocky beaches, tide pools and blasting marine geysers.

At the very least, drive up to the **Cape Perpetua Overlook** for a colossal coastal view from 800ft above sea level – the highest point on the coast. While you're up there, check out the historic **West Shelter** observation point built by the Civilian Conservation Corps in 1933.

If you have more time to spend, stop at the **visitor center** (☎541-547-3289; www.fs.usda.gov/siuslaw; 2400 Hwy 101; vehicle fee $5; ⊙9:30am-4:30pm Jun-Aug. 10am-4pm Sep-May) to plan your day. High points include **Devil's Churn**, where waves shoot up a 30ft inlet to explode against the narrowing sides of the channel, and the **Giant Spruce Trail**, which leads to a 500-year-old Sitka spruce with a 10ft diameter.

The Drive » It's 22 miles to Florence, but only 12 to the Sea Lion Caves.

12 Florence

Looking for a good, old-fashioned roadside attraction? North of Florence is the **Sea Lion Caves** (☎541-547-3111; www. sealioncaves.com; 91560 Hwy 101; adult/child $14/8; ⊙9am-5pm; 🚗), an enormous sea grotto that's home to hundreds of groaning sea lions. Open to the public since the 1930s, the cave is accessed by an elevator that descends 208ft to the sea lions' stinky lair.

Here's the deal: it can be fascinating, but you might feel a little taken when you realize the view is exactly the same as what was on the monitor up in the gift shop – and there's not even free fudge samples down there. But if money's no object, you'll enjoy watching the sea lions cavort, especially if you have kids in tow.

The Drive ⟫ The Oregon Dunes start just south of Florence and continue for the next 50 miles.

✗ p175

13 Oregon Dunes National Recreation Area

As you drive south, you start to notice something altogether different: sand. Lots of it. Stretching 50 miles, the **Oregon Dunes** are the largest expanse of oceanfront sand dunes in the US. Sometimes topping heights of 500ft, these mountains of sand undulate inland up to 3 miles. Hikers and birdwatchers stick to the peaceful northern half of the dunes, and the southern half is dominated by dune buggies and dirt bikes.

At Mile 200.8, the **Oregon Dunes Overlook** is the easiest place to take a gander if you're just passing through. To learn more about trails and off-road vehicles, visit the **Oregon Dunes Visitors Center** (☎541-271-6000;

www.fs.usda.gov/siuslaw; 855 Hwy 101; ⊙8am-4:30pm Mon-Sat Jun-Aug, Mon-Fri Sep-May). For the area's biggest dunes, the 6-mile **John Dellenbeck Trail** (at Mile 222.6) loops through a wilderness of massive sand peaks.

The Drive ⟫ Reedsport is about halfway into the dunes area, some 22 miles south of Florence.

14 Reedsport

Reedsport's location in the middle of the Oregon Dunes makes it an ideal base for exploring the region. Check out the **Umpqua Lighthouse State Park**, offering summer tours of a local 1894 **lighthouse** (☎541-271-4631; www.oregonstateparks.org; 1020 Lighthouse Rd; adult/child $8/4; ⊙10am-5pm May-Oct, hours vary Nov-Apr). Opposite is a whale-watching platform, and a nearby nature trail rings freshwater **Lake Marie**, which is popular for swimming.

Want to see how Oregon's largest land mammal spends its free time? You can spy a herd of around 120 Roosevelt elk meandering about at the **Dean Creek Elk Viewing Area**, 3 miles east of town on Hwy 38.

The Drive ⟫ Enjoy the sand for another 27.5 miles, until you reach Coos Bay and the end of the dunes.

THREE CAPES LOOP

South of the town of Tillamook, Hwy 101 veers inland from the coast. An exhilarating alternative route is the slow, winding and sometimes bumpy Three Capes Loop (p177), which hugs the shoreline for 30 miles and offers the chance to go clamming. En route you'll traverse Cape Meares, Cape Lookout and Cape Kiwanda – three stunning headlands that you'd otherwise miss entirely.

⑮ Coos Bay

The no-nonsense city of Coos Bay and its modest neighbor North Bend make up the largest urban area on the Oregon coast. Coos Bay was once the largest timber port in the world. The logs are long gone, but tourists are slowly taking their place.

In a historic art-deco building downtown, the **Coos Art Museum** (☎541-267-3901; www.coosart.org; 235 Anderson Ave; adult/child $5/2; ⏱10am-4pm Tue-Fri, from 1pm Sat)provides a hub for the region's art culture with rotating exhibits from the museum's permanent collection.

Cape Arago Hwy leads 14 miles southwest of town to **Cape Arago State Park** (☎800-551-6949; www.oregonstateparks.org), where grassy picnic grounds make for great perches over a pounding sea. The park protects some of the best tide pools on the Oregon coast and is well worth the short detour.

The Drive » Highway 101 heads inland for a bit then gets back to the coast 24 miles later at Bandon.

⑯ Bandon

Optimistically touted as Bandon-by-the-Sea, this little town sits happily at the bay of the Coquille River. Its **Old Town**

WHALE-WATCHING

Each year, gray whales undertake one of the longest migrations of any animal on earth, swimming from the Bering Strait and Chukchi Sea to Baja California – and back. Look for them migrating south in winter (mid-December through mid-January) and north in spring (March through June).

district has been gentrified into a picturesque harborside shopping location, offering pleasant strolling and window-shopping.

Along the beach, ledges of stone rise out of the surf to provide shelter for seals, sea lions and myriad forms of life in tide pools. One of the coast's most interesting rock formations is the much-photographed **Face Rock**, a huge monolith with some uncanny facial features that does indeed look like a woman with her head thrown back – giving rise to a requisite Native American legend.

The Drive » Follow the coastline another 24 miles south to Port Orford. This part of the drive isn't much to look at, but not to worry: there's more scenery to come.

TRIP HIGHLIGHT

⑰ Port Orford

Perched on a grassy headland, the hamlet of Port Orford is located on one of the most scenic stretches of coastal highway, and there are stellar

views even from the center of town. If you're feeling ambitious, hike the 3-mile trail up **Humbug Mountain** (☎541-332-6774; www.oregonstateparks.org; Hwy 101), which takes you up, up, up past streams and through prehistoric-looking landscapes to the top, where you'll be treated to dramatic views of Cape Sebastian and the Pacific.

Speaking of prehistoric scenery: your kids may scream at the sight of a Tyrannosaurus rex in front of **Prehistoric Gardens** (☎541-332-4463; www.prehistoricgardens.com; 36848 US 101; adult/child $12/8; ⏱9am-6pm summer, 10am-5pm rest of year; 🖼), 12 miles south of town. Life-size replicas of the extinct beasties are set in a lush, first-growth temperate rainforest; the huge ferns and trees set the right mood for going back in time.

The Drive » The scenery starts to pick up again, with unusual rock formations lining the 28-mile drive to Gold Beach.

✗ p175

Classic Trip

⑱ Gold Beach

Passing through the tourist hub of Gold Beach, you can take a jet boat excursion up the scenic **Rogue River**. But the real treat lies 13 miles south of town, when you enter the 12-mile stretch of coastal splendor known as the **Samuel Boardman State Scenic Corridor**, featuring giant stands of Sitka spruce, natural rock bridges, tide pools and loads of hiking trails.

Along the highway are well over a dozen roadside turnouts and picnic areas, with short trails leading to secluded beaches and dramatic viewpoints. A 30-second walk from the parking area to the viewing platform at **Natural Bridge Viewpoint** (Mile 346, Hwy 101) offers a glorious photo op of rock arches – the remnants of collapsed sea caves – after which you can decide whether you want to commit to the hike down to **China Beach**.

The Drive » It's just 34 miles from Gold Beach to the California border, and 28 to Brookings.

🍴 🛏 p175

⑲ Brookings

Your last stop on the Oregon coast is Brookings. With some of the warmest temperatures on the coast, Brookings is a leader in Easter lily-bulb production; in July, fields south of town are filled with bright colors and a heavy scent. In May and June you'll also find magnificent displays of flowers at the hilly, 30-acre **Azalea Park** (☎541-469-1103; 640 Old County Rd).

History buffs take note: Brookings has the distinction of being the location of the only WWII aerial bombing on the US mainland. In 1942, a Japanese seaplane succeeded in bombing nearby forests with the intent to burn them, but they failed to ignite. The Japanese pilot, Nobuo Fujita, returned to Brookings 20 years later and presented the city with a peace offering: his family's 400-year-old samurai sword, which is now displayed at the **Chetco Community Public Library** (☎541-469-7738; www.chetcolibrary.org; 405 Alder St; ⏰10am-6pm Mon, Fri & Sat, to 7pm Tue-Thu).

🍴 🛏 p175

Astoria Fish and chips at Bowpicker (p174)

Eating & Sleeping

Astoria ❶

✖ Bowpicker
Seafood **$**

(📞503-791-2942; www.bowpicker.com; cnr 17th & Duane Sts; dishes $8-12; ⏱11am-6pm Wed-Sun) On just about every list of great seafood shacks is this adorable place in a converted 1932 gillnet fishing boat, serving beer-battered chunks of albacore and steak fries and that's it. Some say it's the best fish-and-chips in the US.

🛏 Hotel Elliott
Historic Hotel **$$**

(📞503-325-2222; www.hotelelliott.com; 357 12th St; d/ste from $229/249; 😀❄🤖) Standard rooms have charming period elegance at this historic hotel. For more space, get a suite (the 'presidential' boasts two bedrooms, two bathrooms, a grand piano and a rooftop deck). There's also a rooftop terrace with great views, and a wine bar open Wednesday to Sunday.

Seaside ❸

✖ Osprey
Breakfast **$$**

(📞503-739-7054; 2281 Beach Dr; mains $10-15; ⏱7:30am-3pm Thu-Tue; 👶) Simply a lovely place to eat, a little away from the masses of tourists, in shabby beachside-chic surrounds (fire-heated in winter). There are also a few outdoor benches. Mains range from American breakfast classics to *arepa* (corn-and-cheese cakes topped with eggs) and *nasi goreng* (Indonesian fried rice). Lunch on creative sandwiches, mac 'n' cheese, burgers and south-of-the-border treats.

Cannon Beach ❹

✖ Newman's at 988
French, Italian **$$$**

(📞503-436-1151; www.newmansat988.com; 988 Hemlock St; mains $26-39; ⏱5:30-9pm) Expect a fine-dining experience at this small, quality restaurant on the main drag. Award-winning

chef John Newman comes up with a fusion of French and Italian dishes such as marinated rack of lamb and char-grilled portabello mushrooms with spinach and Gorgonzola. Desserts are sublime; reserve ahead.

🛏 Cannon Beach Hotel
Hotel **$$**

(📞503-436-1392; www.cannonbeachhotel.com; 1116 S Hemlock St; d from $160; 😀🤖) This classy, centrally located hotel has just 10 rooms. Standard rooms are lovely, but very small; even the regular suites are tight. A good breakfast at the on-site cafe is included. Two-night minimum in summer.

Lincoln City ❼

✖ Blackfish Cafe
Northwestern US **$$**

(📞541-996-1007; www.blackfishcafe.com; 2733 NW US 101; mains $19-34; ⏱11:30am-3pm & 5-9pm, closed Tue) Blackfish Cafe specializes in cutting-edge cuisine highlighting fresh seafood and local, seasonal vegetables. Chef Rob Pounding is an accomplished master at creating his simple but delicious dishes; try his signature Northwest cioppino. Reserve in summer.

Newport ❾

✖ Local Ocean Seafoods
Seafood **$$**

(📞541-574-7959; www.localocean.net; 213 SE Bay Blvd; mains $17-35; ⏱11am-9pm, to 8pm winter) Popular and with good reason – the food is freshly prepared and very tasty here. Most of the seafood comes straight from the docks. Try the crab po'boy sandwich, shrimp and spicy-noodle salad or pan-fried oysters. The wharf views are pretty, especially on warm days when the walls open up.

🛏 Newport Belle
B&B **$$**

(📞541-867-6290; www.newportbelle.com; 2126 SE Marine Science Dr, South Beach Marina, H Dock; d $165-175; ⏱Feb-Oct; 😀🤖) For a unique stay there's no beating this sternwheeler B&B. The five small but lovely and shipshape rooms all have private bathrooms and water views, while the common spaces are wonderful for relaxing. Best for couples; reservations required.

Yachats ⑩

✖ Yachats Brewing & Farmstore
Gastropub $$

(📞541-547-3884; www.yachatsbrewing.com; 348 US 101; mains $16-24; ⏱11:30am-8pm Mon-Thu, to 9pm Fri & Sat, to 7pm Sun) Order at the bar from the changing menu of eclectic mains or an excellent burger or vegetarian beet burger, and snacks like house-pickled veggies. Pair with beer or kombucha (try the Salal Sour beer for local flavor) and take a seat on the outside patio or by a warm, bright window.

⌂ Heceta Head Lighthouse B&B
B&B $$$

(📞866-547-3696; www.hecetalighthouse.com; 92072 Hwy 101 S; d $299-440; ☺🛜) This 1894 Queen Anne B&B can't help but attract passerby. Located near the lighthouse trail, it's 13 miles south of town on US 101. Inside there are six pretty rooms, all simply furnished with period antiques, along with a classy, museum-like atmosphere. Breakfast is a seven-course gourmet sensation and reservations are definitely recommended.

Florence ⑫

✖ Waterfront Depot
Northwestern US $$

(📞541-902-9100; www.thewaterfrontdepot.com; 1252 Bay St; mains $15-25; ⏱4-10pm) This cozy, atmospheric joint is one of Florence's best restaurants. Come early to snag one of the few waterfront tables, then enjoy your jambalaya pasta or the regulars' favorite, crab-encrusted halibut. There are excellent small plates, a great wine list and spectacular desserts. Reserve ahead – it's well priced and very popular.

Port Orford ⑰

✖ Redfish
Seafood $$$

(📞541-366-2200; www.redfishportorford.com; Hawthorne Gallery, 517 Jefferson St; mains $10-32; ⏱11am-9pm Mon-Fri, 10am-9pm Sat & Sun) At first glance this slick, outrageous-sea-

view restaurant would seem better located in Portland's Pearl District – it's even attached to a highbrow art gallery, owned by glass artist Chris Hawthorne and family. Redfish boasts the freshest seafood in town, so take advantage; the menu changes seasonally. Weekend brunch, too.

Gold Beach ⑱

✖ Anna's by the Sea
Northwestern US $$

(📞541-247-2100; www.annasbythesea.com; 29672 Stewart St; mains $25-42; ⏱5-8:30pm Wed-Sat) One of Gold Beach's best restaurants, this homey spot serves up just a few key seasonally changing mains like black rock cod with sweet onions, oven-seared breast of duck and chicken thighs in chanterelle gravy. Great wine list, but don't expect upscale: it's self-proclaimed as 'Rejecting trendy from the start.' A 20% tip is added to every bill.

⌂ Ireland's Rustic Lodges
Lodge $$

(📞541-247-7718; http://irelandsrusticlodges.com; 29330 Ellensburg Ave; d $80-299; 🛜🐾) A wide variety of accommodations awaits you at this woodsy place. There are regular suites with kitchenettes, rustic one- and two-bedroom cabins, beach houses or even RV sites. A glorious garden sits in front while beach views are out back. Three communal Jacuzzis with faraway ocean views, too.

Brookings ⑲

✖ Mattie's Pancake House
American $

(📞541-469-7211; 15975 US 101 S; mains $5-17; ⏱6am-1:30pm Tue-Sat) This friendly breakfast and lunch spot offers some seriously good pancakes including hearty oatmeal and buckwheat varieties. A short stack ($4.50) will do for most people as each pancake is larger than a human head. There are also lots of omelet and waffle choices plus sandwiches and salads at lunch.

⌂ Harris Beach State Park
Campground $

(📞541-469-2021; www.oregonstateparks.org; 1655 US 101 N; tent/RV sites $20/32; yurts $45; 🐾) Camp above the beach at one of 150 sites or stay in one of six yurts. Showers, flush toilets and coin laundry are among the amenities. Located about a mile north of town.

Three Capes Loop

15

Whether you're coming from Portland or detouring off Hwy 101, the dramatic, ever-changing scenery from forested Cape Meares to sandstone Cape Kiwanda is worth slowing down for.

TRIP HIGHLIGHTS

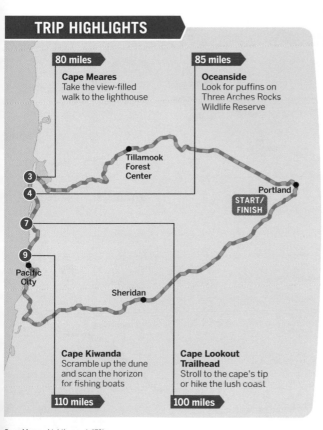

80 miles

Cape Meares
Take the view-filled walk to the lighthouse

85 miles

Oceanside
Look for puffins on Three Arches Rocks Wildlife Reserve

Tillamook Forest Center

3

4

7

9

Pacific City

Sheridan

Portland

START/ FINISH

Cape Kiwanda
Scramble up the dune and scan the horizon for fishing boats

110 miles

Cape Lookout Trailhead
Stroll to the cape's tip or hike the lush coast

100 miles

---

2 DAYS
176 MILES / 283KM

GREAT FOR...

BEST TIME TO GO
May to October to avoid chilling wind and rain.

ESSENTIAL PHOTO
Capture the lens of the Cape Lookout Lighthouse contrasting with the steel sea.

BEST BEACH
Cape Kiwanda has endless sands and a dune to climb.

15 Three Capes Loop

Cape Meares, Cape Lookout and Cape Kiwanda are some of the coast's most stunning headlands, strung together on a slow, winding alternative to US 101. If you start from Portland, you'll drive through towering forests and salmon-filled river country to drive a loop with minimal backtracking. However you tackle this trip, strap on your boots for walks through spruce groves and over dunes to basalt and sandstone precipices.

① Tillamook Forest Center

Learn about the stretch of forest between Portland and the sea at the **Tillamook Forest Center** (☎866-930-4646; www.tillamookforestcenter.org; 45500 Wilson River Hwy; ☺10am-5pm, closed late Nov-Feb), 51 miles from Portland. The interpretive center focuses on the history of wildfire in the region via hands-on exhibits, a 40ft replica fire tower to climb and a suspension bridge over an incredibly scenic part of the Wilson

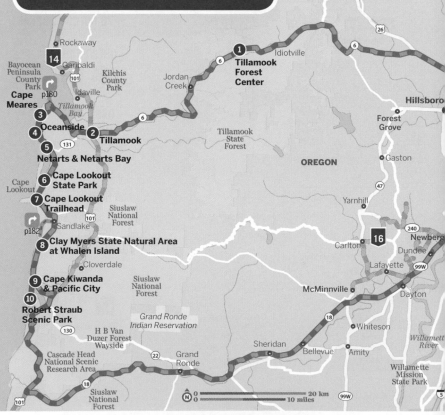

River; the film *Legacy of Fire* is worth watching. Also enjoy over 20 miles of hiking on the **Wilson River Trail**, which wends along this powerful, Douglas fir- and maple-lined river renowned for its steelhead fishing. It's a 2-mile walk to Wilson Falls, where you can splash through rapids moving around big boulders – look for signs of beavers and listen for kingfishers.

The Drive » Head 22 miles west to Tillamook through the scenic Tillamook State Forest.

WASHINGTON
30
Vancouver
Linnton Park
Forest Park
5
26
START/ FINISH
Aloha
Portland
Beaverton
amington
10
Kinton Tigard p260
Midway King City Tryon Creek State Park
19
99W
liddleton
Sherwood
5
Wilsonville Molalla River State Park
Willamette Greenway State Park Canby
Aurora
Hubbard
oodburn
211
Garvais McKee
Mt Angel
Silverton
213

---

② Tillamook

Best known for its huge cheese industry, Tillamook is a nondescript town that's worth a stop to down some dairy. The famed **Tillamook Cheese Factory** (☏800-542-7290; www.tillamookcheese.com; 4175 N US 101; ⏰8am-6pm Mon-Fri, to 8pm Sat & Sun), 2 miles north of town, produces more than 100 million pounds of the product every year. Line up for free cheese samples, lick down an ice-cream cone or peek into the factory-floor assembly line; there's a cafe too. Aircraft lovers should stop at the gargantuan **Tillamook Naval Air Museum** (☏503-842-1130; www.tillamookair.com; 6030 Hangar Rd; adult/child $10.50/7.25; ⏰10am-4pm Wed-Sun), 2 miles south of town on the way to the next stop.

The Drive » Hwy 6 turns into Hwy 131 Scenic Route as it heads west. Shortly after the Tillamook Naval Air Museum take the right signposted for

---

Cape Meares. Drive a mile around the Tillamook Estuary then uphill 2 miles to the cape.

TRIP HIGHLIGHT

③ Cape Meares

The first trailhead of Cape Meares has two trails through luxurious spruce forest: a 2.1-mile trail down to rocky **Meares Beach** or a quarter-mile stroll to **Big Spruce**, heralded as the largest Sitka spruce in Oregon (it's 144ft tall and 15.5ft in diameter). A half-mile further driving down Hwy 131 leads you to a second, much more developed parking area with paved paths to the perhaps-haunted 1889 **Cape Meares Lighthouse** (www.friendsofcapemeares lighthouse.com; Bayshore Dr; ⏰11am-4pm Apr-Oct). There are many viewpoints and information panels along the quarter-mile walk. A shorter dirt path leads to the impressive **Octopus Tree**, a legendary eight-limbed spruce that mystifies science.

🔗 LINK YOUR TRIP

14 **Highway 101 Oregon Coast**

Highway 101 leads straight into Tillamook. Follow this trip's directions from there.

16 **Willamette Valley Wine Tour**

Follow the directions from Robert Straub Scenic Park toward Portland and you'll hit McMinnville. From here you can follow the Willamette Valley Wine Tour.

DETOUR:
BAYOCEAN PENINSULA COUNTY PARK

Start: ❷ Tillamook

At a humble fork in the road, where Hwy 131 veers left toward Cape Meares, turn right to Bayocean Peninsula County Park and follow the road about 2 miles. Today you'd hardly guess that this was once the site of a very swanky planned resort community, built in 1906. In 1914 the town had 2000 residents, even though access was by steamship. The residents built a jetty in 1917 to ease the often-rough boat landings. Within a few years, shifting currents caused by the jetty made the beach begin to disappear; the townspeople extended the jetty and the problem amplified, with more and more structures getting devoured by the ocean. By the late 1930s most of the remaining houses were abandoned and in 1953 the post office closed. In 1971 the last building, a car garage, crumbled into the sea. Today a commemorative sign is all that is left. It's a beautiful, isolated sandy stretch, great for hiking along the beach and bird-watching.

The Drive » Descend 3 miles down the cape then turn right to Oceanside.

TRIP HIGHLIGHT

❹ Oceanside

This tiny village of cozy beach houses perched over a long, flat white-sand beach is the most charming on this route and a great stop for lunch, dinner or overnight. The **Three Arches Rocks Wildlife Reserve** can be seen at the far right if you're facing the ocean. With binoculars you'll be able to see the orange beaks and yellow head tufts of tufted puffins, one of this coast's most recognizable birds, out on these towering rocks. Picnic or fly kites on the beach, search for agates in the winter months or just chill out in the seaside vibe.

The Drive » Turn left onto Hwy 131 again and drive 2 miles to Netarts.

 p183

---

❺ Netarts & Netarts Bay

Take a sharp turn on Happy Camp Rd to reach a small parking lot for a pretty stretch of white beach protected by a wide, flat sandbar island. Or you can continue on Hwy 131 another quarter mile to Crab Ave on the left to head into 'town,' which is a couple of ramshackle motels and deli markets. It's not the most scenic stop, but it may be easier to park here than the more popular beaches on busy weekends.

The Drive » Follow the Scenic Route signs that lead to a road veering left, which winds along Netarts Bay, known for its clamming. After a few miles

you'll rejoin Hwy 131 to Cape Lookout.

 p183

---

❻ Cape Lookout State Park

Besides great camping, there are several trails that fan out from this lovely, protected, white-sand beach area. Take the 2.3-mile (one-way) **North Trail** through lush forest and over cliffs to the summit of Cape Lookout, or the 2.4-mile (one-way) **Cape Trail** that goes through coastal rainforest to a panoramic lookout on the cape. Otherwise, try the easier 1.8-mile (one-way) **South Trail** over to a secluded beach off the cape.

The Drive » Climb a little over a mile uphill then drive another 1.5 miles along the cape to the Cape Lookout Trailhead.

🛏 p183

Cape Kiwanda Dunes and beach (p182)

TRIP HIGHLIGHT

❼ Cape Lookout Trailhead

You can access the same trails (at different points) that are found at Cape Lookout State Park from here. If you're after a short stroll, take the trail to the far left of the parking lot then walk straight at the first junction about 300ft along. In half a mile you'll be rewarded with a viewpoint – on a clear, sunny day you can see all the way to Cape Kiwanda.

The Drive >> After descending about 5 miles from Cape Lookout you'll pass inland dunes on your right, a popular ATV spot. At the next junction turn right and continue about 4 miles.

❽ Clay Myers State Natural Area at Whalen Island

Whalen Island is a wildlife-filled, wooded island that's surrounded by the Sand Creek Estuary. A trail makes a relatively flat but gorgeous 1.4-mile loop from the parking lot through low forest to fringing white-sand beaches. Wildlife that

181

CLAMMING

If you're around Netarts Bay at a minus tide, you're likely to see groups of rubber-booted, bucket-wielding foragers combing the beach. Want to get in on the clamming action? First, everyone 14 and older needs a $10 shellfish license, available at sporting goods stores (there are a few in Tillamook) or through the Oregon Department of Fish & Wildlife (www.dfw.state.or.us) website, where you can also check the regulations, limits and seasonal closures. Cockles, little necks, gaper clams and other species are all present, but razor clams are the real prize. In all cases, show up about an hour before the lowest tide with a bucket, shovel and/or a clam gun, look for small holes in the sand, then dig fast!

may be spotted here includes deer, otter, bear and (gulp!) cougar. It also has some of the best tent camping on this trip, but given the animal life, you probably don't want to leave out any food.

The Drive » Go south 7 miles on Hwy 131 along the coast until the road veers inland at Cape Kiwanda.

🛏 p183

TRIP HIGHLIGHT

❾ Cape Kiwanda & Pacific City

The best beach of the Three Capes sits in front of tiny Pacific City, south of the towering sandstone, dune-covered Cape Kiwanda. Wide and lush with sand space to spare, you can hike the cape via the dune (under a quarter of a mile, but straight up). Back on the beach, dory fishers haul their boats in or out from the beach around 6am and sunset when the weather is calm. You can buy fish from them or order it at many local restaurants.

The Drive » Head south through Pacific City then turn right at the first crossroads.

🍴🛏 p183

❿ Robert Straub Scenic Park

You can access the wild and rugged part of Cape Kiwanda Beach via this little park at the Nestucca Sand Spit, where the legendary – and Chinook salmon–friendly – Little Nestucca River meets the sea. The beach here is less protected and thus is windier and has stronger surf and currents. You can find shelter from the elements in the grass-covered dunes.

DETOUR: SANDLAKE

Start: ❼ Cape Lookout Trailhead

About 2 miles before Whalen Island is a turnoff leading to Sandlake, a spit of land that's home to 1076 acres of sand dunes. Folks from all over the Pacific Northwest come here to camp, drink beer and tool around in their ATVs. You can join the fun watching the spills and thrills or, if that doesn't sound good, plug your ears and race back to the highway.

Eating & Sleeping

Oceanside ❹

✕ Roseanna's Cafe International $$

(☎503-842-7351; www.roseannascafe.com; 1490 Pacific Ave; mains $7-30; ⏰9am-8pm Sun-Thu, to 9pm Fri & Sat) All around the best place to eat on this stretch of coastline is this little cafe in Oceanside. Choose from pastas, seafood and veggie options served in a sailor-shabby-chic seaside setting with a touch of elegance.

🛏 Oceanfront Cabins Cabin $

(☎888-845-8475; www.oceanfrontcabins.com; 1610 Pacific Ave; cabins $80-165; 🐾) Basic cabins, some with kitchens, steps from the beach in the cute little hamlet of Oceanside.

Netarts & Netarts Bay ❺

✕ The Schooner Seafood $$

(☎503-815-9900; www.theschooner.net; 2065 Netarts Boat Basin Rd; mains $13-34; ⏰11:30am-9pm Sun-Thu, to 10pm Fri & Sat) Wonderful bay views from the glass-enclosed eating area make the cocktails and locally sourced meals (oysters, fish, beef and more) even better.

Cape Lookout State Park ❻

🛏 Cape Lookout State Park Campground Campground $

(☎800-452-5687; www.oregonstateparks.org; tent/RV sites $21/31, yurts $47-57) Thirty-eight full hookups, 173 tent sites, 13 yurts and six cabins are available at this beauty of a campground, which is right along the beach but never feels crowded, thanks to well-positioned sites and plenty of trees. Showers and flush toilets available. Book early.

Clay Myers State Natural Area at Whalen Island ❽

🛏 Whalen Island, Tillamook County Park Campground $

(☎May-Oct 503-965-6085, Oct-Apr 503-322-3522; www.co.tillamook.or.us/gov/Parks/Campgrounds.htm; Sandlake Rd; sites $38) There are 34 adorable wooded campsites steps from a private, sheltered beach; no hookups but there is a dump site. Hike around the small, wooded island for utter escape. Swim in the shallows (warmer than the ocean) in summer and pick huckleberries in fall. Keep food stashed securely since there are sometimes bears in the area.

Cape Kiwanda & Pacific City ❾

✕ The Grateful Bread Cafe $

(☎503-965-7337; www.gratefulbreadbakery.com; 34805 Brooten Rd; mains $5-15; ⏰8am-3pm Thu-Mon) Start with heaping portions of fresh and delicious soups, salads, tacos, dory-caught fish, veggie and meat dishes, then finish with fabulous fresh breads, cookies, desserts and maybe a souvenir tie-dyed T-shirt.

✕ Pelican Pub & Brewery American $$

(☎503-965-7007; https://pelicanbrewing.com; 33180 Cape Kiwanda Dr; mains $15-28; ⏰8am-10pm Sun-Thu, to 11pm Fri & Sat) This beloved brewpub in Pacific City offers decent pub grub and a good selection of award-winning beers, but the setting – with tables inches from the sand – is the highlight.

🛏 Inn at Cape Kiwanda Hotel $$$

(☎888-965-7001; www.innatcapekiwanda.com; 33105 Cape Kiwanda Dr; r from $289; 🛜) A classy and popular place that offers luxurious sea-view rooms, balconies and a location to die for.

Willamette Valley Wine Tour

16

Country roads lead through Pinot Noir–covered hills to small wineries with fresh, bucolic views and renowned vintages.

TRIP HIGHLIGHTS

14 miles

Carlton
Charming small town with tasting rooms and eateries

8 miles

Brick House Vineyards
A quintessential Oregon winery complete with compost heaps and friendly dogs

3

4

Newberg
START/ FINISH

6

Lafayette

5

McMinnville
Find food and wine action in the historic downtown

22 miles

Domaine Drouhin Oregon
The majestic setting and wines offer a whiff of France

33 miles

2 DAYS
50 MILES / 80KM

GREAT FOR...

BEST TIME TO GO
April to August for sunshine on green hills.

ESSENTIAL PHOTO
Domaine Drouhin Oregon: take a picture of Pinot Noir vines with a view of the valley.

BEST SCENERY
Stop 6 through stop 8: take in the hillside beauty of the Dundee Hills appellation.

16 | Willamette Valley Wine Tour

Oregon's Willamette Valley stretches over 100 miles from Eugene to Portland and more than 500 wineries lie within its six subappellations. Most of these are approachable, family-run operations dedicated to producing small quantities of high-quality Pinot Noir and sometimes other varietals. Organic, sustainable practices are the norm. This trip takes in the top half of the valley where you'll find the greatest concentration of wineries amid scenic farmlands.

❶ Newberg

The gateway to the Willamette Valley wine country was founded as a Quaker settlement and ironically was 'dry' for most of its early history. It's the biggest town in the area (population 23,600) and the one whose historic architecture has been most surrounded and overwhelmed by strip malls and fast-food joints. Still, it's a convenient place to stay and start your trip.

The Drive >> Take Hwy 240 west where the landscape

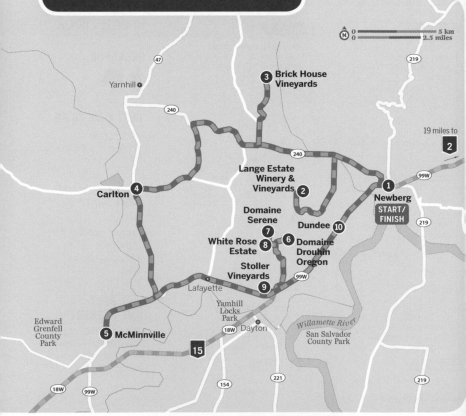

quickly turns into the beautiful vineyard-covered countryside you came here for. Turn right on Red Hills Rd and follow the signs up to Lange, 3.5 miles from the turnoff. The last half is on a well-maintained gravel road.

 p191

---

❷ Lange Estate Winery & Vineyards

Your first tasting is at the **Lange Estate Winery & Vineyards** (📞503-538-6476; www.langewinery.com; 18380 NE Buena Vista Dr, Dundee; tastings from $15; 🕙11am-5pm), founded by one of the valley's earlier families. Here you'll find all the makings of an authentic Willamette Valley winery: gorgeous views, good wines and shaggy dogs. It's very much a family affair and it's known for its good-value Pinot Noir called Three Hills Cuvee.

LINK YOUR TRIP

2 **Columbia River Gorge & Mt Hood**

Head back through Portland and east on Historic Highway 30.

15 **Three Capes Loop**

Take the loop backwards by driving to Pacific City from Hwy 99W.

The Drive » Head back down to Hwy 240, turn left, drive about 3 miles and turn right at Ribbon Ridge Rd. After about 2.5 miles, turn right on Lewis Rogers Lane to Brick House Vineyards.

TRIP HIGHLIGHT

❸ Brick House Vineyards

Lying within the Ribbon Ridge appellation, **Brick House Vineyards** (📞503-538-5136; www.brickhouse wines.com; 18200 Lewis Rogers Lane, Newberg; tastings $20; 🕙by appointment only) is another classically Oregonian winery. Brick House's owner, Doug Tunnell, is a former CBS foreign correspondent and an Oregon native. He's also one of the state's pioneers in organic farming. And the winery is great. Stand in the barn and look out over the vines and you'll get a sense of the unpretentious charm that makes the Willamette Valley so special. The winery itself occupies a converted barn and the Pinot Noir, Chardonnay and Gamay Noir poured here are as fine as the experience is fresh.

The Drive » Go back down Ribbon Ridge Rd and turn right on Hwy 240. After about 2 miles turn left onto Stag Hollow Rd, then right on Carlton–Chehalem Creek Rd, which eventually turns into Carlton's Main St.

TRIP HIGHLIGHT

❹ Carlton

It's hard to come up with a better descriptive word for Carlton than 'adorable.' Just a few streets wide, the town is made up almost entirely of pretty, historic buildings that house an impressive number of tasting rooms, great restaurants, antique shops, a jam maker and a fabulous French-style bakery. Nearby **Anne Amie Vineyards** (📞503-864-2991; www.anne amie.com; 6580 NE Mineral Springs Rd; flights $15; 🕙10am-4:45pm daily Mar-Dec, Thu-Mon only Jan & Feb) has stellar sparkling rosé and dessert wines. Carlton makes a great stop for lunch, and it's also a lovely place to stay overnight. Whenever you're here, be sure to wander around town aimlessly to turn up plenty of delicious surprises.

TOP TIP: SPIT & DRIVE

Some words of advice: when tasting wine, learn to spit. That bucket is there for a reason. Spitting will actually mark you as a pro rather than an amateur.

The Drive » Go south on Tualatin Valley Hwy 47. After about 4.5 miles turn right on Hwy 19 which goes right into downtown McMinnville.

✗ p191

✗ p191

TRIP HIGHLIGHT

❺ McMinnville

At the heart of the region's wine industry lies McMinnville. Stay within its historic, red-brick downtown district and you'll find older buildings, art galleries, boutiques and fine restaurants, along with a small-town feel as kids play on sidewalks and tourists stroll up and down the main artery of 3rd St; head outside this area and this image is dimmed by modern housing communities and shopping areas. It's a great place to stay, eat and end your tour of the wine region.

As you'd expect, there are also several wineries and tasting rooms that you can easily find by taking a stroll around downtown. The most special is **Eyrie Vineyards** (☑503-472-6315; www.eyrie vineyards.com; 935 NE 10th Ave; tastings $40; ☺tastings by appointment only, 11am & 2pm Thu-Mon). The late owner, David 'Papa Pinot' Lett, planted the region's first vines (including the first Pinot Gris in the USA) in 1965 and the first wines were produced in 1970. Today David's

son, Jason, runs the operation.

The Drive » Head northeast on Hwy 99W. After 8 miles turn left at OR 18W/SE Dayton Bypass then take an immediate right onto NE MacDougall Rd. After half a mile turn left on NE Breyman Orchards Rd and follow the signs to Domaine Drouhin.

✗ 🛏 p191

TRIP HIGHLIGHT

❻ Domaine Drouhin Oregon

You may be on day two at this point and it's time for a little more glamour. Owned by renowned Burgundy producer Maison Joseph Drouhin, **Domaine Drouhin Oregon** (☑503-864-2700; www.domainedrouhin.com; 6750 NE Breymen Orchards Rd, Dayton; flights $20; ☺11am-4pm) is famed as much for its history as it is for its Pinot Noir. The winery owes its existence in part to the 1979 Gault Millau 'Wine Olympics,' a blind tasting held in France. In the competition, McMinnville's Eyrie Vineyards placed in the top 10, holding its own against France's most esteemed Pinots, including one from the respected Maison Joseph Drouhin. This stoked Drouhin's already existing interest in the Willamette Valley (Drouhin first visited the valley in 1961), and he soon decided it was time to extend the family's operation. In 1988

he opened Domaine Drouhin Oregon under the management of his daughter, winemaker Véronique Drouhin. She still makes the wine and the top picks are named after her three children. Today the winery is one of the most elegant and scenically located in the valley and the wines, which are made from grapes planted in the French style with vines close together, have a distinct old-world touch.

The Drive » Go straight out the driveway across Breyman Orchards Rd (don't turn) and follow the signs for Domaine Serene.

Willamette Valley Pinot Noir grapes

7 Domaine Serene

Domaine Serene (☎503-864-4600; www.domaineserene.com; 6555 NE Hilltop Lane, Dayton; tastings $25; ⊙ tasting room 11am-4pm Mon-Thu, to 5pm Fri-Sun) is one of the Willamette Valley's best-known wineries heralded, as would be expected, for its Pinot Noir. It's a grand, modern place with a stunning wine cellar and lovely views over the rolling hills and vineyards that sweep across the valley. Along with Pinot Noir, the winery produces highly regarded Chardonnays. You can go with the standard tasting-room-only wine tasting or tour the entire winery, including the cellar, as part of the VIP tour – that, however, will cost you extra.

The Drive » Turn right out of the driveway and don't blink or you'll miss White Rose Estate, your next stop.

8 White Rose Estate

A short hop down the road is **White Rose Estate** (☎503-864-2328; www.whiteroseestate.com; 6250 NE Hilltop Lane, Dayton; tastings $25; ⊙11am-5pm), where you can take in wonderful views from the lawn before descending into the tasting room, which is built directly into the hillside and above the cellars, in order to maintain an optimal temperature for the barrels below. Jesús Guillén, Oregon's first-ever Latino head winemaker, put the winery on the map with its 'neo-classical' (whole-cluster fermentation) Pinot Noirs. Before his passing in November 2018, Jesús was profiled in a documentary about the state's pioneering minority winemakers called 'Red, White and Black,'

189

TOP TIP:
MARK YOUR CALENDAR

Many Willamette Valley wineries are open for tastings only on certain days of the week (usually Wednesday through Sunday or just the weekend) while others offer visits by appointment only. But on Memorial Day and Thanksgiving Day weekends, nearly all of the valley's wineries open their doors to the public – no reservations required. These are widely publicized and very busy weekends. Inside tip: most wineries also open their doors on the weekends prior to these...for those in the know.

produced by Bertony Faustin of **Abbey Creek Vineyards** (☎503-389-0619; www.abbeycreek vineyard.com; 31441 NW Commercial St, North Plains; tastings $10; ⊙noon-5pm Sat & Sun).

The Drive » Go back down Breyman Orchards Rd and turn right at NE MacDougall Rd. Stoller Vineyards is about a mile along.

- - - - - - - - - - - - - - - - - -

⑨ Stoller Vineyards

On the site of what was once the biggest turkey farm in Oregon, **Stoller Vineyards** (☎503-864-3404; www.stollerfamilyestate. com; 16161 NE McDougall Rd, Dayton; tasting flights $20; ⊙11am-5pm) is one of the most ecologically sustainable wineries in the country, if not the world. The winery building holds the US Green Building Council's gold-level certification for Leadership in Energy and Environmental Design, plus the architecture (that looks like a cross between a grain elevator and a barn – but prettier) is true to the site's history. It produces well-heralded Pinot Noirs and Chardonnays.

The Drive » Backtrack east on NE MacDougall Rd, drive a little over a mile then turn right onto Hwy 99W. You'll be in central Dundee in under 4 miles.

- - - - - - - - - - - - - - - - - - -

⑩ Dundee

Dundee is the hub of the Dundee Hills, the Willamette Valley's preeminent subappellation, where you've already visited three superb wineries. Now it's time to see what the region can produce for lunch and chances are you won't be disappointed. Although Dundee isn't the most scenic of the region's towns, it's pleasant enough with a few parks and early 20th-century homes. The real draw, however, is that it's teeming with fabulous restaurants.

🛏 p191

Eating & Sleeping

Newberg ❶

✕ Painted Lady — Northwestern US $$$

(☎503-538-3850; www.thepaintedladyrestaurant.com; 201 S College St; prix fixe $95-110; ⏰5-10pm Wed-Sun) Accomplished chefs Allen Routt and Jessica Bagley use their wide travel and culinary experiences at this renowned restaurant in a renovated 1890s Victorian house. The multicourse set menus include choices of appetizer, like Dungeness crab with miso custard, mains like dry-aged New York strip steaks with pea puree, and desserts like honey lavender mousse, with the option of a wine pairing.

Carlton ❹

✕ The Horse Radish — American $$

(☎503-852-6656; www.thehorseradish.com; 211 W Main St; small-plate combos $12-18; ⏰noon-3pm Sun-Thu, to 10pm Fri & Sat) Gourmet meals, cheese plates and a wine bar in the heart of Carlton, with weekly dinner specials (6pm to 8pm Friday and Saturday) featuring dishes like BBQ shrimp and cheddar grits, or green-chili-stuffed chicken breasts with black beans and rice. There's live music on Friday and Saturday nights.

McMinnville ❺

✕ Valley Commissary — American $

(☎503-883-9177; 920 NE 8th St; mains $8-15; ⏰7am-3pm Mon-Fri, brunch 9am-3pm Sat & Sun; 🖥) Bolster your belly before wine tasting at this breezy, elevated daytime joint. For breakfast and brunch, try the pulled pork, egg and sweet potato burrito, or chicken and waffles with fried sage and hot sauce butter. Come noon, opt for the pork-belly sandwich with housemade kimchi, a chickpea burger with smoked lime yogurt, or the spring veggie grilled cheese.

✕ Joel Palmer House — Northwestern US $$$

(☎503-864-2995; www.joelpalmerhouse.com; 600 Ferry St, Dayton; 3-course menu from $65; ⏰4:30-9:30pm Tue-Sat) Renowned for its dishes built around wild mushrooms and Oregon truffles (often handpicked by the chef, Christopher Czarnecki), this highly lauded restaurant is just a few miles northwest of McMinnville, in Dayton. It's one of Oregon's finest eateries, turning local ingredients into unforgettable fine cuisine. Reservations recommended.

🛏 McMenamins Hotel Oregon — Hotel $$

(☎503-472-8427; www.mcmenamins.com; 310 NE Evans St; d $135-200; 😊✱🛰😺) Expect the typical McMenamins eccentricities, such as eclectic artwork, at this cool hotel. Most of the classic old rooms share bathrooms, which are kept in good order. There's also an unbeatable rooftop restaurant-pub, mandatory for drinks on warm summer nights.

Dundee ❿

🛏 Black Walnut Inn & Vineyard — Inn $$$

(☎503-538-8663; www.blackwalnutvineyard.com; 9600 NE Worden Hill Rd; r $270-650; 🛰) One of the Willamette Valley's most luxurious lodgings, the Black Walnut Inn has beautiful suites each with its own individual charms – a vineyard view, antique French furniture, walk-in closets, private gardens, whatever you fancy. The family who runs it includes travelers and chefs, and the whole thing is designed to feel like a special occasion.

Journey Through Time Scenic Byway

17

An epic drive across windswept plains, desolate badlands and forested mountain passes. Visit ghost towns, fossil beds, small rural towns and excellent museums.

TRIP HIGHLIGHTS

3 miles

Maryhill Museum of Art
World-class collection with Rodin and royal Romanian exhibits

75 miles

John Day Fossil Beds Clarno Unit
Ancient fossils hide in spectacular palisade cliffs

START

2

Grass Valley

5

Kimberly

8

7

FINISH

Baker City

Prairie City

John Day Fossil Beds Painted Hills Unit
Wow! Surreal rolling hills with banded color

205 miles

John Day Fossil Beds Sheep Rock Unit
Fossilized goodies in green rock formations

160 miles

3 DAYS
363 MILES / 584KM

GREAT FOR...

BEST TIME TO GO
June to September for warm temperatures and less rain.

 ESSENTIAL PHOTO

John Day Fossil Beds Painted Hills Unit: the love-child of a *National Geographic* spread and a Mark Rothko painting.

 BEST FOR HISTORY

The Thomas Condon Paleontology Center.

John Day Fossil Beds Painted Hills (p197)

17 Journey Through Time Scenic Byway

Unless you count the futuristic-looking windmills around the town of Wasco, a more precise name for this state scenic byway would be Journey Back in Time Scenic Byway. From the moment you leave Hwy 84 it's truly a time warp: ghost towns lie off the roadside, fossils expose millions of years of history, and even the restaurants and hotels make you feel you've driven into decades past.

❶ Stonehenge

Although it's not part of the official byway, the perfect place to kick off your time travel is at the full-scale replica of **Stonehenge** (US Hwy 97). Built by eccentric businessman Sam Hill as a memorial to the 13 men in Klickitat County killed in WWI, the site is a completed version of the Salisbury Plain monument, although its detractors argue that the keystone is incorrectly aligned with the stars. It's just east of Hwy 97,

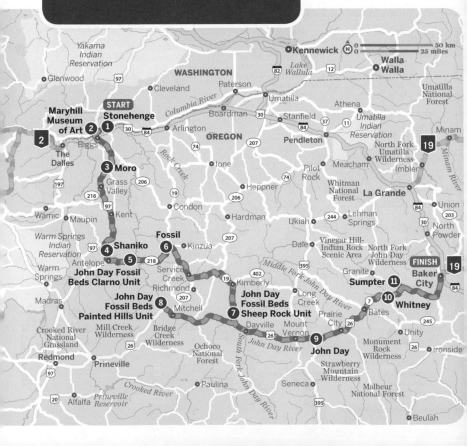

on the Washington side of the Columbia River.

The Drive » Turn left on Hwy 14 and drive about 4 miles to the Maryhill Museum of Art.

TRIP HIGHLIGHT

❷ Maryhill Museum of Art

The spectacular **Maryhill Museum of Art** (🖉509-773-3733; www.maryhillmu seum.org; 35 Maryhill Museum Dr; adult/child $12/5; ⏱10am-5pm mid-Mar–mid-Nov), set in a mansion on a bluff above the Columbia River, was another Sam Hill project. Among its eclectic exhibits is a noteworthy collection of Rodin sculptures, a room full of decadent objects once belonging to Queen Marie of Romania

LINK YOUR TRIP

2 Columbia River Gorge & Mt Hood

From The Dalles, it's only about 30 miles east along Hwy 84 and the Columbia River Gorge to Maryhill.

19 Hells Canyon Scenic Byway

The Hells Canyon Scenic Byway begins in Baker City, right where this trip ends, so they link up perfectly.

and Native American artifacts.

The Drive » Make a right on Hwy 14 then another right 2 miles later onto Hwy 97, which takes you over the Columbia River via the Sam Hill Memorial Bridge. Tip: fill up on gas at Biggs Junction, where the scenic byway officially begins. From here it's about 20 miles to the next stop, past grassy hills, wind farms and homesteads.

----

❸ Moro

In Moro you'll find **Sherman County Historical Museum** (www. shermanmuseum.org; 200 Dewey St; adult/student $5/1; ⏱10am-5pm May-Oct). For a small-town museum it has some surprisingly interesting exhibits, including on the history of wheat production, Native Americans and rural living in the days of old. The town is also home to a handful of antique shops that are worth a browse.

The Drive » South on Hwy 97 you'll be treated to breathtaking views of several volcanoes in the distance, including Mt Hood, Mt Jefferson and Mt Adams. Continue for 35 miles through the near-deserted towns of Grass Valley and Kent.

----

❹ Shaniko

This wee ghost town (population 37) was once the wool-shipping center of the US. Its decrepit old buildings make for good photo ops, and

its architectural grand dame, the Shaniko Hotel, is one of the finer historic buildings in eastern Oregon. (It's been mid-refurbishment but closed for years.) A few shops and a tiny museum are open through summer.

The Drive » Continue south on Hwy 218. About a mile out, the road narrows and winds as it descends through sagebrush-covered hills to the minuscule settlement of Antelope. Turn east here onto Hwy 218 and drive about 16 miles to the next stop.

TRIP HIGHLIGHT

❺ John Day Fossil Beds Clarno Unit

Dramatically eroded palisade cliffs mark your arrival at the John Day Fossil Beds **Clarno Unit** (www.nps.gov/joda; Hwy 218), your first stop in the John Day Fossil Beds National Monument trilogy. The short trails and fossil remains plunge you into a time more than 40 million years ago, when the region was subtropical forest. From the base of the palisades, wander the half-mile Geologic Time Trail to the Trail of Fossils, and you'll see boulder-sized fossils of logs, seeds and other remains from the ancient forest. The quarter-mile Arch Trail leads to a natural arch in the striking palisade cliffs.

The Drive » Continue 18 miles northeast to Fossil.

 p199

➏ Fossil

The town of Fossil (population 447) is aptly named given that it's in the middle of paleontology heaven. It's a good stop for lunch and you can browse the town's very small **Fossil Museum** (📞541-763-2113; 1st St; admission by donation; ⏰1-4pm Wed-Mon May-Oct) or dig for fossils in the **public digging area** (📞541-763-4303; 404 Main St; per person $5; ⏰May-Oct). You're pretty much guaranteed to find something and there's usually someone around to help explain what you've dug up.

The Drive » Head 20 miles southeast on Hwy 19 to the tiny Service Creek (population 2), an old stagecoach stop that consists of a recommended inn and a rafting-put-in-cum-campground on the John Day River. It's exceptionally scenic along the river valley for the next 40 miles to the next stop.

TRIP HIGHLIGHT

➐ John Day Fossil Beds Sheep Rock Unit

The rust-colored walls of the river canyon narrow and then open up again before reaching the spectacular John Day Fossil Beds Sheep Rock Unit. Continue 3 miles south to the **Thomas Condon Paleontology Center** (📞541-987-2333; www.nps.gov/joda; 32651 Hwy 19, Kimberly; ⏰9am-5pm Jun-Aug, 10am-5pm Mar-May & Sep-Oct, 10am-5pm Tue-Sat Nov-Feb). This is where everything comes together. With giant murals and exhibits of fossilized skulls, skeletons, leaves, nuts and branches, the center brings the region's history to life.

After filling your head with paleontology, drive across the highway to the historic **Cant Ranch House** (www.nps.gov/joda; ⏰summer only) for a picnic or snack on the wooden tables overlooking the John Day River. Then backtrack the 3 miles (north) to the **Blue Basin Area** parking lot at the Sheep Rock Unit. Hike the 0.6-mile Island in Time Trail and the 3-mile Blue Basin Overlook Trail. The former passes replicas of large mammal fossils and ends in a massive amphitheater of towering greenish pinnacles, while the latter leads around and above the amphitheater.

The Drive » From Hwy 19 turn west onto Hwy 26, from where it's 36 miles to Mitchell. At 25 miles check out the tree on the north side of the road covered with shoes. It's been there as long as anyone can remember – string a pair up for good luck.

DEEBROWNING/GETTY IMAGES ©

✓ TOP TIP: SHORT CUT TO MITCHELL

Taking Hwy 207 from Service Creek 30 miles to Mitchell will shave about 50 miles off your route. It also saves you from having to backtrack east along Hwy 26, although you'll miss some exceptional scenery along the John Day River.

Maryhill Museum of Art (p195)

From Mitchell it's another 10 miles to the Painted Hills Unit.

TRIP HIGHLIGHT

⑧ John Day Fossil Beds Painted Hills Unit

This is a detour off the official byway but it's arguably the most striking unit of the John Day Fossil Beds, so you won't want to miss it. The goal is to see the low-slung, colorfully banded **Painted Hills** (www.nps. gov/joda; Burnt Ranch Rd) at sunset, when the evening light emphasizes the ochres, blacks, beiges and yellows of the eroded hillsides; an honorable reason to stay overnight in Mitchell. At the site, choose from four trails including the 0.5-mile Painted Hills Overlook and Trail (the most picturesque of the area) and the Painted Cove Trail, which takes you via boardwalk around a hill (five to 10 minutes) to see the area's popcorn-textured clay stone up close.

The Drive ≫ Backtrack east along Hwy 26 and pass the Hwy 19 junction to Picture Gorge, a canyon hemmed in by stone pillars known as Picture Gorge Basalts. Two miles along is the Mascall Formation Overlook, where you'll get spectacular views of the John Day River, Strawberry Mountains, Picture Gorge and Mascall and Rattlesnake Formations. It's another 36 miles to John Day.

✕ ⊨ p199

⑨ John Day

After so many small towns, the one-stoplight town of John Day (population 1821) feels like a metropolis. Make your way to the outstanding **Kam Wah Chung State Heritage Site** (☎541-575-2800; www. oregonstateparks.org; 125 NW Canton St; ⊙9am-noon & 1-5pm May-Oct, limited

ROCK ART

If you're heading east through Picture Gorge (on Hwy 26), at the far end you'll see a sign on the left and a gravel parking area big enough for about two cars. There's a little footpath from the pullout. Walk down the footpath and then hang onto the rock wall on your left, lean around and you'll see some red pictographs. They're really cool. And you can't hurt them because you can't reach them.

hours rest of year), which served as an apothecary, community center, temple and general store for Chinese gold miners and settlers from the late 19th century until the 1940s. Today it's a widely acclaimed museum, featuring the history of the building and the region's Chinese past.

The Drive » Drive east past stop-for-the-night-worthy Prairie City into the lush, conifer-clad Blue Mountains. Up the first grade, pull off at the Strawberry Mountain Overlook for views of the John Day River valley and the Strawberry

Mountains. Continue northeast over Dixie Pass (elevation 5280ft), swing left onto Hwy 7, cross Tipton Summit (elevation 5124ft) and you'll drop into a lovely valley.

✕ ⛺ p199

⑩ Whitney

This isolated and unsignposted prairie settlement, a ghost town in the best sense of the description, was once a busy logging town and the primary stop on the Sumpter Valley Railroad. Its sagging wooden

buildings, which lie on either side of a short dirt road that branches south from Hwy 7, are certainly worth a stop. Find it between mile markers 15 and 16.

The Drive » About 9 miles east turn left on Sumpter Valley Hwy, then drive another 3 miles or so to Sumpter.

⑪ Sumpter

Once home to 3500 people, the town today is a sleepy cluster of Old West buildings huddled along a dusty main drag. The official attraction is the **Sumpter Valley Dredge**, a massive relic of gold-mining engineering sitting beside the river. The dredge's 72-bucket 'digging ladder' extracted some 9 tons of gold.

The Drive » Once you return from here to Hwy 7, it's 26 miles to the Eastern Oregon hub of Baker City.

Eating & Sleeping

John Day Fossil Beds Painted Hills Unit (Mitchell) ❽

✖ Tiger Town Brewing   Chicken $

(☏541-462-3663; www.tigertownbrewing.
com; 108 Main St; 6/10-piece wings $6/9, beer
$5; ◷noon-8pm Wed-Sat, 9am-5pm Sun)
'Tiger Town' was the nickname for modern-day
Mitchell's Main St, a lively stretch that was
frowned upon by those on Piety Hill (where the
churches are). This namesake brewery is in a
hip, black-interior brewpub with some outdoor
seating, although the outrageous smoked
chicken wings (and much more) are prepared in
the adjacent food cart. There's great beer too
with around six house brews on tap.

⛺ Historic Oregon Hotel   Hotel $

(☏541-462-3027; www.theoregonhotel.net;
104 E Main St, d with/without bath from $65/55;
🛜) This creaky, old-fashioned but cute hotel
is in the friendly little town of Mitchell, about
10 miles southeast of the fossil beds' Painted
Hills Unit. The good-sized rooms are individually
decorated, themed from grandma's floral to
cowboy. Most have shared bathrooms and the
three private bathroom rooms have bathtubs
but no shower. It was for sale when we passed
so changes are surely afoot. Call ahead to make
sure it's open in winter.

John Day ❾

✖ Outpost   American $$

(☏541-575-0250; www.outpostpizzapubgrill.
com; 201 W Main St; breakfast $8-12, dinner

mains $14-21; ◷5:30am-9pm Mon-Sat, to
8pm Sun) Expect enormous portions of
down-home American comfort food at this
Western-style joint: biscuits and gravy on two
giant platters, huge omelets, skillet breakfasts
with their own gravitational pull – plus salads,
sandwiches, pizzas, burgers, steaks and pasta,
and homemade cinnamon rolls for breakfast.
There's a good atmosphere, friendly service and
upscale rustic decor.

⛺ Dreamers Lodge   Motel $

(☏800-654-2849; www.dreamerslodge.com;
144 N Canyon Blvd; r $59-95, ste from $109;
🐶❄🛜🖥) One of John Day's better-value
places, this decent motel offers good-sized
rooms with nice touches – comfy old armchairs,
in-room coffee, mini fridge and microwave – and
it's off the main drag. Rates plunge if there are
lots of vacancies.

Prairie City ❾

⛺ Hotel Prairie   Hotel $$

(☏541-820-4800; www.hotelprairie.com; 112
Front St; d $97-159; 🐶❄🖥) Actually located
in Prairie City, 13 miles east of John Day, and
a much cuter town, this historic 1905 hotel
with nine suites (one with kitchenette) caters
especially to bicyclists. There's a subdued,
classy atmosphere – rooms are simple and
not at all fancy, but comfortable; out back is
a nice modern patio for hanging out. Cafe on
premises, and breakfast included. It's by far the
most interesting hotel option in this region, and
has great service to boot.

Blue Mountains Loop

From Oregon Trail wagon stops to million-acre forests and rodeo towns, this loop shows off eastern Oregon's rural variety.

TRIP HIGHLIGHTS

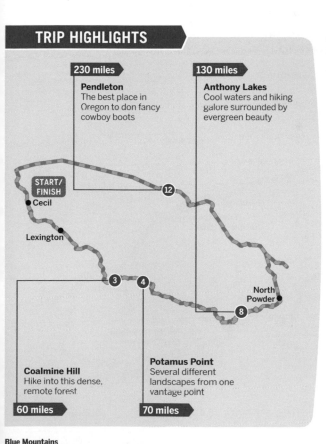

230 miles

Pendleton
The best place in Oregon to don fancy cowboy boots

130 miles

Anthony Lakes
Cool waters and hiking galore surrounded by evergreen beauty

START/ FINISH
● Cecil

Lexington

12

3   **4**

North Powder ●

8

Coalmine Hill
Hike into this dense, remote forest

60 miles

Potamus Point
Several different landscapes from one vantage point

70 miles

**3 DAYS
240 MILES / 386KM**

GREAT FOR...

BEST TIME TO GO
June to September, the only time all the roads are open!

ESSENTIAL PHOTO
Potamus Point, for a panorama of a Wild West quilt of color.

BEST FOR HISTORY
Oregon Trail Interpretive Park, with its 100-year-old Oregon Trail wagon ruts.

18 Blue Mountains Loop

This trip takes you way off the beaten path through country that feels as if the pioneer days never ended. Start in the grain kingdoms of Morrow County before heading up and up into deep, remote, wildlife-filled forests. Just as you start craving a real cup of coffee, you'll descend back to civilization via the good ole cow-poking towns of Union and La Grande to lively, Western-chic Pendleton.

❶ Cecil

Turning onto Hwy 74 from the Columbia River Gorge, stratified river country is quickly replaced by grassy fields and hillside tracts of space-age windmills. The first town you come to is the sheep- and grain-farming hamlet of Cecil, which was founded in the late 1800s, when William Cecil stopped here on the Oregon Trail to fix his wagon and ended up opening a wagon repair shop. Take Cecil's

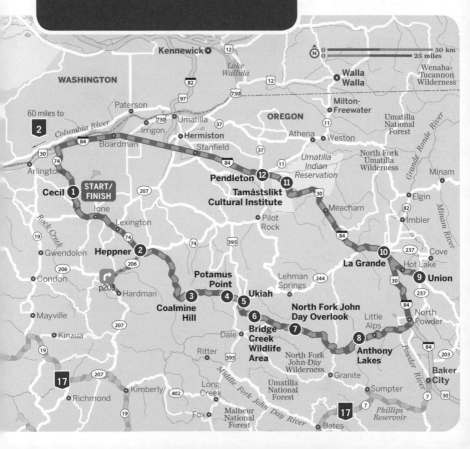

one road to the left off Hwy 74 to check out the ancient **Cecil Store**, a photogenic Old West–style building with a ghost town feel to it.

The Drive » Continue 32 miles down Hwy 74 through the grain-elevator-dominated towns of Morgan (a ghost town), Ione and Lexington. The scenery here is the highlight: picture-perfect homesteads and grazing horses along a meandering creek bed.

---

❷ Heppner

Welcome to the big smoke (although 'spoke' may be more fitting) of Morrow County. Heppner has a massive grain elevator, a small grid of wide streets and a few stately brick buildings. The town's pride and joy is the majestic **Historic**

LINK YOUR TRIP

2 Columbia River Gorge & Mt Hood

It's about 60 miles east along Hwy 84 from The Dalles to the turnoff for Hwy 74.

17 Journey Through Time Scenic Byway

From Baker City, take the mountainous half of this route via Ukiah or I-84 to Pendleton to create a loop.

DETOUR: HARDMAN

Start: ❷ Heppner

Once a stagecoach stop named 'Rawdog,' Hardman's demise began in the late 1880s, when Heppner was chosen as the location for the train stop. The town's last business closed in 1968 and today it's one of the region's most scenic ghost towns. The most attractive building is the renovated dance hall. It's a 40-mile round-trip drive south from Heppner along Hwy 207.

Morrow County Court-house (☎541-676-9061; 100 Court St; ☺8am-5pm Mon-Fri), built in 1903 and still in use, making it one of the oldest continuously used courthouses in the state. It's also said to be haunted, perhaps by the 275 people who lost their lives in the 1903 Heppner Flood. Call if you want a tour.

Another worthwhile stop is the **Morrow County Museum** (www.morrowcountymuseum.com; 444 N Main St; $3; ☺1-5pm Tue-Fri Mar-Oct), where you'll find a collection of pioneer and rural artifacts. Then, before you hit the road again, check in at the **US Forest Service Ranger Station** (☎541-676-9187; 117 S Main St; ☺7:45am-4:30pm Mon-Fri) for maps, trail and road information.

The Drive » Main St leads into Hwy 206/207. After about a mile, turn left toward Willow Creek Reservoir on Hwy 53. From here it's 24 miles to Cutsforth Park, where

the Umatilla National Forest officially starts. It's another 2 miles from here to Coalmine Hill.

🛏 p207

TRIP HIGHLIGHT

❸ Coalmine Hill

The best way to explore the pine- and fir-tree loveliness of the 1.4-million-acre **Umatilla National Forest** is on foot. Stop at the **Coalmine Hill Trailhead** to tackle the 2.5-mile one-way **Bald Mountain Trail**, where you'll be rewarded with a view over Butter Creek. At about 1.25 miles you'll pass **Gibson Cave**, which provided shelter to Native American families long ago. During the 1930s Great Depression, a man named Gibson lived here and became known as a modern caveman.

The Drive » Head south on NF-270 a little over a mile then turn right on NF-021/Western Raite Lane/Western Rt Rd. Continue 6 miles before hanging a right on Arbuckle Mt Rd/NF-180. Follow Arbuckle Mt Rd for about 2.5 miles, before turning right on NF-030 then right onto NF-5316 5 miles on, and finally right 1.5 miles later on NF-360.

④ Potamus Point

This is the best viewpoint of the trip, looking over North Fork John Day River. In winter herds of elk can be seen from here, but unfortunately the road is closed at this time. In the summer months, enjoy the vistas of mountain ponds and unusual rock formations.

The Drive » Backtrack to NF-030 then take a quick right onto NF-5316. After around 6 miles, turn right on NF-053. After 10 miles this turns into OR-244 E/Ukiah-Hilgard Hwy and, a little over a mile later, you'll be back to civilization in Ukiah.

⑤ Ukiah

Nestled within the Camas Prairie, this tiny town is surrounded by rolling grasslands and cut by clear Camas Creek. It's the low, flat heart of the Blue Mountains and a pleasant place for a leg stretch, but there's not much on offer besides the small supply shop.

The Drive » Travel west on OR-244 W/Main St/Ukiah-Hilgard Hwy for a little over a mile, then turn right at Granite-Ukiah Rd 52 and travel 4 miles. The entrance to the wildlife area is on the right side of the road.

⑥ Bridge Creek Wildlife Area

This protected area is known mostly as a wintering ground for elk, but in summer (the only time of year it's accessible without specialty equipment – plus you need a permit to enter between December 1 and April 30) you'll see plenty of birdlife, including mountain bluebirds and horned larks. For a bit of exercise, take the 0.2-mile-long Ron Bridges Memorial Trail for views over Bridge Creek Flats. The trailhead is on the right, 1 mile after the wilderness area on Granite-Ukiah Rd 52.

The Drive » Drive 9 miles east on Granite-Ukiah Rd 52.

⑦ North Fork John Day Overlook

Pull over for spectacular views (when it's clear) over the patchwork of color of the John Day Wilderness to the north, the majestic Strawberry Mountains to the south and the river-filled Bridge Creek Flats to the southeast. If it's early or late in season you may be able to spot elk.

The Drive » Continue east on Granite-Ukiah Rd 52 then turn left on NF-73. Drive around 16 miles, then turn right toward NF-300/172 and follow the signs to Anthony Lakes.

VDB PHOTOS/SHUTTERSTOCK ©

⑧ Anthony Lakes

Known for its powdery winter skiing, Anthony Lakes is also a trove of excellent hiking in summer, with alpine landscapes, five lakes and craggy granite peaks. **Anthony Lake**, the only lake accessible by car, is the biggest and most crowded. Better, take the 1-mile hike to **Black Lake**, which is just as beautiful, to find serious tranquility. Find the trailhead at the Anthony Lakes Campground.

Pendleton Woolen Mills (p206)

The Drive ❯❯ Head back to NF-73 and turn right into Anthony Lake Rd, which eventually turns into Anthony Lakes Hwy. After about 9 miles of winding downhill through pines, turn left on Ellis Rd/Ermey Davis Rd and take the first right on River Lane. This will lead you onto OR-237 N/La Grande-Baker Hwy toward Union. The total distance is 36 miles.

🛏 p207

---

❾ Union

One of eastern Oregon's most likeable, unpretentious towns, Victorian-era, brick-solid Union is like a smaller, cuter version of La Grande and is a quieter place to spend the night if you're ready for a stop. While you're here, learn more about cowboys then and now at the **Union County Museum** (☎541-562-6003; www.ucmuseumoregon.com; 333 South Main St; adult/child $5/free; ☺10am-4pm Mon-Sat, 1-4pm Sun).

The Drive ❯❯ Get back on the La Grande-Baker Hwy. In about 13 miles you'll see the first exit for La Grande.

🛏 p207

---

❿ La Grande

Apart from its pleasant historic area downtown, La Grande is really just a stop for food, gas and lodging. Some 13 miles west of town, however, is the **Oregon Trail Interpretive Park** (☎541-963-7186; I-84 exit 248; day-use $5; ☺9am-7pm Tue-Sun Memorial Day-Labor Day), a great place for a visceral feeling of what it was like for Oregon pioneers crossing the Blue Mountains. Paths wind through the forest to ruts left by pioneer wagons – still visible after 150 years. Find the park on well-marked roads from freeway exit 248.

The Drive ❯❯ Continue on I-84 towards Pendleton. About 25 miles along you'll find yourself descending Emigrant Hill on

TOP TIP: NAVIGATING FOREST ROADS

It's easy to get lost in this tangle of forest roads, so make sure you fill up your tank in Heppner, bring plenty of water, snacks and emergency supplies, and let the ranger station know where you're going. Keep meticulous track of the route you've taken so that in a worst case scenario you can at least backtrack. Cell-phone reception and GPS coverage are iffy at best so don't expect to rely on anything besides your wits.

a 6% downgrade. Stop at the Cabbage Hill Viewpoint to experience something akin to looking down from the heavens. Just before Pendleton, take exit 216 to the Tamástslikt Cultural Institute. Total distance: 50 miles.

✗ ⊨ p207, p216

- - - - - - - - - - - - - - - - - -

⑪ Tamástslikt Cultural Institute

You've learned all about the pioneers so now it's time to delve into the cultures that were here long before covered wagons. State-of-the-art exhibits weave voices, memories and artifacts through an evolving history of the region at this grand **cultural center** (☎541-429-7700; www.tamastslikt. org; 47106 Wild Horse Blvd; adult/child $10/7; ☺10am-5pm Mon-Sat).

The Drive » Get back onto I-84 W. In about 2.5 miles you'll see the first exit for Pendleton.

- - - - - - - - - - - - - - - - - -

TRIP HIGHLIGHT

⑫ Pendleton

Eastern Oregon's largest city, 'wild and woolly'

Pendleton is a handsome old town famous for its wool shirts and rowdy, big-name rodeo. The town has managed to retain a glint of its cow-poking past, though in the last few years at least one small boutique winery has popped up, not to mention art galleries and antique shops.

Take a free tour of **Pendleton Woolen Mills** (☎541-276-6911; www. pendleton-usa.com; 1307 SE Court Pl; ☺8am-6pm Mon-Sat, 9am-5pm Sun), which has been weaving blankets for more than 100 years, and is especially known for Native American designs.

The Drive » From here it's about 70 miles to the Hwy 74 turnoff to Cecil, where the loop began.

✗ ⊨ p207

Eating & Sleeping

Heppner ❷

🛏 Northwestern Motel & RV Park
Motel $

(📞541-676-9167; www.heppnerlodging.com; 389 N Main St; r from $64, tent & RV sites $12-22; ❄🛜🐾) Kitschy outside with red-and-white paint, green shamrocks and garden gnomes a go-go, this motel's clean, stylish rooms are a big surprise. Each one has a theme, including cowboy, zebra and Caribbean. Tent and RV camping is available across the street, and for breakfast there's a small cafe next door run by the same people.

Anthony Lakes ❽

🛏 Anthony Lakes Campground
Campground $

(📞541-894-2393; www.anthonylakescamp grounds.com; 47500 Anthony Lakes Hwy; tent sites $10-14; ⏰Jul-Sep) Though it's 35 miles from town, this rustic but splendid campground is worth the drive (bring mosquito repellent!). It's high up and opens only after the snow melts, so call first.

Union ❾

🛏 Union Hotel
Hotel $

(📞541-562-1200; www.thehistoricunionhotel. com; 326 N Main St; d $97-135, RV sites $35; 😊❄🛜🐾) Fifteen miles southeast of La Grande, in the town of Union, is this very atmospheric old hotel and definitely the best pick in the area. All 16 rooms are decorated individually, and none has a TV or telephone, though three come with kitchenette (there are common rooms with a TV and library).

La Grande ❿

✕ Side A Brewing
Gastropub $$

(📞541-605-0163; www.sideabeer.com; 1219 Washington Ave; mains $10-22; ⏰11am-9pm Sun-Tue, to 10pm Wed & Thu, to 11pm Fri & Sat) Hip, hustling and delicious, Side A is an excellent addition to La Grande's eating and drinking scene. Make new friends at the family-style seating and chat over great burgers, mac and cheese or a flat iron steak. The 'dirty fries' smothered in fresh herbs, cherry peppers, Parmesan cheese and smoked aioli are legendary. Pair with one of the full-flavored beers on tap.

Pendleton ⓬

✕ Hamley's Steakhouse
American $$

(📞541-278-1100; www.hamleysteakhouse.com; 8 SE Court Ave; steaks $34-56, dinner mains $19-26; ⏰4-9:30pm Sun-Tue, to 10:30pm Wed & Thu, to midnight Fri & Sat) This 150-seat steakhouse has been gorgeously done up with wood floors, stone accents and tin ceilings. There's a bar with sports on TV and the bathrooms have 'interesting' art work. Food is decent, with large portions. Hamley's empire also includes a first-rate Western store with a saddle-making workshop in back, a cafe and a wine cellar.

✕ Great Pacific Wine & Coffee Co
American $

(📞541-276-1350; www.greatpacific.biz; 403 S Main St; drinks $2-7, mains $6-14; ⏰10am-9pm Mon-Thu, to 10pm Fri & Sat) This trendy-for-Pendleton coffee shop serves up hot and cold sandwiches, salads, baked stuffed croissants and gourmet Naples-style pizzas. There are plenty of java choices, wine by the glass and even microbrews on tap. Occasional live music.

🛏 Working Girls Old Hotel
Hotel $

(📞541-276-0730; www.pendletonunderground tours.org; 17 SW Emigrant Ave; d $75-95; 😊❄🛜) Run by Pendleton Underground Tours, this former bordello offers five large, beautiful and antique-filled rooms. Only one is en suite; two have private hallway bathrooms (only three rooms are rented at the same time, unless everyone's willing to share bathrooms). There's a guest kitchen and parlor. Best for those who don't need much service (there's no reception). Reservations required.

Hells Canyon Scenic Byway

19

North America's deepest river gorge is more than just scorching temperatures and desolate landscapes. You'll find both, but you'll also find forested ridge tops, peaceful river valleys and hamlets.

TRIP HIGHLIGHTS

70 miles

Joseph
Western trendiness feels awfully good after all those greasy spoons

135 miles

Hat Point
A breathtaking view from heaven to hell

Elgin   Wallowa   Imnaha   **5**

3

START   La Grande

7

FINISH

9   Richland

National Historic Oregon Trail Interpretive Center
Imagine doing this trip in a covered wagon

Hells Canyon Dam
The dramatic canyons around here form the best scenery

280 miles

240 miles

---

4 DAYS
280 MILES / 450KM

GREAT FOR...

BEST TIME TO GO
June to September, when the Imnaha–Halfway road is open.

 ESSENTIAL PHOTO
Capture the majesty of an 8000ft rise from river to peak at Hat Point.

 BEST DAY
Exploring Hells Canyon's vistas and valleys, stops 6 to 9.

Hells Canyon Scenic Byway

In this remote corner of Oregon, at the foot of the Seven Devils Mountains, lies one of the Pacific Northwest's most spectacular sights: Hells Canyon, measuring 8043ft deep from peak to river. The few roads that access the canyon are open much of the year, but the mountains above that offer spectacular vistas are only open in summer, once the snows have melted and temperatures soar.

❶ La Grande

The Oregon Trail crossed this valley, and pioneers rested here before traversing the challenging Blue Mountains. La Grande is the best place in the region to stock up on provisions (trail mix? sunscreen? water?) before driving into the boondocks. Despite the number of services and the few blocks of historical brick architecture, the city isn't that memorable.

The Drive » Take I-82 east and you'll soon be in farmlands

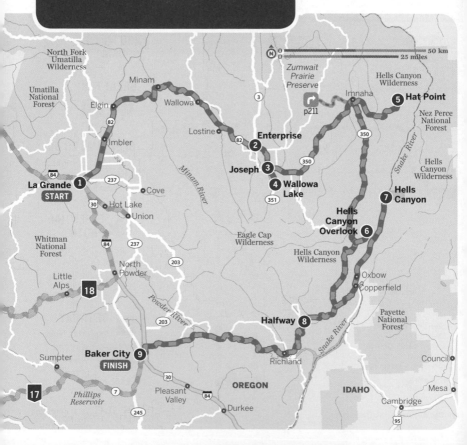

hemmed in by mountains. After the tiny town of Minam, the road veers right to run along the Minam River through a beautiful, slim valley with pine-covered hillsides. You'll eventually drive through the small settlements of Wallowa and Lostine.

🍴 🛏 p207, p216

- - - - - - - - - - - - - - - -

❷ Enterprise

Unlike nearby Joseph (which has argu-ably become *too* cute), Enterprise maintains its good old small-town atmosphere. In fact, its downtown – two blocks of handsome buildings – feels quite lonesome at times. It's a good, economical place to rest for the night and get any gear you may realize you need after all (fish hooks? bug spray?).

LINK YOUR TRIP

17 Journey Through Time Scenic Byway

It's a seamless link: start in Baker City, where the Journey Through Time Scenic Byway ends.

18 Blue Mountains Loop

From La Grande, drive south 25 miles on Hwy 84 to North Powder, or northwest toward Pendleton to hook up with this varied circuit.

DETOUR: ZUMWAIT PRAIRIE PRESERVE

Start: ❺ Hat Point

If you have a high-clearance vehicle and three to five hours to spare, detour up to Zumwait Prairie Preserve. Owned by the Nature Conservancy, this 51-sq-mile preserve is the largest remaining grassland of its kind in the US. Several trails meander through the prairie, which is home to a vast number of hawks and eagles. To get there, take the dirt Camp Creek Rd, which departs Little Sheep Creek Hwy about 1 mile south of Imnaha.

The Drive » Joseph is only 6 miles down I-62.

🍴 🛏 p216

- - - - - - - - - - - - - - - -

TRIP HIGHLIGHT

❸ Joseph

If ever there was a trendy eastern Oregon town, it's Joseph. You can see its wealth right on the brick sidewalks, where well-groomed planter boxes and huge bronze statues sit proudly on every downtown corner. In fact, Joseph is noted for its cast-bronze sculp-tures, thanks in part to **Valley Bronze** (📞541-432-7445; www.valleybronze.com; 18 S Main St; tours adult/child $15/free; ⏲ tours 11am). You can also visit the **Wallowa County Museum** (📞541-432-6095; www.co.wallowa.or.us; 110 S Main St; adult/child $4/2; ⏲ 10am-4pm Memorial Day-late Sep), housed in an 1888 bank building and notable for its displays on pioneer and Nez Percé histories.

Stock up on maps and information about Hells Canyon and surround-ing areas at the **Wallowa Mountains Forest Service Office** (📞541-426-4978; www.fs.usda.gov; 201 E Second St; ⏲ 8am-4:30pm Mon-Fri).

The Drive » Drive 6 miles south on Wallowa Lake Rd (Hwy 351).

🍴 🛏 p216

- - - - - - - - - - - - - - - -

❹ Wallowa Lake

Over 5 miles long and glacially formed, Wal-lowa Lake sits at the foot of the Wallowa Moun-tains, dominated at its southern end by 9617ft Chief Joseph Mountain. Giant old-growth conifers tower over a grassy beach area here, and families lounge in the sun, fish and otherwise frolic away the summer afternoons. A major trailhead starts at the southern end of Wallowa Lake Rd. One popular trail from here is the 6-mile (one-way) jaunt to the gorgeous **Aneroid Lake**. Otherwise ascend 8255ft-high Mt Howard the easy way, on the **Wallowa Lake Tramway** (☎541-432-5331; www.wallowalaketramway. com; 59919 Wallowa Lake Hwy; adult/child $35/25; ☉10am-5pm late May-Sep), for stunning views over the lake and surrounding area.

The Drive ❯❯ Backtrack to Joseph then take Hwy 350 east. After leaving Joseph, the road passes a highway sign that tellingly reads 'Open Range Next 23 Miles,' before meeting up with Little Sheep Creek, which it follows all the way to Imnaha. It's 30 miles to Imnaha, then another 24 miles to Hat Point.

✕ ⏸ p216

TRIP HIGHLIGHT

❺ Hat Point

Now it's time to leave civilization behind. Get an early start for the 30-mile drive to **Imnaha**, one of the most isolated towns in the US. You may want to stay the night here (if you didn't in Joseph or Enterprise) before tackling the route ahead.

The area around Imnaha has some of the most dramatic scenery of the trip. A 24-mile gravel road leads to Hat Point (elevation 6982ft) from Imnaha. The good news: only the first 5 or 6 miles are steep. The road follows a spectacular forested ridge, offering

stunning views along the way. Be sure to stop at the **Granny View Vista** pullout. By the time you get to Hat Point, you'll wonder if the views could get any better. They do. Atop Hat Point stands the 82ft **Hat Point lookout tower**, a fire lookout offering dizzying 360-degree views of the Seven Devils, the Wallowas and Hells Canyon itself. And, yes, you can climb to the top. Without a doubt, this is one of the grandest views in the Pacific Northwest. From around July through September, the road is usually passable for all passenger cars.

The Drive ❯❯ Head 24 miles back to Imnaha and follow the gravel Upper Imnaha Rd south for 30 miles to USFS Rd 39 (also called Wallowa Mountain Loop Rd). This is a dusty, scenic drive along the Imnaha River valley. If you wish to avoid the dust, backtrack along Little Sheep Creek Hwy to USFS Rd 39 and swing left.

✕ ⏸ p217

❻ Hells Canyon Overlook

Whichever route you take, after joining USFS Rd 39, continue southeast until the turnoff for the Hells Canyon Overlook. This is the *only* overlook into Hells Canyon that's accessible by paved road, so take advantage of it. Although you don't get the same 360-degree views as from

THINAIR28 / GETTY IMAGES ©

Hat Point, it's a marvelous vista nonetheless.

The Drive ❯❯ This southern end of USFS Rd 39 is bucolic, with meadows and old farmhouses flanking the river. When you reach Hwy 86, turn left toward Copperfield and Oxbow.

TRIP HIGHLIGHT

❼ Hells Canyon

At Copperfield, you'll reach the Snake River and officially be at the very bottom of Hells Canyon. Down here, it's hot, hot, hot, and the canyon has absolutely no problem living up to its name. Cross the Snake

Hells Canyon Snake River

River into Idaho and turn onto Idaho's Forest Rd 454 (also called Hells Canyon Dam Rd), which eventually dead-ends at Hells Canyon Dam. Here you will find the **Hells Canyon Visitors Center** (www.fs.usda.gov; ◷8am-4pm May-Oct), which is a must if you need hiking trail information. The **Stud Creek Trail** begins immediately below the visitor center and passes some great spots to relax above the river and ponder the immensity of your surroundings.

North of Hells Canyon Dam and the visitor center, the Snake River returns to its natural flowing self, descending through epic scenery and roaring rapids. You can float those rapids by signing on with **Hells Canyon Adventures** (☏800-422-3568; www.hellscanyonadventures.com; 4200 Hells Canyon Dam Rd; jet-boat tours adult/child from $100/70; ◷May-Sep), which offers rafting and jet-boat trips into an otherwise inaccessible area. If there's time for a hike, tackle the 4.5-mile (out and back) **Allison Creek Trail**, which you'll pass about 12 miles north of Oxbow (10 miles before the dam); it has a total elevation gain of about 1200ft up Allison Creek Canyon.

The Drive ›› From Hells Canyon, return by way of Hwy 86 to Halfway.

🛏 p216

- - - - - - - - - - - - - - - - - - -

❽ Halfway

Halfway is an idyllic little town lying on the southern edge of the Wallowa Mountains, surrounded by beautiful meadows dotted with old barns and hay fields. It's also a friendly spot with just enough tourist services to make it a decent base to explore the Hells Canyon Dam area.

TOP TIP: OLLOKOT CAMPGROUND

One of our favorite spots to go is Ollokot Campground, not just for camping, but because it's so beautiful in there with the river and the trees. It's just off the Wallowa Mountain Loop Rd (USFS Rd 39), an hour or so's drive from Imnaha.

The **Pine Ranger Station** (☏541-742-7511; 38470 Pine Town Lane; ⊙7:45am-4:30pm Mon-Fri), 1 mile south of Halfway, acts as the region's tourist information office.

The **Pine Valley Museum** (115 E Record St; admission by donation; ⊙10am-4pm Fri, Sat & Sun Memorial Day–Labor Day) is located right in the middle of town and displays a few of the region's old photos and relics. It's open on weekdays and by request for a $5 suggested donation.

The Drive » You're way more than halfway there! It's 54 miles through pastoral countryside to the end of the trail at Baker City.

🛏 p217

- - - - - - - - - - - - - - - - - -

`TRIP HIGHLIGHT`

❾ Baker City

In the gold-rush days, Baker City was the largest metropolis between Salt Lake City and Portland, and a heady mix of miners, cowboys, shopkeepers and loggers kept the city's many saloons, brothels and gaming halls boisterously alive. Today the city's wide downtown streets and historical architecture recall its rich bygone days, while a little gentrification is filling shops with gourmet goodies.

To remind yourself how easy your modern road trip is, stop in at the evocative **National Historic Oregon Trail Interpretive Center** (☏541-523-1843; www.blm. gov; 22267 Hwy 86; adult/child $8/free; ⊙9am-6pm Apr-Oct, to 4pm Thu-Sun Nov-Mar), one of the best museums in the state. Lying atop a hill 7 miles east of town along Hwy 86, the center contains interactive displays, artifacts and films that brilliantly illustrate the day-to-day realities of the pioneers who crossed this region in the 1800s. Outside, you can stroll on the 4-mile interpretive path and spot the actual Oregon Trail.

🍴 🛏 p217

National Historic Oregon Trail Interpretive Center Old wagon

Eating & Sleeping

La Grande ❶

✕ Nells-N-Out
American $

(📞541-963-5733; 1704 Adams Ave; mains $3-8; ⏱10:30am-10pm) Long-running drive-thru burger joint offering some of eastern Oregon's best fast food. Choose from a huge menu of burgers, plus hotdogs, sandwiches, wraps, salads and sides like battered green beans and jalapeño poppers. The milkshakes are legendary. A few shady picnic tables available.

🛏 Hot Lake Springs
Hotel $$

(📞541-963-4685; www.hotlakesprings.com; 66172 Hwy 203; d from $169, hot springs per hour $25; 😀❄🛜) Eight miles southeast of La Grande is this grand hotel in a historic building that was once a luxury resort, then old folks home and then asylum. Peacocks greet you at the faded entrance. Don't just stop by, guest privacy is highly respected here and you need a reservation. There's also a spa, restaurant, museum, art gallery, bronze foundry (tours available) and several hot-spring pools.

Enterprise ❷

✕ Terminal Gravity Brewing
Pub Food $

(📞541-426-3000; www.terminalgravitybrewing. com; 803 SE School St; mains $9-17; ⏱11am-9pm, to 8pm Sun & Mon) One of Oregon's best breweries is in little Enterprise. There's limited inside seating, but on a warm day you'll want to be at a picnic table outside with a tasty IPA and a buffalo burger anyway. Sandwiches and salads dominate the menu, with a few specials such as beer mac 'n' cheese.

🛏 Ponderosa Motel
Motel $

(📞541-426-3186; www.theponderosamotel. com; 102 E Greenwood St; r from $90;❄🛜🖥) Right downtown is this well-run motel with an attractive log-and-stone facade. The excellent rooms are clean and comfortable, with lodge-like furniture. Prices skyrocket during special events and drop in low season. Plus, if you like puns, its tagline is 'You'll sleep like a log.'

Joseph ❸

✕ Embers Brewhouse
Pub Food $$

(www.embersbrewhouse.com; 206 N Main St; mains $10-24; ⏱11am-9pm Mon-Sat, noon-8pm Sun) Pizza, sandwiches, salads and microbrews all go down easy in this relaxed pub. On summer evenings the place to be is on the front deck, with people-watching opportunities and views of the Wallowas.

🛏 Bronze Antler B&B
B&B $$

(📞541-432-0230; www.bronzeantler.com; 309 S Main St; d $145-267; 😀❄🛜) This restored arts-and-crafts home offers three elegant rooms, each with private bathroom, plus one luxurious suite with steam shower and jets in the tub. There's also a bocce court in the yard, and your friendly hosts know the area well. A cat roams the premises.

It's definitely the coziest place in town, plus it's very professionally run.

Wallowa Lake ❹

✕ Vali's Alpine Restaurant
Hungarian $$

(📞541-432-5691; www.valisrestaurant.com; 59811 Wallowa Lake Hwy; mains $16-28; ⏱5pm & 7pm seatings Wed-Sun Memorial Day-Labor Day) Hungarian specialties such as cabbage rolls, chicken paprika, beef kabobs and schnitzel are all excellent here; there's a set menu item each night (with a mix of options on Fridays). Do not miss dessert. Credit cards are not accepted, and reservations are required.

This has been a long-time eastern Oregon favorite and it continues to uphold its reputation year after year.

🛏 Wallowa Lake State Park
Campground $

(📞541-432-4185; www.oregonstateparks. org; 72214 Marina Lane; tent/RV sites $20/32, yurts $45; 🖥) This popular lakeside state park offers more than 200 campsites, along with two yurts. Flush toilets, showers and firewood are available.

Imnaha ⑤

✖ Imnaha
Store & Tavern   Pub Food $

(📞541-577-3111; 102 Hat Point Rd; mains $7-18; 🕘9am-9pm) This store, restaurant and tavern is pretty much Imnaha's only option. It stocks minimal supplies but has a reliable bar menu and offers tent sites ($6).

Hells Canyon ⑦

🛏 Hells Canyon B&B   B&B $

(📞541-785-3373; www.hcbb.us; 49922 Homestead Rd; s/d/tr $80/98/109; 😊❄️📶) Simple but great-value B&B in the Oxbow area, with low-slung simple rooms and an awesome deck.

Halfway ⑧

🛏 Pine Valley Lodge   Lodge $$

(📞541-742-2027; www.pvlodge.com; 163 N Main St; r $80-150; 😊❄️📶🐾) Halfway's fanciest accommodations, with 14 artistic and very comfortable rooms in four buildings, all surrounded by flowery gardens. There's a

great porch with wicker rocking chairs, and tiny rooms that can be added to regular doubles (from $20); one cabin is also available. Some rooms have kitchenette; breakfast included.

Baker City ⑨

✖ Lone Pine Cafe   Breakfast $

(📞541-523-1805; 1825 Main St; breakfasts $5.50-12; 🕘8am-3pm) Baker City's best breakfast choice, this brick-interior, casual cafe serves hearty egg and potato dishes plus a few extras like brioche French toast and huevos rancheros. It has tasty lunch offerings too with burgers and sandwiches. All of the bread is freshly made in-house.

🛏 Geiser Grand Hotel   Hotel $$

(📞541-523-1889; www.geisergrand.com; 1996 Main St; d $109-289, ste $149-339; 😊❄️📶🐾) Baker City's downtown landmark and fanciest lodging is this meticulously restored Italian Renaissance Revival building, designed by John Bennes, an architect with his fingerprints all over Oregon's coolest buildings. The elegant rooms are spacious and decorated with old-style furniture, while the restaurant offers fine food and has a stunning stained-glass ceiling. There's a great old saloon, too.

To Bend & Back

20

You may be tempted to make a beeline for Bend – with its sunshine, microbrews and amazing array of outdoor activities – but take time to enjoy the spectacular stop-offs along the way.

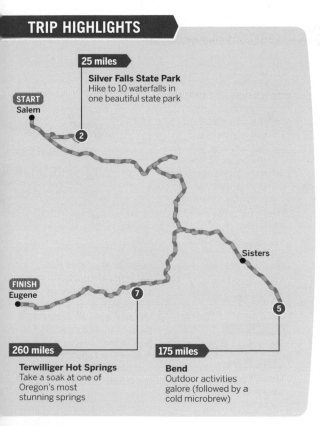

TRIP HIGHLIGHTS

25 miles

Silver Falls State Park
Hike to 10 waterfalls in one beautiful state park

START
Salem

2

Sisters

FINISH
Eugene

7

5

260 miles

Terwilliger Hot Springs
Take a soak at one of Oregon's most stunning springs

175 miles

Bend
Outdoor activities galore (followed by a cold microbrew)

**5 DAYS
280 MILES /
450KM**

GREAT FOR...

BEST TIME TO GO

April to October, though there's always something to do.

ESSENTIAL PHOTO

South Falls in Silver Falls State Park

BEST MUSEUM

Bend's High Desert Museum offers great insight into the area.

20 | To Bend & Back

Pack your snowshoes, swimsuit, hiking boots, day pack and kayak: you'll need them all in Bend. This high desert town enjoys glorious weather and blue skies 250 days a year – not to mention microbreweries and a quirky character for when you're ready to have fun. Along the drive to Bend, you'll experience waterfalls, hot springs and miles and miles of forest, making this an ideal trip for the outdoor adventurer.

❶ Salem

Your trip begins in the state capital, just an hour south of Portland. Before setting off on your journey, stop for a little pioneer history at the **Willamette Heritage Center** (📞503-585-7012; www.willametteheritage.org; 1313 Mill St SE; adult/child $8/4; ◷10am-5pm Mon-Sat), which includes two homes, a parsonage, a Presbyterian church and a mill, all looking much like they did in the 1840s and '50s.

If you've got kids in tow, thrill them with a stop in the **Enchanted Forest** (📞503-371-4242; www.enchantedforest.com; 8462 Enchanted Way SE,

Turner; adult/child $13.50/12, ride tickets $1; ◷10am-4pm, longer hours in summer), **7** miles south of Salem. This theme park is a fun fantasyland offering rides, a haunted house, a European village and a Western town, among other things. Opening hours vary, so check the website.

The Drive » Head 10 miles southeast on Hwy 22, then take Hwy 214 10 miles west to Silver Falls.

 p225

TRIP HIGHLIGHT

❷ Silver Falls State Park

Hoping to glimpse a waterfall or two on your trip? How about 10? Oregon's largest state park packs in 10 waterfalls ranging in height from 27ft to 177ft, and you can see each and every one of them by hiking an 8-mile loop trail known as the **Trail of Ten Falls**. The best place to start is the South Falls parking lot, where you can kick off

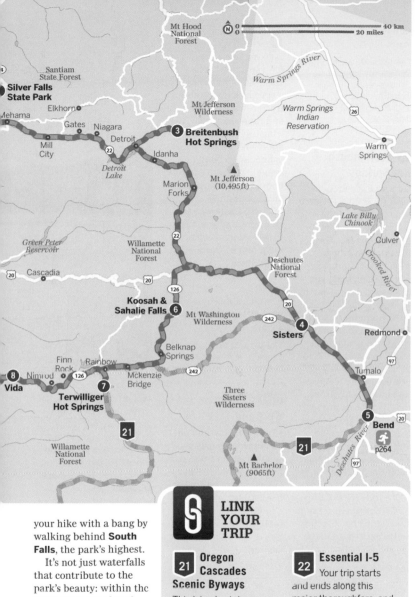

your hike with a bang by walking behind **South Falls**, the park's highest.

It's not just waterfalls that contribute to the park's beauty: within the 9000 acres stand cool forests of Douglas fir, western hemlock, big-leaf maples and cedars, with ferns, Oregon grape and

LINK YOUR TRIP

21 Oregon Cascades Scenic Byways

This trip also takes you to Bend via different routes; mix and match to build your dream itinerary.

22 Essential I-5

Your trip starts and ends along this major thoroughfare, and you can pick it up going in either direction.

salmonberry covering the forest floor.

The Drive » Head back to Santiam Hwy/Hwy 22 and continue west for 40 miles, then strike north for 10 miles on Breitenbush Rd, just past Detroit Lake.

---

❸ Breitenbush Hot Springs

Set above the Breitenbush River on a 154-acre reserve inside Willamette National Forest, Breitenbush Hot Springs is as Oregon as it gets. Along with a fantastically relaxing soak, you'll get a solid dose of earthy Oregonian mellowness. Hot mineral water burbles out of several springs at a scorching 180°F to 200°F (82°C to 93°C) and is cooled to prime soaking temperatures with water from the river. There are seven pools in all. Three overlook a pretty meadow and one of these is a silent pool. Another four pools are arranged in order of temperature, from 100°F to 107°F (37°C to 41°C). Elsewhere, a sauna sits over an open spring and is entirely heated by the steam.

The Drive » Head back to Hwy 22 and drive south for 31 miles. This scenic stretch of road will meet up with Hwy 20, and then it's 26 more miles to Sisters.

---

❹ Sisters

Looking like a movie set for a spaghetti Western, Sisters was once a stagecoach stop and trade town for loggers and ranchers. Today, it's a bustling tourist destination whose main street is lined with boutiques, art galleries and eateries housed in Western-facade buildings.

There's nothing specific here that you have to see – unless you're in town for the **Outdoor Quilt Show** (☏541-549-0989; www.sistersoutdoor quiltshow.org; ⊙2nd Sat Jul) – but it's still a cute town to mosey around in for a while.

The Drive » From Sisters it's a quick 20-minute hop down to Bend.

TRIP HIGHLIGHT

❺ Bend

Hip, outdoorsy, and enjoying ridiculously good weather, Bend is the darling of the high desert. You could spend a week here, hiking, paddling, climbing, mountain biking – the list goes on. Stop by the **Bend Visitor Center** (☏541-382-8048; www.visitbend.com; 750 NW Lava Rd; ⊙9am-5pm Mon-Fri, 10am-4pm Sat & Sun) to explore your options.

With the lovely Deschutes River carving its way through the heart of the city, Bend also offers an attractive downtown:

explore its boutiques, galleries, breweries, dining options on foot (p264).

To learn more about the area, don't miss the superb – and rather extensive – **High Desert Museum** (☏541-382-4754; www.highdesertmuseum.org; 59800 Hwy 97; adult/child $12/7; ⊙9am-5pm May-Oct, 10am-4pm Nov-Apr; ⊕), which covers everything from Native American culture to live animal displays on 135 acres of pine forest.

The Drive » Take Hwy 20 north, curving back through Sisters, then go south where Hwy 126/McKenzie Hwy splits off. Look for the turnoff to the

JORDAN SIEMENS/GETTY IMAGES ©

Hiking in Bend

Koosah and Sahalie Falls about 5 miles later. Total distance: 57 miles.

✕ 🛏 p225, p235

---

6 Koosah & Sahalie Falls

Right off the roadside of McKenzie Hwy are two of Oregon's most impressive waterfalls. The McKenzie River plunges 120ft over Sahalie Falls, the more dramatic of the two: after a good snowmelt, it drenches everything around it in mist as it roars into the frothy pool below.

Only 0.3 miles downstream, Koosah Falls measures 90ft and is wider and easier going than its upstream neighbor. The stretch of the McKenzie River between the falls is utterly spectacular, with roaring cascades that tumble over basalt boulders, through massive logjams and into deep, dark pools.

The Drive » Keep following Hwy 126 another 24 miles and turn left on Aufderheide Rd. Continue on for 8 miles more.

TRIP HIGHLIGHT

7 Terwilliger Hot Springs

Also known as Cougar Hot Springs for its proximity to Cougar Reservoir, this wildly popular hot springs near Terwilliger Reservoir has a beautiful setting among the trees in the Willamette National Forest.

The Drive » Keep following Hwy 126 another 19 miles to the town of Vida.

FIRE ON MT WASHINGTON

About a mile after you join Hwy 20, the lush greenery dwindles and the trees start to look like a weird art project involving charred toothpicks. This is the handiwork of a pair of wildfires – the Bear Butte Fire and the Booth Fire – that joined together in the summer of 2003 to become the B&B Complex Fire, burning over 90,000 acres of the Cascades.

It's hard not to want to stare at the devastation. But keep your eyes on the road for now, because you can pull over at the Mt Washington Viewpoint, between Miles 84 and 85. Here you'll find dramatic views of the mountains and seven interpretive signs that give you the full picture.

❽ Vida

Oregon is known for its wooden bridges, and in Vida is the state's second-longest, **Goodpasture Bridge**. A wooden truss bridge, it's painted white and looks almost like a small-town church – albeit a 237ft-long church that straddles a river. It's right on the highway, so you can stop for a picture (it is a rather good-looking bridge) or just point and say, 'Oooooh,' as you whiz past. Look for it on the left after Mile 26.

The Drive » You're on the home stretch: it's just under 30 miles to Eugene.

❾ Eugene

It's back to civilization in dynamic and liberal Eugene, full of energetic college students, pretty riverside parks and a plethora of restaurant choices.

Where to start? For great fun and a quintessential introduction to Eugene's peculiar vitality, try to time your visit to catch the **Saturday Market** (📞541-686-8885; www.eugenesaturdaymarket.org; 8th Ave & Oak St; ⏰10am-5pm Sat Apr–mid-Nov). Otherwise, wander the **5th Street Public Market** (📞541-484-0383; www.5stmarket.com; cnr 5th Ave & High St; ⏰shops 10am-7pm Mon-Sat, 11am-6pm Sun), an old mill that now anchors several dozen restaurants, cafes and boutique stores.

To wrap up your trip with a bit of culture, stop by the **Jordan Schnitzer Museum of Art** (📞541-346-3027; http://jsma.uoregon.edu; 1430 Johnson Lane; adult/child $5/free; ⏰11am-5pm Tue-Sun, to 8pm Wed). This renowned museum offers a 13,000-piece rotating permanent collection with an Asian art specialty. Highlights include a 10-panel Korean folding screen and a standing Thai Buddha in gold leaf.

✕ ⏢ p225, p243

Eating & Sleeping

Salem ❶

✖ Wild Pear
Deli $

(☎503-378-7515; www.wildpearcatering.com; 372 State St; mains $11-15; ⏰10:30am-6:30pm Mon-Sat) A popular deli, Wild Pear serves up tasty soups, sandwiches and salads, along with fancier options like a lobster melt. There's also a Greek wrap, charcuterie plate, pizzas, homemade pastries and even a traditional pho (Vietnamese noodle soup) – all combined with good, efficient service.

✖ Word of Mouth Bistro
Bistro $

(☎503-930-4285; www.wordofsalem.com; 140 17th St NE; mains $9-16; ⏰7am-3pm Wed-Sun) If crème brûlée French toast sounds good, then make a beeline for this friendly and excellent bistro. Other tasty treats include cinnamon-roll pancakes, an asparagus and Brie omelet, toasted breakfast burritos and a filet mignon Benedict. Gourmet sandwiches, salads and burgers rule the lunch menu (weekdays only).

⌂ Grand Hotel
Hotel $$

(☎503-540-7800; www.grandhotelsalem.com; 201 Liberty St SE; r from $200; ❄ @ ⏰📶🐾) This upscale hotel is next to the city's conference center. Most standard rooms have sitting areas, and all are stylish, modern and elegant. It's geared toward business travelers, with amenities like indoor pool, spa, gym, restaurant and lounge; a breakfast buffet is also included.

Bend ❺

✖ Victorian Café
Breakfast $$

(☎541-382-6411; www.victoriancafebend.com; 1404 NW Galveston Ave; mains $13-26; ⏰7am-2pm) One of Bend's best breakfast spots, the Victorian Café is especially awesome for its eggs Benedict (nine kinds). It's also good for sandwiches, burgers, salads and bloody Marys. There's really nice outdoor seating in summer. Be ready to wait for a table, especially on weekends.

✖ El Sancho
Mexican $

(☎458-206-5973; www.elsanchobend.com; 335 NE Dekalb Ave; tacos $2.75-3.25; ⏰11am-10pm) Fantastic, great-value Mexican served in a cool

atrium-like setting that opens up in summer or is heated in winter. Every taco, from the chipotle chicken to Oaxacan cheese and green chile, is as good as you'll find anywhere. Extras include fried plantains, tamales, chicken tortilla soup and kick-ass margaritas and pisco sours.

⌂ Mill Inn
Inn $

(☎541-389-9198; www.millinn.com; 642 NW Colorado Ave; d $105-170; ⏰📶) A 10-room boutique hotel with small, classy rooms decked out with velvet drapes and comforters; four share outside bathrooms. Full breakfast and hot-tub use are included, and there are nice small patios on which to hang out.

Eugene ❾

✖ Beppe & Gianni's Trattoria
Italian $$

(☎541-683-6661; www.beppeandgiannis.net; 1646 E 19th Ave; mains $15-26; ⏰5-9pm Sun-Thu, to 10pm Fri & Sat) One of Eugene's most beloved restaurants, Beppe & Gianni's serves up homemade pastas and excellent desserts. Expect a wait, especially on weekends.

✖ Krob Krua Thai Kitchen
Thai $

(☎541-636-6267; www.krobkrua.com; 254 Lincoln St; mains $7-9; ⏰11am-9pm Tue-Sun) Superb Thai curries, noodles, salads, soups and wok-fired dishes are served at this joint in the same space as **WildCraft Cider Works** (☎541-735-3506; www.wildcraftciderworks.com; ⏰11:30am-9pm Tue-Thu, to 11pm Fri & Sat, to 8pm Sun), where you can enjoy your food in the tasting room and wash it down with a cider. Spring for the Dungeness crab and shrimp dumplings, the namesake *krob krua* noodles with beef, or the green curry fried rice.

⌂ Campbell House
Inn $$$

(☎541-343-1119; www.campbellhouse.com; 252 Pearl St; r $130-350; ⏰❄ @ 📶🐾) A large inn with 20 rooms and lovely common spaces, Campbell House also has a lush garden, popular for weddings. Choose from small, cozy rooms, spacious suites with Jacuzzi and fireplace, or a two-bedroom suite. Well located on a hill in an upscale neighborhood; hot breakfast included.

Classic Trip

Oregon Cascades Scenic Byways

21

Oregon's Central Cascades are a bonanza of natural wonder. Scenic byways pack in lush forests, thundering waterfalls, snowcapped mountains, high desert and lakes galore.

TRIP HIGHLIGHTS

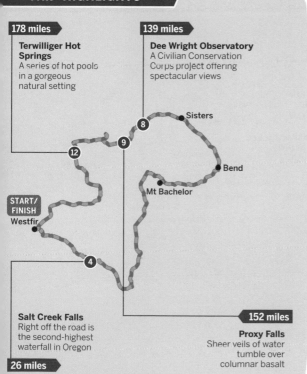

178 miles

Terwilliger Hot Springs
A series of hot pools in a gorgeous natural setting

139 miles

Dee Wright Observatory
A Civilian Conservation Corps project offering spectacular views

Sisters

8

9

12

Bend

Mt Bachelor

START/ FINISH
Westfir

4

Salt Creek Falls
Right off the road is the second-highest waterfall in Oregon

26 miles

152 miles

Proxy Falls
Sheer veils of water tumble over columnar basalt

**4 DAYS
240 MILES / 386KM**

GREAT FOR...

BEST TIME TO GO
June through September to avoid seasonal road closures.

ESSENTIAL PHOTO
Salt Creek Falls, the second-highest waterfall in Oregon.

BEST HOT SPRINGS

Terwilliger Hot Springs at Cougar Reservoir.

oxy Falls (p231) Lower Proxy Falls

21 Oregon Cascades Scenic Byways

The region around Oregon's Central Cascades is, without a doubt, some of the most spectacular terrain in the entire state. But one scenic byway just isn't enough to see it all. Here you have our version of an Oregon sampler platter: a loop that brings together several of the best roads to create a majestic route full of the state's best features.

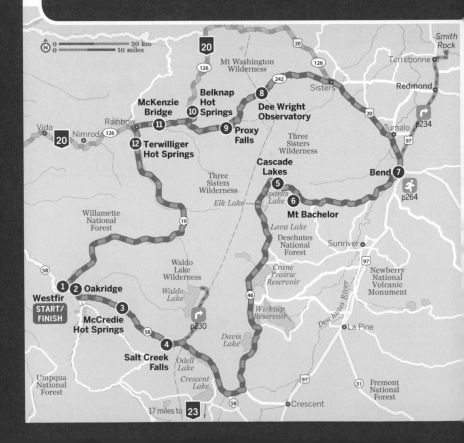

❶ Westfir

Before you spend several days enjoying abundant natural wonders, start with a quick photo op of an entirely man-made one: Oregon's longest covered bridge, the 180ft **Office Bridge**. Built in 1944, the bridge features a covered walkway to enable pedestrians to share the way with logging trucks crossing the Willamette River.

If you plan to do some exploring or mountain biking in the area, pick up a map of the Willamette National Forest at **Middle Fork Ranger Station** (☏541-782-2283; www. fs.usda.gov; 46375 Hwy 58; ⏰8am-4:30pm Mon-Fri).

LINK YOUR TRIP

20 **To Bend & Back**
One trip isn't enough to cover the Cascades; this complementary route offers alternate paths through the same countryside.

23 **Crater Lake Circuit**
Crater Lake is a must-see, and it's just south of the Cascades. Take Hwy 97 south from Bend to join this route.

The Drive » Oakridge is just a few miles to the east on either Hwy 58 or Westfir–Oakridge Rd.

🛏 p235

❷ Oakridge

Oakridge is one of Oregon's mountain-biking hot spots. There are hundreds of miles of trails around town, ranging from short, easy loops to challenging single-track routes. For novice riders, the **Warrior Fitness Trail** is a mostly flat 12-mile loop. The **Larison Creek Trail** is a challenging ride through old-growth forests, and the 16-mile **Alpine Trail** is considered the 'crown jewel' of the local trails for its 7-mile downhill stretch.

The Drive » From Oakridge, Hwy 58 climbs steadily up the Cascade Range's densely forested western slope. Your next stop is about 10 miles east of Oakridge; park on the right just past Mile Marker 45.

❸ McCredie Hot Springs

Because **McCredie Hot Springs** (☏541-782-2283; www.fs.usda.gov; Hwy 58, Oakridge; ⏰dawn-dusk) lies just off the highway, it's a very popular spot for everyone from mountain bikers fresh off the trails near Oakridge to truckers plying Hwy 58. Despite this, it's worth a stop, if only because it's the site of one of the largest – and hottest –

thermal pools in Oregon. If you can hit it early in the morning or late in the evening midweek, you could have the place to yourself.

There are five pools in all: two upper pools that are often dangerously hot (as in don't-even-dip-your-foot-in hot), two warm riverside pools and one smaller, murkier, but usually perfectly heated pool, tucked back into the trees. **Salt Creek** rushes past only steps from the springs and is ideal for splashing down with icy water.

The Drive » Keep heading east another 12 miles and pull off the highway at the signed parking lot.

TRIP HIGHLIGHT

❹ Salt Creek Falls

At 286ft, this monster of a waterfall is Oregon's second-highest. After a good snowmelt, this aqueous behemoth really roars, making for one of the most spectacular sights on the trip. Walk from the parking lot to the viewpoint and there below, in a massive basalt amphitheater hidden by the towering trees, 50,000 gallons of water pour every minute over a cliff into a giant, dark, tumultuous pool. Be sure to hike the short trail downhill toward the bottom of the falls. It's lined with rhododendrons that put on a colorful show

Classic Trip

in springtime, and the views of the falls on the way down are stunning.

Salt Creek Falls is also the starting point for some excellent short hikes, including a 1.5-mile jaunt to **Diamond Creek Falls** and a 4.75-mile walk to **Vivian Lake**.

The Drive » Continue 19 miles along Hwy 58 until you reach the Cascade Lakes Scenic Byway (Hwy 46), which winds its way north through numerous tiny lakes and up to Mt Bachelor. This road is closed from November to May; as an alternative, follow Hwy 97 to Bend.

DETOUR: WALDO LAKE

Start: ❹ Salt Creek Falls

There's no shortage of lakes in the area, but lovely Waldo Lake stands out for its amazing clarity. Because it's at the crest of the Cascades, water doesn't flow into it from other sources; the only water that enters it is rainfall and snowfall, making it one of the purest bodies of water in the world. In fact, it's so clear that objects in the water are visible 100ft below the surface. You can swim in the summer months (it's too cold in the winter), and if you're feeling ambitious after playing 'I Spy' on the lakebed, you can hike the **Waldo Lake Trail**, a 22-mile loop that circumnavigates the lake.

To get there, head 2 miles east of Salt Creek Falls on Hwy 58, and turn left at the Waldo Lake Sno-Park; follow the signs for eight more miles to the lake.

❺ Cascade Lakes

We could get all scientific and explain how lava from nearby volcanoes created the lakes around this area, or we could just tell you that Hwy 46 isn't called the Cascade Lakes Scenic Byway for nothing. The road winds past lake after beautiful lake – **Davis Lake**, **Crane Prairie Reservoir**, **Lava Lake**, **Elk Lake** – all worth a stop. Most have outstanding camping, trout fishing, boating and invigorating swimming ('invigorating' being a euphemism for *cold*).

We love **Sparks Lake** for its scenic beauty set against the backdrop of Mt Bachelor, and it's perfect for peaceful paddling. If you find yourself without a boat, **Wander-**lust Tours** (☎800-862-2862; www.wanderlusttours.com; 61535 S Hwy 97, Suite 13; day tour adult/child $80/60; ⊗8am-5pm) can hook you up with a guided canoe or kayak tour.

The Drive » Mt Bachelor is just a few miles past Sparks Lake. If Hwy 46 is closed for the season, you can backtrack from Bend to reach Mt Bachelor.

🛏 p235

❻ Mt Bachelor

Glorious Mt Bachelor (9065ft) provides Oregon's best skiing. Here, Central Oregon's cold, continental air meets up with the warm, wet Pacific air. The result is tons of fairly dry snow and plenty of sunshine, and with 370in of snow a year, the season begins in November and can last until May.

At **Mount Bachelor Ski Resort** (☎800-829-2442; www.mtbachelor.com; adult/child lift tickets $99/56, cross-country day pass $21/14; ⊗Nov-May; 🚡), rentals are available at the base of the lifts. Mt Bachelor grooms about 35 miles of cross-country trails, though the day pass may prompt skiers to check out the free trails at **Dutchman Flat Sno-Park**, just past the turnoff for Mt Bachelor on Hwy 46.

The Drive » Ready to add a little civilization to your rugged outdoor adventure? Head east to Bend, which is just 22 miles away.

JORDAN SIEMENS/GETTY IMAGES ©

Mountain biking near Bend

7 Bend

Sporting gear is de rigueur in a town where you can go rock climbing in the morning, hike through lava caves in the afternoon, and surf, on a river, into the sunset. Plus, you'll probably be enjoying all that activity in great weather, as the area gets more than 250 days of sunshine each year (don't forget the sunscreen!).

Explore downtown on foot (p264), and be sure to check out the excellent High Desert Museum (p222). It charts the exploration and settlement of the Pacific Northwest, but it's no slog through history. The fascinating Native American exhibit shows off several wigwams' worth of impressive artifacts, and the live animal exhibits and living history are sure to be hits with the kids.

The Drive » Head 22 miles north to Sisters, then drive northwest along Hwy 242. This is part of the McKenzie Pass–Santiam Pass Scenic Byway – closed during the winter months. Your next stop is 15 miles from Sisters.

✖ 🛏 p225, p235

8 Dee Wright Observatory

Perched on a giant mound of lava rock, built entirely of lava rock, in the middle of a field of lava rock, stands the historic Dee Wright Observatory. The structure, built in 1935 by Franklin D Roosevelt's Civilian Conservation Corps, offers spectacular views in all directions. The observatory windows, called 'lava tubes,' were placed to highlight all the prominent Cascade peaks that can be seen from the summit, including Mt Washington, Mt Jefferson, North Sister, Middle Sister and a host of others.

The Drive » Head west on Hwy 242 for 13 miles to Mile Marker 64 and look for the well-signed Proxy Falls trailhead.

9 Proxy Falls

With all the waterfalls around the Central Cascades – hundreds of them in Oregon alone – it's easy to feel like 'You've seen one, you've seen 'em all.' Not so fast. Grab your camera and see if you're not at least a little impressed by photogenic Proxy Falls. If there were a beauty contest for waterfalls, Proxy would certainly be in the running, scattering into sheer veils down

Classic Trip

WHY THIS IS A CLASSIC TRIP
CELESTE BRASH, WRITER

Lakes, waterfalls, hot springs, volcanos and high desert – how much more natural variety could you ask for in a road trip? I love driving these stretches of empty highway and, even more, stopping to enjoy the quiet wilderness in all its variations along the way – especially the hot springs. After outdoorsy days, nothing beats a fantastic meal and a cold beer in Bend.

Above: Sparks Lake (p230)
Left: Dee Wright Observatory (p231)
Right: Salt Creek Falls (p229)

a mossy wall of columnar basalt. It's not even like the falls make you work for it: it's an easy 1.3-mile loop from the parking area. If you want to save the best for last, take the path in the opposite direction from what the sign suggests, so you hit Upper Proxy Falls first and you can build up to the even better Lower Proxy Falls.

The Drive » Nine miles from the falls, turn right on Hwy 126 (McKenzie Hwy); Belknap is just 1.4 miles away.

🔟 Belknap Hot Springs

Although nudity is the norm at most hot springs, Belknap is the sort of hot spring resort you can take your grandmother to and neither of you will feel out of place. Two giant swimming pools filled with 103°F (40°C) mineral water provide optimum soaking conditions in a family environment. The McKenzie River rushes by below, trees tower over everything, and everyone has a good time. An excellent alternative to camping, the resort has rooms for nearly all budgets.

The Drive » Head southwest on Hwy 126 for 6 miles to reach your next stop.

🛏 p235

233

Classic Trip

⑪ McKenzie Bridge

Although from the road it looks like there is nothing but trees, there's actually plenty to do around here, including fishing on the McKenzie River and hiking on the nearby **McKenzie River National Recreation Trail**. To learn more about all your recreational options, stop at the **McKenzie Ranger Station** (☎541-822-3381; www.fs.fed.us/r6/willamette; 57600 McKenzie Hwy; ☉8am-4:30pm Mon-Sat in summer), about 2 miles east of town. The rangers are fonts of information, plus you can find everything you ever wanted to know about the McKenzie River trail, including maps and books.

↱ DETOUR: SMITH ROCK

Start: ❼ Bend

Best known for its glorious rock climbing, **Smith Rock State Park** (☎800-551-6949; www.oregonstateparks.org; 9241 NE Crooked River Dr; day-use $5) boasts rust-colored 800ft cliffs that tower over the pretty Crooked River, just 25 miles north of Bend. Non-climbers can enjoy miles of hiking trails, some of which involve a little rock scrambling.

The Drive » About 6 miles west of McKenzie Bridge, turn left on Hwy 19 (aka Aufderheide Memorial Dr) just past Rainbow. After almost 8 miles, you'll come to the parking lot from which you'll take a 0.25-mile trail through old-growth forest.

🔖 p235

TRIP HIGHLIGHT

⑫ Terwilliger Hot Springs

In a picturesque canyon in the Willamette National Forest is one of the state's most stunning hot springs. From a fern-shrouded hole, scorching water spills into a pool that maintains a steady minimum temperature of 108°F (42°C). The water then cascades into three successive pools, each one cooler than the one above it. Sitting there staring up at the trees is an utterly sublime experience. After hiking back to the car, you can even jump into Cougar Reservoir from the rocky shore below the parking lot.

The Drive » From Terwilliger Hot Springs, take Aufderheide/Hwy 19 south 41 miles to return to Westfir.

VOLCANO SIGHTS

The Cascades are a region of immense volcanic importance. Lava fields can be seen from McKenzie Pass and along Hwy 46, and road cuts expose gray ash flows. Stratovolcanoes such as South Sister and Mt Bachelor, and shield volcanoes like Mt Washington, tower over the landscape. Although it's not instantly obvious when you drive to the center of **Newberry National Volcanic Monument** (39 miles south of Bend), you're actually inside the caldera of a 500-sq-mile volcano. What could be stranger than that? It's still active.

Eating & Sleeping

Westfir ①

� Westfir Lodge
Lodge $

(☎541-782-3103; www.westfirlodge.com; 47365 1st St; d $99-199; ⊜ ❄ 🛜) A stone's throw from Oregon's longest covered bridge is this spacious B&B lodge with eight homey guest rooms. Some rooms share bathrooms down the hall. Check out the central vault, left over from when this building used to be a lumber company office.

Cascade Lakes ⑤

� Cultus Lake Resort
Cabin $$

(☎541-408-1560; www.cultuslakeresort.com; Hwy 46; cabins $85-175; ⊙mid-May–Sep; 🐾) This pleasant lakeside resort offers several homey cabins with a two-night minimum; from July 4 to Labor Day they rent by the week only. There's a restaurant (closed Monday) and marina, too. New owners are still finding their feet but have their heart in the business.

� Sparks Lake Campground
Campground

(Hwy 46; campsites free; ⊙Jul-Sep) One of the most scenically situated campgrounds on the Cascade Lakes Scenic Byway, with views of Mt Bachelor and meadows. Pit toilets available; no water. First-come, first-served.

Bend ⑦

✕ Blacksmith
American $$$

(☎541-318-0588; www.bendblacksmith.com; 211 NW Greenwood Ave; mains $16-44; ⊙4-10pm Mon-Thu, to midnight Fri & Sat, to 9pm Sun) This upscale restaurant offers cowboy comfort food with a twist, such as cider-brined pork chop with Brussels sprouts, Cajun beef medallions and grilled shrimp with housemade grits. Or you can tackle the 24oz bacon-glazed Tomahawk rib-eye ($72). Happy hour offers shrimp ceviche and three kinds of mac 'n' cheese (smoked, bacon and truffle).

✕ Deschutes Brewery & Public House
Pub $$

(☎541-382-9242; www.deschutesbrewery.com; 1044 NW Bond St; ⊙11am-10pm Sun-Thu, to midnight Fri & Sat) Bend's first microbrewery serves good, hearty food (fish-and-chips, burgers, salads) at its beautiful two-story restaurant. Noteworthy beers include Mirror Pond Pale Ale, Black Butte Porter and Obsidian Stout, as well as anything on the seasonal or pub-only menu. Deschutes' Red Chair NWPA was voted 'world's best beer' in the 2012 World Beer Awards.

� McMenamins Old St Francis School
Hotel $$

(☎541-382-5174; www.mcmenamins.com; 700 NW Bond St; r from $189; ⊜ ❄ 🛜) One of McMenamins' best venues, this old schoolhouse has been remodeled into a hotel – two rooms even have side-by-side clawfoot tubs. The fabulous tiled saltwater Turkish bath alone is worth the stay; nonguests can soak for $5. A restaurant-pub, three bars, a movie theater and artwork complete the picture.

Belknap Hot Springs ⑩

� Belknap Hot Springs Lodge
Resort $$

(☎541-822-3512; www.belknaphotsprings. com; 59296 Belknap Springs Rd; tent/RV sites $30/40, d $110-185, cabins $135-550; ⊜ ❄ ⛱ 🐾) Located 5 miles east of McKenzie Bridge, this large mountain resort has something for everyone – camping, RV sites, rustic cabins, modern lodge rooms and even mountain homes (off-site). The reason to visit or stay, however, is the spring-fed pools; nonguests pay $8/15 per hour/day.

McKenzie Bridge ⑪

� Cedarwood Lodge
Cabin $$

(☎541-822-3351; www.cedarwoodlodge. com; 56535 McKenzie Hwy; cabins $135-195; ⊙closed Nov-Apr; 🛜) Ensconce yourself in one of eight rustic, comfortable, fully equipped cabins set above the McKenzie River.

Essential I-5

22

Taking the direct route? That doesn't mean you have to miss out on Oregon's road-trip staples. Right off I-5 lie pioneer history, covered bridges and even a little Shakespeare.

TRIP HIGHLIGHTS

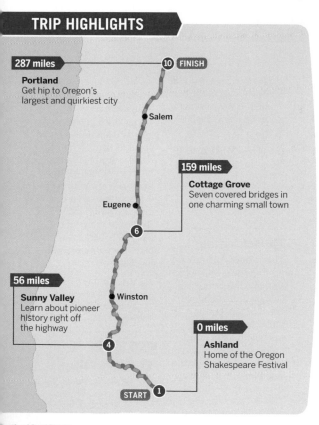

287 miles

10 FINISH

Portland
Get hip to Oregon's largest and quirkiest city

● Salem

159 miles

Cottage Grove
Seven covered bridges in one charming small town

Eugene ●

6

56 miles

Sunny Valley
Learn about pioneer history right off the highway

● Winston

4

0 miles

Ashland
Home of the Oregon Shakespeare Festival

START ● **1**

1–2 DAYS
300 MILES /
483KM

GREAT FOR...

BEST TIME TO GO

March through October, when everything is open.

 ESSENTIAL PHOTO

Any of the covered bridges of Cottage Grove.

 BEST FOR CULTURE

A night of theater at Ashland's Shakespeare Festival.

Portland Pearl District

22 Essential I-5

The word 'interstate' seldom evokes a road-tripper's dream itinerary, but I-5 will dash those preconceived notions. Oregon's major thoroughfare takes you through mountains, farmland and forests, and there's plenty to see and do along the way — provided you know which exits to take. Just off the highway, you'll find historical sites, roadside attractions and more. It's also the jumping-off place for many of Oregon's back-road gems.

TRIP HIGHLIGHT

❶ Ashland

Prithee, fair traveler, begin thine trip in Ashland, and get thee to the box office, for the players of the **Oregon Shakespeare Festival** (OSF; ☎541-482-4331; www.osfashland.org; cnr Main & Pioneer Sts; tickets $30-136; ☺Tue-Sun Feb-Oct) do strut and fret upon three stages each year from February through October. Back in the Victorian era, Ashland was known for its sulfurous mineral springs that smell not unlike rotten eggs. But now the festival's 10 productions are Ashland's primary claim to fame, drawing visitors from all over. The whole town gets in on the act, with nods to the bard found at every turn. Explore the town's historic heart on foot (p262).

The Drive » From Ashland, head 11 miles north on I-5 and take exit 30, then go west on OR-238 for 6 miles.

✕ 🛏 p243, p251

❷ Jacksonville

This former gold-prospecting town is the oldest settlement in southern Oregon and a National Historic Landmark. Small but endearing, the town's main drag, California St, is lined with well-preserved brick-and-wood buildings dating from the 1880s. But the way to get in touch with local history is to wander the 32-acre **Jacksonville Cemetery**, at the top of Cemetery Rd, which you access at East E St and N Oregon St. Its historic pioneer grave sites chronicle wars, epidemics and other causes of untimely deaths.

The Drive » Take Oregon St north and it will meet up with I-5 in Gold Hill. The well-signed Vortex is a bit over 4 miles north of Gold Hill on Sardine Creek Rd.

❸ Gold Hill

Some attractions will suck you in more than others, but Gold Hill's **Oregon Vortex** (☎541-855-1543; www.oregonvortex.com; 4303 Sardine Creek L Fork Rd; adult/child $13.50/9.75; ☺9am-4pm Mar-Oct, to 5pm Jun-Aug; 🚗) has gravitational pull on its side, luring visitors with its unexplained phenomena: how did that broom stand up on its own? What made that water run uphill? Detractors will try to explain away the mysterious events that have drawn crowds since the 1930s, but it just sounds like, 'Blah, blah, physics, blah.' Isn't it more fun to just believe?

The Drive » Backtrack to I-5 and go north 27 miles to exit 71. Sunny Valley is right off the highway.

TRIP HIGHLIGHT

❹ Sunny Valley

Sunny Valley serves as a quick, convenient

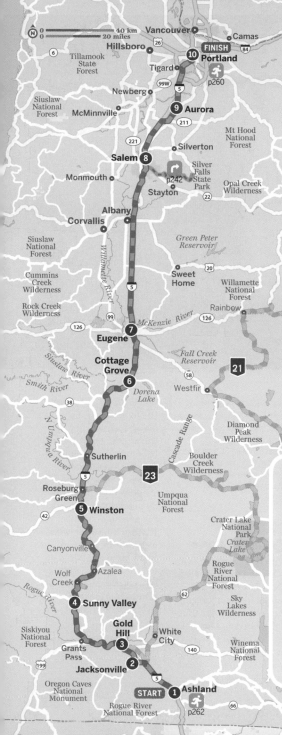

stop for a little Oregon pioneer history. Visible from the highway, you could mistake it for a Western-themed rest stop, thanks mostly to the **Applegate Trail Interpretive Center** (☎541-472-8545; www.rogueweb.com/interpretive; I-5 exit 71; $6; ⏲10:30am-4:30pm Thu-Sun late May-Sep), an excellent little museum gussied up like a spaghetti-Western storefront, where history is brought to life with taxidermy and sound effects.

If the museum's closed, you can still check out the **covered bridge** that crosses **Grave Creek** and the namesake grave itself, belonging to one Martha Crowley, a pioneer girl who died of typhoid fever on the Applegate wagon train.

The Drive » Get back on I-5 and travel 71 miles to exit 112. Take Hwy 99 N for just under 9 miles.

LINK YOUR TRIP

21 Oregon Cascades Scenic Byways

From Eugene, drive 42 miles east to Westfir to kick off a tour of some of the state's most beautiful scenery.

23 Crater Lake Circuit

Hop off at Medford for an inland loop that includes the serene and mysterious Crater Lake.

PAUL W HARVEY IV/SHUTTERSTOCK ©

❺ Winston

Tiny Winston itself isn't much of a drawcard, but 10 miles southwest is the **Wildlife Safari** (541-679-6761; www.wildlifesafari.net; 1790 Safari Rd, I-5 exit 119; adult/child $22/16; 9am-6pm;) – an animal attraction you don't even have to get out of your car for. You can drive around the 600-acre park dotted with inquisitive ostriches, camels, giraffes, lions, tigers and bears (oh, my!) among other exotic animals, then hop right back on the highway and keep driving.

The Drive » Follow OR-42 north to I-5, then travel 48 miles north to get to Cottage Grove. To get to the Mosby Creek bridges, go east on Main St, pass under I-5, then continue 2.5 miles on Mosby Creek Rd and turn left on Layng Rd to access trailhead parking.

TRIP HIGHLIGHT

❻ Cottage Grove

With seven covered bridges around town, Cottage Grove has rightfully earned its nickname of the Covered Bridge Capital of Oregon. The most famous bridge here is a small, open-top railroad trestle that had a cameo at the beginning of the movie *Stand By Me,* when the four preteen boys set off on their journey into the woods. The rails have been paved over, and the **Mosby Creek Trestle Bridge** is now part of the **Row River Trail**, easily accessible for hikers, bikers and film buffs. It's also kind of a twofer, as it crosses the creek just a couple hundred feet from Lane County's oldest covered bridge, the photogenic **Mosby Creek Bridge** built in 1920.

The Drive » Take Mosby Creek Rd back to I-5, then travel north 17.5 miles and take exit 192 for Eugene.

Cottage Grove Covered bridge

7 Eugene

Fun-loving Eugene is full of youthful energy, liberal politics and alternative lifestylers, making it a vibrant stop along your I-5 travels. Here you'll find a great art scene, exceptionally fine restaurants, boisterous festivals, miles of riverside paths and several lovely parks. A hike up wooded **Skinner Butte**, directly north of downtown, provides good orientation and a bit of exercise (though you can drive up if you're feeling lazy).

If you want to get a dose of history while you're at it, stop at the **Museum of Natural and Cultural History** (📞541-346-3024; http://natural-history.uoregon.edu; 1680 E 15th Ave; adult/child $5/3; ⏰11am-5pm Tue-Sun). Housed in a replica of a Native American longhouse, this museum contains good displays on Native American artifacts and fossils.

The Drive » Get back on I-5 and travel north 66 miles to the capital of Oregon.

✕ 🏠 p243, p225

8 Salem

Given that you're driving across the Beaver State, be sure to stop by and pay homage – perhaps even sing a few bars of 'Oregon, My Oregon' – at the **Oregon State Capitol** (📞503-986-1388; www.oregon legislature.gov; 900 Court St NE; ⏰8am-5pm Mon-Fri). The third Oregon capitol building (the first two burned down) is a sleek, deco-style structure faced with gray marble. The most notable features of the capitol are four Works Progress Administration–era murals lining the rotunda. Check the schedule – you might be able to catch a free tour.

DETOUR: SILVER FALLS STATE PARK

Start: **8** Salem

Sure, most of Oregon's 100-plus waterfalls are tucked away in the mountains, but that doesn't mean you have to take a whole separate trip. You can see 10 of them just 22 miles east of Salem at spectacular **Silver Falls State Park** (📞503-873-8681; www. oregonstateparks.org; day fee $5, tent sites/RV sites/cabins $19/29/43). Take an 8-mile loop to see them all, or skip straight to the tallest, 177ft **South Falls**.

The Drive » Take I-5 north another 20 miles, then take exit 278 toward Aurora.

 p225

9 Aurora

Originally built as a religious commune, the town of Aurora still has a common purpose, but now it's antique shops galore (rather than the Golden Rule–based teachings of founder Wilhelm Keil). Dozens of shops line the main streets with offerings that range from rustic to quirky to garage-sale-esque.

If you like your antiques big and chunky instead of dainty and fragile, then make your way immediately to the awesome **Aurora Mills Agricultural Salvage Yard** (📞503-678-6083; www.auroramills.com; 14971 First St NE; ◷10am-5pm Tue-Sun). An enormous, two-story building houses a cornucopia of vintage signs, architectural elements and dazzling miscellany that has the ability to both inspire and overwhelm.

The Drive » Aurora is practically a suburb of Portland, so hop back on I-5 and drive 25 miles to reach downtown and your final destination.

TRIP HIGHLIGHT

10 Portland

Stay for more than 10 minutes and you're bound to feel like you're in an episode of *Portlandia* at some point. Quirky, friendly and laid-back – but with a slightly disproportionate number of hipsters sporting bushy beards and skinny jeans – Portland is a must-do on any I-5 itinerary. Stop a while to experience some of the best food, art, beer and music the Pacific Northwest has to offer.

If you didn't book a room at the McMenamin brothers' Kennedy School (p243), you should at least pop into this former elementary school that's now a hotel, brewpub and movie theater. Wander the halls to check out its colorful collection of mosaics, collages and other cool artworks.

Be sure to poke around the hip boutiques, cafes, bars, bike shops and bookstores along three east-side streets: N Mississippi Ave, NE Alberta St and SE Hawthorne Blvd. Then head downtown and explore some of its best stop-offs (p260).

p243

Eating & Sleeping

Ashland ❶

✖ Standing Stone Brewery
International $$

(☎541-482-2448; www.standingstonebrewing.com; 101 Oak St; mains $15-25, small plates $3-11; ☼11am-midnight) Popular and friendly brewery-restaurant with a confusing but good menu offering everything from burgers and pizzas to BBQ ribs to tacos and enchiladas. Wash it all down with some microbrews or a cocktail. There's a great back patio, too.

⎩ Palm
Boutique Hotel $$

(☎541-482-2636; www.palmcottages.com; 1065 Siskiyou Blvd; d $141-289; ⊜❄🎐💺🐾) Fabulous small motel remodeled into 16 charming garden-cottage rooms and suites (some with kitchens). It's an oasis of green on a busy avenue, complete with grassy lawns and a saltwater pool. A house nearby harbors three large suites (from $249). Lots of ecopractices from zero gasoline use to free charging stations for electric vehicles.

⎩ Country Willows
B&B $$

(☎541-488-1590; www.countrywillowsinn.com; 1313 Clay St; d $135-225, ste $225-310; ⊜❄@🎐💺) Only minutes from downtown is this luxurious B&B on 5 acres in the 'countryside.' The nine rooms, suites and a cottage sport a mix of antiques and contemporary furniture; some suites are as big as small apartments and have a kitchenette or private deck.

Eugene ❼

✖ McMenamins North Bank
American $$

(☎541-343-5622; www.mcmenamins.com; 22 Club Rd; mains $16-32; ☼11am-11pm Sun-Thu, to midnight Fri & Sat) Gloriously located on the banks of the mighty Willamette, this relatively modest (for a McMenamins) pub-restaurant boasts some of the best views in Eugene. Grab a riverside patio table on a warm, sunny day and order a cheeseburger with the Hammerhead ale.

⎩ C'est La Vie Inn
B&B $$

(☎541-302-3014; www.cestlavieinn.com; 1006 Taylor St; r from $180; ⊜❄@🎐) This gorgeous Victorian house, run by a friendly French woman and her American husband, is a neighborhood showstopper. Beautiful antique furniture fills the living and dining areas, while the four tastefully appointed rooms (each named for a French artist) offer comfort and luxury. Hosts provide a full breakfast, as well as afternoon port and other nice touches.

Portland ❿

✖ Little Big Burger
Burgers $

(☎503-274-9008; www.littlebigburger.com; 122 NW 10th Ave; burgers $5-6; ☼11am-10pm) Owned by the same folks who own Hooters, this burger chainlet keeps things appealingly simple, with a six-item menu of mini burgers made from prime ingredients. Try a beef burger topped with cheddar, Swiss, chèvre (goat's cheese) or blue cheese, with a side of truffled fries – then wash it down with a root-beer float.

⎩ Ace Hotel
Boutique Hotel $$

(☎503-228-2277; www.acehotel.com; 1022 Harvey Milk St; s with shared bath from $200, d with private bath from $285; P⊜❄@🎐💺) A well-established brand, the Ace fuses industrial, minimalist and retro styles to great effect. From the photo booth in its lobby to the salvaged-wood furniture in its rooms, the hotel feels very chic and very Portland. There's a Stumptown coffee shop and underground bar on-site, and **Clyde Common bistro** (www.clydecommon.com; mains $25-40; ☼6-11pm Sun-Wed, to midnight Thu-Sat, brunch 10am-3pm Sat & Sun) adjoins the lobby. The location can't be beat.

⎩ Kennedy School
Hotel $$

(☎503-249-3983; www.mcmenamins.com; 5736 NE 33rd Ave, r $135-235; 🎐; 🖥/0) This former elementary school is now home to a hotel (sleep in old classrooms!), a restaurant with a great garden courtyard, several bars, a microbrewery and a movie theater. Guests can use the soaking pool for free. The whole school is decorated in the McMenamins' distinctive art style – mosaics, fantasy paintings and historical photographs.

Crater Lake Circuit

23

*Make it a (big) day trip or stay a week –
serene, mystical Crater Lake is one of Oregon's
most enticing destinations. The best route
takes you on a heavily forested, waterfall-
studded loop.*

TRIP HIGHLIGHTS

199 miles

Toketee Falls
Two tiers flow
dramatically over
columnar basalt

95 miles

Crater Lake
Clear, blue, serene –
this famous lake is like
no other

Roseburg

(6)

(4)

(3)

Medford

Ashland

START/
FINISH

Prospect
Take a short hike to
the Avenue of Giant
Boulders

57 miles

**2–3 DAYS
365 MILES / 587KM**

GREAT FOR...

BEST TIME TO GO
Late May to mid-
October, when all the
roads are open.

 **ESSENTIAL
PHOTO**
No surprise here:
Crater Lake.

 **BEST
WATERFALL**
Two-tiered Toketee
Falls is our favorite.

Crater Lake Circuit

The star attraction of this trip is Crater Lake, considered by many to be the most beautiful spot in all of Oregon. The sight of the still, clear and ridiculously blue water that fills an ancient volcanic caldera is worth the trip alone, but the drive there is lined with beautiful hikes, dramatic waterfalls and natural hot springs, all right off the highway.

❶ Ashland

A favorite base for day trips to Crater Lake, Ashland is bursting at the seams with lovely places to sleep and eat (though you'll want to book your hotel room far in advance during the busy summer months). Home of the Oregon Shakespeare Festival (p238), it has more culture than most towns its size, and is just far enough off the highway to resist becoming a chain-motel hub.

It's not just Shakespeare that makes

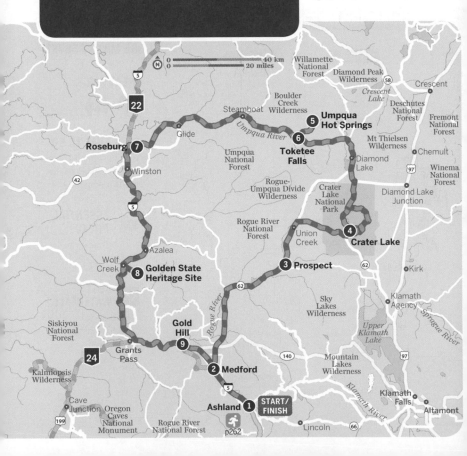

Ashland the cultural heart of southern Oregon. If you like contemporary art, check out the **Schneider Museum of Art** (☑541-552-6245; http://sma.sou.edu; 1250 Siskiyou Blvd; suggested donation $5; ⊙10am-4pm Mon-Sat).

Ashland's historic downtown and lovely **Lithia Park** make it a dandy place to go for a walk (p262) before or after your journey to Crater Lake.

The Drive » Medford is 13 miles north of Ashland on I-5.

 p243, p251

---

❷ Medford

Southern Oregon's largest metropolis is where you hop off I-5 for your trek out to Crater Lake, and it can also serve as a suitable base of operations if you want a cheap,

LINK YOUR TRIP

24 Caves of Highway 199

Go from forest to caves to beach with this trip that starts in Grants Pass, between Medford and Roseburg.

22 Essential I-5

Join up with this tour of Oregon's major thoroughfare at Ashland, Medford or Roseburg.

---

convenient place to bunk down for the night.

On your way out, check out the **Table Rocks**, impressive 800ft mesas that speak of the area's volcanic past and are home to unique plant and animal species. Flowery spring is the best time for hiking to the flat tops, which were revered Native American sites. After **TouVelle State Park** (www.oregonstateparks.org; Table Rock Rd; parking $5), fork either left to reach the trailhead to Lower Table Rock (3.5-mile round-trip hike) or right for Upper Table Rock (2.5-mile round-trip hike).

The Drive » The drive along Hwy 62 isn't much until after Shady Cove, when urban sprawl stops and forest begins. Your next stop is 45 miles northeast in Prospect.

 p251

---

❸ Prospect

No wonder they changed the name of Mill Creek Falls Scenic Area – that implies you're just going to see another waterfall

(not that there's anything wrong with that). But the real treat at **Prospect State Scenic Viewpoint** is hiking down to the **Avenue of Giant Boulders**, where the Rogue River crashes dramatically through huge chunks of rock and a little bit of scrambling offers the most rewarding views.

Take the trail from the southernmost of two parking lots on Mill Creek Dr. Keep left to get to the boulders or right for a short hike to two viewpoints for **Mill Creek Falls** and **Barr Creek Falls**. If you've got one more falls-sighting left in you, take the short hike from the upper parking lot to the lovely **Pearsony Falls**.

The Drive » Follow Hwy 62 for another 28 miles to reach the Crater Lake National Park turnoff at Munson Valley Rd.

TRIP HIGHLIGHT

❹ Crater Lake

This is it: the main highlight and reason for being of this entire trip is Oregon's most beautiful body of fresh water,

Crater Lake (☏541-594-3000; www.nps.gov/crla; 7-day vehicle pass winter/summer $15/25). This amazingly blue lake is filled with some of the clearest, purest water you can imagine – you can easily peer 100ft down – and sits inside a 6-mile-wide caldera, created when Mt Mazama erupted nearly 8000 years ago. Protruding from the water and adding to the drama of the landscape is **Wizard Island**, a volcanic cinder cone topped by its own mini crater called Witches Cauldron.

Get the overview with the 33-mile **Rim Drive** (☺Jun–mid-Oct), which offers over 30 viewpoints as it winds around the edge of Crater Lake. The gloriously still waters reflect surrounding mountain peaks like a giant dark-blue mirror, making for spectacular photographs and breath-taking panoramas.

You can also camp, ski or hike in the surrounding old-growth forests. The popular and steep mile-long **Cleetwood Cove Trail**, at the northern end of the crater, provides the only water access at the

Crater Lake National Park Crater Lake

cove. Alternatively, get up close on a two-hour **boat tour** (☎888-774-2728; www.travelcraterlake.com; Cleetwood Cove boat dock; ⏱late Jun–early Sep).

The Drive » Head north on Hwy 138 for 41 miles and turn right on Rd 34.

✕ ⊨ p251

---

❺ Umpqua Hot Springs

Set on a mountainside overlooking the North Umpqua River, Umpqua is one of Oregon's most splendid hot springs, with a little bit of height-induced adrenaline thanks to its position atop a rocky bluff.

Springs are known for soothing weary muscles, so earn your soak at Umpqua by starting with a hike – it is in a national forest, after all – where you'll be treated to lush, old-growth forest and waterfalls punctuating the landscape. Half a mile from the parking lot is the scenic **North Umpqua Trail** (www.fs.usda.gov).

The Drive » The turnout for Toketee Falls is right on Hwy 138, 2 miles past the Umpqua turnoff.

❻ Toketee Falls

More than half a dozen waterfalls line this section of the Rogue-Umpqua Scenic Byway, but the one that truly demands a stop is the stunning, two-tiered **Toketee Falls** (USFS Rd 34). The falls' first tier drops 40ft into an upper pool behind a cliff of columnar basalt, from where the water crashes another 80ft down the rock columns into yet another gorgeous, green-blue pool below. One tiny disclaimer: although the hike is just 0.4 miles, there's a staircase of 200 steps down to the viewpoint, so climbing back up to your car is a bit of a workout.

The Drive » From here, the scenery tapers back down to only moderately spectacular as you leave the Umpqua National Forest. It's just one hour to Roseburg.

❼ Roseburg

Sprawling Roseburg lies in a valley near the confluence of the South and North Umpqua Rivers. The city is mostly a cheap, modern sleepover for travelers headed elsewhere (such as Crater Lake), but it does have a cute, historic downtown area and is surrounded by award-winning wineries.

Don't miss the excellent **Douglas County Museum** (☎541-957-7007; www.umpquavalleymuseums.org; 123 Museum Dr, I-5 exit 123; adult/child $8/2; ◷10am-5pm Tue-Sat; ⛄), which displays the area's cultural and natural histories. Especially interesting are the railroad derailment photos and *History of Wine* exhibit. Kids have an interactive area and live snakes to look at.

The Drive » Go south on I-5 for 47 miles and take the Wolf Creek exit. Follow Old State Hwy 99 to curve back under the interstate. Golden is 3.2 miles east on Coyote Creek Rd.

✗ p251

❽ Golden State Heritage Site

Not ready to return to civilization quite yet? Stop off in the ghost town of **Golden**, population zero. A former mining town that had over 100 residents in the mid-1800s, Golden was built on the banks of Coyote Creek when gold was discovered there.

A handful of structures remain, as well as some newfangled interpretive signs that tell the tale of a curiously devout community that eschewed drinking and dancing, all giving a fascinating glimpse of what life was like back then. The weathered wooden buildings include a residence, the general store/post office, and a classic country church. Fun fact: the town was once used as a location for the long-running American Western TV series *Gunsmoke*.

The Drive » Go south another 45 miles on I-5 and take exit 43. The Oregon Vortex is 4.2 miles north of the access road.

❾ Gold Hill

Just outside the town of Gold Hill lies the Oregon Vortex (p238), where the laws of physics don't seem to apply – or is it all just an optical illusion created by skewed buildings on steep hillsides? However you see it, the place is definitely bizarre: objects roll uphill, a person's height changes depending on where they stand, and brooms stand up on their own...or so it seems.

Eating & Sleeping

Ashland ❶

✗ Morning Glory   Cafe $

(☎541-488-8636; 1149 Siskiyou Blvd; mains $10-17; ⏰8am-1:15pm) This casual cafe is one of Ashland's best breakfast joints. Creative dishes include crab omelet, vegetarian hash with roasted chilies, and shrimp cakes with poached eggs. For lunch there's gourmet salad and sandwiches. Go early or late to avoid a long wait.

⌂ Columbia Hotel   Hotel $$

(☎541-482-3726; www.columbiahotel.com; 262 1/2 E Main St; d $104-189; ⊜❄🛜) Awesomely located 'European-style' hotel – which means most rooms share outside bathrooms. It's an especially great deal for downtown Ashland, with 24 quaint vintage rooms (no TVs) and a historic feel. Park in back for fewer stairs to climb.

Medford ❷

✗ Organic Natural Café   Cafe $

(☎541-773-2500; www.organicnaturalcafe.com; 226 E Main St; mains $8-12; ⏰9am-7pm Mon-Sat; ⊘) Step up to the cafeteria here and order a panini-style sandwich or burger (choose from vegetarian/buffalo/organic beef). There's a salad bar, along with fresh juices and fruit smoothies. The theme – in case you haven't guessed yet – is all about local, organic and gluten-free.

✗ Porters Dining
at the Depot   American $$

(☎541-857-1910; www.porterstrainstation.com; 147 N Front St; mains $14-39; ⏰4-11pm Tue-Sat, to 10pm Sun & Mon) This gorgeous, arts-and-crafts-style restaurant is decked out in dark-wood booths and boasts an awesome patio next to the train tracks. Steak, seafood and pasta dishes dominate the menu, though the food won't blow you away. The attached bar stays open later.

Crater Lake ❹

✗ Crater Lake
Lodge Dining Room   Northwestern US $$$

(☎541-594-2255; www.craterlakelodges.com; dinner mains $24-43; ⏰7-10am, 11:30am-2:30pm & 5-9pm mid-May–mid-Oct) Crater Lake's finest dining is at the lodge, where you can feast on Northwestern cuisine from a changing menu that includes dishes like bison meatloaf and elk chops with huckleberry sauce. Try for a table with a lake view (there are only a few). Dinner reservations are recommended.

⌂ Crater Lake
Lodge   Lodge $$

(☎888-774-2728; www.craterlakelodges.com; r from $197; ⏰late May–mid-Oct; ⊜🛜) This grand old lodge has 71 simple but comfortable rooms (no TV or telephone), but it's the common areas that are most impressive. Large stone fireplaces, rustic leather sofas and a spectacular view of Crater Lake from the patio make this place special. There's a fine dining room, too.

⌂ Mazama
Campground   Campground $

(☎888-774-2728; www.craterlakelodges.com; Mazama Village; tent/RV sites $22/32; ⏰Jun–mid-Oct; 🛜📶) Located 7 miles from the lake and open approximately mid-June through September or October (depending on the weather), this is the park's main campground. There are over 200 wooded sites, showers and a laundry; some sites are first-come, first-served.

Roseburg ❼

✗ McMenamins
Roseburg
Station Pub   American $$

(☎541-672-1934; www.mcmenamins.com; 700 SE Sheridan St; mains $8-17; ⏰11am-11pm Mon-Thu, to midnight Fri & Sat, to 10pm Sun) This is a beautiful, cozy pub-restaurant in subdued McMenamins style – dark-wood paneling and lots of antique chandeliers. Typical burgers, sandwiches and salads dominate the menu. It's in an old train depot; sit and order a microbrew on the sunny patio in summer, or cozy up in the little dark bar on a bleak day.

Caves of Highway 199

24

Short but scenic, Hwy 199 strings together a hit parade of natural wonders, from wildflower-covered mountain trails to marble caves and redwood forests, culminating in the Pacific Coast.

TRIP HIGHLIGHTS

150 miles

Jedediah Smith Redwoods State Park
An impressive grove of old-growth redwoods

62 miles

Kerby
Stop if for no other reason than the It's a Burl Gallery

START
Grants Pass

4

Cave Junction

6

8

FINISH
Crescent City

Oregon Caves National Monument
Duck, shimmy and climb through this underground wonder

83 miles

2 DAYS
154 MILES / 248KM

GREAT FOR...

BEST TIME TO GO
April through October, when the caves are open.

ESSENTIAL PHOTO
You, on the banks of the scenic Smith River.

BEST BOTANY LESSON
Check out the carnivorous *Darlingtonia* plant on the Eight Dollar Mountain Boardwalk Trail.

Jedediah Smith Redwoods State Park (p258)

Caves of Highway 199

Think Hwy 199 is just a convenient connector from the interstate to the coast and Hwy 101? Well, you could buzz through it in a couple of hours and think, 'My, what pretty trees we passed.' But take your time and you'll discover an amazing amount of natural diversity, all conveniently packaged into one compact area. Prepare to picnic, hike, climb, swim and explore all along the Redwood Hwy.

❶ Grants Pass

As a modern and not particularly scenic city, Grants Pass isn't a huge tourist destination, but its location on the banks of the Rogue River makes it a portal to adventure. White-water rafting, fine fishing and jet-boat excursions are the biggest attractions, and there's good camping and hiking in the area. If you're here on a Saturday between mid-March and Thanksgiving, be sure to check out the **Outdoors Growers' Market** (www.

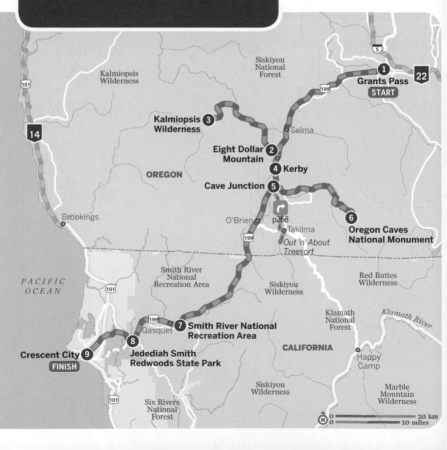

growersmarket.org; cnr 4th & F Sts; ⏰9am-1pm Sat mid-Mar–late-Nov), a farmers and craft market that draws the city together.

Since the theme of this trip is caves, be sure to stop by the **visitor center** and snap a picture with the local caveman statue for posterity.

The Drive » Take Hwy 199 24 miles southwest and turn right on Eight Dollar Rd, just 3.5 miles past Selma. The trailheads mentioned in the next stop are less than a mile from the turnout.

 p259

② Eight Dollar Mountain

If seeing some rare, carnivorous plants would just about make your trip, you've come to the right place. This area is

LINK YOUR TRIP

14 Highway 101 Oregon Coast

From Crescent City, drive 26 miles north to Brookings to kick off your Oregon coastal adventure.

22 Essential I-5

Grants Pass is right on this major thoroughfare that gets you where you're going and has some fun along the way.

one of the only places on earth where you'll find the *Darlingtonia californica* (also called the Pitcher Plant, the Cobra Lily and 'that little plant that eats bugs'). Beautiful and deadly (but not to humans), this lily-like plant gobbles up insects and digests them. The **Eight Dollar Mountain Boardwalk Trail** offers easy viewing of the *Darlingtonia* with a gentle stroll on a boardwalk trail – or if you refuse to be coddled, opt for the still-not-that-strenuous 1-mile hike that overlooks the Illinois River.

The Drive » Continue west on USFS Rd 4201 (Eight Dollar Rd). The next stop is 16 long, winding miles from the boardwalk, taking a little over an hour to navigate.

③ Kalmiopsis Wilderness

One of Oregon's largest wilderness areas, the remote Kalmiopsis Wilderness is famous for its rare plant life. About 150 million years ago, the area was separated from North America by a wide gulf and vegetation evolved on its own, so by the time the mountains fused to the continent, the plant life was very different from that of the mainland. These unique plant species are showcased on the steep, 0.75-mile hike to **Babyfoot**

Lake. In addition to the carnivorous *Darlingtonia,* the pink-flowered *Kalmiopsis leachiana* and rare Port Orford cedar are found almost nowhere else on earth.

The Drive » Backtrack to US 199. Turn right and go 2.7 miles south to Kerby.

TRIP HIGHLIGHT

④ Kerby

With a population of just 400 – and sometimes listed as a ghost town – tiny Kerby still has a surprising amount going for it. First of all, there's the **Kerbyville Museum** (📞541-592-5252; 24195 Redwood Hwy; adult/child $5/2; ⏰11am-3pm Tue-Sat, noon-3pm Sun Apr-Oct), which is located in an 1880s pioneer home and offers insight into pioneer life and Native American history.

And for real roadside fun, try the whimsical **It's a Burl Gallery** (📞800-548-7064; 24025 US 199; ⏰8am-5pm), which looks like a hobbit home right on the highway. Part gallery, part attraction, it features fantastical carvings, driftwood sculptures and elaborate tree houses. At the very least, stop by and admire the garden gallery.

The Drive » Go 2.4 short miles south on US 199 to the town of Cave Junction.

 p259

❺ Cave Junction

Relatively bustling among the towns along US 199, Cave Junction is the jumping-off point for the Oregon Caves National Monument. The local terroir – taking advantage of both coastal and inland climates – lends itself nicely to Pinot Noir and Chardonnay, which you can sample at several local wineries.

While you're out here in the middle of nowhere, stop in to **Taylor's Country Store** (📞541-592-5358; http://taylorsausage.com; 202 S Redwood Hwy; mains $3-12; 🕑6am-7pm Mon-Thu, to 8:30pm Fri, 7am-7pm Sat, 8am-7pm Sun). It looks like a hole in the wall from outside, but opens up to a bustling store and restaurant surrounding a meat counter. Meals are amazingly cheap, it's a very local scene and it even has live music on Friday nights. The family have been making their sausages with recipes from their European ancestors since the 1930s.

The Drive ›› Drive southeast on OR-46 for 19 miles.

🍴 🛏 p259

TRIP HIGHLIGHT

❻ Oregon Caves National Monument

The 'Marble Halls of Oregon' are the highlight of any US 199 trip. During your spelunking adventure at **Oregon Caves National Monument** (📞541-592-2100; www.nps.gov/orca; 19000 Caves Hwy; tours adult/child $10/7; 🕑tours 9am-6pm Jun-Aug, closed Dec-Mar, hours vary rest of year), expect to climb, twist, duck and wiggle your way through the 3 miles of passages and stairs on the 90-minute tour. Your reward is myriad cave formations, such as cave popcorn, pearls, moon milk, classic pipe organs, columns and stalactites.

Guided tours run at least hourly – half-hourly in July and August. Dress warmly, wear good shoes and be prepared to get dripped on. For safety reasons, children less than 42in tall are not allowed on tours.

A handful of short nature trails surround the area, such as the 0.75-mile **Cliff Nature Trail** and the 3.3-mile **Big Tree Trail**, which loops through old-growth forest to a huge Douglas fir.

The Drive ›› Backtrack to US 199 and head south. After about 15 minutes you'll cross the state line into California. The Smith River Information Center is 34 miles southwest of Cave Junction.

🛏 p259

---

❼ Smith River National Recreational Area

For about 16 miles, Smith River weaves back and forth alongside the Redwood Hwy, making this stretch of the **Six Rivers National Forest** the prettiest part of the drive. In summer you can stop off for a swim in the clear, emerald waters; in winter you can try to land a trophy-sized salmon or steelhead (or at least something modest for dinner).

DETOUR: TREETOP TREK

Start: ❺ Cave Junction

Why settle for a motel when you can sleep in a tree house? The **Out 'n' About Treesort** (📞541-592-2208; www.treehouses.com; 300 Page Creek Rd; tree houses $150-330; 😊) in Takilma, near Cave Junction, offers 16 different kinds of tree houses that sleep between two and six guests. If your fear of heights or the booked-up rooms (reservations are crucial) are keeping you from a treetop sleepover, consider stopping by for a **zipline** or a **horseback trail ride**.

Oregon Caves National Monument Passageway

Short, easy and right off the highway, the 2-mile **Myrtle Creek Trail** (www.redwoodparksconservancy.org; US 199 & South Fork Rd) is a popular hike that's lush and green. As you traipse through wildflowers, ferns, cedars and red alder, look for unusual species that will bring out the botany enthusiast in you.

To learn more about the area, stop by the **Smith River Information Center** (☎707-457-3131; www.fs.usda.gov; 10600 US 199, Gasquet; ☺8am-4:30pm Mon-Fri).

The Drive ≫ Drive 9.2 miles west on US 199 to get to the Jedediah Smith Redwoods State Park visitor center.

The Drive ≫ Go 4.5 miles west to the junction of Hwy 101, then take 101 south 4.5 more miles into Crescent City.

TRIP HIGHLIGHT

❽ Jedediah Smith Redwoods State Park

Tree-huggers can find plenty to hug in this forest filled with centuries-old redwoods, spruce, hemlock and Douglas firs – and with 20 miles of hiking and nature trails, there's a lot to explore, even if you choose not to canoodle. **Jedediah Smith Redwoods State Park** (☎707-465-7335; www.parks.ca.gov; Hwy 199, Hiouchi; day-use parking fee $8; ☺sunrise-sunset; **P**) is a blissfully undeveloped spot full of old-growth redwoods, which can grow up to 300ft tall. The park's best scenery can be found at **Stout Grove**. To get there, go south on South Fork Rd. After half a mile, turn right on Douglas Park Rd then continue onto the narrow, unpaved Howland Hill Rd for one of the best redwood routes anywhere.

❾ Crescent City

You've made it! After nonstop trees, mountains and rivers, you get a change of pace when US 199 dead-ends at the Pacific Ocean. Slightly scruffy Crescent City is hardly the crown jewel of the Pacific Coast, but **Beachfront Park** (Howe Dr; **P**) is a great harborside beach for families, with picnic tables, a bicycle trail and no waves.

The **Battery Point Lighthouse** (☎707-464-3089; www.delnortehistory.org; South A St; adult/child $5/1; ☺10am-4pm Apr-Sep, 10am-4pm Sat & Sun Oct-Mar) offers tours, but only at low tide, and only April through September. But if you luck out (call first) you'll see the keeper's quarters and over 150 years of artifacts, plus a spectacular ocean view from the top.

Nearby, you can hike through the wetlands at the 5000-acre **Tolowa Dunes State Park** to find sand dunes, beaches strewn with driftwood, two lakes and more than 250 species of birds.

✖ ⊨ p259

Eating & Sleeping

Grants Pass ❶

✕ Taprock   American $$

(☎541-476-2501; www.taprock.com; 971 SE
6th St; mains $12-31; ☺8am-10pm) Gorgeous,
multimillion-dollar restaurant perched above
the Rogue River. The menu has something
for everyone – steaks, burgers, seafood,
sandwiches and salads. There's also breakfast
and awesome deck seating with water views.

🛏 Buona Sera Inn   Motel $

(☎541-476-4260; www.buonaserainn.com; 1001
NE 6th St; s/d from $67/74; ☻🛜🛏) Lovingly
renovated motel with 14 comfortable, and even
slightly luxurious, country-style rooms. All have
quality linens and boast a fridge and microwave;
some come with kitchenette.

Kerby ❹

🛏 Kerbyville Inn   B&B $

(www.kerbyvilleinn.com; 24304 Redwood Hwy;
r $85-125; ❄🛜) The five suites here are all
very spacious and have kitchenettes and spa
tubs. Each is named after a wine – Chardonnay,
Burgundy and so on. The owners are super-
friendly. Bookable through www.airbnb.com.

Cave Junction ❺

✕ Wild River Brewing
& Pizza Co   Pizza $$

(☎541-592-3556; www.wildriverbrewing.com;
249 N Redwood Hwy; pizzas $10-29, sandwiches
$5-9; ☺11am-9pm Mon-Thu, to 10pm Fri & Sat,
noon-9pm Sun) This is a link in a small but good
restaurant-brewery chain. There are large
family tables inside, but if it's sunny, the back
deck (overlooking a creek) is the place to be.
Lots of sandwiches are available, too.

🛏 Country Hills
Resort   Campground, Cabin $$

(☎541-592-3406; www.countryhillsresort
com; 7901 Caves Hwy; tent/RV sites $18/32,
r/cabins from $70/90; 🛜) This rustic resort

has five country-style, dimly lit motel rooms
and six cabins that come with kitchenettes. It
also offers beautiful creekside camping and
full-hookup RV sites. It's 8 miles from Cave
Junction, on the way to Oregon Caves; reserve
ahead in summer. Don't rely on the wi-fi to work.

Oregon Caves National Monument ❻

🛏 Oregon Caves Chateau   Lodge $$

(☎541-592-3400; www.oregoncaveschateau.
com; 20000 Caves Hwy; r $117-212; ☺May-Oct;
☻) Situated near the entrance to the Oregon
Caves, this impressive, historic lodge has huge
windows facing the forest, 23 simple, vintage
rooms and a fine restaurant (open 5:30pm to
8pm) overlooking a plunging ravine. Snacks
and great milkshakes are served at the old-
fashioned soda fountain (open 7am to 5pm). It
was closed for repairs at time of research but
scheduled to reopen by summer 2020.

Crescent City ❾

✕ Good Harvest Cafe   American $

(☎707-465 6028; 575 Hwy 101 S; mains $7-16;
☺7:30am-9pm Mon-Sat, from 8am Sun; 🖉🐾)
This popular family owned cafe is in a spacious
location across from the harbor. It's got a bit of
everything – all pretty good – from soups and
sandwiches to full meals and smoothies. Fine
beers, a crackling fire and loads of vegetarian
options make this among the best dining spots
in town.

🛏 Curly Redwood Lodge   Motel $

(☎707-464-2137; www.curlyredwoodlodge.
com; 701 Hwy 101 S; r $79-107; 🅿☻❄🛜)
The motel is a marvel: its paneling came from
a single curly redwood tree that measured over
18ft thick in diameter. Progressively restored
and polished into a gem of mid-20th-century
kitsch, the inn is like stepping into a time
capsule and a delight for retro junkies. Rooms
are clean, large and comfortable (request one
away from the road).

STRETCH
YOUR LEGS
PORTLAND

Start/Finish Stumptown Coffee Roasters

Distance 2 miles

Duration 3 hours

With green spaces galore, the world's largest independent bookstore, art, handcrafted beer, a vibrant food culture and a livability rating that's off the charts, Portland is made for walking. This route takes you to the highlights of downtown.

Take this walk on Trips

Coffee & Doughnuts

Start with coffee at **Stumptown Coffee Roasters** (www.stumptowncoffee.com; 128 SW 3rd Ave; ◔6am-7pm Mon-Fri, 7am-7pm Sat & Sun; 🛜), which has been roasting its own beans since 1999. A minute's walk away is **Voodoo Doughnut** (www.voodoo doughnut.com; 22 SW 3rd Ave; doughnuts from $2; ◔24hr), which bakes quirky treats.'

The Walk » Head toward the waterfront on pedestrian-only SW Ankeny St.

Saturday Market & Tom McCall Waterfront Park

Victorian-era architecture and the lovely **Skidmore Fountain** give the area beneath the Burnside Bridge near-European flair. Hit it on a weekend to catch the chaotic **Saturday Market** (www. portlandsaturdaymarket.com; 2 SW Naito Pkwy; ◔10am-5pm Sat, 11am-4:30pm Sun Mar-Dec), an outdoor crafts fair with yummy food carts. From here you can explore the **Tom McCall Waterfront Park** (Naito Pkwy) along the Willamette River.

The Walk » Walk north under the Burnside Bridge through the park, then turn left on NW Couch St and right into NW 3rd Ave.

Chinatown

The ornate **Chinatown Gateway** (cnr W Burnside St & NW 4th Ave) define the southern edge of Portland's so-called Chinatown – but you'll be lucky to find any Chinese people here at all. The main attraction is the **Lan Su Chinese Garden** (www.lansugarden.org; 239 NW Everett St; adult/student $11/8; ◔10am-7pm mid-May–mid-Oct, to 5pm mid-Oct–mid-Mar, to 6pm mid-Mar–mid-May), a one-block haven of tranquility, ponds and manicured greenery. For a drink with a view, head to the rooftop bar of the Hoxton hotel, **Tope** (www.thehoxton.com; 15 NW 4th Ave; tacos $4.25-5.25, snacks $2-19; ◔4-10pm Sun & Mon, to 11pm Tue-Thu, to midnight Fri & Sat).

The Walk » Make your way west on NW Davis St to NW 8th Ave.

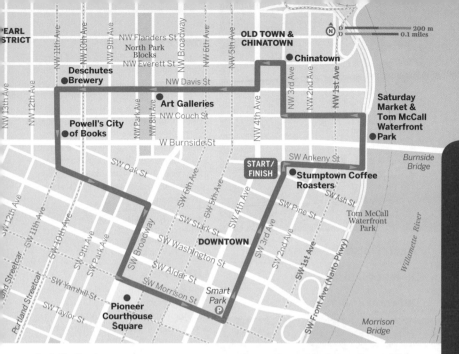

Art Galleries

Several top-notch galleries can be found on this block. They're open late the first Thursday of each month, when new exhibits open and crowds of appreciative gawpers stroll through the area.

The Walk » Continue up NW Davis St to NW 11th Ave.

Deschutes Brewery

Since walking makes you thirsty and you're in Beervana (a group is lobbying to make this Portland's official name), it's high time for a pint and/or lunch. Grab a table under the arches framing the restaurant at **Deschutes Brewery** (www.deschutesbrewery.com; 210 NW 11th Ave; ⊙11am-10pm, to midnight Fri & Sat).

The Walk » Walk south on NW 11th Ave one block to find yourself in the Pearl District's upmarket shopping area.

Powell's City of Books

Powell's City of Books (www.powells.com; 1005 W Burnside St; ⊙9am-11pm) is, until someone proves otherwise, the world's largest independent bookstore. Find a whole, awe-inspiring city block of new and used titles and prepare to get lost.

The Walk » Cross W Burnside St then turn left on SW Stark St and right on SW Broadway to SW Morrison St.

Pioneer Courthouse Square

End your walk in the heart of downtown Portland. This brick plaza is nicknamed 'Portland's living room' and is the most visited public space in the city. When it isn't full of hacky-sack players, sunbathers or office workers lunching, the square hosts concerts, festivals, rallies, farmers markets – and even summer Friday-night movies, **Flicks on the Bricks** (https://thesquarepdx.org/events; ⊙7pm Fri Jul & Aug). Around the square is an endless array of shopping, restaurants and food carts.

The Walk » Head east three blocks down SW Morrison St, turn left on SW 3rd Ave and in six blocks you'll be back at Stumptown Coffee Roasters.

261

STRETCH YOUR LEGS
ASHLAND

Start/Finish Town Plaza

Distance 2 miles

Duration 2 hours

With a historic downtown right on the edges of a beautifully designed park, Ashland's best assets are all within easy walking distance of each other – including the ever-popular Oregon Shakespeare Festival.

Take this walk on Trips

Town Plaza

People have been 'taking the waters' in Ashland ever since a lithia-water spring was discovered in 1907; early visitors flocked here to enjoy its supposed health benefits. Sample the coveted mineral water at the **Lithia Fountain** on the Town Plaza, or just enjoy watching unsuspecting tourists take a drink and quickly spit it out: the water tastes and smells like rotten eggs, and just to enhance the experience, it's also carbonated.

The Walk » Right behind the plaza is the northern tip of Lithia Park. Head south to explore the 1.4-mile stretch of greenery; because it's so narrow, it's hard to get lost.

Lithia Park

Listed on the National Register of Historic Places, fetching Lithia Park has been around since 1892. The 93-acre park got a dramatic upgrade in 1914, thanks to the hiring of Golden Gate Park's John McLaren as landscape architect. Today the park includes fountains, a Japanese garden, tennis courts, a duck pond and a band shell – not to mention miles of tree-lined trails. Enjoy colorful blossoms in spring, lush greenery in summer and dazzling, changing colors in fall.

The Walk » When you're done exploring the park, head back to the plaza and turn right on E Main St. One short block later, turn right on Pioneer St.

Shakespeare Theatres

Even if you don't have tickets to the Oregon Shakespeare Festival (p238), you can join the fun during festival season. Plan ahead to catch a **backstage tour** that takes you behind the scenes of the three stages, including the outdoor Elizabethan stage. For something more spur-of-the-moment, there are free, half-hour **Green Shows** (www.osfashland. org/greenshow; 15 S Pioneer St; ☻6.45pm Tue-Sun Jun–mid-Oct) in the festival courtyard before each night's performance.

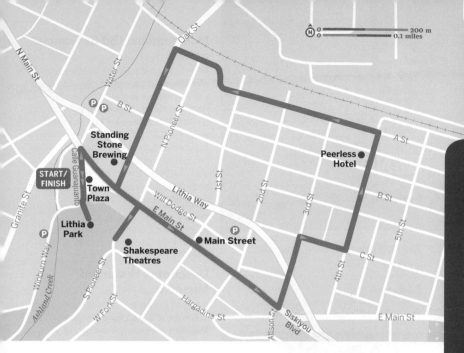

The Walk » Make your way back to Main St and turn right again to explore the historic downtown.

Main Street

The few blocks of Main St between Oak St and N 3rd St are the heart of town, lined with historical buildings that have been turned into shops, cafes and fun boutiques. The 1910 Columbia Hotel (p251) is Ashland's oldest hotel and it contains the oldest phone booth in Oregon, complete with pressed-tin ceiling.

The Walk » Keep heading east until you reach N 3rd St, then turn left. Turn right on C St, then left on N 4th St. You'll pass a mishmash of commercial buildings as you head toward the old rail yard area.

Peerless Hotel

Built in 1900, the **Peerless Hotel** (☏541-488-1082; www.peerlesshotel.com; 243 4th St; d $199-310; ☻✲☎) started as a modest boarding house for railroad workers, with 10 rooms and one bath. The build-

ing was restored (and baths added) in 1994, and the process included uncovering and restoring the photogenic, 10ft-tall Coca-Cola sign painted on the exterior brick walls back in 1915.

The Walk » Head west along A St to make your way through the historic railroad district. Turn left on Oak St and get ready for refreshments.

Standing Stone Brewery

Sure, there's the craft microbrew made right on the premises. And, yes, there's the sampler tray that lets you try six at once. But Standing Stone Brewery (p243) is about more than just beer: the varied menu offers everything from nachos to Thai curry to wild salmon, and there's a kids' menu with lots of non-beer drink options. There's even live music on the back patio during the summer.

The Walk » Just south is the Town Plaza, where you began the walk.

STRETCH YOUR LEGS
BEND

Start/Finish McMenamins Old St Francis School

Distance 2 miles

Duration 2 hours

Pretty, compact and occasionally even a little sleepy, downtown Bend has a friendly, laid-back vibe and a small-town feel. Discover public art, quirky businesses, bustling brewpubs and local history on this 2-mile tour of downtown.

Take this walk on Trips

McMenamins Old St Francis School

Former students would hardly recognize their old parochial school today, with its quirky murals, fantastical light fixtures and pronounced sense of whimsy. McMenamins Old St Francis School (p235) has been repurposed as a fun-loving hotel, but you don't have to be an overnight guest to enjoy recess. The movie theater, brewpub, outdoor bar and Turkish soaking pool are all open to the public.

The Walk » From the front doors of the school, go left and follow Bond St two short blocks southwest to Idaho Ave, where you'll find the next stop between Bond St and Wall St.

Deschutes Historical Museum

Located in another former grade-school building, the **Deschutes Historical Museum** (www.deschuteshistory.org; 129 NW Idaho Ave; adult/child $5/2; ☺10am-4:30pm Tue-Sat) has plenty to teach you about local history, showing off historical photos and artifacts that illuminate the lives of pioneers, Native Americans, loggers and everyday citizens.

The Walk » Cross Wall St to admire the historic Trinity Episcopal Church. Head northeast on Wall St then go left on Louisiana Ave to Drake Park.

Drake Park

Nature's never far away in Bend; if you can't hit the trails, slopes or river, Drake Park provides a quick fix right downtown. The Deschutes River flows through the park, slowing briefly to form scenic **Mirror Pond**. Grab a bench, spread a picnic, feed the geese or stroll the paths of this pretty, tree-lined park surrounded by some of Bend's most attractive arts-and-crafts homes. If you're lucky, you might catch a performance of **Shakespeare in the Park** (www.shakespearebend.com; tickets $25-75; ☺late Aug).

The Walk » Cross the pedestrian bridge and continue on Nashville Ave for three blocks.

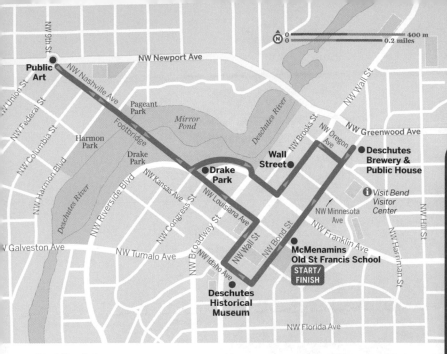

Public Art

In the roundabout at the intersection of Newport Ave and Nashville Ave is a metal horse sculpture called *Bueno Homage to the Buckaroo*. It's part of the **Roundabout Art Route** (www.roundabout artroute.com), which has beautified 20 local roundabouts with large-scale sculptures. This is the only one that's walking distance from downtown, but it might inspire you to jump in your car and visit them all.

The Walk » Double back across the river over the pedestrian bridge, turning left on the path that follows Riverside Blvd. When the path ends, continue onto Franklin Ave and turn left on Wall St one block later.

Wall Street

Bend's charming downtown is epitomized in the stretch of Wall St between Franklin Ave and Oregon Ave. Wander in and out of stores and boutiques and check out the historic **Tower Theatre** (www.towertheatre.org; 835 NW Wall St), built in 1940. Be sure to stop and indulge your sweet tooth (as well as any children you may have in tow) at **Cravin's Candy Emporium** (www.powellsss.com; 818 NW Wall St; ⏰10am-9pm Mon-Sat, to 8pm Sun; 👫).

The Walk » Go right on Oregon Ave and left on Bond St, another street with lots of shops to explore; the brewery will be half a block down on your right.

Deschutes Brewery & Public House

The Deschutes Brewery & Public House (p235) is just one stop on the 'Bend Ale Trail,' a group of several local microbreweries that will help you reach 'beervana.' The best way to experience its extensive beer menu? The six-beer sampler – though choosing even six can be difficult. The food is no afterthought: the brewery serves a wide range of way-better-than-pub grub.

The Walk » Follow Bond St southwest to return to your starting point.

British Columbia

Follow winding roads into the deep forests of
northern Vancouver Island, where bald eagles
patrol and black bears munch dandelions,
or point your wheels north toward Whistler,
where dramatic glazed mountaintops scrape
the sky. Then coast back down to explore
dynamic Vancouver or quaint Victoria. Healthy
living reaches its zenith in British Columbia
(BC). You'll eat well, drink well and play
well. From islands to glaciers to world-class
vineyards, this region beckons for road trips
and doesn't disappoint.

Capilano Suspension Bridge (p273)
PETER ADAMS/GETTY IMAGES ©

267

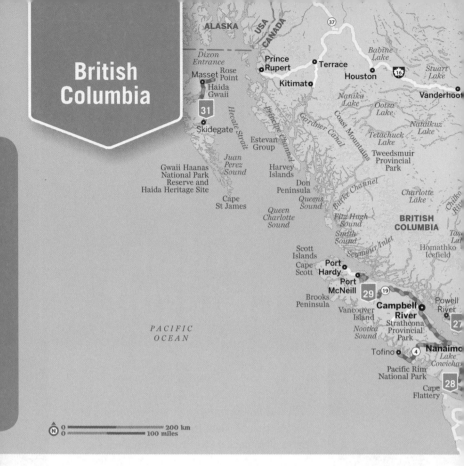

British Columbia

ALASKA
USA
CANADA

Dixon Entrance
Prince Rupert • Terrace
Masset Rose Point
Haida Gwaii
Kitimat
Houston
Babine Lake
Stuart Lake
Vanderhoof

Skidegate
Nanika Lake
Ootsa Lake
Natalkuz Lake
Tetachuck Lake
Tweedsmuir Provincial Park

Hecate Strait
Juan Perez Sound
Estevan Group
Harvey Islands
Don Peninsula
Queens Sound

Gwaii Haanas National Park Reserve and Haida Heritage Site
Cape St James
Queen Charlotte Sound
Fitz Hugh Sound
Smith Sound
Charlotte Lake
Chilko River

BRITISH COLUMBIA

Scott Islands
Cape Scott
Port Hardy
Port McNeill
Brooks Peninsula
Vancouver Island
Nootka Sound
Seymour Inlet
Homathko Icefield

PACIFIC OCEAN

Campbell River
Strathcona Provincial Park
Powell River

Tofino
Pacific Rim National Park
Nanaimo
Lake Cowichan
Cape Flattery

0 ——— 200 km
0 ——— 100 miles

DON'T MISS

First Nations Culture

With state-of-the-art museums, art galleries, totem poles and modern communities, Native culture is accessible on Trips **26** **29** **31**

Local Refreshments

In-house roasted coffee, local breweries, countless wineries and unique cideries will tempt your taste buds on Trips **27** **28** **30**

Dramatic Beaches

Long Beach with its endless sand, remote Botanical Beach and forested China Beach await on Trips **28** **29**

Ancient Forests

Looking up at the towering old-growth trees in Cathedral Grove, Goldstream Provincial Park and Capilano will leave you dizzy on Trips **25** **27** **29**

Wildlife

While never a sure bet, you have a chance to spot a bear, a bald eagle or a pod of whales on Trips **28** **29** **32**

31 **Haida Gwaii Adventure 2 Days**
Experience remote wilderness and fascinating First Nations culture on these edge-of-the-earth islands.

32 **Around the Kootenays 5–6 Days**
Admire alpine meadows and rugged sawtooth ridges, with scenic lakes and nice towns in between.

Vancouver & the Fraser Valley

25

This tour has something for everyone – parks, beaches, mountains, vineyards, hot springs and a big dollop of history, starting with an exploration of the coveted oceanfront city of Vancouver.

TRIP HIGHLIGHTS

7 km

Capilano Cliffwalk
Exhilarating glass-and-steel walkway that makes tightrope walking seem a cinch

11 km

Grouse Mountain Nature Reserve
Orphaned grizzlies, domesticated wolves, owls, beehives and more

3

2

1

START

FINISH

North Vancouver

Burnaby

4

Mission

Harrison Hot Springs

Stanley Park Seawall
Fresh air and to-die-for views, all on Vancouver's doorstep

0 km

Fort Langley
Step back in time and experience BC at its birth

67 km

2 DAYS
186KM / 116 MILES

GREAT FOR...

BEST TIME TO GO
June to September for warm days and ripened fruit.

ESSENTIAL PHOTO
Wobbling over the Capilano Suspension Bridge.

BEST FOR FAMILIES
Fort Langley offers family fun for all ages. And you might strike it rich panning for gold!

25

Vancouver & the Fraser Valley

As you step onto the swinging Capilano Suspension Bridge, get eyed up by a grizzly bear atop Grouse Mountain or watch your children hone their bartering skills over wolverine skins at Fort Langley, you might wonder what happened to the promised pretty valley drive. But don't worry; it's here. With dramatic mountains rising on either side, a tour along the Fraser River is as action-packed as it is scenic.

TRIP HIGHLIGHT

❶ Stanley Park

Just steps from downtown Vancouver (also worth a walk around; p340), but seemingly worlds away, **Stanley Park** (www.vancouver.ca/parks; West End; P ⛨; ☒19) is a spectacular urban oasis, covered in a quarter of a million trees that tower up to 80m (260ft). Rivaling New York's Central Park, this peninsula is a favorite hangout for locals, who walk, run or cycle around the 9km

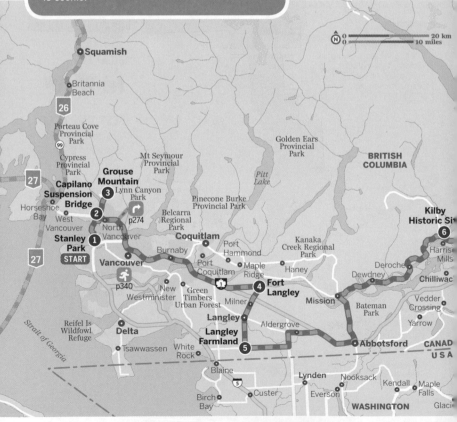

(5.5-mile) super-scenic **seawall** that circles the outer edge of the park. The pathway offers shimmering views of Burrard Inlet and passes impressive **totem poles**, squat **Brockton Point Lighthouse** and log-strewn **Third Beach**, where you can also take a dip. Watch for the dramatic **Siwash Rock**, standing sentry off the western shoreline. Meaning 'he is standing up,' it was named after a traditional First Nations legend that indicates it is a man transformed into

stone; the hole in the rock is where he kept his fishing tackle.

Looking out across tree-fringed English Bay, Second Beach has a heated outdoor **swimming pool** (open May to September) that's wildly popular with families. From here, a long sandy beach stretches south along Beach Ave. Looking for some kid-friendly action? The park's eastern shoreline is home to a fantastic **water park** (Lumberman's Arch; ⊙10am-6pm Jun-Sep; 👪) that will keep your youngsters happily squealing for hours.

Also in the park is the ever-popular **Vancouver Aquarium** (📞604-659-3400; www.vanaqua.org; 845 Avison Way; adult/child C$38/21, ⊙9:30am-6pm Jul & Aug, 10am-5pm Sep-Jun; 👪; 🚌19). One of the city's biggest attractions, it's home to penguins, otters and a plethora of BC marine critters.

The Drive » Head north on Stanley Park Causeway and cross the beautiful Lions Gate Bridge to North Vancouver.

Head east on Marine Dr for a block and turn left onto Capilano Rd, heading north for 2.4km (1.5 miles).

🛏 p277

- - - - - - - - - - - - - - - -

TRIP HIGHLIGHT

❷ Capilano Suspension Bridge

Not for the faint of heart, **Capilano Suspension Bridge Park** (📞604-985-7474; www. capbridge.com; 3735 Capilano Rd, North Vancouver; adult/ child C$47/15; ⊙8am-8pm May-Aug, reduced hours; 🅿 👪; 🚌236) is home to one of the world's longest (140m/460ft) and highest (70m/230ft) pedestrian suspension bridges, swaying gently over the roiling waters of Capilano Canyon. As you gingerly cross, try to remember that the steel cables you are gripping are embedded in huge concrete blocks on either side. This is the region's most popular attraction, hence the summertime crowds. The grounds here include rainforest walks, totem poles and

🔗 LINK YOUR TRIP

26 Sea to Sky Highway

Head northwest from Vancouver, rather than east, and wind your way up into the mountains.

27 A Strait Hop

Drive onto the ferry at Horseshoe Bay in West Vancouver.

some smaller bridges strung between the trees that offer a lovely squirrel's-eye forest walk. You can also test your bravery on the **Cliffwalk**, a glass-and-steel walkway secured with horizontal bars to a granite cliff face and suspended 90m (295ft) over the canyon floor. Deep breath...

The Drive » Continue north on Capilano Rd. This turns into Nancy Greene Way, which ends at the next stop.

❸ Grouse Mountain

One of the region's most popular outdoor hangouts, **Grouse Mountain** (☎604-980-9311; www.grousemountain.com; 6400 Nancy Greene Way, North Vancouver; adult/child C$56/29; ⏰9am-10pm; 🅿 🚻; 🚌236) rises 1231m (4039ft) over North Vancouver's skyline. In summer, Skyride gondola tickets to the top include access to lumberjack shows, bird of prey displays and alpine hiking trails plus a **nature reserve** that's home to orphaned grizzly bears and timber wolves. You can also brave the two-hour, five-line **zipline course** (C$89, excluding Skyride) or the 'Eye of the Wind' tour, which takes you to the top of a 20-story wind turbine tower for spectacular 360-degree views. In winter, Grouse is a very popular magnet for local and visiting skiers and snowboarders.

The Drive » Return south down Nancy Greene Way and Capilano Rd, taking a left onto Edgemont Blvd, which leads to Hwy 1. Head east, following the highway through Burnaby, crossing the Second Narrows Bridge and then the impressive 10-lane Port Mann Bridge. Continue on Hwy 1, exiting at 88 Ave East and following signs to Fort Langley. Trip takes round an hour.

❹ Fort Langley

Little Fort Langley's tree-lined streets and 19th-century storefronts make it one of the Lower Mainland's most picturesque historic villages. Its main heritage highlight is the evocative **Fort Langley National Historic Site** (☎604-513-4777; www.parkscanada.gc.ca/fortlangley; adult/child C$8/4; ⏰10am-5pm; 🚻; 🚌562), perhaps the region's most important old-school landmark.

A fortified trading post since 1827, this is where James Douglas announced the creation

DETOUR:
LYNN CANYON PARK

Start: ❷ **Capilano Suspension Bridge**

For a free alternative to Capilano, divert to **Lynn Canyon Park** (www.lynncanyon.ca; Park Rd, North Vancouver; ⏰10am-5pm Jun-Sep, noon-4pm Oct-May; 🅿 🚻; 🚌228 then 227), a temperate rainforest area that's home to its own lofty but slightly smaller suspension bridge. There are also plenty of excellent hiking trails and some great tree-hugging picnic spots here. Check out the park's **Ecology Centre** (☎604-990-3755; www.lynncanyonecologycentre.ca; 3663 Park Rd, North Vancouver; by donation; ⏰10am-5pm Jun-Sep, 10am-5pm Mon-Fri & noon-4pm Sat & Sun Oct-May; 🚻) for displays on the region's rich biodiversity. If you're really keen on local flora, drop into a bookstore on your travels and pick up a copy of the *Vancouver Tree Book* (David Tracey, 2016). It details many of the regions leafy wonders and shows you how to spot them while you're here. While you're weaving around the trails at Lynn Canyon or any other tree-hugging hot spot you discover during your drive, look out for cedars, hemlocks, Douglas fir and more. To find the park, head east on Hwy 1 from Capilano Rd and turn left on Lynn Valley Rd.

of British Columbia in 1858, giving the site a legitimate claim to being the province's birthplace. Chat with costumed re-enactors knitting, working on beaver pelts or sweeping their pioneer homes. Also open to explore are re-created artisan workshops and a **gold-panning area** that's very popular with kids. And when you need a rest, sample baking and lunchtime meals from the 1800s in the **Lelem' Cafe**.

Be sure to check the fort's website before you arrive: there's a wide array of events that bring the past back to life, including a summertime evening campfire program that will take you right back to the pioneer days of the 1800s.

The Drive » Head south out of the village on Glover Rd, crossing Hwy 1 and then taking a slight left so that you're traveling south on 216th St. The next stop is just past 16th Ave.

 p277

- - - - - - - - - - - - - - - -

❺ Langley Farmland

The vine-covered grounds of **Chaberton Estate Winery** (☏604-530-1736; www.chabertonwinery.com; 1064 216 St, Langley; ☺10am-6pm, to 8pm Thu-Sat, 11am-6pm Sun) is the setting for the Fraser Valley's oldest wine-making operation, here since 1991. The French-influenced, 22-hectare (55-

DETOUR: HOPE

Start: ❼ Harrison Hot Springs

Hope's nickname is the 'Chainsaw Capital' and this rather unusual moniker certainly draws attention. The name was earned by the wooden sculptures peppered throughout the town. Hope is a small community at the eastern edge of the Fraser Valley, set beneath the shadow of the Cascade Mountains. The 70-plus chainsaw sculptures are the products of both local and visiting artists. Most depict wildlife, including the Sasquatch who is believed to live in the nearby woods.

If Hope looks oddly familiar, you may be dating yourself. The original *Rambo* movie was filmed here in 1982. For a self-guided tour map of the sculptures and *Rambo* locations, drop into the visitor center on the edge of town. Hope is 40km (25 miles) east of Harrison Hot Springs on Hwy 7.

acre) vineyard specializes in cool-climate whites: its subtle, Riesling-style Bacchus is dangerously easy to drink. There's also a handy bistro here.

Head south and right on 4th St to the charming **Vista D'oro** (☏604-514-3539; www.vistadoro.com; 346 208th St, Langley; ☺11am-5pm Thu-Sun Mar-Dec), a working farm and winery where you can load up on fresh pears, plums, apples and stripy heirloom tomatoes. Sample preserves such as piquant mango lime salsa and sweet rhubarb and vanilla jam. Also pick up a bottle of its utterly delicious, port-style walnut wine that's made from nuts grown just outside the shop. It's

definitely small batch, so if you see it buy it.

The Fraser Valley is home to countless farms, producing everything from tulips to cheese. Many accept visitors, give tours and sell their wares in farm shops. If you're keen to visit some more, go to www.circlefarmtour.com for details.

The Drive » Return north up 216th St and turn right on North Bluff Rd. Continue east for four blocks and turn left onto 248th St, which takes you to the Fraser Hwy. Head east toward Abbotsford, and then north on the Abbotsford Mission Hwy over the Fraser River to Hwy 7. Turn right and follow the road along the river. Approximately 1½ hours.

TOP TIP: TRAFFIC REPORTS

Traffic over the Lions Gate Bridge and along Hwy 1 can be heavy enough to bring you to a standstill at times. Check the website of DriveBC (www.drivebc.ca) for traffic, construction and incident reports.

❻ Kilby Historic Site

To get to **Kilby Historic Site** (☎604-796-9576; www.kilby.ca; 215 Kilby Rd; adult/child C$10/8; ⊙11am-4pm Jul & Aug, reduced hours Sep-Jun), **turn right onto School Rd and then right again onto Kilby Rd. The clocks turn back to the 1920s when you enter this site**, all that remains of the once thriving Harrison Mills community. Join a tour led by costumed interpreters as you explore the general store, hotel, post office and working farm, complete with friendly farm animals. Save time for treats made with traditional ice cream.

The Drive ➤➤ Return to Hwy 7 and carry on east, passing through farmland and hazelnut orchards. Turn left on Hwy 9, which takes you to Harrison Hot Springs, for a total drive of 21km (13 miles).

❼ Harrison Hot Springs

Set on the edge of Harrison Lake with views to forest-carpeted mountains, Harrison Hot Springs (www.tourismharrison.com) is a resort town that draws both locals and visitors to its sandy beach, warm lagoon and lakeside promenade. While the lake itself is glacier-fed, two hot springs bubble at the southern end of the lake and the warm water can be enjoyed year-round at the town's upscale resort (p277) and the indoor public pool. If you're smart, you'll time your Harrison visit for the area's biggest cultural festival. July's multiday Harrison Festival of the Arts (www.harrisonfestival.com) has been running for more than 30 years, bringing live music, gallery shows, creative workshops and more to the area's beachfront streets.

🛏 p277

Eating & Sleeping

Stanley Park ❶

🛏 Listel Hotel
Boutique Hotel $$$

(📞604-684-8461; www.thelistelhotel.com; 1300 Robson St, West End; d from C$340; 🅿️ ❄️ @ 🛜; 🚌5) A lounge-cool sleepover with famously friendly front-deskers. Rooms at the Listel have a relaxed West Coast feel and typically feature striking original artworks. But it's not all about looks; cool features include glass water bottles in the rooms, a daily wine reception (from 5pm) and the free use of loaner e-bikes if you want to explore nearby Stanley Park.

🛏 Sylvia Hotel
Hotel $$

(📞604-681-9321; www.sylviahotel.com; 1154 Gilford St, West End; d from C$199; 🅿️ @ 🛜🐾; 🚌5) This ivy-covered 1912 charmer enjoys a prime location overlooking English Bay. Generations of guests keep coming back – many requesting the same room every year – for a dollop of old-world ambience, plus a side order of first-name service. The rooms, some with older furnishings, have an array of comfortable configurations; the best are the large suites with kitchens and waterfront views.

Fort Langley ❹

🍽 Veggie Bob's Kitchen
Vegan $

(📞604-888-1223; www.veggiebobs.com; 9044 Glover Rd; mains C$8-12; 🕙11am-8pm Tue-Sun; 🍴; 🚌562) Veggie Bob's recently went 100% vegan without having to change the fundamentals of its American heartland meets Mexican menu. Unlikely new favorites include a vegan hot dog smeared with mac 'n' cheese, the ever-popular quesadilla with guacamole, and a doorstep-sized apple pie for desert. Seating is coffee-bar style amid an array of sculpted busts.

🍽 Wendel's Bookstore & Cafe
Cafe $

(📞604-513-2238; www.wendelsonline.com; 9233 Glove Rd; dishes C$8-16; 🕙7:30am-10pm; 🛜🍴; 🚌562) It's difficult to work out if Wendel's is a bookstore attached to a cafe or a cafe attached to a bookstore. Both are equally visit-worthy. This is certainly more than a soup and sandwich hangout for bibliophiles. You can get baby back ribs here, and the homemade desserts (including caramel and pecan cheesecake) are surely from another sweeter planet.

Harrison Hot Springs ❼

🛏 Harrison Hot Springs Resort
Hotel $$

(📞604-796-2244; www.harrisonresort.com; 100 Esplanade Ave; r from C$160; 🅿️ ➿ ❄️ 🛜🐾) This fabled resort on the lakefront in Harrison Hot Springs exudes peace. Open since 1886, it has an art-deco flair and offers good service. The hot-spring pools are set in an inner courtyard complete with trees and fairy lights. There is also a divine-smelling spa, numerous restaurants and a concierge who can arrange everything from fishing trips to golf.

Classic Trip

Sea to Sky Highway

The coastal scenery here is magnificent – as are the deep forests, crashing waterfalls and lofty mountains. When you can see it all in a day, it's almost too good to be true.

26

TRIP HIGHLIGHTS

132 km

Audain Art Museum
Dramatic art gallery housing historic and contemporary BC art

 10 FINISH

9

84 km

Brandywine Falls
Your knees will turn to jelly as you look over the plummeting water

56 km

5

Brackendale Eagles
Soaring, hunting and hanging out in their hundreds

● Squamish

3

35 km

Britannia Mine Museum
Grab your hard hat for a look into a mining community

● Horseshoe Bay
START

1–2 DAYS
132KM / 82 MILES

GREAT FOR...

BEST TIME TO GO
November to March has the best snow; June to September offers sunny hiking, plus driving without chains.

ESSENTIAL PHOTO
Get the ultimate snowy-peak picture from Tantalus Lookout.

 BEST FOR OUTDOORS
Ski Olympic-style down Whistler Mountain.

Classic Trip

26 Sea to Sky Highway

Drive out of North Vancouver and straight onto the wild west coast. This short excursion reveals the essence of British Columbia's shoreline with majestic sea and mountain vistas, outdoor activity opportunities, wildlife-watching possibilities and a peek into the regional First Nations culture and pioneer history that's woven along the route. There's even freshly roasted, organic coffee along the way. How much more 'BC' can you get?

❶ Horseshoe Bay

Standing at the foot of Horseshoe Bay as clouds and mist drift in across the snowcapped mountains of Howe Sound, may well make you feel like you've stepped into Middle Earth. Green-forested hills tumble down around the village, which has a small-town vibe that doesn't attest to its proximity to Vancouver. Grab a coffee and some fish-and-chips from one of the many waterfront cafes and watch the bobbling boats from the seaside park. This first stop is all about slowing down and taking it all in.

Have a wander through the **Spirit Gallery** (☎604-921-8972; www.spirit-gallery.com; 6408 Bay St, Horseshoe Bay, West Vancouver; ⏲10am-6pm; 🚌257), which is filled with classic and contemporary First Nations art and design from the region. You'll find everything from eye glasses to animal hand-puppets, prints, pewter and carvings.

The Drive ❯❯ Head north for 25km (15.5 miles) on Hwy 99, which curves around the coast and follows Howe Sound. You'll be traveling between steep mountainsides, down which waterfalls plummet, and the often misty ocean where islands are perched like sleeping giants. Watch out for Tunnel Point Lookout on the western side of the highway for a vantage point across the sound.

TOP TIP: GAS STATION?

There is nowhere to fill your tank between North Vancouver and Squamish, a distance of around 50km (31 miles). This is mountain driving so make sure you've got at least half a tank when you set out.

❷ Porteau Cove Provincial Park

Once popular with regional First Nations communities for sturgeon fishing, Porteau Cove is one of the oldest

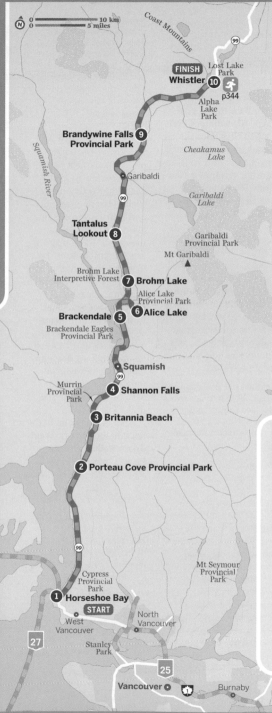

archaeological sites on the northwest coast. These days it's a haven for divers, with a sunken ship and reefs supporting countless species of marine life, such as octopus and wolf eels. The rocky beach is good for exploring, with plenty of logs to clamber on, and in summer the water is just about warm enough for a quick dip.

The Drive » From here, the sound narrows and as you continue 8km (5 miles) north on Hwy 99, the mountains from the opposite shore begin to loom over you.

TRIP HIGHLIGHT

❸ Britannia Beach

Don a hard hat and hop on a bone-shaking train that trundles you through a floodlit mine tunnel. With hands-on exhibits, gold panning,

LINK YOUR TRIP

25 Vancouver & the Fraser Valley

Highway 99 begins in North Vancouver where you can divert onto this multifarious exploration of Vancouver and its fertile hinterland.

27 A Strait Hop

This shore-tracking tour of Vancouver Island and the Sunshine Coast goes through Horseshoe Bay (the first stop on this trip).

an engaging film and entry into the dizzying 20-story mill, the **Britannia Mine Museum** (📞604-896-2260; www.britanniaminemuseum.ca; Hwy 99; adult/child C$30/19; 🕙9am-5pm; 🚻) has plenty to keep you (and any kids in tow) busy. Factor in a couple of hours here.

The Drive ›› Continue 7km (4.25 miles) north on Hwy 99, through the lush green Murrin Provincial Park.

 p287

❹ Shannon Falls

Torpedoing 335m 1099ft) over the mountaintop, **Shannon Falls** (www.bc-parks.ca; Hwy 99, Squamish) is the third-largest flume in the province. Historically, the medicine

people of the Squamish First Nation trained alongside these falls. A short, picturesque walk through the woods leads to a viewing platform.

You can also hike from here to the peak of the **Stawamus Chief** (two to three hours round-trip) or hop back in your car and continue another minute or two along Hwy 99 to the **Sea to Sky Gondola** (📞604-892-2551; www.seatoskygondola.com; 36800 Hwy 99, Squamish; adult/child C$42/14; 🕙10am-6pm May-Oct, reduced hours Nov-Apr) where a cable-car zips you up to a summit lodge at 885m (2904ft). From here you can walk across a shaky suspension bridge to access a network of above-the-treeline trails.

The Drive ›› Continue north on Hwy 99, past the Stawamus Chief and through Squamish, where you can stop for gas or sample from a raft of craft

breweries and distilleries. Carry on along the highway, taking a left on Depot Rd and then another left onto Government Rd. The next stop is a few minutes up the road on your right.

TRIP HIGHLIGHT

❺ Brackendale

Brackendale is home to one of the largest populations of wintering bald eagles in North America. Visit between November and February to see an almost overwhelming number of these massive, magnificent birds feasting on salmon in the Squamish River. A path running alongside the riverbank offers a short walk and plenty of easy eagle-spotting opportunities. Across the river are the tall trees of **Brackendale Eagles Provincial Park**, where the beady-eyed birds perch in the night.

Also in this neighborhood is the historic **West Coast Railway Heritage Park** (📞604-898-9336; www.wcra.org; 39645 Government Rd, Squamish; adult/child C$25/15; 🕙10am-3pm; 🚻). This large, mostly outdoor museum is the final resting place of British Columbia's legendary *Royal Hudson* steam engine and has dozens of other historic railcars, including working engines and cabooses, sumptuous sleepers and a cool vintage mail car. Check out

---

THE STAWAMUS CHIEF

Towering 700m (2297ft) above the waters of Howe Sound like 'The Wall' in *Game of Thrones*, the Chief is the world's second-largest freestanding granite monolith. The three peaks have long been considered a sacred place to the Squamish people; they once came here seeking spiritual renewal. It's also the nesting grounds of peregrine falcons, who are increasingly returning to the area.

The views from the top are unbelievable. The sheer face of the monolith has become a magnet to rock climbers, while hikers can take a steep trail starting from the base station of the Sea to Sky Gondola to one or all of the three summits.

the handsome Round-house building, housing the park's most precious trains and artifacts.

The Drive » Hwy 99 leaves the Squamish River 5km (3 miles) north of Brackendale and heads into the trees. The next stop is on the right.

----

6 Alice Lake

Delve into an old-growth hemlock forest for hiking and biking trails as well as lakeside picnic opportunities. Surrounded by a ring of towering mountains and offering two sandy beaches fringed by relatively warm water in summer, **Alice Lake Provincial Park** (www. discovercamping.ca; Hwy 99, Brackendale; campsites C$43) is a popular spot for a dip, a walk and an alfresco lunch.

Next stretch your legs on the 6km (3.75-mile) **Four Lakes Trail**, an easy hike that does a loop around all four lakes in the park, passing through stands of Douglas fir and western red cedar. Keep your eyes (and your ears) peeled for warblers, Steller's jays and chickadees as well as for the box turtles that sometimes sun themselves on the logs at Stump Lake.

The Drive » Continue north along Hwy 99 for around 6km (3.75 miles) to Brohm Lake.

LOOK FAMILIAR?

The mine complex at Britannia Beach has been used as a film location for more than 50 movies and TV shows. *The X-Files, Smallville, Dark Angel* and *Insomnia* are just a few of the names on its list of appearances.

If you carry on to Shannon Falls and have any teens with you, they may experience severe déjà vu. These falls featured in *Twilight: Breaking Dawn*.

----

7 Brohm Lake

Less developed than Alice Lake Provincial Park, **Brohm Lake Interpretive Forest** has 10km (6.25 miles) of walking trails, many of them easy and flat. The lake is warm enough for summer swimming as the sun filters down onto the tree-studded shoreline.

Archaeological digs from this area have unearthed arrowheads and tools from early First Nations communities that date back 10,000 years. The area was later the scene of a logging mill and today is home to **Tenderfoot Fish Hatchery** (☎604-898-3657; 1000 Midnight Way, Brackendale; ☺8am-3pm), a facility aimed at replenishing depleted chum and Chinook salmon stocks, which fell from around 25,000 in the 1960s to around 1500 in the early 1980s. You can visit the hatchery and take a self-guided tour by following a 3km (2-mile) trail from Brohm Lake.

The Drive » Continue up Hwy 99 just over 3km (2 miles) to the next stop.

----

8 Tantalus Lookout

This viewpoint looks out across the Tantalus Mountain Range. Tantalus was a character in Greek mythology who gave us the word 'tantalize'; apparently the mountains were named by an explorer who was tempted to climb the range's snowy peaks, but was stuck on the other side of the turbulent Squamish River. In addition to Mt Tantalus, the Greek hero's entire family is here – his wife Mt Dione, his daughter Mt Niobe, his son Mt Pelops and his grandson Mt Thyestes.

The Squamish people once used this area to train in hunting and believe that long ago, hunters and their dogs were immortalized here, becoming the soaring mountain range. Those stone hunters must be rather tantalized themselves; the forested

Classic Trip

WHY THIS IS A CLASSIC TRIP
BRENDAN SAINSBURY, WRITER

If you live in BC (as I do), this is where you take any visiting friend or relative to instantly impress them. It's BC's greatest hits in one morning (or afternoon) – mountains, water, forests, wildlife, First Nations myths, and a rugged but well-maintained road that never strays far from the wilderness. A stop in Squamish for coffee and a quick 'run' up the Chief is de rigueur.

Above: View to the Stawamus Chief (p282), Squamish
Left: Welcome figure carved out of western red cedar by Sessiyam Ray Natraoro of Squamish Nation, Squamish Lil'wat Cultural Centre (p286)
Right: Mountain biking, Whistler (p286)

slopes of the mountains are home to grizzly bears, elk, wolverines, wolves and cougars.

The Drive » Follow Hwy 99 22km (13.7 miles) north through the woods, skirting the edge of Daisy Lake before reaching the next stop on your right.

- - - - - - - - - - - - - - -

`TRIP HIGHLIGHT`

❾ Brandywine Falls Provincial Park

Surging powerfully over the edge of a volcanic escarpment, **Brandywine Falls** (www.env.gov.bc.ca/bcparks/explore/parkpgs/brandywine_falls; Hwy 99) plunge a dramatic 70m (230ft) – a straight shot into the pool below. Follow the easy 10-minute trail through the woods and step out onto the viewing platform, directly over the falls.

From here you can also see **Mt Garibaldi**, the most easily recognizable mountain in the Coast Range. Its distinctive jagged top and color has earned it the name Black Tusk. This mountain is of particular significance to local First Nations groups who believe the great Thunderbird landed here. With its supernatural ways, it shot bolts of lightning from its eyes, creating the color and shape of the mountaintop.

A 7km (4.25-mile) looped trail leads further through the park's dense forest and ancient lava

Classic Trip

beds to **Cal-Cheak Suspension Bridge**.

The Drive » Continue north for 17km (10.5 miles) along Hwy 99, passing Creekside Village and carrying on to the main Whistler village entrance (it's well signposted and obvious once you see it).

- - - - - - - - - - - - - - - -

❿ Whistler

Nestled in the shade of the formidable Whistler and Blackcomb Mountains, Whistler has long been BC's golden child. Popular in winter for its world-class ski slopes and in summer for everything from hiking to one of North America's longest ziplines, it draws fans from around the world. It was named for the furry marmots that fill the area with their loud whistle, but there are also plenty of berry-snuffling black bears about.

The site of many of the outdoor events at the 2010 Winter Olympic and Paralympic Games, Whistler village is well worth a stroll (p344) and is filled with an eclectic mix of stores, flash hotels

THE STORY BEGINS

As you enter the **Squamish Lil'wat Cultural Centre** (☎604-964-0990; www.slcc.ca; 4584 Blackcomb Way; adult/child C$18/5; ⏱10am-5pm daily Apr-Oct, Tues-Sun Nov-Mar) in Whistler, take a look at the carved cedar doors you're passing through. According to the center's guide map, the door on the left shows a grizzly bear – protector of the Lil'wat – with a salmon in its mouth, representing sharing. The carving references a mother bear and cub that walked into the center during construction. The door on the right, depicting a human face and hands up, symbolizes the Squamish welcoming all visitors.

and seemingly countless cafes and restaurants.

Crisscrossed with over 200 runs, the **Whistler-Blackcomb** (☎604-967-8950; www.whistlerblackcomb. com; day-pass adult/child C$178/89) sister mountains are linked by a 4.4km (2.75-mile) gondola that includes the world's longest unsupported span. Ski season runs from late November to April on Whistler and to June on Blackcomb. **Ziptrek Ecotours** (☎604-935-0001; www.ziptrek.com; 4280 Mountain Sq, Carleton Lodge; adult/child from C$119/99; 🚲) offers year-round zip-line courses that will have you screaming with gut-quivering pleasure.

While you're here, be sure to take in the wood-beamed **Squam-**

ish Lil'wat Cultural Centre, built to resemble a traditional longhouse. It's filled with art, images and displays that illuminate the traditional and contemporary cultures of the Squamish and Lil'wat Nations.

A short stroll away, **Audain Art Museum** (☎604-962-0413; www. audainartmuseum.com; 4350 Blackcomb Way; adult/child $18/free; ⏱10am-5pm, to 9pm Fri, closed Tue) is home to an array of paintings from BC icons, including Emily Carr and EJ Hughes, plus a collection of historic and contemporary First Nations works. Allow at least an hour here.

🍴 🛏 p287

Eating & Sleeping

Britannia Beach ❸

✖ Galileo Coffee
Company   Cafe $

(☏604-896-0272; www.galileocoffee.com; 173
Hwy 99; baked goods from C$4; ⊙6am-2pm,
from 7am Sat & Sun; 🛜) Lovable small-
batch coffee roaster that's commandeered
a clapboard house next to Hwy 99 that once
belonged to the Britannia Mine manager. The
sweet snacks are everyone's favorite carb-load
and the coffee is essential rocket fuel to help
you up the Chief.

Squamish ❹

✖ Howe Sound Pub
& Brewing Company   Pub Food $$

(☏778-654-3358; www.howesound.com;
37801 Cleveland Ave; mains C$15-26; ⊙11am-
midnight, to 1am Fri, from 8am Sat & Sun; 🛜)
This wood-beamed, ever-popular brewpub has a
deck with views of the Chief, where you can get
comfortable and partake of some irresistible
yam fries and bold Devil's Elbow IPA. Or head
inside for handmade pizzas, burgers and
sandwiches, and elevated pub classics including
mussels in a honey pale ale broth.

🛏 Howe Sound Inn   Inn $$

(☏604-892-2603; www.howesoundinn.com;
37801 Cleveland Ave; d C$145; 🛜) Quality rustic
is the approach at this comfortable inn, where
the rooms are warm and inviting with plenty
of wooden furnishings. Recover from your
climbing escapades in the property's popular
sauna – or just head to the downstairs brewpub,
which serves some of BC's best housemade
beers. Inn guests can request free brewery
tours.

Even if you're not staying, it's worth stopping
in at the restaurant here for great pub grub with
a gourmet twist.

Whistler ❿

✖ 21 Steps
Kitchen & Bar   Canadian $$

(☏604-966-2121; www.21steps.ca; 4433
Sundial Pl; mains C$18-41; ⊙5:30-11pm; 🖉)
Offering small plates (C$6 to $16) for nibblers
and main dishes for starving skiers, the chefs
at this casual upstairs spot advertise their work
as 'modern comfort food.' Vegetarians will sigh
contentedly at the 'vegetable tower' (roasted
eggplant, zucchini and squash), pescatarians
will relish the pan-seared trout and visiting
Aussies will get homesick over the Australian
lamb chop in a vermouth reduction.

🛏 Adara Hotel   Boutique Hotel $$

(☏604-905-4009; www.adarahotel.com;
4122 Village Green; r from C$219; 🛜🖳🐾)
Unlike all those lodges now claiming to be
boutique hotels, the sophisticated and
blissfully affordable Adara is the real deal. With
warm wood furnishings studded with orange
exclamation marks, the rooms offer spa-like
baths, cool aesthetics and 'floating' fireplaces
that look like TVs. Boutique extras include fresh
cookies and in-room boot dryers. Prices dip
significantly in shoulder season.

🛏 HI Whistler Hostel   Hostel $

(☏604-962-0025; www.hihostels.ca/whistler;
1035 Legacy Way; dm/r C$43/120; @🛜)
Built as athlete accommodations for the 2010
Winter Olympics, this sparkling hostel is 7km
(4.25 miles) south of the village, near Function
Junction. Transit buses to/from town stop right
outside. Book ahead for private rooms (with
private bathrooms and TVs) or save by staying
in a small dorm. Eschewing the sometimes
institutionalized HI hostel feel, this one has
IKEA-style furnishings, art-lined walls and a
licensed cafe.

There's also a great TV room for rainy-day
hunkering. If it's fine, hit the nearby biking
and hiking trails or barbecue on one of the two
mountain-view decks.

A Strait Hop

27

BC's forested, multi-fjorded coastline stretches for at least 24,000km (15,000 miles). But you don't have to drive that far for a taste of the region's salty, character-packed waterfront communities.

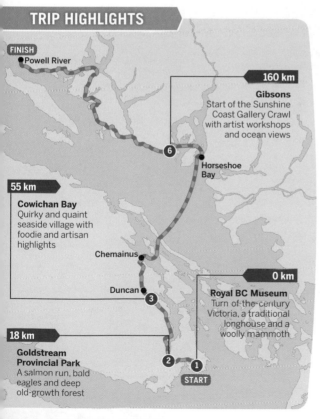

FINISH
● Powell River

160 km

Gibsons
Start of the Sunshine Coast Gallery Crawl with artist workshops and ocean views

 6

● Horseshoe Bay

55 km

Cowichan Bay
Quirky and quaint seaside village with foodie and artisan highlights

● Chemainus

● Duncan

 3

0 km

Royal BC Museum
Turn-of-the-century Victoria, a traditional longhouse and a woolly mammoth

18 km

Goldstream Provincial Park
A salmon run, bald eagles and deep old-growth forest

 2   1

START

2–3 DAYS
351KM / 219 MILES

GREAT FOR...

BEST TIME TO GO
June to September offers the most sunshine and least rain.

ESSENTIAL PHOTO
Clouds draped across mountaintops from the deck of a Horseshoe Bay ferry.

BEST FOR FOODIES
Dive into some delightful regional flavors in Cowichan Bay.

---

27 | A Strait Hop

Perhaps it's the way sunlight reflects across the ever-shifting ocean, or the forest walks and beachcombing that seem an essential part of coastal life. Whatever the reason, the towns and villages snuggled next to the Pacific draw artistic folk from around the world to settle here and create strong communities and beautiful art. Take this leisurely tour for a slice of life on both the mainland and Vancouver Island.

TRIP HIGHLIGHT

1 Victoria

British Columbia's lovely, walkable (p342) and increasingly bike-friendly capital is dripping with colonial architecture and has enough museums, attractions, hotels and restaurants to keep many visitors enthralled for an extra night or two.

Must-see attractions include the excellent **Royal BC Museum** (✆250-356-7226; www. royalbcmuseum.bc.ca; 675 Belleville St; adult/child

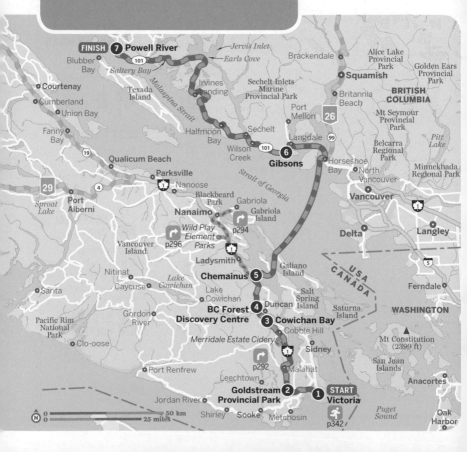

C$17/11, incl IMAX $27/21; 🕙10am-5pm daily, to 10pm Fri & Sat mid-May–Sep; ; 🚍70). Come eye to beady eye with a woolly mammoth and look out for cougars and grizzlies peeking from behind the trees. Step aboard Captain Vancouver's ship, enter a First Nations cedar longhouse, and explore a re-created early colonial street complete with shops, a movie house and an evocative replica Chinatown. A few minutes' stroll away, you'll also find the hidden gem **Miniature World** (📞250-385-9731; www.miniatureworld.com; 649 Humboldt St; adult/child C$16/8; 🕙9am-9pm mid-May–mid-Sep, to 5pm mid-Sep–mid-May; ; 🚍70), an

LINK YOUR TRIP

26 **Sea to Sky Highway**

Join this trip at Horseshoe Bay winding your way up Hwy 99 past the climbing hub of Squamish to the peerless ski-town of Whistler.

29 **Vancouver Island's Remote North**

From Nanaimo explore the more remote flavor of Vancouver Island by pitching north to Qualicum Beach or west to Tofino.

RULE OF THE ROAD

Bone-shaking automobiles began popping up on the roads of British Columbia in the early years of the 20th century, often the toys of rich playboys with too much time on their hands. But for many years BC had few regulations governing the trundling procession of cars around the region: vehicles could drive on either side of the road in some communities, although the left-hand side (echoing the country's British colonial overlords) gradually became the accepted practice.

Aiming to match driving rules in the US (and in much of the rest of the world) – yet managing to confuse the local issue still further – BC began legislating drivers over to the right-hand side of the road in the early 1920s. One of the last areas to make the switch official was Vancouver Island. During the transition period, some minor accidents were reported around the region as forgetful drivers tootled toward each other before veering across at the last minute.

immaculate, old-school attraction crammed with 80 diminutive dioramas themed on everything from Arthurian Britain to a futuristic sci-fi realm.

Also worth visiting is the **Art Gallery of Greater Victoria** (📞250-384-4171; www.aggv.ca; 1040 Moss St; adult/child C$13/2.50; 🕙10am-5pm Tue, Wed, Fri & Sat, to 9pm Thu, noon-5pm Sun; 🚍14), home to one of Canada's best Emily Carr collections. Aside from Carr's swirling nature canvases, you'll find an ever-changing array of temporary exhibitions.

And save time to hop on a not-much-bigger-than-a-bathtub-sized **Victoria Harbour Ferry** (📞250-708-0201; www.victoriaharbourferry.com; fares from C$7; 🕙Mar-Oct).

This colorful armada of tiny tugboats stop at numerous docks along the waterfront, including the Inner Harbour, Songhees Park and Fisherman's Wharf (where alfresco fish and chips is heartily recommended).

The Drive » Follow Hwy 1 (which begins its cross-country journey in Victoria) 19km (12 miles) west onto the sometimes narrow, heavily forested Malahat Dr section, also known as the Malahat Hwy.

✗ 🛏 p297, p305

TRIP HIGHLIGHT

❷ Goldstream Provincial Park

Alongside the Malahat, the abundantly forested **Goldstream Provincial Park** (📞250-478-9414; www.goldstreampark.com;

DETOUR: MERRIDALE ESTATE CIDERY

Start: ❷ Goldstream

After leaving Goldstream, head west off the highway onto Cobble Hill Rd. This weaves through bucolic farmland and wine-growing country. Watch for asparagus farms, beady-eyed llamas, blueberry stalls and verdant vineyards. Stop in at charming **Merridale Estate Cidery** (📞250-743-4293; www. merridalecider.com; 1230 Merridale Rd, Cobble Hill; ⊙11am-5pm, reduced hours Oct-Mar), an inviting apple-cider producer offering many varieties, as well as artisan gin and vodka.

Cobble Hill Rd crosses over the highway and loops east to Cowichan Bay.

2930 Trans-Canada Hwy; **P**) drips with ancient, moss-covered cedar trees and a moist carpet of plant life. The short walk through the woods to the **Freeman King Visitors Centre** (📞250-478-9414; 2390 Trans-Canada Hwy; ⊙9am-4:30pm) is beautiful; once you're there, take in the center's hands-on exhibits about natural history.

The park is known for its salmon spawning season (from late October to December), when the water literally bubbles with thousands of struggling fish. Hungry bald eagles also swoop in at this time to feast on the full-grown salmon.

A short 700m (half-mile) trail leads to Niagara Falls, which is a lot narrower but only 4m (13ft) shorter than its famous Ontario namesake. Hike beyond the falls and you'll reach an impressive railway trestle (which you're not supposed to walk on).

The Drive » From Goldstream, the Malahat climbs north for 8km (5 miles) to its summit with a number of gorgeous viewpoints over Brentwood Bay. Continue on Hwy 1 for another 28km (17.5 miles), following signs east off the highway for Cowichan Bay.

TRIP HIGHLIGHT

❸ Cowichan Bay

With a colorful string of wooden buildings perched on stilts over a mountain-shadowed ocean inlet, Cowichan Bay – Cow Bay to locals – is well worth a stop. Wander along the pier of the **Maritime Centre** (📞250-746-4955; www.classicboats.org; 1761 Cowichan Bay Rd; suggested donation C$5; ⊙9am-4pm Wed-Sun) to peruse some salty boat-building exhibits and intricate models and get your camera out to shoot the handsome panoramic views of the harbor. Duck into the galleries and studios lining the waterfront or stretch your legs on a five-minute stroll to the **Cowichan Estuary Nature Centre** (📞250-597-2288; www.cowichanestuary.ca; 1845 Cowichan Bay Rd; suggested donation C$2; ⊙noon-4pm; 🚻), where area birdlife and marine critters are profiled.

Drop into the **Mud Room** (📞250-710-7329; www.cowbaymudroom.com; 1725 Cowichan Bay Rd; ⊙9am-6pm Jun-Sep, reduced hours in winter) to see potters at work making usable objects like cups and plates. Look for seaside-themed mugs and the popular yellow-glazed dragonfly motif pieces.

The artisans are also at work in Cow Bay's kitchens. This is a great place to gather the makings of a great picnic at **True Grain Bread** (📞250-746-7664; www.truegrain. ca; 1725 Cowichan Bay Rd; ⊙8am-6pm, closed Mon Nov-Feb). Alternatively, drop in for succulent, fresh-made fish-and-chips at the locally loved **Rock Cod Cafe** (📞250-746-1550; www.rockcodcafe.com; 1759 Cowichan Bay Rd; mains C$16-26; ⊙11am-9pm Jul & Aug, to 7pm Sun-Thu, to 8pm Fri & Sat Sep-Jun; 🚻).

The Drive » Return to Hwy 1 and head north a further 12km (7.5 miles).

✕ ⍩ p297

---

④ BC Forest Discovery Centre

You won't find Winnie-the-Pooh in this 40-hectare (100-acre) wood, but if you want to know more about those giants swaying overhead, stop in at the **BC Forest Discovery Centre** (📞250-715-1113; www.bcforestdis coverycentre.com; 2892 Drinkwater Rd; adult/child C$16/11; ⊙10am-4:30pm Apr-Sep, reduced hours Oct-Mar, 🚻). Woodland paths lead you among western yews, Garry oaks and 400-year-old fir trees with nesting bald eagles in their branches. Visit a 1920s sawmill and a 1905 wooden school-

Cowichan Bay Colorful houses

house, and climb to the top of a wildfire lookout tower. Hop on a historical train for a ride around the grounds and check out some cool logging trucks from the early 1900s. Visit the indoor exhibits for the lowdown on contemporary forest management.

The Drive » It's a 20km (12.5-mile) journey to the next stop. Continue north on Hwy 1, turning right onto Henry Rd and then left onto Chemainus Rd.

COUGAR!

Weighing in at up to 70kg (155lb), cougars are stealthy in the extreme and can, on their own, hunt and kill a 300kg (660lb)moose. While they're rarely seen, they can (and do) occasionally attack humans so it pays to be prepared – especially as the majority of the large cats in this region reside on the southern third of Vancouver Island.

Cougars are most active at dusk and dawn and most encounters take place in late spring and summer; however, cougars roam and hunt at any time of the day or night and in all seasons. Almost all human-based cougar attacks are on children, so keep your young ones close when you're outside and pick them up immediately if you see a cougar. Hike in groups of two or more and make enough noise to prevent surprising a cougar.

If you come across a cougar, always give it an avenue of escape. Talk to the cougar in a confident voice, face it and remain upright. Do not turn your back on the cougar. Do not run. Try to back away from the cougar slowly. If the cougar appears aggressive, do all you can to enlarge your image. Don't crouch down or try to hide. Pick up sticks or branches and wave them about. Convince the cougar that you are a threat, not prey. And if a cougar does attack, fight back!

DETOUR: GABRIOLA ISLAND

Start: ❺ **Chemainus**

If you're tempted by those mysterious little islands peeking at you off the coast of Vancouver Island, take the 20-minute BC Ferries (www.bcferries.com) service from Nanaimo's Inner Harbour to **Gabriola Island** (www.gabriolaisland.org). Home to dozens of artists plus a healthy smattering of old hippies, there's a tangible air of quietude to this rustic realm. Pack a picnic and spend the afternoon communing with the natural world in a setting rewardingly divorced from big-city life.

❺ Chemainus

The residents of this tree-ringed settlement – a former resource community that almost became a ghost town – began commissioning **murals** on its walls in the 1980s, part of a forward-thinking revitalization project. The paintings – there are now almost 50 – soon became visitor attractions, stoking the town's rebirth. Among the best are the 17m-long (55ft-) pioneer-town painting of Chemainus c 1891 on Mill St, the 15m-long (50ft-) depiction of First Nations faces and totems on Chemainus Rd, and the evocative Maple St mural showing the waterfront community as it was in 1948.

Pick up a walking-tour map of the murals from the **visitor center** next to Waterwheel Park (where there's also a parking lot). In the same building, the town's small **museum** is well stocked with yesteryear reminders of the old town. Be sure to chat with the friendly volunteers; they'll regale you with real-life stories of the area's colorful past.

The lower part of the town is rather quiet but the southern end of Willow St has many cafes, restaurants and boutique galleries to keep you and your wallet occupied.

The impressive **Chemainus Theatre Festival** (☎250-246-9820; www.chemainustheatrefestival.ca; 9737 Chemainus Rd; tickets from C$25) is also popular, staging shows for much of the year.

The Drive » Head north on Hwy 1 toward Nanaimo. Follow the signs to Departure Bay and catch a BC Ferries vessel to mainland Horseshoe Bay. From there, hop a second 40-minute ferry ride to Langdale on the Sunshine Coast (there are many restaurants in Horseshoe Bay if you're waiting between ferries).

From Langdale, it's a short drive along Hwy 101 to Gibsons.

TRIP HIGHLIGHT

❻ Gibsons

Gibsons *feels* cozy. If you didn't know better, you'd think you were on an island – such is the strong community and almost isolated feel this town exudes. Head straight for the waterfront area – known as **Gibsons Landing** – where you can take in the many bright-painted clapboard buildings that back on to the water's edge, as well as intriguing artisan stores.

A walk along the town's main wooden jetty leads you past a colorful array of houseboats and floating garden plots. You'll also come to the sun-dappled gallery of **Sa Boothroyd** (☎604-886-7072; www.saboothroyd.com; Government Wharf; ☺11am-5pm). The artist is typically on hand to illuminate her browse-worthy and often humorous works. Although her bigger canvases are suitably pricey, there are lots of tempting original trivets, coasters and tea cozies.

Need more culture? Head to the charming **Gibsons Public Art Gallery** (☎604-886-0531; www.gpag.ca; 431 Marine Dr; ☺11am-4pm Jun-Aug, Thu-Mon only Sep-May), which showcases the work of locals artists and changes its displays every month.

BC Forest Discovery Centre (p293)

DETOUR: WILD PLAY ELEMENT PARKS

Start: ❺ Chemainus

Fancy zipping, swinging or jumping from a giant tree? It's an easy 21km (13-mile) drive north on Hwy 1 from Chemainus to **Wild Play Element Parks** (🕿250-716-7874; www.wildplay.com; 35 Nanaimo River Rd; ⏰10am-6pm mid-May–Sep, reduced hours Oct–mid-May; 🚻) for some woodland thrills involving canopy obstacle courses and a daredevil bungee-jump zone.

Check the website for show openings, always a good time to meet the arty locals.

The Drive » Continue along tree-lined Hwy 101; expect glimpses of sandy coves in the forests on your left. The highway leads through Sechelt (handy for supplies) then on to Earls Cove. Hop the BC Ferries service across Jervis Inlet to Saltery Bay. This achingly beautiful 50-minute trip threads past islands and forested coastlines. From Saltery Bay, take Hwy 101 to Powell River.

 p297

❼ Powell River

Powell River is one of the Sunshine Coast's most vibrant communities. It was founded in the early 1900s when three Minnesota businessmen dammed the river to create a massive hydroelectric power plant. Not long after, a pulp mill was built to take advantage of the surrounding forests and handy deepwater harbor, with the first sheets of paper trundling off its steamy production line in 1912. Within a few years, the mill had become the world's largest producer of newsprint, churning out 275 tonnes daily.

Today there's an active and artsy vibe to this waterfront town, including its historic **Townsite** (🕿604-483-3901; www.powellrivertownsite.com; 6211 Walnut Ave, Dr Henderson's House; ⏰noon-4pm Tue-Fri Mar-Oct, 11am-3pm Tue-Fri Nov-Feb) area, which is great for on-foot wandering. Many of Powell River's oldest streets are named after trees and some are still lined with the original mill workers' cottages that kick-started the settlement. The steam-plumed mill is still here, too – although it's shrinking every year and its former grounds are being transformed into parkland. Dip into this history at **Powell River Museum** (🕿604-485-2327; www.powellrivermuseum.ca; 4798 Marine Ave; ⏰10am-4pm mid-Jun–Sep, closed Mon Oct–mid-Jun), which covers the area's First Nations heritage and its tough pioneer days.

If you spend the night in town, catch a film at the quaint **Patricia Theatre** (🕿604-483-9345; www.patriciatheatre.com; 5848 Ash Ave), Canada's oldest continually operating cinema.

✗ ⌂ p297

SUNSHINE COAST GALLERY CRAWL

Along Hwy 101, keep your eyes peeled for jaunty purple flags fluttering in the breeze. These indicate that an artist is at work on the adjoining property. If your eyesight isn't up to the task (or you're the designated driver), pick up the handy Sunshine Coast Purple Banner flyer from area visitor centers and galleries to find out exactly where these artists are located. Some are open for drop-in visits while others prefer that you call ahead. The region is studded with arts and crafts creators, working with wood, glass, clay and just about everything else. For further information, check www.suncoastarts.com.

Eating & Sleeping

Victoria ❶

✕ Jam Cafe
Breakfast $$

(📞778-440-4489; www.jamcafes.com; 542 Herald St; breakfast C$13-17; ⊗8am-3pm; 🛜🅿; 🖥70) No need to conduct an opinion poll: the perennial lines in the street outside Jam suggest that this is the best breakfast spot in Victoria. The reasons? Tasteful vintage decor (if you'll excuse them the moose's head); fast, discreet service; and the kind of creative breakfast dishes that you'd never have the energy or ingenuity to cook yourself.

🛏 Ocean Island Inn
Hostel $

(📞250-385-1789; www.oceanisland.com; 791 Pandora Ave; dm/d from C$36/56; @🛜; 🖥70) The kind of hostel that'll make you want to become a backpacker (again), the Ocean is a fabulous blitz of sharp color accents, global travel memorabilia and more handy extras than a deluxe five-star hotel. Bank on free breakfast (including waffles!), free dinner, a free nightly drink, free bag storage (handy for the West Coast Trail) and free friendly advice.

Cowichan Bay ❸

✕ Masthead Restaurant
Northwestern US $$$

(📞250-748-3714; www.themastheadrestaurant.com; 1705 Cowichan Bay Rd; mains C$22-54; ⊗5-10pm) The patio deck of this charming, 1863 heritage-building restaurant is a fine place for a splurge, and the C$37 three-course BC-sourced tasting menu is surprisingly good value. Seasonal ingredients form the approach here and there are also some good Cowichan Valley wines to try if you're feeling boozily adventurous.

🛏 Dreamweaver
B&B $$

(📞250-748-7688; www.dreamweaverbedand breakfast.com; 1682 Botwood Lane; d from C$135; 🛜) This Victorian-style home welcomes guests with three comfortable, rather floral rooms. It's perched on the edge of the village, just steps away from the restaurants and galleries.

Gibsons ❻

✕ Molly's Reach
Breakfast, Burgers $$

(📞604-886-9710; www.mollysreach.ca; 647 School Rd; mains C$12-17; ⊗8am-3pm) Any Canadian who was near a TV set in the 1970s and '80s will recognize this sunset-yellow harborside abode as the primary filming location for the long-running drama series, *The Beachcombers*.

Powell River ❼

✕ Base Camp
Cafe $

(📞604-485-5826; www.basecamp-coffee.com; 4548 Marine Dr; mains C$8-16; ⊗7am-5pm; 🛜) The town's quintessential community coffee hangout has, no doubt, served as base camp for many energetic Sunshine Coast excursions judging by the breakfasts – be it the maple granola parfait or the curried tofu scramble. The communal tables are great for eavesdropping and the large local map on the wall will help get you oriented while you enjoy the java.

🛏 Old Courthouse Inn
Hotel $$

(📞604-483-4000; www.oldcourthouseinn.ca; 6243 Walnut St; s/d from C$119/139; 🛜) A wonderful slice of yesteryear or an old-fashioned over-cluttered inn, depending on your penchant for antiques, this mock-Tudor hotel keeps one foot in the past, reliving its glory days as the town courthouse. The eight rooms retain the feel of the 1940s, but with modern amenities (wi-fi, TVs) thrown in, and a generous hot breakfast is included in the on-site cafe.

Southern Vancouver Island Tour

28

Begin on the Gulf Islands among uncommon amounts of creativity and tranquility. Then cross through ancient, fern-lined forests to Vancouver Island's wild west coast.

TRIP HIGHLIGHTS

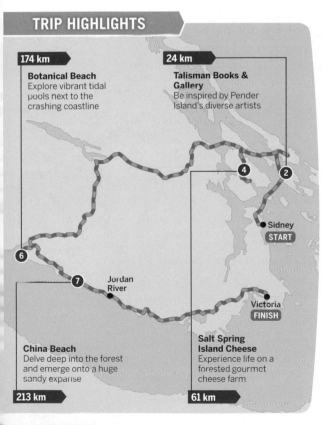

174 km

Botanical Beach
Explore vibrant tidal pools next to the crashing coastline

24 km

Talisman Books & Gallery
Be inspired by Pender Island's diverse artists

China Beach
Delve deep into the forest and emerge onto a huge sandy expanse

213 km

Salt Spring Island Cheese
Experience life on a forested gourmet cheese farm

61 km

Jordan River

● Sidney
START

Victoria
FINISH

4–5 DAYS
290KM / 182 MILES

GREAT FOR...

BEST TIME TO GO
June to September for frequent ferries, warm weather and possible whale sightings.

ESSENTIAL PHOTO

Botanical Beach's crashing waves.

BEST FOR OUTDOORS

Salt Spring Island for cycling and hiking, and kayaking in sun-dappled lakes.

Botanical Beach (p303) Tidal pools

Southern Vancouver Island Tour

Whether you're standing on the deck of a Gulf Islands ferry or on the sandy expanse of China Beach, the untamed ocean is an essential part of life in this part of the world. It seems to foster pods of creativity – small islands where artisans practice crafts from pottery to cheese-making – and it salt-licks the dramatic coastline into shape, with sandy coves fringed by dense, wind-bent woodlands.

❶ Sidney

A short trip north of Victoria, the sunny seaside town of Sidney is ideal for wandering. Along the main street, an almost unseemly number of bookstores jostle for space with boutique shops and cafes. The best for serious bibliophiles is vaguely Dickensian **Haunted Books** (☎250-656-8805; 9807 3rd St; ⏰10am-5pm). When you reach the water, you'll find the **Seaside Sculpture Walk** – showcasing a dozen or so locally

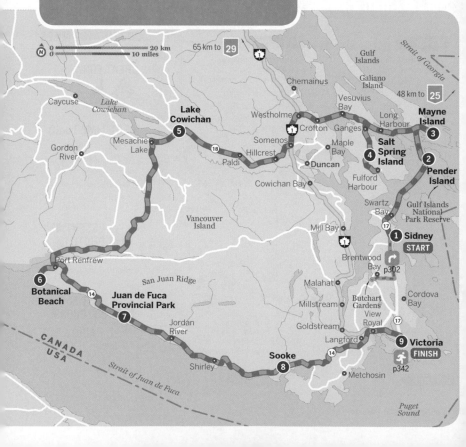

created artworks – plus a picturesque pier with twinkling island vistas.

While you're at the waterfront, visit the compact but brilliant **Shaw Centre for the Salish Sea** (☎250-665-7511; www.salishseacentre.org; 9811 Seaport Pl; adult/child C$17.50/12; ☺10am-4:30pm;). It opens your eyes to the color and diversity in the neighboring Salish Sea with aquariums, touch tanks and plenty of hands-on exhibits. The staff are well-versed and the gift shop is a treasure trove.

The Drive » Follow Hwy 17 (Patricia Bay Hwy) north for 6km (3.75 miles) to its end at the BC Ferries terminal. Board a boat for a beautiful 40-minute crossing to Pender Island.

LINK YOUR TRIP

25 Vancouver & the Fraser Valley

From the Gulf Islands, catch a ferry to Tsawwassen to get a closer look at Vancouver and the farm-dotted Fraser River Valley.

29 Vancouver Island's Remote North

When you reach Hwy 1 after leaving Salt Spring Island, you can carry on north for a taste of off-the-beaten-track Vancouver Island.

OFF THE FENCE

Going strong for nearly 25 years, **Art Off the Fence** started as just that – an artist exhibiting her work all over her fence. Each year in mid-July, a dozen or so additional artists hang their work on the fence and in the orchard of a Pender property, creating a weekend-long grassroots outdoor gallery. Look, shop, enjoy the live music and meet the island locals.

✕ 🍴 p305

----

❷ Pender Island

Arriving on this small island, you are quickly enveloped in a sense of tangible quietude. Narrow roads wind within deep forests where you'll see countless walking trails, quail crossings and confident deer.

Pender is actually two islands – North and South, joined by a small bridge. **Gowland** and **Tilly Point** on South Pender have beach access; head to Tilly Point for tidal pools and Mt Baker views. Sheltered, sandy **Medicine Beach** on the North Island has lots of clamber-worthy logs. While on the beaches, look out for bald eagles, seals and otters.

Pender is also home to many artists. Pick up a copy of the *Pender Island Artists Guide* on the ferry. A great place to start is at **Talisman Books & Gallery** (☎250-629-6944; www.talisman books.ca; 4/4605 Bedwell Harbour Rd, Driftwood Centre, North Pender; ☺10am-5pm, 11am-4pm Sun) in the central Driftwood Centre where you'll also find great cakes and coffee.

For locally produced wine, head to **Sea Star Vineyards** (☎250-629-6960; www.seastarvineyards. ca; 6621 Harbour Hill Dr, North Pender; ☺11am-5pm May-Sep). Using grapes from its own vine-striped hills, it produces tasty small-batch tipples plus a wide array of fruit from kiwis to raspberries.

Also worth a look is **Pender Islands Museum** (www.penderislandsmuseum. ca; 2408 South Otter Bay Rd, North Pender; ☺10am-4pm Sat & Sun Jul & Aug, reduced hours Sep-Jun; P), housed in a 1908 farmhouse. Explore the history of the island through its re-created rooms, vintage photos and evocative exhibits.

The Drive » Return to the ferry terminal on North Pender and board a ferry for the 25-minute voyage through the channel to Mayne Island.

✕ p305

❸ Mayne Island

As the boat pulls into Mayne Island, you're greeted with colorful wooden houses, quaint communities and lots of deer. Head to **Georgina Point Lighthouse** for ocean and mountain-filled views across Active Pass. The water literally bubbles here with the strength of the current. This is a popular spot for eagles to fish and you're also likely to see (and hear) sea lions resting on nearby rocks.

For a quiet retreat, visit the **Japanese Garden** (Dinner Point Rd, Dinner Bay Community Park), dedicated to the many Japanese families who settled on the island from 1900 onward. Once constituting a third of the popula-

tion, they contributed more than half of the island's farming, milling and fish-preservation work. During WWII the government saw them as a national threat and forced their removal. The garden contains traditional Japanese elements within a forest, including shrines and a peace bell.

The Drive ❯❯ Return to the ferry terminal and board a ferry to Long Harbour on Salt Spring Island. The trip takes around 45 minutes to an hour.

 p305

 TRIP HIGHLIGHT

❹ Salt Spring Island

When folks from Vancouver talk about quitting their jobs and making jam for a living, they're likely mulling a move

to Salt Spring. Once a hippie haven and later a yuppie retreat, it's now home to anyone who craves a quieter life without sacrificing everyday conveniences. The main town of **Ganges** has it all, from grocery stores to galleries. It's a wonderful place to explore.

Salt Spring is also home to many an artisan, from bakers to carvers and winemakers. Stop in at **Waterfront Gallery** (☎250-537-4525; www.waterfrontgallery.ca; 107 Purvis Lane, Ganges; ⏰10am-5pm), which carries the work of many local artists with pottery, glassware, knitwear, candles and even birdhouses prominent. Also stop in at **Salt Spring Mercantile** (☎250-653-4321; www.saltspringmercantile.com; 2915 Fulford-Ganges Rd, Fulford; ⏰8:30am-6pm), which sells lots of local products, including Salish Sea Chocolates (try the cherry with hazelnut), jars of fresh chutney and flower-petal-packed soaps.

Save time for **Salt Spring Island Cheese** (☎250-653-2300; www.saltspringcheese.com; 285 Reynolds Rd; ⏰11am-5pm, to 4pm Oct-Apr; ♿) on Weston Creek Farm. Meet the goats and sheep that produce milk for the cheese, see it being made, and be awed by the beautiful finale – taste cheeses adorned with lemon slices, flowers and chilies.

DETOUR: BUTCHART GARDENS

Start: ❶ Sidney

A 16km (10-mile) drive south of Sidney on Hwy 17, turning west on Keating Cross Rd, brings you to Benvenuto Ave and British Columbia's most famous botanical attraction. The century-old **Butchart Gardens** (☎250-652-5256; www.butchartgardens.com; 800 Benvenuto Ave; adult/teen/child $34/17/3; ⏰8:45am-10pm Jun-Aug, reduced hours Sep-May; 🅿75), which originated from an attempt to beautify an old cement factory site, has been cleverly planned to ensure there's always something in bloom, no matter what the season. In summer, there are Saturday night fireworks displays and in winter the twinkling seasonal lights are magical. Whatever time of year you arrive, give yourself at least a couple of hours to enjoy the spectacle.

Ganges, Salt Spring Island Locally made cheese for sale

Head to **Ruckle Park** for ragged shorelines, gnarly arbutus forests and sun-kissed farm-lands. There are trails here for all skill levels as well as great ocean views for a picnic. **Mt Maxwell** offers a steep but worth-while hike and **Cushion Lake** and **St Mary's Lake** are summertime swimming haunts. Fancy exploring sans car? Visit **Salt Spring Adventure Co** (☎250-537-2764; www. saltspringadventures.com; 125 Rainbow Rd, Ganges; rentals/ tours from C$40/65; ⊙9am-6pm May-Sep) to rent kay-aks and join excursions.

The Drive >> Head 7km (4.25 miles) north of Ganges to Vesuvius Bay and take a 25-minute ferry ride to Crofton on Vancouver Island. From the east coast, curve inland for 38km (23.5 miles) along Hwy 18 and the glassy-calm waters of Lake Cowichan.

✗ 🛏 p305

---

⑤ Lake Cowichan

Hop out of the car at Lake Cowichan for some deep breaths at the ultra-clear, tree-fringed lakefront. This is a per-fect spot for swimming or setting out for a hike along the lakeside trails.

The Drive >> From Lake Cowichan, follow South Shore Rd and then Pacific Marine Rd to Port Renfrew and on to Botanical Beach, 66km (41 miles) from Lake Cowichan.

- - - - - - - - - - - - - - - -

TRIP HIGHLIGHT

⑥ Botanical Beach

It's worth the effort to get to **Botanical Beach,** which feels like the end of the earth. Follow the winding road from Port Renfrew and then the sometimes steep pathway down to the beach. The tidal pools here are rich in colorful marine life, including chitons, anemones, gooseneck

MARKET DAY

If you arrive on Salt Spring Island on a summer weekend, the best way to dive into the community is at the legendary Saturday Market where you can tuck into luscious island-grown fruit and piquant cheeses while perusing locally produced arts and crafts.

barnacles, sea palms and purple sea urchins. Surrounded by windblown coastline and crashing waves, this is also a favorite springtime haunt of orcas and gray whales, plus a feeding ground for harbor seals.

The rocks here can be slippery and the waves huge; take care and watch the tide.

The Drive » Head southeast on Hwy 14 for around 40km (25 miles) to nearby Juan de Fuca Provincial Park.

TRIP HIGHLIGHT

❼ Juan de Fuca Provincial Park

Welcome to the dramatic coastal wilderness of **Juan de Fuca Provincial Park** (☎250-474-1336; www.env.gov.bc.ca/bcparks/explore/parkpgs/juan_de_fuca; Hwy 14). There are good stop-off points along this rugged stretch, providing memorable views of the rocky, ocean-carved seafront where trees cling for dear life and whales slide past just off the coast. Our favorite is **China Beach**, reached along a fairly gentle, well-maintained trail through dense forest. The prize is a long stretch of windswept sand. **French Beach** is also popular with day-trippers and requires less of a leg-stretch.

The Drive » Continue southeast along Hwy 14, skirting the coastline to Sooke, 74km (46 miles) away.

❽ Sooke

Once considered the middle of nowhere, seaside Sooke is gaining popularity thanks in part to the thriving 55km (34 miles) Galloping Goose trail, a cycling and hiking path linking it with Victoria. For an introduction to the area, stop at **Sooke Region Museum** (☎250-642-6351; www.sookeregionmuseum.com; 2070 Phillips Rd; ⊙9am-5pm Tue-Sun), which has intriguing exhibits on the district's pioneer past, including the tiny **Moss Cottage**, one of the island's oldest pioneer homes.

The Drive » From Sooke, follow Hwy 14 (Sooke Rd) east, all the way to Hwy 1. Join the eastbound traffic, which will lead you on to nearby Victoria, 40km (25 miles) from Sooke.

🛏 p305

- - - - - - - - - - - - - - - - - -

❾ Victoria

The provincial capital is vibrant, charming and highly walkable (p342). The boat-filled Inner Harbour, magnetic boutique shopping and belly-thrilling cuisine make it understandably popular. Add an outgoing university crowd plus a strong arts community and you get an interesting, diverse population.

🛏 p305

Eating & Sleeping

Sidney ❶

✗ Beacon Cafe
Cafe $

(☏778-426-3663; 2505 Beacon Ave; snacks C$6-11; ⏱8am-4pm) A steadfastly local corner cafe with a few regal touches. Pastries and sandwiches abound, but the place is best enjoyed for its hot smoothies (including apple-pie flavor) and all-day high tea.

🛏 Sidney Pier Hotel & Spa
Hotel $$

(☏250-655-9445; www.sidneypier.com; 9805 Seaport Pl; d/ste C$245/275; @ 🛜🏊) This swish waterfront property fuses West Coast lounge cool with beach pastel colors and is a worthy alternative to staying in Victoria. Many rooms have shoreline views. A spa and large gym add value, plus you're steps from a rather good micro-distillery. There's also an on-site deli-cafe and West Coast–themed restaurant.

Pender Island ❷

✗ Vanilla Leaf Bakery Cafe
Cafe $

(☏250-629-6453; 17/4605 Bedwell Harbour Rd, Driftwood Centre, North Pender; snacks C$3-8; ⏱7am-5pm, from 8am Sun; 🛜) Superb pastries both sweet and savory are served here along with organic coffee. Safeguarded behind a glass partition, you can admire pistachio-cream Danish pastries, steak-and-ale pies and the dangerous-looking 'mile-high apple pie.' It's located in the Driftwood Centre with extra seating (and a summer ice-cream trolley) on a square of lawn outside.

Mayne Island ❸

✗ Bennett Bay Bistro
Canadian $$

(☏250-539-3122; www.bennettbaybistro. com; 494 Arbutus Dr; mains C$15-28; ⏱11:30am-8:30pm) You don't have to be a guest of the **Mayne Island Resort** (www. mayneislandresort.com; d/villa $159/299; 🛜🏊🏊) to dine at its restaurant, and you'll find a menu combining pubby classics like fish-and-chips with elevated dinner features like pasta and steaks. Go for the seafood, though. Reservations recommended.

Salt Spring Island ❹

✗ Tree House Cafe
Canadian $$

(☏250-537-5379; www.treehousecafe.ca; 106 Purvis Lane, Ganges; mains C$12-18; ⏱8am-4pm, to 10pm Wed-Sun, reduced hours Sep-Jun) At this magical outdoor dining experience, you'll be sitting in the shade of a large plum tree as you choose from a menu of North American–style pastas, Mexican specialties and gourmet burgers and sandwiches. There's live music Wednesday to Sunday nights in summer.

🛏 The Cottages on Salt Spring Island
Cottage $$$

(☏250-931-7258; www.cottagesonsaltspring. com; 315 Robinson Rd; cottages from C$300; P 🛜🏊) A small 'village' of deluxe cottages spread over lakeside grounds 3km (2 miles) northeast of Ganges. The semi-detached cottage units have huge modern interiors (most have three levels) with king-size beds, full kitchens and spectacular bathrooms equipped with tubs and separate showers. All have two bedrooms.

Sooke ❽

🛏 Sooke Harbour House
Hotel $$$

(☏250-642-3421; www.sookeharbourhouse. com; 1528 Whiffen Spit Rd; d from C$329; 🛜🏊) Whether you opt for the 'Emily Carr' or the 'Blue Heron,' each of the 28 guest rooms here has a decadent tub or steam shower, while most also have wood-burning fireplaces, balconies and expansive sea views.

Victoria ❾

🛏 Abigail's Hotel
B&B $$$

(☏250-388-5363; www.abigailshotel.com; 906 McClure St; d from C$249; P @ 🛜; �7) A boutique hotel with the ambience of a B&B, the historic Abigail's is Victoria's most Victorian accommodations despite the fact it was only built in 1930 with a mock Tudor facade. Near-perfect rooms come with heavy drapes, shapely furniture and marble bathrooms. In the morning, you can swan downstairs for a spectacular breakfast.

Vancouver Island's Remote North

29

Throw yourself head-first into Vancouver Island's natural side. Ancient forests, diving orca, wild sandy beaches, quaint villages and a peek into First Nations cultures make it a well-rounded trip.

TRIP HIGHLIGHTS

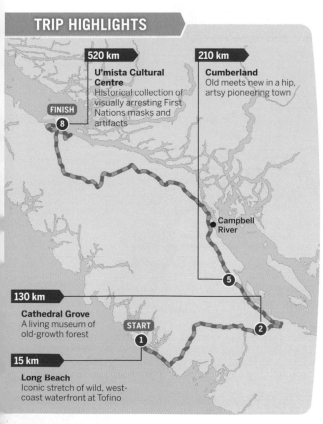

520 km

U'mista Cultural Centre
Historical collection of visually arresting First Nations masks and artifacts

210 km

Cumberland
Old meets new in a hip, artsy pioneering town

FINISH
8

Campbell River

5

130 km

Cathedral Grove
A living museum of old-growth forest

START
1

2

15 km

Long Beach
Iconic stretch of wild, west-coast waterfront at Tofino

2–3 DAYS
537KM / 336 MILES

GREAT FOR...

BEST TIME TO GO

May to September for the most sunshine and the least chance of relentless rain.

 ESSENTIAL PHOTO

The forest of totem poles watching over the sea at Alert Bay.

 BEST FOR STORM WATCHERS

Watch massive, frothy waves crashing onto Long Beach, especially in winter.

29

Vancouver Island's Remote North

Following this trip is like following Alice down the rabbit hole – you'll feel you've entered an enchanted land that's beyond the reach of day-to-day life. Ancient, moss-covered trees will leave you feeling tiny, as bald eagles swoop above and around you like pigeons. You'll see bears munching dandelions and watching you inscrutably. And totem poles, standing like forests, will seem to whisper secrets of the past. Go on. Jump in.

TRIP HIGHLIGHT

1 Tofino

Packed with activities and blessed with stunning beaches, former fishing town Tofino sits on Clayoquot (clay-kwot) Sound, where forests rise from roiling waves that continually batter the coastline. Visitors come to surf, whale-watch, kayak, hike and hug trees. For the scoop on what to do, hit the **visitor center** (☎250-725-3414; www.tourismtofino. com; 1426 Pacific Rim Hwy;

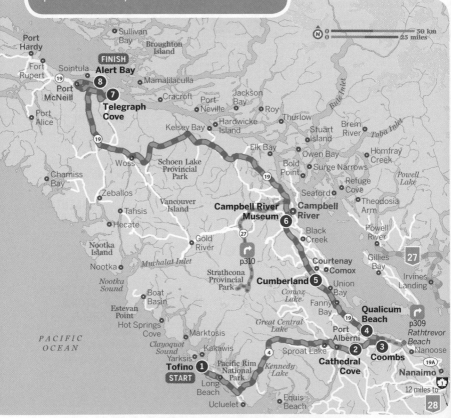

⊙ 9am-8pm Jun-Aug, reduced hours Sep-May).

The area's biggest draw is **Long Beach**, part of Pacific Rim National Park. Accessible by car along the Pacific Rim Hwy, this wide sandy swath has untamed surf, beachcombing nooks and a living museum of old-growth trees. There are plenty of walking trails; look for swooping eagles and huge banana slugs. Tread carefully over slippery surfaces and never turn your back on the mischievous surf.

Kwisitis Visitor Centre (Wick Rd; ⊙ 10am-5pm May-Oct, Fri-Sun only Mar, Apr, Nov & Dec) houses exhibits on the region, including a First Nations canoe and a look at what's in the watery depths.

LINK YOUR TRIP

27 A Strait Hop
From Qualicum Beach, travel south on Hwy 19 to Nanaimo, where you can hook up with this water-hugging circuit of the Georgia Strait.

28 Southern Vancouver Island Tour
Drive east from Coombs on Hwy 4A, then south on Hwy 1 for a vision of the island's more cultivated side.

DETOUR: RATHTREVOR BEACH

Start: ❸ **Coombs**

It's only around 20 minutes from Coombs, but Rathtrevor Beach feels like it's a million miles away. Visit when the tide is out and you'll face a huge expanse of sand. Bring buckets, shovels and the kids, who'll spend hours digging, catching crabs and hunting for shells. The beach is in a provincial park just east of Parksville, and is backed by a forested picnic area. To get there from Coombs, drive east on Hwy 4A, connecting to Hwy 19 northwest and then turning off at Rathtrevor Rd.

While you're in Tofino, don't miss Roy Henry Vickers' **Eagle Aerie Gallery** (📞250-725-3235; www.royhenryvickers.com; 350 Campbell St; ⊙ 10am-5pm), housed in an atmospheric traditional longhouse. Vickers is one of Canada's most successful and prolific indigenous artists.

If you're freshly arrived in Tofino and want to know what makes this place so special, head down First St and join the undulating 1.2km (0.75-mile) gravel trail to **Tonquin Beach** where a magical parting of the trees reveals a rock-punctuated swath of sand well-known for its life-affirming sunsets.

The Drive ≫ Follow Pacific Rim Hwy 4 southeast, and then north as it turns into the Mackenzie Range. Mountains rise up on the right as you weave past the unfathomably deep Kennedy Lake. The road carries on along the racing Kennedy River. Continue to the next stop, just past Port Alberni. This longish 140km (87 miles) leg should take a little over two hours.

 p313

 TRIP HIGHLIGHT

❷ Cathedral Grove

To the east of Port Alberni, **Cathedral Grove** (www.bcparks.ca; MacMillan Provincial Park; P) is the spiritual home of tree huggers and the mystical highlight of MacMillan Provincial Park. Look up – way, waaaaay up – and the vertigo-inducing views of the swaying treetops will leave you swooning. Extremely popular in summer, its accessible forest trails wind through dense woodland, offering glimpses of some of British Columbia's oldest trees, including centuries-old Douglas firs more than 3m (10ft) in diameter. Try hugging that.

The Drive » Continue east for 17km (10.5 miles) on Hwy 4, past Cameron Lake, with swimming beaches and supposedly a resident monster. From Hwy 4, follow Hwy 4A for 2km (1.25 miles) into Coombs.

-----

❸ Coombs

The mother of all pit stops, **Coombs Old Country Market** (📞250-248-6272; www.oldcountry market.com; 2326 Alberni Hwy; ⏰9am-6pm Feb-Dec) attracts huge numbers of visitors almost year-round. You'll get inquisitive looks from a herd of goats that spends the summer season on the grassy roof, a tradition here for decades. Nip inside for giant ice-cream cones, heaping pizzas and all the deli makings of a great picnic, then spend an hour or two wandering around the attendant stores, which are filled with unique crafts, clothes and antiques.

The Drive » Continue east for 9km (5.5 miles) on Hwy 4A, crossing Hwy 19 to Parksville on the coast. Turn left and follow the coastline west past pretty French Creek for 11km (6.75 miles) and on to Qualicum Beach.

-----

❹ Qualicum Beach

A small community of classic seafront motels and a giant beachcomber-friendly bay, Qualicum Beach is a favorite family destination. This coastline is thick with shellfish; many of the scallops, oysters and mussels that restaurants serve up come from here. Wander the beach for shells, and look for sand dollars – they're readily found here.

JAIME KOWAL/GETTY IMAGES ©

📍 DETOUR: STRATHCONA PROVINCIAL PARK

Start: ❻ Campbell River Museum

BC's oldest protected area and also Vancouver Island's largest park, **Strathcona** (📞250-474-1336; www.env.gov.bc.ca/bcparks/explore/parkpgs/strath) is a 40km (25-mile) drive west on Hwy 28 from Campbell River. Centered on Mt Golden Hinde, the island's highest point (2200m/7218ft), it's a pristine wilderness crisscrossed with trail systems that deliver you to waterfalls, alpine meadows, glacial lakes and looming crags.

On arrival at the main entrance, get your bearings at **Strathcona Park Lodge & Outdoor Education Centre**. It's a one-stop shop for park activities, including kayaking, guided treks and rock climbing for all ages.

The Drive » While it's slower than Hwy 19, Hwy 19A is a scenic drive, following the coast north past the Fanny Bay Oyster Farm and Denman Island. After 55km (34 miles) turn left just north of Union Bay to connect with Hwy 19. Turn right, continue north for 5km (3 miles) and take the exit for Cumberland.

✗ 🛏 p313

TRIP HIGHLIGHT

❺ Cumberland

Founded as a coal-mining town in 1888, Cumberland was one of BC's original pioneer settlements, home to workers from Japan, China and the American South. These days,

Tofino Long Beach (p309)

it's officially a 'village' with a main street that's still lined with early 20th-century wood-built stores. But Cumberland has also moved with the times. Instead of blacksmiths and dry-goods shops, you'll find cool boutiques, espresso bars and a local community who've pioneered one of the finest mountain-biking networks in BC in an adjacent forest. You can get kitted out for two-wheeled action at **Dodge City Cycles** (250-336-2200; www.dodgecitycycles.com; 2705 Dunsmuir Ave; bike rentals per 2/24hr C$50/120; 9am-6pm

Mon-Sat, 10am-2:30pm Sun). If you prefer something more sedentary take time to peruse the very impressive **Cumberland Museum** (250-336-2445; www.cumberlandmuseum.ca; 2680 Dunsmuir Ave; adult/child C$5/4; 10am-5pm Jun-Aug, closed Mon Sep-May), which explores the area's coal-mining past.

The Drive >> Carry on north on Hwy 19, with mountain and island views. Turn right onto Hamm Rd, heading east across farmland and passing a bison farm. Turn left onto Hwy 19A, which skirts Oyster Bay. The next stop is on your left, on the outskirts of Campbell River. Total distance: 55km (34 miles).

 p313

----

❻ Campbell River Museum

Stretch your legs and your curiosity with a wander through the **Museum at Campbell River** (250-287-3103; www.crmuseum.ca; 470 Island Hwy; adult/child C$8/5; 10am-5pm mid-May–Sep, from noon Tue-Sun Oct–mid-May). Hop behind the wheel of an early logging truck, explore a settler's cabin, see First Nations masks and watch footage of the removal of the legendary, ship-destroying

311

TOP TIP:
PACIFIC RIM PARK PASS

First-timers should drop by the **Pacific Rim Visitors Centre** (☎250-726-4600; www.pacificrimvisitor.ca; 2791 Pacific Rim Hwy, Ucuelet; ☻10am-4:30pm Tue-Sat) for maps and advice on exploring this spectacular region. If you're stopping in the park, you'll need to pay and display a pass, available here.

Ripple Rock, which was blasted with the largest non-nuclear explosion in history.

The Drive » From Campbell River, head northwest on Hwy 19. As you inch into Vancouver Island's north, follow the signs and an increasingly narrow road for 16km (10 miles) to Telegraph Cove. En route, you'll pass Beaver Cove with its flotilla of logs waiting to be hauled away for milling. It's a beautiful drive, but isolated. Fuel up before you head out.

❼ Telegraph Cove

Built on stilts over the water in 1912, Telegraph Cove was originally a station for the northern terminus of the island's telegraph. A salmon saltery and sawmill were later added. Extremely popular with summer day-trippers, the board-walk and its many houses

have been charmingly restored, with plaques illuminating their original residents. During the season, the waters off the cove are also home to orcas. See (and hear) them on a trip with **Prince of Whales** (☎888-383-4884; www.princeofwhales.com; half-day trip adult/child C$130/95). You might also encounter minke and humpback whales as well as dolphins and porpoises.

The Drive » Return to Hwy 19 and carry on for 26km (16 miles) to Port McNeill, from where you can catch a BC Ferries vessel for the 45-minute journey to Alert Bay on Cormorant Island.

✗ ⌂ p313

TRIP HIGHLIGHT
❽ Alert Bay

This spread-out island village has an ancient and mythical appeal underpinned by its strong First Nations culture and community. In some respects, it feels like an open-air museum. On the southern side is an old pioneer fishing settlement and the traditional **Namgis Burial Grounds**, where dozens of gracefully weathering totem poles stand like a forest of ageless art.

Next to the site of the now-demolished St Michael's Residential School is a much more enduring symbol of First Nations community. The must-see **U'mista Cultural Centre** (☎250-974-5403; www.umista.ca; 1 Front St; adult/child C$12/5; ☻9am-5pm Tue-Sat Sep-Jun, daily Jul & Aug) houses ceremonial masks and other items confiscated by the Canadian government in the 1920s and now repatriated from museums around the world.

Continue over the hill to the Big House, where **traditional dance performances** (cnr Wood St & Hill St; ☻Thu-Sat Jul & Aug) are held for visitors. One of the world's tallest totem poles is also here. Alert Bay is home to many professional carvers and you'll see their work in galleries around the village.

Head to the **visitor center** (☎250-974-5024; www.alertbay.ca; 118 Fir St; ☻9am-5pm Mon-Fri Jun, Sep & Oct, daily Jul & Aug) for more information.

⌂ p313

TOP TIP:
VANCOUVER ISLAND NORTH

For maps, activities, tide charts and photos to inspire you, visit www.vancouverislandnorth.ca.

Eating & Sleeping

Tofino ❶

✕ Sobo   Canadian $$

(☏250-725-2341; www.sobo.ca; 311 Neill St; mains C$17-36; ⏱11:30am-9pm) It's hard not to love a restaurant whose name is short for 'sophisticated bohemian,' a label that might have been invented with Tofino in mind. Once a humble food truck, Sobo is now an ultra-contemporary bricks-and-mortar bistro with floor-to-ceiling windows. The salads are exceptional and the pizzas aren't far behind.

⌂ Ecolodge   Hostel $$

(☏250-725-1220; www.tbgf.org; 1084 Pacific Rim Hwy; r incl breakfast from C$159; P @ 🛜) This quiet, wood-built education center on the grounds of the botanical gardens is popular with families and groups for its selection of rooms, large kitchen and on-site laundry. There's a bunk room that's around C$45 per person per night in summer for groups of four. Rates include garden entry.

Qualicum Beach ❹

✕ Fish Tales Cafe   Seafood $$

(☏250-752-6053; www.fishtalescafe.com; 3336 Island Hwy W; mains C$18-30; ⏱11.30am-9pm Tue-Sun) Anglophilia is alive and well in this diminutive timber-framed restaurant where fish-and-chips and mushy peas are served against a backdrop of model ships, Union Jack tea towels and horse brasses. It's understandably popular with UK expats who sit around reminiscing about their school days.

⌂ Free Spirit Spheres   Cabin $$$

(☏250-757-9445; www.freespiritspheres.com; 420 Horne Lake Rd; spheres from C$314) When it comes to extravagantly unconventional accommodations, these three wooden spheres, handmade by owner-inventor Tom Chudleigh and suspended like giant eyes within the forest canopy, score 10 out of 10. Compact two- to three-person spheres have pull-down beds, built-in cabinets and mini-libraries rather than TVs and are a perfect way to commune with BC's giant trees.

Cumberland ❺

✕ The Wandering Moose   Cafe $

(☏250-400-1111; www.wanderingmoose.ca; 2739 Dunsmuir Ave; mains C$6-12; ⏱10am-4pm Thu-Sat & Mon-Tue, from 9am Sun; 🛜) The redbrick walls of Cumberland's original post and customs house contrast with a more flamboyant interior. A forthright blackboard greets you on entry advertising wraps, burritos and breakfast muffins. Drop off the kids by the dollhouse and enjoy the reverie.

Telegraph Cove ❼

✕ Seahorse Cafe   Cafe $

(☏250-527-1001; www.seahorsecafe.org; mains C$7-10; ⏱8am-6pm May, Jun & Sep, 7am-8pm Jul & Aug) This popular little dockside cafe has plenty of outdoor picnic tables for you to relax at while digging into generous around-the-world 'snacks' like barbecued Bavarian smokies, Canadian bison burgers, Swedish crepes, Baja tacos and Greek salads.

⌂ Telegraph Cove Resort   Resort $$

(☏250-928-3131; www.telegraphcoveresort. com; campsites/cabins/lodge rm from C$38/150/220) This well-established heritage resort provides accommodations in forested tent spaces as well as a string of rustic, highly popular cabins on stilts overlooking the marina. A new 24-room lodge built from local wood to resemble the nearby Whale Interpretive Centre (p357) manages to look fabulous without spoiling the fishing-village ambience.

Alert Bay ❽

⌂ Alert Bay Cabins   Cabin $$

(☏604-974-5457; www.alertbaycabins.net; 390 Poplar Rd; cabins C$145-200) A clutch of well-maintained cabins, each with kitchens or kitchenettes, this is a great retreat-like option if you want to get away from it all. Cabins accommodate four to six people. Call ahead and the staff will even pick you up from the ferry; otherwise it's a 2.5km (1.5-mile) walk.

Classic Trip

Okanagan Valley Wine Tour

30

Weave your way between golden hills and the shimmering Okanagan Lake. This route will leave you with a trunkful of first-class wine and, depending on the season, juicy cherries and peaches.

TRIP HIGHLIGHTS

2 km

Mission Hill Family Estate
This wine finds its way into many a restaurant across BC; try it at its source

3 km

Old Vines
Dishing up all kinds of gourmet-prepared local produce on a vineyard terrace

● Kelowna

❷
❶
START

❺

FINISH
❼

Carmelis Goat Cheese Artisan
Whether in blue or gelato form, it's handmade and delicious

35 km

Summerhill Pyramid Winery
The pyramid experience is intriguing, as is the wine

27 km

**2 DAYS
35KM / 22 MILES**

GREAT FOR...

BEST TIME TO GO

July and September bring hot sunny days – perfect for a slow-paced meander.

 ESSENTIAL PHOTO

View from the terrace at Mission Hill Family Estate winery.

 BEST FOR FOODIES

Stop for fresh peaches, nectarines, apricots, cherries, raspberries and watermelons in season.

Classic Trip

30 Okanagan Valley Wine Tour

Filling up on sun-ripened fruit at roadside stalls has long been a highlight of traveling through the Okanagan on a hot summer day. Since the 1980s, the region has widened its embrace of the culinary world by striping its hillsides with grapes. Over 180 vineyards take advantage of the Okanagan's cool winters and long summers. Ice wine, made from grapes frozen on the vine, is a unique take-home tipple. And when you're done soaking up the wine, you can soak up the scenery at the countless beaches along the way.

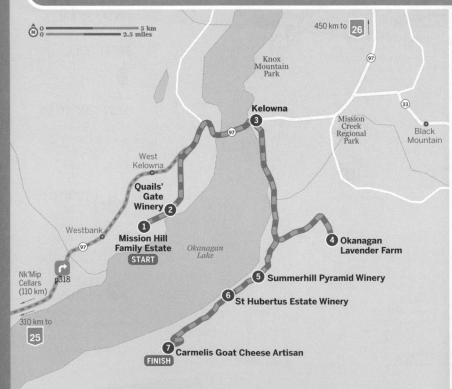

❶ Mission Hill Family Estate

Begin your leisurely taste-tripping trawl on the western shore of the 100km-long Okanagan Lake, the region's centerpiece. Following Boucherie Rd north, between the lake and Hwy 97, will bring you to Westbank's **Mission Hill Family Estate** (☎250-768-6400; www.missionhillwinery.com; 1730 Mission Hill Rd, West Kelowna; ☺10am-7pm; Ⓟ). The estate is a modernist reinterpretation of mission buildings, reached through imposing gates and dominated by a 26m (85ft) bell-tower. Several tours and tastings are available, with some that

LINK YOUR TRIP

25 Vancouver & the Fraser Valley

Follow Hwys 3A and 3 from the southern end of Okanagan Lake to Hope and the pastoral Fraser Valley.

26 Sea to Sky Highway

Head northwest from Okanagan Lake on Hwy 97 through Kamloops to Hwy 99 for this spectacular melding of mountains and sea.

LOCAL KNOWLEDGE: WHAT'S RIPE WHEN

Say that 10 times fast. It's even trickier when you've got a mouthful of plump raspberries. Farms sell their ripened fruit at stalls along the road, and fresh fruit and veggie markets are plentiful. Harvest times bring lower prices and top nosh. Here's what to watch for when:

Strawberries June and July

Raspberries July

Cherries June to August

Apricots July and August

Peaches July to September

Pears August and September

Apples September to October

Table grapes September to October

include lunch. Aside from checking out vineyards and barrel cellars, you may be lucky enough to see an amazing (and rare) tapestry by French-Russian artist Marc Chagall hanging in one of the rooms.

The winery's Terrace restaurant sits atop a glorious terrace overlooking vineyards and lake. Its spectacular food matches the setting. Nearby, a grassy amphitheater hosts summer concerts (accompanied by wine, of course). You can also visit the shop for souvenir bottles. Try Oculus, the winery's premium and unique Bordeaux blend.

The Drive » Return to Boucherie Rd and continue 2km (1.25 miles) north, following the lakeshore.

❷ Quails' Gate Winery

Charming stone and beam architecture reigns at **Quails' Gate Winery** (☎250-769-4451; www.quailsgate.com; 3303 Boucherie Rd, West Kelowna; ☺10am-8pm; Ⓟ). Tours run throughout spring and summer and begin in an on-site pioneer home built in 1873. Tastings are held throughout the day – the rhubarby Chenin Blanc and pleasantly peppery reserve Pinot Noir are recommended. The winery's Old Vines restaurant is a foodie favorite, with a menu showcasing seasonal BC ingredients and a commitment to sourcing sustainable seafood.

Classic Trip

Or you could just chill at vine-side picnic benches.

The Drive ⟫ Head 9km (5.5 miles) northeast on Boucherie Rd before merging with Hwy 97. Cross the lake at the new William R Bennett Bridge and head for the 'east coast' town of Kelowna, the Okanagan capital.

 p323

----

❸ Kelowna

The wine industry has turned Kelowna into a bit of a boomtown. The pop-ulation has almost dou-bled since the early 1990s and property prices have risen accordingly. A wan-der (especially along Ellis St) will unearth plenty of art galleries and lakeside parks, along with cafes and wine bars.

Continue your wine ed-ucation at the **Okanagan Wine and Orchard Mus-eum** (☏778-478-0325; www.kelownamuseums.ca; 1304 Ellis St; by donation; ☺10am-5pm Mon-Sat, 11am-4pm Sun). Housed in the historic Laurel Packinghouse and expanded to include fruit memorabilia in 2016, the museum offers a look at celebrated bottles, labels and equipment, along with an overview of wine-making in the region. There's a separate section on fruit packing.

With vineyards cozied up to Knox Mountain, **Sandhill Wines** (☏250-979-4211; www.sandhillwines.ca; 1125 Richter St; ☺10am-6pm; P), formerly known as Calona Vineyards, was the Okanagan's first winery, kicking off production in 1932. Its architecturally striking tasting room is an atmospheric spot to try the ever-popular, melon-note Pinot Blanc, along with the port-style dessert wine that makes an ideal cheese buddy. You'll find the winery north of Hwy 97.

The Drive ⟫ Head south of Kelowna on Lakeshore Rd, keeping Okanagan Lake on your right. Take a left onto Dehart Rd and follow it to Bedford Rd. Turn right and then right again so that you're heading south on Takla Rd. The 10km (6.25-mile) drive should take less than 15 minutes.

🍴 🛏 p323

----

❹ Okanagan Lavender Farm

Visiting **Okanagan Lav-ender Farm** (☏250-764-7795; www.okanaganlavender.com; 4380 Takla Rd; tours C\$5-15; ☺10am-5pm, tours 10:15am, 11:30am & 2:30pm Jun-Aug; P 🐾) is a heady experience. Rows and rows of over 60 types of lavender waft in the breeze against the back-drop of Okanagan Lake.

↪ DETOUR: NK'MIP CELLARS

Start: ❷ Quails' Gate

Add a day to your visit and head for this multifarious **cultural center** (☏250-495-7901; www.nkmipdesert.com; 1000 Rancher Creek Rd; adult/child C\$12/8; ☺9:30am-4:30pm May-Sep, shorter hours Oct-Apr; P) just east of Osoyoos, part of a First Nations empire that includes a desert golf course, the noted winery **Nk'Mip Cellars**, a resort and more. The architecturally slick cultural center celebrates the Syilx people of the Okanagan Nation and the delicate desert ecosystem where they traditionally live. Those with a little reptilian courage can also check out the on-site rattlesnake enclosure.

Save a bit more time to sample one of the region's most distinctive wineries at Nk'Mip Cellars, North America's first indigenous-owned and -operated winery when it opened in 2003. Tastings of five different wines cost C\$5. The place is known for its ice wines and is open 10am to 6pm in the summer (to 5pm November to March). The two Nk'Mip sites are located about 112km (70 miles) south of Westbank along Hwy 97.

Kelowna Vineyard

Classic Trip

WHY THIS IS A CLASSIC TRIP
BRENDAN SAINSBURY, WRITER

Even as a BC resident you still have to sometimes pinch yourself when traveling through the Okanagan to check that you haven't been accidentally teleported over to France or Italy. Not only do the vine-striped hills and glassy water vistas resemble Provence or Lake Garda, the quality and quantity of the wines have also burgeoned to challenge the hegemony of the European stalwarts cross the 'pond.'

Above: Terrace (by architect Tom Kundig), Mission Hill Family Estate (p317)
Left: Summerhill Pyramid Winery
Right: Grapes growing by Okanagan Lake

You can enjoy a guided or self-guided tour of the acreage and pop into the shop. Your wine-soaked palate will be well and truly cleansed.

The Drive » Retrace your route back to Lakeshore Rd, heading south and then veering left onto Chute Lake Rd after 6.5km (4 miles).

TRIP HIGHLIGHT

⑤ Summerhill Pyramid Winery

In the hills along the lake's eastern shore, you'll soon come to one of the Okanagan's most colorful wineries. **Summerhill Pyramid Winery** (📞250-764-8000; www.summerhill. bc.ca; 4870 Chute Lake Rd; 🕘9am-6pm; P) combines a traditional tasting room with a huge pyramid where every Summerhill wine ages in barrels, owing to the belief that sacred geometry has a positive effect on liquids. The winery's vegan-friendly Sunset Organic Bistro is much loved and the Ehrenfelser ice wine is particularly delightful.

The Drive » Return to Lakeside Rd and continue south for 2.5km (1.5 miles). The next stop is across from Cedar Creek Park.

✖ p323

⑥ St Hubertus Estate Winery

Lakeside **St Hubertus Estate Winery** (📞250-764-7888; www.st-hubertus.

Classic Trip

bc.ca; 5225 Lakeshore Rd, near Kelowna; ⊙10am-5:30pm May-Oct, noon-4pm Mon-Sat Nov-Apr) is another twist on the winery approach. Visiting is like being at a traditional northern European vineyard, complete with Bavarian architectural flourishes.

Despite its emphasis on Germanic wines, including Riesling, St Hubertus isn't conservative: try its floral, somewhat spicy Casselas and the rich Marechal Foch. While there are no formal tours, you can stroll around the vineyard or head to the complimentary tasting room to try four different wines. There's also a shop selling artisan foods and, of course, wine.

✓ TOP TIP: WINE FESTIVALS

The Okanagan stages four major multiday seasonal wine festivals (www.thewinefestivals.com) throughout the year. Time your visit right and dip into one of these:

Winter Festival January

Spring Wine Festival May

Summer Wine Festival August

Fall Wine Festival October

The Drive » Continue south on Lakeside for 4km (2.5 miles) and then take the left turning onto Rimrock Rd. Follow it for 200m (220yd) to a T-junction and take a right onto Timberline Rd.

TRIP HIGHLIGHT

❼ Carmelis Goat Cheese Artisan

End your tour by treating your driver to something they can sample at **Carmelis Goat Cheese Artisan** (☎250-764-9033; www.carmelisgoatcheese.com;

170 Timberline Rd; ⊙10am-6pm May-Sep, 11am-5pm Mar, Apr & Oct; Ⓟ 🛝). Call ahead to book a tour of the dairy, milking station and cellar. Even without the tour, you can sample the cheeses. For those who prefer something milder, try the super-soft unripened versions like feta and yogurt cheese. The showstopper is the goat's-milk gelato which comes in 24 different flavors.

THE OGOPOGO

For centuries, traditional First Nations legends have told of a 15m (50ft) sea serpent living in Okanagan Lake. Called the N'ha-a-itk (Lake Demon), it was believed to live in a cave near Rattlesnake Island, just offshore from Peachland. People would only enter the waters around the island with an offering, otherwise they believed the monster would raise a storm and claim lives.

Beginning in the mid-1800s, Europeans also began reporting sightings of a creature with a horse-shaped head and serpent-like body. Nicknamed Ogopogo, the serpent has been seen along the length of the 129km (80 mile) lake, but most commonly around Peachland. In 1926, 30 carloads of people all claimed to have seen the monster and film footage from 1968 has been analyzed, concluding that a solid, three-dimensional object was moving through the water.

Cryptozoologist Karl Shuker suggests that the Ogopogo may be a type of primitive whale like the basilosaurus. Keep your eyes peeled, but if you don't have any luck spotting it, you can visit a statue of the Ogopogo at Kelowna's City Park.

Eating & Sleeping

Quail's Gate ❷

✗ Old Vines Restaurant — Bistro $$$

(☎250-769-2500; www.quailsgate.com; 3303 Boucherie Rd, Quails' Gate Estate, West Kelowna; mains from C$23; ⊙11am-10pm) Using only the freshest ingredients available, this terrace-style restaurant draws crowds. At brunch, try the Dungeness crab cakes with coconut, cilantro and pineapple, and the daikon radish salad. Or dig into smoked quail or prawn risotto at lunch. Wash it all down with some of the region's top wine.

Kelowna ❸

✗ RauDZ Regional Table — Fusion $$

(☎250-868-8805; www.raudz.com; 1560 Water St; mains from C$17; ⊙5-10pm) Noted chef Rod Butters has defined the farm-to-table movement with his casual bistro that's a temple to Okanagan produce and wine. The dining room is as airy and open as the kitchen. The seasonal menu takes global inspiration for its Mediterranean-infused dishes, which are good for sharing, and serves steaks and seafood. Suppliers include locally renowned Carmelis goat's cheese.

✗ Little Hobo Soup & Sandwich Shop — Cafe $

(☎778-478-0411; www.facebook.com/littlehobokelowna; 596 Leon Ave; mains from C$7; ⊙8am-2pm Mon-Fri) This unadorned sandwich shop is hugely popular and for good reason: the food is excellent. Custom sandwiches are good, but the daily specials really shine (meatloaf, pasta, pierogi etc) and the variety of soups is simply superb.

✗ Kelowna Farmers Market — Market $

(☎250-878-5029; www.kelownafarmers andcraftersmarket.com; cnr Springfield Rd & Dilworth Dr; ⊙8am-1pm Wed & Sat Apr-Oct) The farmers market has more than 150 vendors, including many with prepared foods. Local artisans also display their wares. It's east of downtown near the Orchard Park Shopping Centre, off Hwy 97.

▭ Hotel Eldorado — Hotel $$

(☎250-763-7500; www.hoteleldoradokelowna. com; 500 Cook Rd; r from C$180; P ⊛ ❋ � �) This historic lakeshore retreat, south of Pandosy Village, has 19 heritage rooms where you can bask in antique-filled luxury. A modern, low-key wing has 30 more rooms and six opulent waterfront suites. It's classy, artful and funky all at once. Definitely the choice spot for a luxurious getaway.

▭ Hotel Zed — Motel $$

(☎250-763-7771; www.hotelzed.com; 1627 Abbott St; r from C$90; P ⊛ ❋ ⏛ ⏛) An old Travelodge has been reborn as this funky throwback to a 1960s that never existed. The rooms come in many shapes and sizes; all are in cheery colors. Extras such as free bike rentals, Ping-Pong, hot tub, comic books in the bathrooms and much more are way cool. It's perfectly located downtown, across from City Park.

Summerhill Pyramid ❺

✗ Summerhill Pyramid Bistro — Bistro $$

(☎250-764-8000; www.summerhill.bc.ca; 4870 Chute Lake Rd, Summerhill Pyramid Winery; mains from C$15; ⊙11am-11pm) Acclaimed chef Jeremy Luypen has created excellent locally sourced and organic menus for lunch and dinner. In between, there is an exquisite selection of small dishes, which go well with an afternoon of organic wine tasting.

Haida Gwaii Adventure

31

Far-flung and isolated, the lush Haida Gwaii ('Islands of the People') are steeped in superlatives – most stunning scenery, freshest seafood and most accessible First Nations culture.

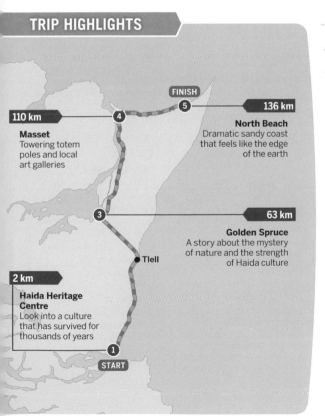

110 km

④

Masset
Towering totem poles and local art galleries

FINISH

⑤

136 km

North Beach
Dramatic sandy coast that feels like the edge of the earth

③

63 km

Golden Spruce
A story about the mystery of nature and the strength of Haida culture

● **Tlell**

2 km

Haida Heritage Centre
Look into a culture that has survived for thousands of years

①

START

**2 DAYS
136KM / 85 MILES**

GREAT FOR...

BEST TIME TO GO

July and August: more likely sunshine and less vicious wind.

 ESSENTIAL PHOTO

Capture the islands' wilderness from Tow Hill's viewpoint.

 BEST FOR CULTURE

Gain insight into the resurgence of Haida culture at the Haida Heritage Centre.

31 Haida Gwaii Adventure

You'll be welcomed to what feels like the edge of the earth. Once known as the Queen Charlotte Islands, this rugged northwestern archipelago maintains its independent spirit, evident in its quirky museums, rustic cafes, down-to-earth art and nature-loving locals. You'll feel closer to the natural world than ever before, and some of the Northern Hemisphere's most extraordinary cultural artifacts are found here.

TRIP HIGHLIGHT

① Skidegate

If you're not bringing your car, you can rent a car in advance of your BC Ferries arrival in Skidegate on Graham Island (or air arrival in Sandspit). Spend some time perusing the clapboard houses or fueling up at the home-style pub or cafes in nearby Queen Charlotte. Save an hour or two for the unmissable: the **Haida Heritage Centre** (☎250-559-7885; www.haidaheritagecentre. com; Second Beach Rd; adult/ child C$16/5; ☺9am-5pm Jul & Aug, reduced hours Sep-Jun), a striking crescent of totem-fronted cedar longhouses that's arguably British Columbia's best First Nations attraction. Check out ancient carvings and artifacts recalling 10,000 years of Haida history and look for the exquisite artworks of the legendary Bill Reid, such as huge canoes and totem poles.

Hitting Hwy 16, head north to explore the distinctive settlements that make latter-day Haida Gwaii tick. You'll wind along stretches of rustic waterfront and through shadowy woodland areas while a permanent detachment of beady-eyed eagles follows your progress.

The Drive » Follow Hwy 16 north along the shoreline. Take a few minutes to walk down to the beach when you see the pullout and signage for Balancing Rock just out of Skidegate. At 35.4km (22 miles) you'll enter the flat, arable land around Tlell River. Turn left at Wiggins Rd when you see signs for Crystal Cabin, then right on Richardson Rd.

② Tlell

Crystal Cabin (☎250-557-4383; www.crystalcabingallery. com; 778a Richardson Rd; ☺9am-6pm May-Sep, reduced hours Oct-Apr) features the works of 20 Haida artists at the jewelry workshop of April and Sarah Dutheil, second-generation artisans and sisters who were taught by their father, local legend and authority on island geology, Dutes. April has written on Haida Gwaii agate collecting and is happy to explain Dutes' Tlell Stone Circle, which is just

✓ TOP TIP: GETTING THERE

From mainland Prince Rupert in northern BC, take the **BC Ferries** (☎250-386-3431; www.bcferries.com) service to Skidegate on Graham Island. The crossing usually takes seven to eight hours.

outside the cabin. There are many forms of art here, including carvings from argillite, a local rock that can only be carved by Haida artisans.

The Drive » Continue 21.7km (13.5 miles) northwest along Hwy 16. This incredibly straight route was a walking trail until 1920 when a road was built by placing wooden planks end-to-end along the ground. Watch for deer by the road and shrub-like shore pines along the now-paved route.

✕ p331

TRIP HIGHLIGHT

❸ Port Clements

At Port Clements, head around through town on Bayview Ave until it turns south and becomes a gravel road. Follow this for 3.5km (2 miles) to the **Golden Spruce Trail**. The easy 15-minute (one-way) walk through the forest leads to the banks of the Yakoun River and the site of the legendary Golden

LINK YOUR TRIP

29 Vancouver Island's Remote North

After a seven-hour boat ride from Skidegate to Prince Rupert you travel along the inside passage on a 22-hour ferry to Port Hardy. From here drive 40 km (25 miles) along Hwy 9 to Port McNeill to pick up this trip.

DETOUR:
GWAII HAANAS
NATIONAL PARK RESERVE

Start: ❶ **Skidegate**

Famed for its mystical élan, **Gwaii Haanas National Park Reserve** (www.pc.gc.ca/en/pn-np/bc/gwaiihaanas) covers much of Haida Gwaii's southern section, a rugged region only accessible by boat or floatplane. The reserve is the ancient site of Haida homes, burial caves and the derelict village of Ninstints with its seafront totem poles (now a Unesco World Heritage site). Visitors often remark on the area's magical and spiritual qualities, but you should only consider an extended visit if you are well prepared.

It is essential to contact **Parks Canada** (☎250-559-8818, reservations 877-559-8818; Haida Heritage Centre at Kay Llnagaay, Skidegate; ◷office 8:30am-noon & 1-4:30pm Mon-Fri) in advance, as access to the park is very limited and most visitors will find it best to work with officially sanctioned tour operators.

Spruce. Tragically cut down in 1997 by a deranged environmentalist, the tree – a 45m (150ft), 300-year-old genetic aberration with luminous yellow needles – was revered by local Haida as the transformed spirit of a little boy. The tree's death was traumatic for many island residents. You can see a seedling taken from a cutting from the felled tree in Millennium Park in Port Clements. For a gripping read, pick up *The Golden Spruce: A True Story of Myth, Madness and Greed* by John Vaillant (2006).

Head back to the village and nip into **Port Clements Museum** (☎250-557-4576; www.portclementsmuseum.ca; 45 Bayview Dr; adult/child C$5/free; ◷10am-4pm Jun–mid-Sep, from 2pm Sat & Sun mid-Sep–May), where you're welcomed by a forest of rusty logging machinery. Learn about early logging practices and check out toys and tools from pioneering days. You'll also encounter a stuffed albino raven, another genetic aberration that was also revered until it electrocuted itself on local power lines.

The Drive » Head north along Hwy 16, which hugs Masset Inlet to the northern coast. Continue north to Masset and Old Masset, 43.5km (27 miles) from Port Clements. Hwy 16 is officially the Yellowhead Hwy and Mile 0 is at Masset. From here Yellowhead Hwy runs to Winnipeg, Manitoba, although you'll have to take the ferry between Haida Gwaii and Prince Rupert.

🛏 p331

TRIP HIGHLIGHT

❹ Masset

Masset primarily occupies the rather stark, institutional buildings of a disused military base and the adjoining **Old Masset** is a First Nations' village where wood-fired homes are fronted by broad, brooding totem poles. There are several stores here where visitors can peruse and buy Haida carvings and paintings.

Also in Masset is the **Dixon Entrance Maritime Museum** (☎250-626-6066; www.massetbc.com/visitors/maritime-museum; 2183 Collinson Ave; adult/child C$3/free; ◷1-6pm daily Jun-Aug, 2-4pm Sat & Sun Sep-May). Housed in what was once the local hospital, the museum features exhibits on the history of this seafaring community, with displays on shipbuilding, medical pioneers, military history, and nearby clam and crab canneries. Local artists also exhibit their work here.

The Drive » Head east off Hwy 16 along a well-marked road signposted for North Beach and Naikoon Provincial Park. The next stop is 27.4km (17 miles) from Masset.

🛏 p331

DON JOHNSTON/GETTY IMAGES ©

Gwaii Haanas National Park Reserve Sea lions

RETURN OF THE HAIDA

The Haida are one of Canada's First Nations peoples, and had lived here for thousands of years before Europeans turned up in the 18th century. Centered on the islands, these fearsome warriors had no immunity to such diseases as smallpox, measles and tuberculosis that were brought by the newcomers, and their population of tens of thousands was quickly decimated. By the early 20th century, their numbers had fallen to around 600.

Since the 1970s, the Haida population – and its cultural pride – has grown anew, and the Haida now make up about half of the 5000 residents on the islands. In 2009, the Government of British Columbia officially changed the name of the islands from the Queen Charlottes to Haida Gwaii ('Islands of the People') as part of the province's reconciliation process with the Haida.

Historically, one of the most vibrant of First Nations cultures, the Haida have very strong narratives and oral history. Legends, beliefs, skills and more are passed down from one generation to the next and great importance is placed on the knowledge of past generations. Today the Haida seek to live in harmony with their environment. Traditional laws recognize the stunning nature of the islands and embrace both the past and look to the future.

To learn more about the Haida, visit www.haidanation.ca.

TRIP HIGHLIGHT

❺ Rose Spit

The region's wild northern tip is home to **Naikoon Provincial Park** (☎250-626-5115; www.env. gov.bc.ca/bcparks; off Hwy 16). This dense, treed park has more than 96km (60 miles) of white-sand beach and is the area's most popular destination for summertime nature fans.

Continue along the tree-lined dirt road until you reach **Tow Hill**, a steep, dense and easily enjoyed short forest walk (1km/0.6 miles each way). Look out for trees where strips of bark have been carefully removed for Haida basket-making over the decades, then catch your breath at the summit while you gaze over the impenetrable coastal forest stretching into the mist.

Finally, head for the park's extreme coastal tip and **North Beach**. Leave the car here and tramp along the wave-smacked sandy expanse, where locals walk in the surf plucking Dungeness crabs for dinner. With the wind watering your eyes, you'll feel closer to nature than you've ever felt before.

✖ p331

Eating & Sleeping

Tlell ❷

✗ Haida House
at Tllaal
Seafood $$

(📞855-557-4600; www.haidahouse.com; 2087 Beitush Rd; mains from C$20; ⏰5-7:30pm Tue-Sun mid-May–mid-Sep) This Haida-run restaurant next to the river in Tlell at the end of Beitush Rd has excellent, creative seafood and other dishes with island accents, such as Haida favorites with berries. Also rents plush rooms at this magical spot in the forest.

Port Clements ❸

🛏 Golden Spruce Motel
Motel $

(📞250-557-4325; www.goldenspruce.ca; 2 Grouse St; r from C$90; 🅿😊🛜) Urs, the owner of this simple yet comfortable motel, gives a warm welcome and has a good breakfast cafe. Some rooms have kitchenette and there are firepits outside for guest use.

Masset ❹

🛏 Copper Beech House
B&B $$

(📞250-626-5441; www.copperbeechhouse. com; 1590 Delkatla Rd; r from C$120; 🅿😊❄🛜) This legendary B&B in a rambling old 1920s 'character house' on Masset Harbor is owned and managed by writer Susan Musgrave. It has five unique rooms, and there's always something amazing cooking in the kitchen.

Rose Spit ❺

✗ Moon Over
Naikoon Bakery
Bakery $

(📞250-626-5064; 16443 Tow Hill Rd; snacks from C$3; ⏰8am-5pm Jun-Aug) Embodying the spirit of its location, on a road to the end of everything, this tiny community center and bakery is housed in an old school bus in a clearing about 6km (3.75 miles) east of Masset. The baked goods and coffee are brilliant. Keep your eyes open for the sign as the bus can't be seen from the road.

🛏 All The Beach
You Can Eat
Cabin $$

(📞250-626-9091; www.allthebeachyoucaneat. com; Km 15, Tow Hill Rd; cabins from C$120; 🅿) On beautiful North Beach, five cabins are perched in the dunes, back from the wide swath of sand that runs for miles east and west. Like other properties with rental cabins out here, there is no electricity; cooking and lighting are fueled by propane. It's off the grid and out of this world. Generally you can get cell-phone reception on the beach at low-tide.

🛏 Agate Beach
Campground
Campground $

(📞250-557-4390; www.env.gov.bc.ca/bcparks; Tow Hill Rd, North Shore, Naikoon Provincial Park; tent & RV sites C$18; 🅿) This stunning, wind-whipped campground is right on the beach on the north shore. Frolic on the sand, hunt for its namesake rocks and see if you can snare some flotsam.

Around the Kootenays

32

Multiple mountain ranges, pockets of mining history and relaxed small towns with idiosyncratic art scenes, BC's Kootenay region is the quiet, unpublicized alternative to the Rocky Mountain national parks.

TRIP HIGHLIGHTS

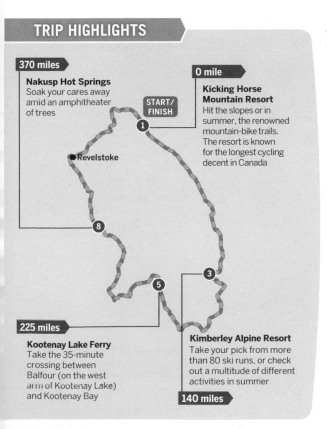

370 miles

Nakusp Hot Springs
Soak your cares away amid an amphitheater of trees

● Revelstoke

START/ FINISH
1

8

5

3

0 mile

Kicking Horse Mountain Resort
Hit the slopes or in summer, the renowned mountain-bike trails. The resort is known for the longest cycling decent in Canada

225 miles

Kootenay Lake Ferry
Take the 35-minute crossing between Balfour (on the west arm of Kootenay Lake) and Kootenay Bay

Kimberley Alpine Resort
Take your pick from more than 80 ski runs, or check out a multitude of different activities in summer

140 miles

5–6 DAYS
835KM / 519 MILES

GREAT FOR...

BEST TIME TO GO
June to September when roads and trails are snow-free and accessible.

ESSENTIAL PHOTO
Summit of Mt Revelstoke.

BEST FOR OUTDOORS
Biking, hiking and – best of all – white-water rafting.

Kicking Horse River White-water rafting (p334)

Around the Kootenays

The commanding ranges of the Monashee, Selkirk and Purcell Mountains striate the Kootenays, with the Arrow and Kootenay Lakes adding texture in the middle. This drive allows you to admire their placid alpine meadows and rugged sawtooth ridges while popping into appealing towns such as Revelstoke, Golden, Nelson and Radium Hot Springs in between. Herein lie plenty of launchpads for year-round outdoor adventures.

TRIP HIGHLIGHT

❶ Golden

Golden sits at the confluence of two rivers, three mountain ranges and five national parks – all of them less than 90 minutes drive away.

The town is the center for white-water rafting trips on the turbulent and chilly Kicking Horse River. Along with the powerful grade III and IV rapids, the rugged scenery that guards the sheer walls of the Kicking Horse Valley makes

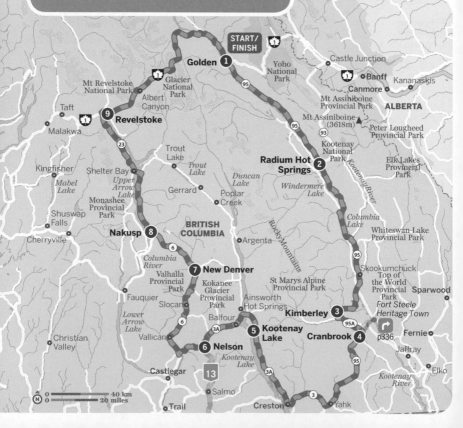

this rafting experience one of North America's best.

Indelibly linked to Golden is the **Kicking Horse Mountain Resort** (☎250-439-5425; www.kickinghorseresort.com; Kicking Horse Trail; 1-day lift ticket adult/child winter C$94/38, summer C$42/21), 6km (3.75 miles) to the west – a ski resort that opened in 2000 and is known for its abundance of expert runs. In the summer, the resort and its gondola are handed over to mountain bikers and, more recently, climbers keen to tackle several newly installed via ferrata routes.

The Drive » Head south on Hwy 95 through the Columbia River Wetlands, a hugely important ecological area that's home to 260 species of bird and numerous animals, including grizzly bears. In just over an hour, you will arrive in Radium Hot Springs.

✕ 🛏 p339

LINK YOUR TRIP

13 International Selkirk Loop

In Nelson, branch south on Hwy 6 toward the US border to join this designated Scenic Drive through BC and Washington State.

❷ Radium Hot Springs

Lying just outside the southwest corner of Kootenay National Park, Radium Hot Springs is a major gateway to the entire Rocky Mountains national park area.

The town itself isn't much more than a gas and coffee pit stop. The main attraction is the namesake **hot springs** (☎250-347-9485; www.pc.gc.ca/hotsprings; off Hwy 93; adult/child $7/5; ⏰9am-11pm), 3km (2 miles) north of town at the jaws of Kootenay National Park (you can hike in via the Sinclair Canyon). One of three hot springs in the Rockies region, Radium is the only one that is odorless. Keeping its water between 37°C (100°F) and 40°C (103°F), the facility is more public baths than fancy spa, although the exposed rock and overhanging trees make for a pleasant setting.

The Drive » Heading south, Hwy 93/95 follows the wide Columbia River valley between the Purcell and Rocky Mountains. It's not especially interesting, unless you're into the area's industry (ski resort construction), agriculture (golf courses) or wild game (condo buyers). South of Skookumchuck on Hwy 93/95, the road forks. Go right on Hwy 95A and within 30 minutes you'll be in Kimberley.

❸ Kimberley

Welcome to Kimberley, a town famous for its erstwhile lead mine, contemporary alpine skiing resort and Canada's largest cuckoo clock.

For well over half a century, Kimberley was home to the world's largest lead-zinc mine, the Sullivan mine, which was finally decommissioned in 2001. Since 2015, the local economy has switched track somewhat and now hosts Canada's largest solar farm.

In the 1970s, Kimberley experimented with a Bavarian theme in the hope of attracting more tourists. Remnants of the Teutonic makeover remain. The central pedestrian zone is named the Platzl and you can still bag plenty of tasty schnitzel and sausages in its restaurants, but these days the town is better known for the **Kimberley Alpine Resort** (☎250-427-4881; www.skikimberley.com; 301 N Star Blvd; 1-day lift pass adult/child C$75/30) with 700 hectares (1730 acres) of skiable terrain.

For a historical detour, take a 15km (9.25-mile) ride on **Kimberley's Underground Mining Railway** (☎250-427-7365; www.kimberleysundergroundminingrailway.ca; Gerry Sorensen Way; adult/child C$25/10; ⏰tours 11am, 1pm & 3pm May-Sep, trains to resort 10am Sat & Sun), where a tiny train putters through the steep-walled Mark Creek Valley toward some sweeping mountain vistas.

The Drive ≫ It's a short 30-minute drive southeast out of Kimberley on Hwy 95A to Cranbrook where you'll merge with Hwy 95 just east of the town.

- - - - - - - - - - - - - - - - - -

❹ Cranbrook

The region's main commercial center with a population of just under 20,000, Cranbrook is a modest crossroads. Hwy 3/95 bisects the town, which is a charmless array of strip malls.

The main reason for stopping here is to visit the multifarious **Cranbrook History Centre**

(☑250-489-3918; www. cranbrookhistorycentre.com; 57 Van Horne St S, Hwy 3/95; adult/child C$5/3; ⊙10am-5pm Tue-Sun). Dedicated primarily (though not exclusively) to train and rail travel, the center displays some fine examples of classic Canadian trains, including the luxurious 1929 edition of the Trans-Canada Limited, a legendary train that ran from Montréal to Vancouver. Also on-site is a fabulous model railway, the town museum (with plenty of First Nations and pre-human artifacts) and the elegant Alexandra Hall, part of a grand railway hotel that once stood in Winnipeg but was reconstructed in Cranbrook in 2004. The

center has recently been undergoing major renovations to rehouse some of its prized locomotives, but remains open with minimal disruption.

The Drive ≫ Take Hwy 3 (Crowsnest Hwy) out of Cranbrook. The road is shared with Hwy 95 as far as Yahk, beyond which you pass through the Purcell Mountains to Creston. North of Creston, turn onto Hwy 3A and track alongside the east shore of Kootenay Lake. This leg takes around 2½ hours.

✕ ⊨ p339

- - - - - - - - - - - - - - - - - -

> **TRIP HIGHLIGHT**

❺ Kootenay Lake

Lodged in the middle of the Kootenays between the Selkirk and Purcell Mountains, Kootenay Lake is one of the largest bodies of freshwater in BC. It's crossed by a year-round toll-free **ferry** (☑250-229-4215; www2.gov. bc.ca/gov/content/trans portation/passenger-travel) that runs between the two small communities of Kootenay Bay on the east bank, and Balfour on the west. The ferry's a worthwhile side trip if traveling between Creston and Nelson for its long lake vistas of blue mountains rising sharply from the water. Ferries run every 50 minutes throughout the day and the crossing takes 35 minutes. On busy summer weekends, you may have to wait in a long

DETOUR: FORT STEELE HERITAGE TOWN

Start: ❹ **Cranbrook**

Fort Steele is an erstwhile gold rush town that fell into decline in the early 1900s when it was bypassed by the railway which went to Cranbrook instead. In the early 1960s, local authorities elected to save the place from total oblivion by turning it into a **heritage site** (☑250-426-7342; www.fortsteele.ca; 9851 Hwy 93/95; adult/youth C$18/12 summer; ⊙10am-5pm mid-Jun–Aug, shorter hours winter) of pioneering mining culture. Buildings were subsequently rescued or completely rebuilt in vintage 19th-century style to lure in tourists. The site today consists of old shops, stores and a blacksmith, plus opportunities to partake in gold-panning, go on train rides or see a performance in a working theater.

In summer there are all manner of activities and re-creations, which taper off to nothing in winter, although the site stays open.

line for a sailing or two before you get passage.

The Drive » From where the ferry disembarks in Balfour on the western shore of Kootenay Lake, take Hwy 3A along the north shore of the West Arm for 32km (20 miles) before crossing the bridge into the town of Nelson.

TOP TIP: TIME ZONES

Take note if you've got an urgent appointment. This drive straddles two different time zones. Golden and the Eastern Kootenays, including Radium Hot Springs and Cranbrook, are on Mountain Time, while Revelstoke and the Western Kootenays, including Nelson, are one hour behind on Pacific Time.

6 Nelson

Nelson is an excellent reason to visit the Kootenays and should feature on any itinerary in the region. Tidy brick buildings climb the side of a hill overlooking the west arm of deep-blue Kootenay Lake, and the waterfront is lined with parks and beaches. The thriving cafe, culture and nightlife scene is a bonus. But what really propels Nelson is its personality: a funky mix of hippies, creative types and rugged individualists (many locals will tell you it's the coolest small town in BC). You can find all these along Baker St, the pedestrian-friendly main drag where wafts of patchouli mingle with hints of fresh-roasted coffee.

Founded as a mining town in the late 1800s, Nelson embarked on a decades-long heritage-preservation project in 1977. Almost a third of Nelson's historic buildings have been restored to their original architectural splendor. Pick up the superb *Herit-*age *Walking Tour* from the visitor center, which gives details on more than 30 buildings and offers a good lesson in Victorian architecture.

The town is also an excellent base for hiking, skiing, kayaking the nearby lakes, and – in recent years in particular – mountain-biking. Free-riding pedal-heads have plenty of favorite spots in British Columbia and the Rockies, but many particularly enjoy Nelson's unique juxtaposition of top-notch single-track and cool bikey ambiance. The surrounding area is striped with great trails, from the epic downhill of **Mountain Station** to the winding **Svoboda Road Trails** in West Arm Provincial Park.

The Drive » Heading north from Nelson to Revelstoke, Hwy 6 threads west for 16km (10 miles) before turning north at South Slocan. The road eventually runs alongside pretty Slocan Lake for about 30km (18.5 miles) before reaching New Denver, 97km (60 miles) from Nelson.

 p339

7 New Denver

With only around 500 residents, New Denver is a historic little gem that slumbers away peacefully right on the clear waters of Slocan Lake. Chapters in its not-so-sleepy history have included silver mining and a stint as a WWII Japanese internment camp. Details of the former can be found at the **Silvery Slocan Museum** (📞250-358-2201, www.newdenver.ca/silvery-slocan-museum; 202 6th Ave; by donation; ⊙9am-5pm Jul-Aug, Sat & Sun only Sep-Jun), located in an 1897 Bank of Montreal building.

The Drive » It is an attractive but relatively straightforward 46km (28.5-mile) drive from New Denver to Nakusp on Hwy 6 via Summit Lake Provincial Park. Look out for mountain goats on the rocky outcrops.

TRIP HIGHLIGHT

8 Nakusp

Situated right on Upper Arrow Lake, Nakusp was forever changed by BC's orgy of dam building in the 1950s and

1960s. The water level here was raised and the town was relocated to its current spot, which is why it has a 1960s-era look. It has some attractive cafes and a tiny museum. If you missed Radium Hot Springs or just can't get enough of the Rocky Mountains' thermal pleasures, divert to **Nakusp Hot Springs** (☎250-265-4528; www.nakusphotsprings.com; 8500 Hot Springs Rd; adult/child C$10.50/9.50; ⊙9:30am-9:30pm), 12km (7.5 miles) northeast of town.

The Drive » Head north on Hwy 23 along the east shore of Arrow Lake for 48km (30 miles). You'll need to cross this lake, too, on a ferry between Galena and Shelter Bay. Hwy 23 continues on the west shore and will take you all the way to Revelstoke, 52km (32 miles) north of Shelter Bay.

- - - - - - - - - - - - - - - - - -

❾ Revelstoke

Gateway to serious mountains, Revelstoke doesn't need to blow its own trumpet – the ceaseless procession of freight trains through the town center makes more than enough noise. Built as an important point on the Canadian Pacific transcontinental railroad that first linked Eastern and Western Canada, Revelstoke echoes not just with whistles but with history. If you haven't yet been satiated with Canadian railway memorabilia, you can sample a bit more at the **Revelstoke Railway Museum** (☎250-837-6060; www.railwaymuseum.com; 719 Track St W; adult/child C$10/5; ⊙9am-5pm May-Sep, shorter hours Oct-Apr; P).

Revelstoke's compact center is lined with heritage buildings, yet it's more than a museum piece. **Grizzly Plaza**, between Mackenzie and Orton Aves, is a pedestrian precinct and the heart of downtown, where free live-music performances take place every evening in July and August.

Notwithstanding, this place is mainly about the adjacent wilderness and its boundless opportunities for hiking, kayaking and, most of all, skiing. North America's first ski jump was built here in 1915. One year before, Mt Revelstoke became Canada's seventh national park. From the 2223m (7293ft) summit of **Mt Revelstoke**, the views of the mountains and the Columbia River valley are excellent. To ascend, take the 26km (16-mile) Meadows in the Sky Parkway, 1.6km (1-mile) east of Revelstoke off the Trans-Canada Hwy. Open after the thaw, from mid-May to mid-October, this paved road winds through lush cedar forests and alpine meadows and ends at Balsam Lake, within 2km (1.25 miles) of the peak. From here, walk to the top or take the free shuttle.

The Drive » Keep your eyes on the road or, better yet, let someone else drive as you traverse the Trans-Canada Hwy (Hwy 1) for 148km (92 miles) between Revelstoke and Golden. Stunning mountain peaks follow one after another as you go.

🍴 🛏 p339

Eating & Sleeping

Golden ❶

✗ Wolf Den   Pub Food $$
(☎250-344-9863; www.thewolfsdengolden.ca;
1105 9th St; dinner mains from C$14; ⏱4-10pm)
An excellent pub with live music on Sundays. It's
hugely popular with locals, who love the burgers
and hearty fare, which is way above average.
The beer menu includes some of BC's best on
tap. It's just south of the river from downtown.

⊨ Dreamcatcher Hostel   Hostel $
(☎250-439-1090; www.dreamcatcherhostel.
com; 528 9th Ave N; dm/r from C$32/90;
P ⊕ ⊛ 🛜) Run by two veteran travelers, this
centrally located hostel has everything a budget
traveler could hope for. There are three dorm
rooms, five private rooms, a vast kitchen and
a comfy common room with a stone fireplace.
Outside there's a garden and a barbecue.

Cranbrook ❹

✗ Retro Cafe   French $
(☎250-428-2726; www.retrocafe.ca; 1431
NW Blvd, Creston; mains from C$8; ⏱7am-
4pm Mon-Fri, to 3pm Sat) A French mirage in
Creston, 'retro' will probably be the last thing
on your mind as you scour the hand-scrawled
blackboard and tuck into *très délicieux* crepes.

⊨ Valley View Motel   Motel $
(☎250-428-2336; www.valleyviewmotel.
info; 216 Valley View Dr, Creston; r from C$75;
P ⊕ ⊛ 🛜) In motel-ville Creston, this is your
best bet. On a view-splayed hillside, it's clean,
comfortable and quiet.

Nelson ❻

✗ All Seasons Cafe   Fusion $$$
(☎250-352-0101; www.allseasonscafe.com;
620 Herridge Lane; mains from C$22; ⏱5-

10pm) Sitting on the patio here beneath little
lights twinkling in the huge maple above you
is a Nelson highlight; in winter, candles inside
provide the same romantic flair. The eclectic
menu changes with the seasons but always
celebrates BC foods. Presentations are artful;
service is gracious.

⊨ Hume
Hotel & Spa   Hotel $$
(☎250-352-5331; www.humehotel.com; 422
Vernon St; r from C$120; P ⊕ ⊛ 🛜) This 1898
classic hotel maintains its period grandeur. The
43 rooms vary greatly in shape and size; ask for
the huge corner rooms with views of the hills
and lake. Rates include a delicious breakfast. It
has several appealing nightlife venues.

Revelstoke ❾

✗ Modern
Bakeshop & Café   Cafe $
(☎250-837-6886; www.themodernbake
shopandcafe.com; 212 Mackenzie Ave; mains
from C$6; ⏱6:30am-5pm Mon-Sat; 🛜) Try
a croque monsieur (grilled ham-and-cheese
sandwich) or an elaborate pastry for a taste of
Europe at this cute art-deco cafe. Many items,
such as the muffins, are made with organic
ingredients. Discover the baked 'boofy uptrack
bar' for a treat. Nice seating outside.

⊨ Regent
Hotel   Hotel $$
(☎250-837-2107; www.regenthotel.ca; 112 1st
St E; r from C$110; P ⊕ ⊛ 🛜🏊) The poshest
place in the center is not lavish, but it is comfy.
The 42 modern rooms bear no traces of the
hotel's 1914 roots and exterior. The restaurant
and lounge are justifiably popular. Many guests
bob the night away in the outdoor hot tub.

STRETCH
YOUR LEGS
VANCOUVER

Start/Finish Gastown

Distance 10km (6.25 miles)

Duration 3 to 4 hours

Wandering around Vancouver, with its visually arresting backdrop of sparkling ocean and snow-dusted mountaintops, you discover there's more to this city than appearances. It's a kaleidoscope of distinctive neighborhoods, strongly artistic and just as hip as it is sophisticated.

Take this walk on Trip

Gastown

Crammed into a dozen, often brick-paved blocks, trendy Gastown is where the city began. Century-old heritage buildings now house cool bars and quirky galleries, with the landmark **steam clock** (cnr Water & Cambie Sts; ⓈWaterfront) whistling to a camera-wielding coterie of onlookers every 15 minutes. Tucked along handsome historic rows, swish boutiques, artisan stores and chatty coffee shops invite leisurely browsing and laid-back java sipping. And when you need a fuel-up, **Brioche** (www.brioche.ca; 401 W Cordova St; mains C$10-16; ⊘7am-9pm Mon-Fri, 8am-9pm Sat & Sun; ⓈWaterfront) is a colorful, comfy place to stop for lunch.

The Walk ≫ Follow Water St east, turning right on Carrall St and heading south for three blocks to Pender St and Chinatown.

Chinatown

North America's third-largest **China-town** (www.vancouver-chinatown.com) is a highly wanderable explosion of sight, sound and aromas. Check out the towering **Millennium Gate** (cnr W Pender & Taylor Sts; ⓈStadium-Chinatown) and visit the tranquil **Dr Sun Yat-Sen Classical Chinese Garden** (www.vancouverchinese garden.com; 578 Carrall St; adult/child C$14/10; ⊘9:30am-7pm mid-Jun–Aug, 10am-6pm Sep & May–mid-Jun, 10am-4:30pm Oct-Apr; ⓈStadium-Chinatown). Save time for the **Chinese Tea Shop** (www.thechineseteashop. com; 101 E Pender St; ⊘1-6pm Wed-Mon; ⌨3), and slip into colorful apothecary stores for a fascinating eyeful of traditional Chinese medicine.

Have lunch at the deservedly popular, locally beloved New Town Bakery – and buy some pork buns to go.

The Walk ≫ Follow Keefer St and Keefer Pl west, crossing the roundabout at the end and continuing along the footpath to Beatty St. Turn left and walk three blocks to Robson St. Turn right, crossing Granville St, and continue along Robson to Hornby St.

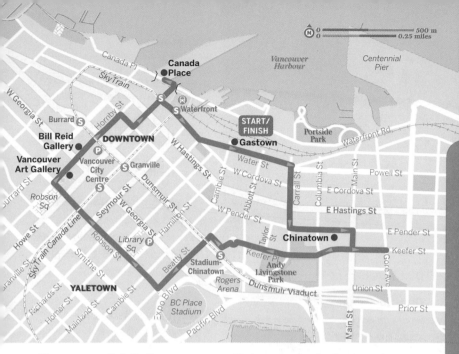

Vancouver Art Gallery

A palatial former courthouse building, the grand home of the **Vancouver Art Gallery** (www.vanartgallery.bc.ca; 750 Hornby St; adult/child C$24/6.50; ⊙10am–5pm Wed-Mon, to 9pm Tue; 🚌5) showcases contemporary exhibitions, work by time-honored masters, and blockbuster international traveling shows. Check out **FUSE** (C$29; ⊙8pm-midnight), a regular late-night party event where you can hang out with the city's young creatives over wine and live music. Check ahead for regular gallery talks and tours.

The Walk >> Exit the gallery on the Hornby St side and walk two blocks northeast along Hornby.

Bill Reid Gallery

The **Bill Reid Gallery of Northwest Coast Art** (www.billreidgallery.ca; 639 Hornby St; adult/youth/child C$13/6/free; ⊙10am–5pm May-Sep, 11am-5pm Wed-Sun Oct-Apr; ⓢBurrard) showcases carvings, paintings and jewelry from Canada's most revered Haida artist as well as his fellow First Nations creators. On the mezzanine level you'll view an 8.5m-long bronze of intertwined magical creatures.

The Walk >> Continue up Hornby St to Pender St. Turn right and then left onto Howe St. Follow this towards the water.

Canada Place

Shaped like a series of sails jutting into the sky over the harbor, **Canada Place** (www.canadaplace.ca; 999 Canada Place Way; 🅿 🕴; ⓢWaterfront) is a cruise-ship terminal, convention center and pier where you can stroll the waterfront and enjoy handsome views of the grand North Shore mountains. Save time to snap photos of the floatplanes landing and taking off alongside, framed by Stanley Park in the background. Next door, check out the grass-roofed convention-center expansion and the tripod-like **Olympic Cauldron**, a permanent reminder of the 2010 Games.

The Walk >> Backtrack up Howe St for one block and turn left onto W Cordova St. After three blocks, edge left onto Water St and back into Gastown.

STRETCH YOUR LEGS
VICTORIA

Start/Finish Chinatown

Distance 6km (3.75 miles)

Duration 5 hours

It's not sugar coating – the seaside provincial capital really is as charming and beautiful as it first appears. Filled with funky boutiques, excellent museums, unique neighborhoods and a jewel of a park, Victoria makes for a blissful wander.

Take this walk on Trips

Chinatown

Settled in 1858, Chinatown announces itself with a bright, traditional gate, and stretches two packed blocks along Fisgard St. Pop into **Fantan Trading Ltd** (551 Fisgard St; ⊙11am-5pm; 🚌70) for a maze of made-in-China goods or **Fan Tan Home & Style** (www.fantanvictoria.com; 541 Fisgard St; ⊙9:30am-5:30pm; 🚌70) for beautiful wooden and woven items. Dine at **Venus Sophia** (www.venussophia.com; 540 Fisgard St; afternoon tea C$14-30; ⊙10am-6pm Jul & Aug, from 11am Wed-Sun Sep-Jun; 🖋; 🚌70), a tearoom with a vegetarian twist, then breathe in and slide along super-narrow **Fan Tan Alley**. It's home to many small boutiques and vintage shops.

The Walk ≫ At Chinatown's gate, turn right onto Government St.

Government Street

With everything from book emporiums to ice-cream parlors, Government St is a great stretch of pavement to pound. Visit **Silk Road** (www.silkroadteastore.com; 1624 Government St; ⊙10am-5:30pm Mon-Sat, 11am-5pm Sun; 🚌70) for heavenly teas, and detour onto Johnson St for quirky independent stores. Hungry? Continue along Government St, turn left onto Fort St and then around the corner onto Broad St for the phenomenal **Pagliacci's** (www.pagliaccis.ca; 110 Broad St; mains C$17-29; ⊙11:30am-10pm Sun-Thu, to 11pm Fri & Sat; 🚌70), a local pasta place.

The Walk ≫ Continue eight blocks south on Government St.

Inner Harbour

Watched over by the grand Empress Hotel, the handsome **Parliament Buildings** (www.leg.bc.ca; 501 Belleville St; ⊙ tours 9am-5pm mid-May–Aug, from 8:30am Mon-Fri Sep–mid-May; 🚌70) and Royal BC Museum (p290), the Inner Harbour is Victoria's most photogenic location. On lazy summer afternoons, walk down along the waterfront promenade to check out the boats bobbing like candy-colored

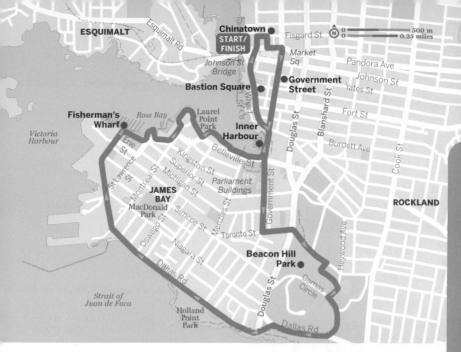

corks and enjoy a full roster of artisan market stalls and top-notch street performers.

The Walk >> Continue south on Government St to Toronto St. Turn left and follow this east for three blocks to Beacon Hill Park.

Beacon Hill Park

An idyllic fusion of planted gardens and wild and woody sections, Beacon Hill Park is naturally popular. There's a playground, an excellent petting zoo and a heron-nesting zone worth cricking your neck to see. Head south and you'll find one of North America's tallest totem poles and eventually Dallas Rd, a breeze-licked oceanside walk where whale sightings aren't uncommon.

The Walk >> Follow Dallas Rd to its end.

Fisherman's Wharf

At **Fisherman's Wharf** (www.fishermans wharfvictoria.com; just off Fisherman's Wharf Park; P; ☐30), fishing boats share dock space with a floating community of houseboats. Wander along the sun-dappled boardwalks and visit the galleries – then add a hunger-busting pit stop. **Barb's** (www.barbsfishandchips.com; 1 Dallas Rd, Fisherman's Wharf; meals C$10-23; ⏱11am-dusk mid-Mar–Oct; ☐30) is hard to resist for fish-and-chips, and kids' eyes will pop at the counter of **Jackson's Ice-Cream**.

The Walk >> Follow the shoreline footpath east along the water from Fisherman's Wharf, all the way back to the Inner Harbour. Alternatively, jump on one of the cute harbour ferries. From the Inner Harbour, follow Wharf St north.

Bastion Square

Historic **Bastion Square** (☐24) hosts a popular seasonal **artisan market** along with cafes and buskers. This is also a great area to come for dinner. **ReBar** (50 Bastion Sq; mains C$16-18; ⏱11:30am-9pm Mon-Fri, from 10am Sat, 10am-8pm Sun; 🖋; ☐70) is a favorite among Victorians for good reason.

The Walk >> Carry on up Wharf St to Fisgard St to complete the loop.

STRETCH YOUR LEGS
WHISTLER

Start/Finish Town Plaza

Distance 2.7km

Duration 4 hours

This super-scenic, gable-roofed village has some top cultural attractions plus enticing shops and restaurants where you can rub shoulders with ski bunnies and bike barons. Feeling energetic? The outdoor pursuits are virtually endless.

Take this walk on Trip

Town Plaza

There's something about the Whistler shopping scene that makes money run through your fingers like water. From boutique hat shops to PEI ice-cream outlets, the options are an interesting (and often worthwhile) distraction here. You'll find plenty of the prerequisite sports-gear and souvenir stores, among less likely neighbors like cigar emporiums. Town Plaza is ringed with shops and is the best place to start browsing.

The Walk » From Town Plaza, head west directly opposite the gazebo, between Deer Lodge and the Delta Whistler. Walk a block down Main St and swing a right to the museum.

Whistler Museum

The **Whistler Museum & Archives** (www. whistlermuseum.org; 4333 Main St; suggested donation C$5; ⊙11am-5pm, to 9pm Thu) features paraphernalia from the 2010 Winter Olympics, plus displays on geology, wildlife and village history. Look for exhibits on Myrtle Philip, one of the area's early pioneers and check out the notorious 'Toad Hall' photo, a happy group of nude skiers from the 1970s.

The Walk » Return east up Main St towards the Village Stroll and carry on north to Olympic Plaza.

Olympic Plaza

Surrounded by cafes and home to a fantastic children's playground, Olympic Plaza is the location of one of Canada's finest destination bakeries, **Purebread** (www.purebread.ca; 4338 Main St; baked goods C$3-6; ⊙8am-6pm), and **Whistler Brewhouse** (www.mjg.ca/brewhouse; 4355 Blackcomb Way; ⊙11:30am-midnight, to 1am Fri & Sat), which offers smooth drinks such as Lifty Lager and 5 Rings IPA.

In summer, catch a performance at the outdoor theater.

The Walk » Follow the footpath at the end of the Village Stroll – this leads to Lorimer Rd. Turn right and follow it over the bridge, then turn right onto Blackcomb Way.

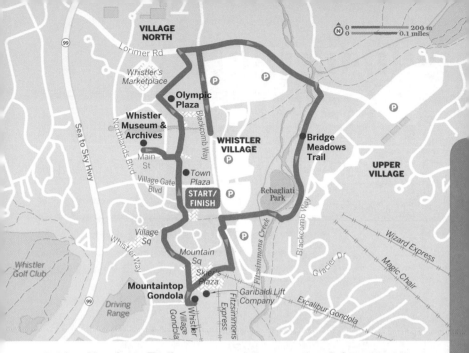

Bridge Meadows Trail

A few minutes' walk along Blackcomb Way brings you to the striking Audain Art Museum (p286) and its region-defining BC and First Nations artworks. Afterwards, retrace your steps along Blackcomb and turn right onto Lorimer Rd for the nearby Squamish Lil'wat Cultural Centre (p286).

Next door, follow nature-hugging Bridge Meadows Trail south along Fitzsimmons Creek. Veer right at the covered wooden bridge and cross to Rebagliati Park, with its forest and waterside meadow views. Continue west through the woods to Blackcomb Way.

The Walk » Cross over Blackcomb Way and follow the footpath south until you reach a set of stairs. Turn right and descend back to the Village Stroll.

Mountaintop Gondola

Hop on the Whistler Village Gondola, sans skis. At the top, the **Peak 2 Peak Gondola** (www.whistlerblackcomb.com/discover/360-experience; 4545 Blackcomb Way; adult/child C$63/32; ⊙10am-5pm) links Whistler with Blackcomb. In summer, you can head to the top of Whistler Peak (via the Peak Express chairlift) and admire the view from the new **Cloudraker Skybridge**, a 130m (140yd) suspension bridge with a see-through base.

The Walk » Return down to Whistler and the Village Stroll.

Beer at the GLC

If your knees are a little wobbly after all that gondola action, steady them with a beer overlooking the slopes at the **Garibaldi Lift Company** (4165 Springs Lane; ⊙11am-1am), the closest bar to the powder. The pub-grub menu includes hearty burgers, but if you're craving something healthier, head to **Hunter Gather** (www.huntergatherwhistler.com; 4368 Main St; mains C$15-29; ⊙noon-10pm), a noisy but cheerful emporium of local food.

The Walk » Continue on the Village Stroll back to Town Plaza.

ROAD TRIP ESSENTIALS

The Pacific Northwest Driving Guide

Short on interstates, long on scenic byways, the Pacific Northwest yields some of the most beautiful drives on the continent.

DRIVING LICENSE & DOCUMENTS

Foreign visitors can legally drive a car in the USA for up to 12 months using their home driver's license. However, an International Driving Permit (IDP) will have more credibility with police than your driver's license, especially if your home license doesn't have a photo or isn't in English. Your national automobile association can provide one for a small fee, and they're usually valid for one year. Always carry your home license together with the IDP.

Driving rules in Canada are similar to the US, although they vary slightly from province to province. Just like in the US, you will need a driver's license and proof of insurance. A foreign license will suffice, though an IDP can save you headaches if your license is in a foreign language.

INSURANCE

Auto insurance is obligatory for car owners in the Pacific Northwest. Rates fluctuate widely, depending on where the car is registered; it's usually cheaper if registered at an address in the suburbs or in a rural area, rather than in a central city. Male drivers under the age of 25 will pay astronomical rates. Collision coverage has become very expensive, with high deductibles, and is generally not worthwhile unless the car is somewhat valuable.

Obtaining insurance, however, is not as simple as walking into an agency, filling out a form and paying for it. Many agencies refuse to insure drivers who have no car insurance – a classic catch-22. Those agencies that will do so often charge much higher rates because they presume a higher risk. The minimum term for a policy is usually six months, but some insurance companies will refund the difference on a prorated basis if the car is sold and the policy voluntarily terminated. Shop around. If you're planning to drive in both the USA and Canada, make sure your insurance is valid on both sides of the border.

RENTING A CAR

Major international rental agencies have offices throughout the Pacific Northwest. To rent a car, you must have a valid driver's license, (usually) be at least 21 years of age and present a major credit card or a large cash deposit. Drivers under 25 often pay a surcharge over the regular rental.

Agencies often have bargain rates for weekend or weeklong rentals, especially outside the peak seasons or in conjunction with airline tickets. Prices vary greatly depending on the type or size of car, pick-up and drop-off locations, number of drivers etc. In general, expect to pay from $30 to $60 per day for a midsize car, more in peak seasons, but you may find rates

---

Driving Fast Facts

Right or left? Drive on the right

Legal driving age 16

Top speed limit 75mph US, 110km/h Canada

Best bumper sticker Sasquatch for President

Driving Problem-Buster

What should I do if my car breaks down? If it's a rental, call the company. If it's your own car, membership in an automobile association will offer 24-hour roadside assistance.

What if I have an accident? If there are no serious injuries and your car is operational, move over to the side of the road. If there are serious injuries, call 911 for an ambulance. Exchange information with the other driver, then file an accident report with the police or Department of Motor Vehicles (DMV).

What should I do if I get stopped by the police? Stay in your car and keep your hands visible. They'll want to see your driver's license and proof of liability insurance. As long as you're not a serious threat, you probably won't end up in jail, although you'll probably get either a ticket or a warning if you've broken a road rule.

What if I don't have a room booked for the night? Chain motels along the highway are a convenient solution if you're willing to give up amenities. You can try to book a last-minute bargain on websites like www.priceline.com or www.hotwire.com.

as low as $14 for an economy car in low season if booked in advance. Rates usually include unlimited mileage, but not taxes or insurance.

You may get better rates by prebooking from your home country. If you get a fly-drive package, local taxes may be an extra charge when you collect the car. Several online travel-reservation networks have up-to-the-minute information on car-rental rates at all the main airports. Compare their rates with any fly-drive package you're considering.

Basic liability insurance covers damage you may cause to another vehicle. Rental companies are required by law to provide the minimum level set by each state, but it usually isn't enough in the event of a serious accident. Many Americans already have enough insurance coverage under their personal car-insurance policies; check your own policy carefully. Foreign visitors should check their travel-insurance policies to see if they cover foreign rental cars. Rental companies charge about $15 per day for this extra coverage.

Insurance against damage or loss to the car itself, called Collision Damage Waiver (CDW) or Loss Damage Waiver (LDW), can cost $10 to $20 per day (and may have a deductible). The CDW may be voided if you cause an accident while breaking the law, however. Again, check your own coverage to see if you have comprehensive collision insurance.

Some credit cards cover CDW for rentals up to 15 days, provided you charge the entire cost of the rental to the card. Check with your credit-card company to determine the extent of coverage.

Most of the big international rental companies have desks at airports, in all major cities and in some smaller towns. Check online or call toll-free for rates and reservations.

BORDER CROSSINGS

All crossings are open 24 hours except Lynden/Aldergrove, which is open 8am to midnight. During the week, expect to wait five to 20 minutes, an hour or more on weekends and during holidays. For up-to-date wait times, check www.cbsa-asfc.gc.ca/bwt-taf/menu-eng.html; it has links to other US–Canada border crossings. Tips and directions can be found at www.vancouver.hm/border.html.

Visa requirements (p57) vary widely for entry to the US and Canada.

Many travelers also cross the border by ferry, principally on journeys from Anacortes to Sidney (near Victoria), BC, and from Port Angeles to Victoria.

Blaine/Douglas (aka Peace Arch) crossing The main overland point of entry from Washington to Vancouver, BC. It's at the northern end of I-5, which continues as Hwy 99 on the Canadian side. This crossing has the longest lines.

Pacific Highway crossing Commercial trucks (and regular vehicles) use this crossing, 3 miles (5km) east of Blaine/Douglas; from I-5, take exit 275 (the one before Blaine). If you're entering Canada with duty-free goods, you'll need to cross here.

Lynden/Aldergrove crossing A good choice during busy times is this little-known crossing about 30 miles (50km) east of Blaine/Douglas. Take exit 256 off I-5, just north of Bellingham, and follow Hwy 539.

Sumas/Huntingdon crossing Best for heading to BC's interior is this crossing 62 miles (100km) east of Blaine/Douglas. Take exit 255 off I-5, just north of Bellingham, and follow Hwy 542 and then Hwy 9.

FERRIES

Washington and BC have two of the largest state-owned ferry systems in the world, and these ferries access some of the most rewarding destinations in the Pacific Northwest. Some boats are passenger only, while others take both vehicles and passengers. Be aware that some summertime ferry routes can have long waits if you're in a car. Bring snacks, as ferry offerings are limited and expensive.

BC Ferries (☑250-386-3431; www.bcferries.com) Operates most of the ferries in BC.

Primary links are between Tsawwassen (south of Vancouver) and Swartz Bay (on Vancouver Island), and to Nanaimo from Tsawwassen and Horseshoe Bay. BC Ferries services also link the Gulf Islands to Tsawwassen.

Black Ball Transport (☑250-386-2202; www.cohoferry.com; 430 Belleville St, Victoria) Privately operated; connects Victoria, BC, with Washington's Port Angeles (on the Olympic Peninsula).

Clipper Navigation (☑800-888-2535; www.clippervacations.com/clipper-ferry) Privately operated; operates the *Victoria Clipper*, a passenger ferry that connects Seattle with Victoria, BC. Stops at the San Juan Islands mid-May through September, and also has whale-watching trips.

Washington State Ferries (WSF; ☑888-808-7977; www.wsdot.wa.gov/ferries) Routes, prices and schedules available on the website; fares depend on destination, vehicle size and trip duration, and are collected either for round-trip or one-way travel depending on the departure terminal. Reserve, as bookings are becoming almost mandatory for some destinations (ie the San Juan Islands).

Road Distances (miles)

	Seattle	Portland	Vancouver	Spokane	Eugene	Ashland	Seaside	Bend	ONP	Walla Walla	Whistler
Portland	172										
Vancouver	141	315									
Spokane	280	351	410								
Eugene	283	110	424	462							
Ashland	460	285	599	637	180						
Seaside	194	80	334	432	181	356					
Bend	330	159	470	396	120	186	247				
ONP	90	146	128	370	265	425	150	305			
Walla Walla	270	245	408	158	352	470	322	286	350		
Whistler	215	390	70	495	498	675	409	640	305	485	
Mt Rainer	85	136	179	212	204	325	279	195	175	173	300

Road-Trip Websites

ROAD CONDITIONS & TRAFFIC

Oregon Trip Check www.tripcheck.com

Washington State Department of Transportation www.wsdot.com/traffic

Drive British Columbia www.drivebc.ca

DRIVING RULES

Oregon Department of Transportation www.odot.state.or.us/forms/dmv/37.pdf

Washington State Department of Transportation www.wsdot.wa.gov/Local Programs/Traffic/Laws

British Columbia Regulations www2.gov.bc.ca/gov/content/transportation/ driving-and-cycling/road-safety-rules-and-consequences

AUTOMOBILE ASSOCIATIONS

American Automobile Association www.aaa.com

Canadian Automobile Association www.caa.ca

MAPS

For a good road atlas or driving maps, try Rand McNally (www.randmcnally.com) and its Thomas Brothers city guides; both are stocked at many bookstores and some gas stations.

ROAD CONDITIONS

A few backcountry roads are in open-range country where cattle forage along the highway. Deer and smaller wildlife are also hazards. Pay particular attention at night.

During winter months – especially at the higher elevations – there will be times when tire chains are required on snowy or icy roads. Sometimes such roads will be closed to cars without chains or 4WD, so it's a good idea to keep a set of chains in the trunk. Make sure they fit your tires, and practice putting them on *before* you're out there next to the busy highway in the cold and dirty snow. Also note that many car-rental companies specifically prohibit the use of chains on their vehicles. Roadside services might be available to attach chains to your tires for a fee.

ROAD RULES

Cars drive on the right-hand side of the road. The use of seat belts and child safety seats is required. It's illegal to talk or text on a cell phone while driving, unless you're on a hands-free device. The maximum legal blood-alcohol content for drivers is 0.08%; in Canada, it's 0.05%.

Speed limits vary depending on the type of road: in the United States, it's generally 55–65mph on highways, up to 75mph on the interstates, 25–35mph in cities and towns, and as low as 15mph in school zones. It's forbidden to pass a school bus when its lights are flashing.

In Canada, speed limits are expressed as kilometers per hour, so if you see a sign that says 'Maximum 60', it doesn't mean 60mph. If you're watching your US odometer, you shouldn't be traveling at more than 37.28mph.

Speed limits are generally 70–90km/h on highways (or 43–56mph), up to 110km/h (68mph) on expressways, 40–50km/h (25–31mph) on residential streets, and 30–50km/h (19–31mph) in school zones.

For tips and rules on driving in the USA, get an Oregon or Washington Driver Handbook at any Department of Motor Vehicles (DMV) office or online.

FUEL

Keep in mind that Oregon law prohibits you from pumping your own gasoline (except on some Native American reservations and remote small-town areas) – all stations are full service, so just sit back and enjoy it.

Gas prices are fairly uniform, but tend to get more expensive in remote rural areas or near airports where rental-car returners don't mind paying extra. Within a given area, prices might differ by about 10 cents per gallon from one place to the next.

The Pacific Northwest Travel Guide

GETTING THERE & AWAY

AIR

Domestic airfares fluctuate significantly depending on season, day of the week, length of stay and flexibility of the ticket for changes and refunds. Still, nothing determines fares more than demand, and when business is slow, airlines drop fares to fill seats. Airlines are competitive and at any time any one of them could have the cheapest fare.

Most air travelers to the Pacific Northwest will arrive at one of the three main airports in the region:

Seattle-Tacoma International Airport (SEA; ☑206-787-5388; www.portseattle.org/Sea-Tac; 17801 International Blvd; ☏) Known locally as 'Sea-Tac,' this is the fastest-growing airport in the US with Delta Airlines being the most dominant carrier.

Portland International Airport (☑503-460-4234; www.flypdx.com; 7000 NE Airport Way; ☏; ☒Red) Consistently voted the best airport in the US (it is); Delta and Alaska Airlines have the most flights.

Vancouver International Airport (YVR; ☑604-207-7077; www.yvr.ca; 3211 Grant McConachie Way, Richmond; ☏) The second-busiest and oft-voted best airport in Canada is a hub for Air Canada and WestJet.

BUS

In car-oriented societies like the USA and Canada, bus travel takes second place. Service is infrequent or inconvenient, networks are sparse and fares can be relatively high. Air travel is often cheaper on long-distance routes, and it can even be cheaper to rent a car than take the bus, especially for shorter routes. However, very long-distance bus trips can be available at decent prices if you purchase or reserve tickets in advance.

The largest nationwide bus company in the USA and Canada, Greyhound (www.greyhound.com) operates to major and minor cities throughout the Pacific Northwest; check its website for destinations and schedules. Bolt Bus (www.boltbus.com) is an expanding and often more budget-friendly alternative with great service between the three major cities in the Pacific Northwest and to California. Tickets can be purchased by phone or online with a credit card and mailed to you if purchased in advance, or picked up at the terminal with proper identification. Buying tickets in advance will save you money, as will traveling on weekdays and during non-holiday times. Children, students, military personnel, veterans and seniors are eligible for discounts as well; check websites for specifics.

Passengers will need to get off the bus and go through immigration and customs procedures at the US–Canada border.

Car Sharing

There are an ever-changing number of car-sharing programs in the US. These programs usually require a membership fee (one-time and/or annual), plus a per-hour car-rental charge. Two of the biggest are Zipcar and Car2go, but there are many that operate only within a city or a few cities. They can be an economical way to rent (or share) a car if you only need wheels for an hour or two at a time.

Book Your Stay Online

For more accommodation reviews by Lonely Planet writers, check out http://hotels.lonelyplanet.com. You'll find independent reviews, as well as recommendations on the best places to stay. Best of all, you can book online.

Travelers need to ensure that they have valid passports and proper visas.

CAR & MOTORCYCLE

Although the quickest way to get to the Pacific Northwest is usually by plane, the best way to get around is by car. If you have the time, it can be less expensive to drive to the Pacific Northwest than to fly and rent a car. And the region is blessed with many scenic highways that make driving long distances a feasible alternative.

Note that driving regulations, such as speed limits and the permissibility of right turns on red lights or making U-turns, can vary somewhat from state to state.

Passports are checked at drive-through immigration points at the border and vehicles may be subject to search. Driving into the US in a vehicle with Canadian license plates or vice versa for short-term tourism is not an issue but importing a vehicle permanently requires considerable paperwork and fees. The availability of gasoline and repair services at the border depends on where you cross but in general a fill-up station and/or mechanic is never too far away.

TRAIN

The Pacific Northwest is well served by **Amtrak** (800-872-7245; www.amtrak.com) in the USA and **VIA Rail** (514-871-6000; www.viarail.ca) in Canada. Trains are comfortable, if slow, and equipped with dining and lounge cars on long-distance routes.

Amtrak's *Coast* Starlight links Los Angeles, CA, to Portland and Seattle via Oakland, CA, and other West Coast cities. The Empire Builder runs from Chicago, IL, to the Pacific Northwest via Minneapolis, MN, and Spokane, WA, where it separates to reach Portland and Seattle. VIA Rail's

Canadian runs between Vancouver and Toronto. Schedules can be very fluid: arrival and departure times become less reliable the further you are from the starting point.

Fares on Amtrak vary greatly, depending on the season and what promotions are going. You can beat the rather stiff full-price fares by purchasing in advance – the further ahead you buy, the better the fare. Round trips are the best deal, but even these can be more expensive than airfares. Children, students, veterans, military personnel, seniors and even AAA members are eligible for discounts; check Amtrak's website for details, and for rail passes, which are a good option for longer travel periods.

Passengers will need to get off the train for passport control and customs at the US–Canada border. You'll need a valid passport and proper visa.

DIRECTORY A–Z

ACCESSIBLE TRAVEL

If you have a physical disability, travel within the Pacific Northwest won't be too difficult. The Americans with Disabilities Act (ADA) requires all public buildings in the US – including most hotels, restaurants, theaters and museums – to be wheelchair accessible. Most sidewalks in the Pacific Northwest are wide and smooth and many intersections have curb cuts and sometimes audible crossing signals.

Lift-equipped buses are the norm in Washington, Oregon and BC, and many taxi companies have wheelchair-accessible cabs. Some municipal bus networks provide door-to-door service for people with disabilities. Most car-rental franchises are able to provide hand-controlled models at no extra charge – but reserve well ahead. All major airlines, Greyhound buses and Amtrak trains allow service animals to accompany passengers (bring documentation for them). Airlines will also provide assistance for connecting, boarding and disembarking if requested with your reservation. Disabled travelers using Washington State Ferries should check www.wsdot.wa.gov/ferries/commuterupdates/ada for information on reduced fares and how to board.

Many state and national parks in the Northwest maintain a nature trail or two for use by travelers in wheelchairs. For a list of accessible trails in Washington State, see www.wta.org/go-outside/basics/ada-accessible-hikes; for Oregon check www.traillink.com/stateactivity/or-wheelchair-accessible-trails.aspx. Meanwhile, BC has a good general website at www.hellobc.com/british-columbia/about-bc/accessibility.aspx.

The America the Beautiful Access Pass (previously known as the Golden Access Passport; these are still honored) is available free to blind or permanently disabled US travelers with documentation. It gives free lifetime access to US national parks and wildlife refuges and 50% off campground use. For more information see www.nps.gov/findapark/passes.htm.

ACCOMMODATIONS

Many lodgings have only nonsmoking rooms, but you can usually smoke outdoors. Air-conditioning is common in inland places but nearly nonexistent along the coast, which is much cooler. Many hotels take pets, but always ask beforehand (there's usually a fee). Wi-fi access is commonplace except in backcountry towns. Children (defined as anything from under six to under 18) can often stay free with their parents.

Except where noted, rates listed in this guide do not include the applicable lodging tax.

Washington Outside Seattle, lodging-tax rates vary by county but are generally around 12% for hotels of about 50 rooms or more. Smaller hotels or B&Bs usually include taxes in their daily rates. Seattle hotel rooms are subject to a tax of 15.6% (less for most B&Bs and historical properties).

Oregon Outside Portland, lodging tax is 6% to 10.5%. In Portland it's 11.5% to 13.5%, depending on the size of the hotel.

Sleeping Price Ranges

The following price ranges refer to a double room at high-season rates, excluding local taxes.

$ less than $100

$$ $100–$200

$$$ more than $200

British Columbia Lodgings in BC attract an 8% provincial sales tax (PST) plus a 5% goods and services tax (GST). Some BC regions levy an additional tax on overnight accommodations of up to 2%.

ELECTRICITY

Type A
120V/60Hz

Type B
120V/60Hz

Eating Price Ranges

These price ranges represent the average cost of a main course.

$ less than $15

$$ $15–$25

$$$ more than $25

FOOD

Try to think of a food that isn't grown, raised or harvested in the Pacific Northwest, and you'll realize why in-the-know gourmands have been putting down roots in the region for decades. Outsiders, who have been slower to discover the abundance, now flock here for the food, seeking a taste of Northwest cuisine prepared by talented chefs who cook local, seasonal foods with an alluring simplicity.

The further you head inland, away from the region's biggest cities, the less you'll find things like pork finished on hazelnuts and discussions about organic produce. Expect more 'traditional' meat and potato dishes, pizzas and burgers, and fewer ethnic restaurants, with the exception of Mexican food. Thanks to a large immigrant population, you can find many excellent, authentic Mexican restaurants throughout the Pacific Northwest.

In the cities, you'll discover diverse ethnic cuisine, from Ethiopian to Ecuadorian, but it's Asian foods that really shine. Vancouver, in particular, offers a high concentration of Japanese, Thai, Chinese and Asian-fusion restaurants, but it's easy to find all types of Asian food everywhere in the Northwest.

As for 'Northwest cuisine,' the nebulous, all-encompassing term doesn't really mean much. Try asking a local, 'What exactly *is* Northwest cuisine?' and you might experience an uncomfortable pause followed by, 'local, seasonal and fresh,' or 'organic and sustainable.' While those words won't conjure up an image of a specific dish or narrow to a section of the spice rack, they hint at what truly defines the regional fare: simplicity.

Farmed & Wild

The diverse geography and climate – a mild, damp coastal region with sunny summers and arid farmland in the east – foster all types of farm-grown produce.

Farmers in these parts grow plenty of fruit, from melons, grapes, apples and pears to strawberries, cherries and blueberries. Veggies thrive here too: potatoes, lentils, corn, asparagus and Walla Walla sweet onions, all of which feed local and overseas populations.

Other well-known farmed products include hazelnuts (also known as filberts; Oregon produces 99.9% of the hazelnuts grown in the US) and herbs, especially lavender and spearmint. Hop farming is another regional specialty. The Northwest is the only region of the country with large-scale hop farms, which provide the sticky, fragrant cones that help add flavor, aroma and bitterness to many beers around the world.

Many wild foods thrive here as well, especially in the damper regions such as the Coast Range. Foragers there seek out year-round wild mushrooms, as well as summertime huckleberries and blackberries.

LGBTIQ+ TRAVELERS

The Pacific Northwest is generally a very gay-friendly place. As elsewhere, gay life is most tolerated in urban centers while attitudes tend to be less accepting in the hinterlands. In the major cities of Seattle, Vancouver and Portland, and even some smaller towns, such as Eugene and Victoria, travelers will find everything from gay religious congregations to gay hiking clubs, while in the rural areas they may want to keep their orientation to themselves.

The Capitol Hill neighborhood is the center of gay life in Seattle. In Vancouver, the West End is gay-centric, while Commercial Dr is more lesbian-oriented. Queer-integrated Portland has no specific gay neighborhood (Sam Adams, Portland's mayor from 2008 to 2012, was the first openly gay mayor of a large US city).

Seattle Gay News (www.sgn.org) A weekly newspaper focusing on gay issues.

Proud Queer (www.pqmonthly.com) Online news serving Portland's gay community.

Vancouver Pride Society (www.vancouverpride.ca) Check out the events link.

Tourism Vancouver (www.tourismvancouver.com/vancouver/gay-friendly-vancouver) Resources for gay-friendly Vancouver.

Local Produce

Finding local products has become a popular pursuit for an increasingly food-aware, eco-minded population, most of whom believe that shipping food long distances wastes precious resources. The year-round availability of fresh produce has spurred a fanaticism for seasonal eating. Many of those food fanatics prefer organic, sustainably produced edibles, and conventional farmers and vintners are working to meet the demand by undergoing the two- to three-year organic-certification process.

Farmers markets have become the best examples of this new hyper-awareness of food sourcing, and a handful operate year-round. Some of the most popular markets go beyond offering produce, with everything from pastries, artisan cheeses, honey and jams to prepared foods such as wood-fired pizzas, roasted peppers, and biscuits and gravy.

If you miss the markets, don't worry. Many grocery stores and specialty food markets prominently label local foods. Large-scale brands such as Tillamook Cheese, which makes cheese, yogurt and ice cream in the coastal town of Tillamook, OR, have a devoted customer base that enjoys supporting local economies. So does the fast-food chain Burgerville, which buys ingredients for its menus from local sources – it offers Walla Walla onion rings, blackberry or hazelnut milkshakes and Tillamook cheddar burgers.

Upscale restaurants also reflect the public's passion for local foods. Some menus name the farms and harvesters who supply specific ingredients. If you're curious, ask servers for details about a restaurant's sourcing practices – most likely they'll be used to such requests.

MONEY

ATMs are widely available. Credit cards are accepted at most hotels, restaurants and shops.

OPENING HOURS

Opening hours can vary throughout the year, usually with longer opening hours in summer, and fewer in winter.

Businesses 9am to 5pm

Post offices and banks 8am or 9am to 5pm Monday to Friday, some 8am or 9am to 2pm Saturday

Restaurants 7am to 11:30am breakfast, 11:30am to 2:30pm lunch, 5pm to 9pm dinner

Shops 9am or 10am to 5pm or 6pm (malls 9pm) Monday to Saturday, noon to 5pm Sunday

Supermarkets 8am to 10pm, open 24 hours in large cities

PUBLIC HOLIDAYS

Holidays falling on a weekend are usually observed the following Monday.

New Year's Day January 1 (USA and Canada)

Martin Luther King Jr Day Third Monday in January (USA)

Family Day Second or third Monday in February (Canada)

Presidents' Day Third Monday in February (USA)

Good Friday Friday before Easter Sunday (Canada)

Easter Sunday in late March or early April (USA and Canada)

Easter Monday Monday after Easter (Canada)

Victoria Day Monday on or preceding May 24 (Canada)

Memorial Day Last Monday in May (USA)

Canada Day July 1, or July 2 if July 1 is Sunday (Canada)

Independence Day July 4 (USA)

Whale-Watching

The Pacific Northwest is one of the world's premier spots for whale-watching. Since the shoreline is so long, if you want to see whales at their peak, pick a particular coastal spot – then find out when most whales will be passing through.

WASHINGTON

You can spot gray and humpback whales from Washington's coastline, especially from Long Beach (near the Oregon border), Westport and Ozette. The most famous kind of whale in this state, however, is the killer whale, or orca.

About 75 resident orcas in several pods live year-round in the Puget Sound and San Juan Islands area, feeding on the plentiful fish. The San Juan Islands in particular are the best place for spotting orcas, since they often swim close to shore. You can take boat tours from the islands or spot them from land – Lime Kiln Point State Park on San Juan Island is an especially good place. And while you're here, be sure to visit the **Whale Museum** (☑360-378-4710; www.whale museum.org; 62 1st St; adult/child $9/4; ☺9am-6pm Sun-Thu, to 8pm Fri & Sat) in Friday Harbor.

The best time to spot orcas is from April to September; numerous charter companies run cruises from the San Juans, Puget Sound and Seattle. You might be able to spot orcas from a ferry too.

Out on the coast, any orcas you might see are part of transient pods that can roam from Alaska to California. These killer whales don't interact with resident pods, and their diet includes seals, sea lions and even small whales.

OREGON

The high capes and headlands of the Oregon coast are excellent vantage points to watch for gray whales. Gray and humpback whales have the longest migrations of any mammal in the world: more than 5000 miles (8000km) from the Arctic to Mexico, and back again. There are both spring and fall migrations; the springtime journey, which peaks in late March, brings the whales closer to shore, while the winter peak is in late December. Favorite whale-watching spots include Cape Arago, Cape Blanco, Cape Perpetua, Cape Meares, Cape Lookout, Ecola State Park, Shore Acres State Park and Yaquina Head Outstanding Natural Area.

Depoe Bay and Newport are especially dedicated to the activity, and here you'll find several tour-boat companies willing to take you out. An organization called **Whale Watching Spoken Here** (www.whalespoken.wordpress.com) rallies hundreds of trained volunteers to assist visitors in spotting whales at various sites all along the Oregon coast. Check the website for details. And be sure to drop into its **Whale Watching Center** (☑541-765-3304; www.whalespoken. org; 119 SW US 101; ☺10am-4pm Wed-Sun winter, 9am-5pm daily summer) in Depoe Bay, offering exhibits and sea views.

BRITISH COLUMBIA

Tofino and Ucluelet – the communities surrounding Pacific Rim National Park Reserve on Vancouver Island – have an estimated 20,000 whales passing through. You're likely to spot a few blowholes around here from March to May. Another good place on land to try spotting whales is Telegraph Cove, where orcas can often be seen; visit the **Whale Interpretive Centre** (☑250-928-3129; www.killerwhalecentre.org; by donation adult/child C$5/3; ☺9:30am-5:30pm mid-May– Oct) here. If you'd rather go for a super close-up, however, there are several boat-tour companies in Victoria.

Labor Day First Monday in September (USA and Canada)

Columbus Day Second Monday in October (USA)

Thanksgiving Day Second Monday in October (Canada); fourth Thursday in November (USA)

Veterans' Day November 11 (USA)

Remembrance Day November 11 (Canada)

Christmas Day December 25 (USA and Canada)

Boxing Day December 26 (Canada)

SAFE TRAVEL

The Pacific Northwest is generally a friendly and safe place to travel, though crime does exist – mostly in bigger cities. Take the usual precautions.

➡ Don't leave valuables visible in your vehicle, whether you're in a busy downtown street or at a remote hiking trailhead, break-ins are frequent.

➡ Pacific Westerners are notoriously terrible at driving in snow and on ice. When the rain freezes, accidents are rife and you may consider staying off the roads.

➡ Climate change means forest fires. If there's smoke pollution from fire, get a N95 mask from a hardware store.

➡ Drivers should watch out for loose cattle and horses in remote countryside areas.

➡ When camping in bear country, use bear containers/boxes or hang food correctly.

➡ While hiking in bear country, wear bear bells or talk loudly to avoid surprising them. Bears will generally avoid people when they can. Never feed bears or other wildlife!

➡ It's unlikely you'll even glimpse a mountain lion (also called a cougar or puma). Adult travelers aren't much at risk of an attack, but unattended children and pets can be. Loud noises and making yourself appear bigger (hold open your jacket) will usually scare them off.

➡ Rattlesnakes live in dry desert country and hikers can sometimes encounter them basking on trails. Give them a wide berth and they'll leave you alone. Wearing thick hiking boots offers some protection, as does staying out of thick underbrush.

TELEPHONE

The US and Canada use GSM-850 and GSM-1900 bands. SIM cards are relatively easy to obtain in both countries.

TOURIST INFORMATION

Oregon, Washington and BC have state and provincial tourist bureaus that offer glossy guides, maps and plenty of other pertinent travel information. Individual cities, towns and regions also maintain visitor centers, which are often run by the local chamber of commerce.

Washington State Tourism (www.experiencewa.com)

Oregon Tourism Commission (www.traveloregon.com)

Destination British Columbia (www.hellobc.com)

VISAS

Requirements vary widely for entry to the US and Canada. Check www.travel.state.gov (USA) and www.cic.gc.ca/english/visit/visas.asp (Canada).

Entering the USA

Getting into the United States can be complicated, depending on your country of origin, as the rules keep changing. For up-to-date information about visas and immigration, check the website of the **US Department of State** (www.travel.state.gov) and the travel section of **US Customs & Border Protection** (www.cbp.gov).

For the most part, all foreign visitors need a visa to enter the US. Exceptions include most citizens from Canada and Bermuda, certain North American Free Trade Agreement (NAFTA) professional workers and those entering under the Visa Waiver Program (VWP). You can determine your eligibility for a Waiver of Tourist Visa (VWT) with the Electronic System for Travel Authorization (ESTA; www.cbp.gov/travel/international-visitors/esta). Visitors should carry their passport (valid for at least six months) and expect to be photographed and have their index fingers scanned.

Practicalities

Radio NPR (www.npr.org) has a progressive yet impartial approach to news and talk radio.

Discount Cards If you plan on visiting many national or state parks or national forests, a recreation pass will save you money – check www.nps.gov/planyour visit/passes.htm for details. For Washington, go to parks.state.wa.us/204/ Passes-permits; for Oregon, www.oregonstateparks.org/ckFiles/files/2012_ pass_summary.pdf

Student Discounts If you're a student, bring along your student ID, which can get you discounts on transportation and admission to sights and attractions.

Hostels Many hostels in the Pacific Northwest are members of HI-USA (www.hi usa.org), which is affiliated with Hostelling International. You don't need a HI-USA card to stay at these hostels, but having one saves you a few bucks per night. You can buy one at the hostel when checking in.

Post The US Postal Service (www.usps.com) and Canada Post (www.canada post.ca) provide dependable, timely service.

Senior Discounts People over the age of 65 (or sometimes younger) often qualify for the same discounts as students; any identification showing your date of birth should suffice. Folks 62 or older visiting national parks can get a Senior Pass (store.usgs.gov/pass/senior.html). For more information, contact the American Association of Retired Persons (www.aarp.org).

Smoking Banned in all indoor public spaces throughout the Pacific Northwest, including bars and restaurants.

Time Oregon (except most of Malheur County, near the Idaho border), Washington, and Vancouver, BC, are in the Pacific zone (GMT minus seven hours in summer, minus eight in winter).

Entering Canada

Most visitors to Canada from major Western countries will need no visa, but requirements change frequently, so check **Citizenship & Immigration Canada** (www.cic.gc.ca/english/visit/visas.asp) before you leave. You can apply for an Electronic Travel Authorization (eTA), required for visa-exempt foreign nationals traveling to or through Canada (C$7; good for up to five years) at www.canada.ca.

Officially, US citizens don't need a passport or visa to enter Canada by land; some proof of citizenship, such as a birth certificate along with state-issued photo identification, will ordinarily suffice. However, since the introduction of tighter border security, officials recommend that US citizens carry a passport to facilitate entry. To return to the US from Canada, everyone, including US citizens, needs a valid passport.

BEHIND THE SCENES

SEND US YOUR FEEDBACK

We love to hear from travelers – your comments help make our books better. We read every word, and we guarantee that your feedback goes straight to the authors. Visit **lonelyplanet.com/contact** to submit your updates and suggestions.

Note: We may edit, reproduce and incorporate your comments in Lonely Planet products such as guidebooks, websites and digital products, so let us know if you don't want your comments reproduced or your name acknowledged. For a copy of our privacy policy visit lonelyplanet.com/privacy.

WRITER THANKS

BECKY OHLSEN

Thanks to editor Ben Buckner for the gig, Celeste Brash for writing the previous edition, Paul Smith for being a great travel companion, and all the dedicated volunteers at the many wonderful tiny museums, state parks, national parks and campgrounds we visited along the way.

ROBERT BALKOVICH

Thank you, as always, to my friends and family for your continued support while I run hither and thither and yon. Special thanks to Karin, for sharing your love of Seattle with me and setting me off on the right foot, and to Lynae for the wonderful home away from home where I made many great memories.

CELESTE BRASH

Thanks to my husband Josh and my kids who have come with me on so many Oregon trips over the years. And to many friends old and new that helped out this time around, including Ticari, Chris and Ashley, Nathan, Dana, Jon and Kara, Ron & Nisa, Elizabeth, Pattye, Rachel Cabakoff, Amanda Castleman, Dave Nevins, Amy Hunter, all my LP co-authors and Ben Buckner for seeing this through.

JOHN LEE

Heartfelt thanks to Maggie for joining me at all those restaurants and for keeping me calm during the brain-throbbing final write-up phase of this project. Thanks also to Max, our crazy-whiskered ginger cat, for sticking by my desk and also reminding me to chase him around the house every once in a while. Cheers also to my brother Michael for visiting from England and checking out some local breweries with me: you really know how to go the extra mile.

CRAIG MCLACHLAN

A hearty thanks to all those who helped out on the road, but most of all, to my exceptionally

THIS BOOK

This 4th edition of Lonely Planet's the *Pacific Northwest's Best Trips* guidebook was researched and written by Becky Ohlsen, Robert Balkovich, Celeste Brash, John Lee, Craig McLachlan, MaSovaida Morgan and Brendan Sainsbury. The previous edition was also written by Becky, Celeste, John and Brendan, as well as Ryan Ver Berkmoes. This guidebook was produced by the following:

Destination Editor Ben Buckner

Senior Product Editors Martine Power, Vicky Smith

Product Editor Rachel Rawling

Regional Senior Cartographer Alison Lyall

Cartographer Rachel Imeson

Book Designer Lauren Egan

Assisting Editors Sarah Bailey, Andrew Bain, James Bainbridge, Judith Bamber, Michelle Bennett, Lucy Cowie, Emma Gibbs, Carly Hall, Jennifer Hattam, Gabrielle Innes, Jodie Martire, Lou McGregor, Monique Perrin, Sarah Reid, Gabrielle Stefanos

Assisting Cartographers Julie Sheridan, Diana von Holdt

Cover Researcher Meri Blazevski

Thanks to Sasha Drew, Andi Jones, Lauren O'Connell, Charlotte Orr, Martin Tyler

beautiful wife, Yuriko, who maintained semi-control of my craft beer intake.

MASOVAIDA MORGAN

Deepest thanks to the many wonderful souls who helped out with tips, suggestions, dining companionship, coffees, rides and nights on the dance floor during this research trip: Katie Doyle, Kurt Berning, Jocelyn Bourgault, Antoinette Foster, Joseph Lewis, Liz & James Nickerson, Tom Campitelli, Leif Jacobsen, Nathan Williams, Ellie & Susa, Hobe & Thomas, Zac Webster, Ross Beach, Bertony & Chris, Luis, Ian & Emily, and Jason & Hannah.

BRENDAN SAINSBURY

Many thanks to all the skilled bus drivers, helpful tourist information staff, generous hotel owners, expert burger flippers, unobtrusive bears and numerous passers-by who helped me, unwittingly or otherwise, during my research trip. Special thanks to my wife Liz, my son Kieran and my mother-in-law Ammy for their company (and patience) on the road.

ACKNOWLEDGE-MENTS

Climate map data adapted from Peel MC, Finlayson BL & McMahon TA (2007) 'Updated World Map of the Köppen-Geiger Climate Classification', *Hydrology and Earth System Sciences*, 11, 1633–44.

INDEX